Roads to Paradise

Roads to Paradise

Reading the Lives of the Early Saints

Alison Goddard Elliott

Published for Brown University Press
by University Press of New England
Hanover and London, 1987

UNIVERSITY PRESS OF NEW ENGLAND

BRANDEIS UNIVERSITY   UNIVERSITY OF NEW HAMPSHIRE
BROWN UNIVERSITY   UNIVERSITY OF RHODE ISLAND
CLARK UNIVERSITY   TUFTS UNIVERSITY
UNIVERSITY OF CONNECTICUT   UNIVERSITY OF VERMONT
DARTMOUTH COLLEGE

Printed in the United States of America

∞

LIBRARY OF CONGRESS CATALOGING IN PUBLICATION DATA
Elliott, Alison Goddard.
Roads to paradise.
Bibliography: p.
Includes index.
1. Hagiography. I. Title.
BX4662.E44 1987 809'.93527 86-40384
ISBN 0-87451-389-8

5 4 3 2 1

This project has been supported by the National Endowment for the Humanities, a federal agency that supports the study of such fields as history, philosophy, literature, and the languages.

To Charlie, who took me to Sant' Onofrio

Contents

EDITOR'S FOREWORD *by Charles Segal*   ix
AUTHOR'S PREFACE   xv

1 Introduction   1

2 Hagiographic Epic   16
    The Ethos of Martyrdom   18
    To Speak a Martyrdom   23

3 Hagiographic Romance   42
    Gradational Structures   45
    The Romance Model   51

4 The Saint Sets Forth: Motifs of Departure   77
    The Childhood of the Hero   77
    The Break with the Past   81
    The "More" Motif   83
    Secret Flight   85
    The Flight from Marriage: Lévi-Strauss
      in the Desert   92

5 The Downward Journey   103
    Symbolic Death and Burial   104
    Unusual Guides   116
    Disguise   119
    The Journey's Goal   120
    Seeking the Woman   126

6 The Ascent: Paradise Regained   131
    Food and Sex   137
    The Peaceable Kingdom   144

7 The Saint as Liminal Hero   168

8 The Road's End: Postscripta   181
  Hagiography and Epic: The Power of Discourse   182
  Hagiography and Romance: 192
    Animals   193
    Liminality   204
    The Persistent Dream   209

  APPENDIX: TABLE OF THEMES AND MOTIFS   215
  BIBLIOGRAPHY   217
    Abbreviations Used   217
    Primary Sources   218
    Secondary Works   221
  INDEX   237

Illustrations

Frescoes in the Campo Santo, Pisa, Fourteenth Century

FIGURE 1. Paphnutius buries St. Onuphrius.   56

FIGURE 2. St. Macarius the Roman and his lions.   64

FIGURE 3. St. Antony, helped by two lions,
buries St. Paul of Thebes.   109

FIGURE 4. The devil, disguised as a lady pilgrim,
tempts a monk at his cave (St. Macarius).   112

FIGURE 5. The monk drives the disguised female
pilgrim from his cave (St. Macarius).   114

FIGURE 6. The devil, disguised as an elderly pilgrim,
tempts a monk in his cell.   121

FIGURE 7. A desert monk at work, plaiting a
basket of leaves.   134

Editor's Foreword

Alison Goddard Elliott died of cancer on September 18, 1984 at the age of forty-seven. She had just been promoted to Associate Professor of Classics, with tenure, at Brown University. She left behind the manuscript of *Roads to Paradise* in a nearly completed state, having entered the manuscript into the Brown University main-frame computer and made revisions systematically as she went along. The editorial work necessary to putting the book into final form consisted mainly in checking and completing references, translating some passages of Greek, Latin, French, and Old French, doing some stylistic retouching, and adding a few details that she had indicated in marginal notes. One chapter required major stylistic revisions, but these did not alter the tone or substance of the work. Had she lived to see the work through the press herself, she would doubtless have made many improvements and refinements. Even as it stands, however, the work certainly achieves her main objectives: to demonstrate with very full documentation the underlying narrative structure of the lives of the early saints, to show their affinities to and differences from the classical myths of the questing hero, and to trace continuities into the literary epics of Medieval Europe.

Roads to Paradise makes a number of different but complementary contributions. First of all, it makes accessible to the general reader a fascinating body of texts generally studied only by specialists. Many of these have never been published in a modern language, much less studied from the point of view of narrative structure. Alison Elliott elucidates this structure and the mythical symbols it contains. Using the recent work of Charles Altman, she demonstrates how the saints' lives show a "gradational" pattern

(attaining "more" holiness), in contrast to the contrastive or di-
chotomizing patterns of the early martyrologies, with their absolute
polarities of right and wrong, Christian and pagan. She shows how
these lives, recounting a quest for the Earthly Paradise, resemble
folktale and mythical narratives, especially romance narratives.
These ascetics' denial of even the most basic physical needs corresponds to contemporary theological concerns with the Fall, the cor-
ruption of the body, the evil of sexuality, and the idealization of a
prelapsarian paradise of corporeal purity. In classical thought the
forms of civic life and social organization differentiate man from
the beasts and constitute the essence of his true estate. Only by
being a "political animal," in Aristotle's celebrated formulation,
does man fulfil his humanity. For the desert saints, on the other
hand, man's real goal is the heavenly kingdom, and civic life constitutes a state of alienation from his "true" condition. Hence to ne-
gate civilized life, to replace culture by nature, is also to bypass the
fallen condition of humankind. To draw closer to the beasts is, paradoxically, to regain a lost proximity to the divine.

In attempting a unified interpretation of texts composed over a
thousand-year period and over a geographical range extending
from Spain to the Byzantine East and from France to Egypt, Alison
Elliott concentrates on the continuities of narrative patterns rather
than on the historical specificity of individual works and their
cultural milieus, although these are not entirely neglected. Nevertheless, the author would not, I think, want to claim that hers is the
only approach. As the subtitle suggests, this book is a "reading"
rather than an exhaustive analysis, and its focus is literary rather
than historical in the narrow sense, although it holds rich implications for further strictly historical study. It uncovers a narrative
model of remarkable tenacity over the centuries and thereby places
hagiography within the larger context of both classical narrative
patterns (e.g. the Greek novel) and the medieval romance. It should
contribute considerably to bringing hagiography into the mainstream of contemporary critical discourse about myth, symbol, and
narrative.

Alison Elliott discusses these texts with a freshness, synoptic vision, and unifying clarity that orient the modern reader in a highly specialized field among remote, often exotic writings. She took delight in these tales, and she conveys that delight to her readers with liveliness and warmth of style, lucidity of thought and presentation, and a sharp focus on the essential details and main outlines of the material. She loves a good story, and she brings these half-forgotten, mythicized biographies to life again with an intellectual rigor that is both demanding and stimulating. She invites and enables us to share her enthusiasm and to join her in the challenge of uncovering and tracing these subsurface patterns.

This work was the major subject of Alison Elliott's research for several years. She brought to it an unusual combination of skills: solid training in both classical and medieval culture; a profound command of Greek, Latin, and the Romance languages and literatures; wide reading in hagiography (the subject of her doctoral dissertation at the University of California, Berkeley), and in anthropological, linguistic, and semiological theories of myth and narrative; and an extraordinary energy, efficiency, and commitment to scholarship. In carrying this ambitious project through to completion in a relatively short period, she could draw upon her earlier work on Prudentius, on the early martyrs, and on her edition of the Old French *Life of Saint Alexis* (see the Bibliographies). That the still richer potential demonstrated by this book will remain unfulfilled is a sore loss to scholars in the field and a grievous sorrow to those who knew Alison personally.

The special circumstances in which this book was brought to completion made very heavy demands on many people, only a few of whom I can name here. The late Craig Manning of Brown University continued to work with me on the manuscript after Alison Elliott's death and brought his characteristic erudition, care, and acumen to many editorial problems. His premature death in February 1986, is a loss felt keenly by all who knew his rare abilities and great promise. Alison Elliott was deeply appreciative of the concern, support, and generous assistance given her by her colleagues in the Department of Classics and in the Medieval Studies Program at Brown. On her behalf I would like to thank especially Professor

Martha Schaffer of Brown University for her ever-resourceful kindness and unfailing patience. Professor Karen Bassi, now of Syracuse University, and Professor Robert Mathiesen of Brown gave unstinting personal and professional help. Professors Kurt and Deborah Raaflaub, Professor Karen Newman, Sandra Wyatt, Frances Bene, Charles McKinley, Alissa Rubin, and Camille Fusco (among many other friends and colleagues) made Alison Elliott's last months of work happier and easier.

To Elli Mylonas' expertise with the computer I owe much saving of time and effort in the last stages of the revision; she has made the production of the text a much easier process than it would otherwise have been. Through the good offices of Professor Gian Biagio Conte of the University of Pisa I was able to obtain photographs of the frescoes of the Lives of the Saints in the Campo Santo at Pisa; and I am deeply grateful to Professor Chiara Frugoni of the Department of Medieval Studies of the University of Pisa for generously providing these photographs and for kind permission to use them in the book. Ruthann Whitten of Brown University typed parts of the manuscript and did much else besides. Professor Froma Zeitlin of Princeton University provided Alison Elliott with out-of-the-way publications at a critical moment and helped in many other ways with characteristic generosity and energy. Dr. Celia Chazelle generously helped with proofreading.

To Alison Elliott's thanks to her family I would like to add my own, particularly to her mother, Dr. Katherine Evans Goddard, for her constant interest and encouragement. Alison's father, Dr. David Goddard, would have enjoyed the achievement represented by this book; he had the pleasure, at least, of knowing of its near-completion.

Special thanks are due to Professor Peter Brown who read the manuscript both in a penultimate and in the final version and made valuable suggestions. Many of his useful bibliographical additions have been incorporated into the notes. His encouragement and interest in the work of a total stranger meant a very great deal to Alison Elliott. Professor Donald Maddox also improved the manuscript by a perspicacious criticism that was both scrupulous and sympathetic. I am grateful to Professor Ernest Sosa, Director of the Brown University Press, and to Professor Stephen Nichols of the University of Pennsylvania for help and advice.

The Hospice Program of Rhode Island and the devoted people on its staff, particularly Ellie Reinhard, R.N., helped make it possible for Alison Elliott to continue to work in her familiar surroundings. For care and compassion beyond the call of professional duty, feeling thanks are also due to Michelle Paquet, M.D., and Joni Jones, R.N., of Rhode Island Group Health Association; Lynne McCabe, R.N., and Ann Devine of Hospice; Peter Black, M.D., and Amy Pruitt, M.D., of Massachusetts General Hospital. It is a tribute to Alison Elliott's own courage, strength, and generosity that so many people involved themselves in her suffering and, directly or indirectly, made it possible for her to complete a task that was so dear to her.

Alison Elliott was fortunate to have had such friends. She was fortunate too to have a life's work of whose importance she was fully convinced and to which she felt a commitment that went far deeper than mere outward academic success. She kept to the end her cheerfulness, zest for work, and her rare combination of personal warmth and intellectual energy. Along with revising *Roads to Paradise*, she even wrote a series of children's stories about a friendly teddy bear named Sid. The sources of such courage and strength are mysterious. In her last months Alison knew the gifts of the spirit that she described in the Lives she studied:

Beatus est ergo qui facit Dei voluntatem super terram. Angeli ministrant ei, et faciunt eum exultare, et ei vires addunt singulis horis, dum est in carne.

(Blessed is he who does the will of God on earth. Angels minister to him, and make him exult, and give him strength during every hour that he is on earth.)

CHARLES SEGAL

Providence, Rhode Island
September 7, 1986

Author's Preface

This book bears witness, I have no doubt, to the presumptuousness of one trained as a scholar of classical and medieval literature with the temporal restrictions all too common to those disciplines—nothing after 300 A.D. for the first, nothing before Charlemagne for the second—who dares to take on a subject not her own. (Here my gratitude to Peter Brown is most pronounced, for both his writings and his more personal guidance have saved me from making the more egregious errors.) The more I read, the more I became convinced that we overlook at our loss the period called, perhaps condescendingly, "the Late Antique." I am also convinced that the loss is as great for the medievalist as it is for the classicist. Prudentius, for all his many verbal borrowings from Vergil, has more in common in spirit with the *Chanson de Roland* or the *Couronnement de Louis* than he does with the classical. This book, while concerned at times with influences and borrowings, is less concerned with verbal echoes than with the way the borrowings were used to create new narrative structures and symbolic constructs.

The scholarly quest is, like the romance one, an unpredictable journey. Discoveries come when least expected, and in mysterious ways. This book owes its genesis to chance. In 1981 I was taken to see the church of Sant' Onofrio on the Janiculum in Rome, a church perhaps most famous as the spot where Tasso is buried. We visited the cloister, and I saw there the charming frescoes depicting the life of the saint painted by the "Cavaliere d'Arpino," works of considerable liveliness although not falling into the category of "Great Art." I enjoyed them thoroughly. But as I gazed, I was struck by a sense of familiarity. In common with the average reader of this book, I am sure, I had never heard of Saint Onuphrius, but I recognized the story of his life. Although I knew Jerome's *Life of Paul of Thebes*, which shares the motif of the two grave-digging lions, my sense of familiarity went deeper than this one detail. I determined to read the *vita* of Onuphrius, and this book is the result.

Writing has been fun. It has been difficult to answer the question "what are you working on?" in anything less than an hour, but I have enjoyed trying. My pleasure, moreover, has been increased by the assistance I have received. The libraries of the American Academy in Rome and the Ecole Normale Supérieure in Paris provided rich and congenial settings for scholarship. My enjoyment of the libraries of the latter city was rendered greater because of a fellowship from the American Philosophical Society to work on a manuscript in the Bibliothèque Nationale; this grant has borne double fruit as I profited from my time there to work on two projects at once, something I could not have done without the generosity of the American Philosophical Society. My family, friends, and colleagues have generously indulged my burgeoning passion for lions and provided me with additional examples, not all of which could I incorporate in this volume. I am grateful for the perspicacious comments of all who have read the manuscript with care and compassion and aided in the task of research in many ways: J. Giles Milhaven, Charles Segal, Robert Mathiesen. I owe an especial debt of gratitude to my research assistant, Craig Manning, whose sensitivity and precise aid in proof reading and in locating lost page numbers and missing references were invaluable. My final debt is to the knowledge, encouragement, and charity of Peter Brown, which were given me at a time that I needed them badly indeed. The errors that remain are mine but would be many more, but for this help. The work, particularly the last section of chapter 6, is also dedicated to the *leunculi* who aided inestimably in its production, largely by warming the manuscript and books as I tried to read.

Providence, Rhode Island
August 1, 1984

Roads to Paradise

Chapter 1

Introduction

In the Middle Ages saints were heroes. Crowds flocked to the shrines of popular saints; preachers filled their sermons with stirring tales of saintly heroism. In times of trouble, men and women prayed to these human intercessors and lavished on their cults both love and money. The stories of their sufferings and heroic contests against the forces of evil inspired men and changed their lives. The great cathedrals bear eloquent witness to the veneration of the most popular figures: St. Peter's in Rome, the cathedral of Saint Mary Magdalen in Vézelay, the splendid pilgrimage church at Santiago de Compostella. Lesser known saints as well had their ardent devotees: Saint Eulalia, a virgin martyr, venerated at Mérida and Barcelona; Saint Onuphrius, a desert hermit whose only clothing was made of palm fronds, the patron of weavers.

In *Thought and Letters in Western Europe*, M. L. Laistner offers a comprehensive and sympathetic picture of the appeal of hagiography for a medieval audience:

> The lives of saints, martyrs, and outstanding figures in the Church owed their popularity to many causes. Their historical accuracy counted but little with the average reader who found in them a good story. If the adventures of the saintly hero conformed to pattern, that was assuredly not regarded as a fault. . . . There is in most men a love of the marvellous. In the early Middle Ages this was the more intense because fortified by the sanctions of religion. When belief in miracles and in frequent manifestations of Divine approval or displeasure was all but universal, . . . what more attractive literature could there be than some hagiography in which the supernatural

played a determining part in the hero's life and made even more manifest his powers after death? In these *Lives*, too, men might read of the customs, manners, and scenery of foreign lands, or of hairbreadth escapes, like those of Findan from his Norman captors when he set out to ransom his sister.[1]

Hagiography, then, offered something for everyone. Laistner, moreover, has put his finger on two very important issues. Unlike his modern counterpart, medieval man was not distressed by the lack of historical accuracy. Still more important to this study is Laistner's second observation, that many of the lives conform to a pattern. Far from being a fault, for a medieval audience this fact added to the appeal of the lives, for in that pattern, as we shall see, was encoded much of the meaning of the story. Modern readers, however, have generally not shared the medieval enthusiasm for saints' lives. The usual objections are to their lack of historical perspective, to their improbable miracles, and to their ubiquitous sameness—to what Hippolyte Delehaye calls their monochrome color, "la teinte monochrome."[2] James Earl puts it more colloquially: "When you've read one saint's Life, you've read them all."[3]

Laistner mentioned "historical accuracy." Although often considered a branch of historiography, hagiography is born from a special set of circumstances that subtly alter its nature. The premise upon which all accounts of saints are based is that the narrative is true, that the saint in question lived and performed the deeds described in his or her biography. Nevertheless the circumstances surrounding the composition of a hagiographic document and the aims for which it was intended cannot be ignored. Delehaye warns:

Of course the literary monuments, the institutions, the works of art in which the memory of the saint lives again bear the impression of these exceptional conditions; and the fundamental mistake would consist in interpreting them without taking account of the spirit that inspired them.[4]

1. Laistner, pp. 282–83. The reference to Findan is to the anonymous *Life of Findan* in *Monumenta Germaniae Historica, Scriptores*, XV, p. 512ff.

2. *Les Passions des martyrs et les genres littéraires* (1921), p. 223.

3. "Literary Problems in Early Medieval Hagiography" (1971), p. 7. For a criticism of this viewpoint, see Olsen, "'De Historiis Sanctorum'" (1980).

4. *Cinq Leçons sur la méthode hagiographique*, p. 8: "Tout naturellement les monuments littéraires, les institutions, les oeuvres d'art où revit la mémoire du saint

According to Delehaye, the task of the hagiographer is not identical to that of the secular biographer or historian: "The saint's story begins, so to speak, at the point where the story of great men ends, and . . . his existence has unlimited prolongations."[5] As important as the history of the saint's life is his history after death. But other, equally significant characteristics distinguish hagiography from history and give it its special quality.

The purpose of hagiography is of paramount importance. It has a double goal: celebration and edification.[6] To aid in meeting both goals, hagiographers not unnaturally employed the lessons they had learned from the rhetorical schools. The imprint of panegyric is often plainly visible. Charlotte D'Evelyn writes of hagiography:

The genre . . . has two objectives: the one, devotional, to honor the saint; the other, instructive, to explain to the hearer or reader the significance for Christian truth of the saint and his life. If only one of these objectives was present the narrative would become history, or biography, or allegory, homily, or treatise, but not legend.[7]

In a homily on St. Gordius, St. Basil the Great explained the purposes of hagiographic encomium:

Thus, whenever we recount the lives of those who were distinguished in holiness, first we praise God through his servants; then we praise the just through the testimony of those who are known to us; we gladden the people through the hearing of fine things. For the life of Joseph is an exhortation to moderation of sexual desires, and the narration of Samson's life is an incitement to courage.[8]

In one of the most influential saints' lives, the *Life of St. Benedict*, Gregory the Great commented, "And some there are that be sooner

---

portent l'empreint de ces conditions exceptionelles, et l'erreur fondamentale consisterait ici à les intérpreter sans tenir compte de l'esprit qui les a inspirés."

5. Ibid., pp. 7–8: "L'histoire [du saint] commence, pour ainsi dire, là où se termine celle des grands hommes, et . . . son existence a des prolongements indéfinis."

6. In *Legends of the Saints* (rpt. 1962), p. 3, Delehaye writes: "to be strictly hagiographical the document must be of a religious character and aim at edification."

7. In a review of Wolpers, *Die englische Heiligenlegende des Mittelalters*, p. 214.

8. *PG* 31, 492.

moved to the love of God by virtuous examples than by godly sermons."[9] We can judge the efficacy of the holy exemplar by the actions of St. Augustine, who tells of his own conversion upon hearing the *Life of St. Antony (Confessions,* VIII.vi.14–15)—a Life that also moved other listeners to imitate the ascetic saint. Three centuries later we find this *vita* exercising its spell on the English St. Guthlac. The author of the *Life of Guthlac,* an otherwise unknown monk Felix, describes the experience as follows: "Cum enim priscorum monachorum solitariam vitam legebat, tum inluminato cordis gremio avida cupidine heremum quaerere fervebat"[10] (While he was reading the solitary life of the first monks, his heart was illuminated and he burned with eager desire to seek the desert).

Laistner's second point, closely related to the first, concerns the way adventures of saintly heroes tend to conform to a pattern. The resemblance between many saints' lives is indeed remarkable. With little or no alteration, the identical story may be told of two distinct saints.[11] St. Jerome was not the first to earn a lion's gratitude by removing a thorn from its paw, nor Paul of Thebes the only one to enjoy the services of lions as grave-diggers.

The sameness of many hagiographic accounts, as well as the frequency of so-called "uncritical" borrowings from one tale to another, have often been commented upon, and always with disfavor. The remarks of Ferdinand Lot are representative: "The insincerity of the pagan aretologists seems unfortunately to have been handed on, along with the literary genre, to the Lives of the Christian Saints. At an early date, it is admitted that no blame attaches to a writer, if in recounting the life of a saintly man, he borrows a fact from another life, for the purpose of edification."[12] Insincerity,

9. Don Edmund Luck, O.S.B., ed., *The Life and Miracles of St. Benedict, by Gregory the Great,* from an old English version by P. W. (Paris, 1608), p. xi.

10. Ed. Colgrave (1956), p. 86. Colgrave dates the *Life* between 730–40. Guthlac had already decided on a religious life, but reading the *Vita sancti Antonii* convinced him to become a hermit; see Kurtz, "From St. Antony to St. Guthlac" (1926), p. 106n.

11. For instance, St. Onuphrius and the lapsed bishop described in the *Verba Seniorum,* discussed below, p. 57. See also the many examples in Delehaye, *Les Passions,* p. 229; also Aigrain, *L'Hagiographie,* p. 149.

12. *The End of the Ancient World* (rpt. 1961), p. 162.

however, is not the right word to describe this phenomenon, for most if not all hagiographers were nothing if not sincere. There are, I suggest, more profound reasons for the many repetitions; it is the task of this volume to illuminate some of them.

One of the most common explanations for this seeming lack of regard for "history" on the part of the hagiographers is what is held to be an undue influence of rhetoric combined with a faulty methodology.[13] The remarks of one scholar concerning Jerome's lives of the hermits typify this attitude:

> One need hardly note that these methods [the use of rhetorical ornamentation, etc.], far from embellishing the narrative, detract from its historical value. Indeed, once the possibility of non-historical additions is admitted, no narrative, especially one involving miracles, can claim unqualified truth. The fact that Jerome did not realize that shows that he lacked to a considerable degree the critical eye which is so necessary to the historian.[14]

But Jerome would probably have concurred happily with this verdict on the grounds that he was not here writing secular history.[15] Similarly, another hagiographer, Prudentius, when he needed to versify a proper name that would not scan correctly according to the laws of classical metrics, gloried in breaking such pagan rules, and boasted of doing so (*Peristephanon* IV, 161–72). The aims and methods of many, if not most, ancient hagiographers were not those of the modern scholar or the classical poet.

Some medieval hagiographers explicitly came to grips with the problem. Gregory of Tours, for instance, gave his *Vita Patrum* the subtitle, *Liber de vita quorumdam feliciosorum* (The Book of the Life of Certain Blessed Men), and in the prologue wrote of his use of the singular noun, *vita:*[16]

> And some ask whether we ought to say "Life" of the saints or "Lives." Aulus Gellius, however, and many other philosophers prefer to say

13. For a comprehensive discussion of the influence of classical rhetoric on hagiography, see Delehaye, *Les Passions.*

14. Coleiro, "St. Jerome's Lives of the Hermits" (1957), p. 164.

15. Compare *De Viris Illustribus,* preface (PL 23, 631–34).

16. In his life of St. Guthlac, quoted in note 10, above, Felix also speaks of the "priscorum monachorum solitariam vitam," the solitary *life* of the first solitary monks.

"Lives." For the authority, Pliny, in the third book of his *Art of Grammar* states: "The ancients spoke of 'Lives,' but the grammarians do not think that the word 'life' has a plural." Therefore, it is plainly better to say "Life" of the Fathers than "Lives," because, although there is a diversity of merits and miracles, nevertheless one life of the body nurtures all men in the world.[17]

Hagiography, moreover, was considered to be ethically rather than factually true. To move men to the love of God was such a noble purpose that other considerations (such as truthfulness) paled before it. Peter Brown observes that in the late ancient world, described by Henri Marrou as the "Civilization of the *Paideia*," men not only sought examples but also tended to "find what is exemplary in persons rather than in more general entities."[18] The author of an anonymous *Life of St. Gregory* written at Whitby around 700 A.D. asked for understanding if he should mistakenly ascribe to his hero deeds performed by another, for if such things were not literally true of one saint, they were of another, and all were equal in Christ.

So, if any reader should know more about all the miracles of this kindly man or how they happened, we pray him for Christ's sake, not to nibble with critical teeth at this work of ours *which has been diligently twisted into shape by love rather than knowledge. . . .* So let no one be disturbed even if these miracles were performed by any other of the holy saints, since the holy Apostle, through the mystery of the limbs of a single body, which he compares to the living experience of the saints, concludes that we are all "members one of another." . . . Hence we know too that all saints have everything in common through the love of Christ of whose body they are members. *Hence if anything we have written did not concern this man . . . yet in his case we have little doubt on the whole that they were true of him, too.*[19]

A final reason for the lack of enthusiasm for hagiography among a previous generation of scholars has been its relationship with

17. *PL* 71, 1010.
18. Peter Brown, "The Saint as Exemplar in Late Antiquity" (1983), p. 2, quoting Marrou, *A History of Education in Antiquity* (1956), pp. 96–101 and 217–26. Cf. Cicero's account of following Scaevola as his model, *De Amicitia* 1.
19. Colgrave, *The Earliest Life of Gregory the Great* (1968), 129–33 (emphasis added).

folklore.[20] Although many (but not all) saints were in fact historic figures, the subject of how the lives of some saints are fabulated is more a branch of folklore or mythology than a historical discipline. Folklore has been seen as popular, unscientific, and unhistoric, none of which characteristics recommended it to the positivist scholarship of prior decades.[21] From my point of view, however, it is precisely this relationship that yields some of the richest fruit. Saints were heroes, no different in the popular imagination from many other beloved figures of story and legend. They worked wonders, defeated the forces of evil, and earned their just reward at the end of a life of trial. Moreover, while every man might not realistically aspire to winning the hand of a princess and acquiring a kingdom, all might hope to resist the wiles of the devil and attain the kingdom of heaven.

Hagiography is not history. Many of the tales, as we have seen, were intended to be exemplary in nature,[22] But even if Jerome and the others were not intending to write history, the charges of sameness are nevertheless valid. In many cases, however, to ascribe the "borrowings" merely to plagiarism is too simple an explanation. Many tales sound alike precisely because they are, in a profound sense, the same story, just as the Monk of Whitby claimed, although the reasons I advance for their identity differ somewhat from his.

The charges of repetitiveness and of liberal "borrowings" are not unique to hagiographic accounts. Furthermore, for a medieval, if not for a modern, audience they may have constituted part of the enjoyment of the text (*plaisir du texte*). Discussing Ian Fleming's James Bond thrillers, Umberto Eco has written: "The reader's pleasure consists in finding himself plunged into a game where he

20. Doble, "Hagiography and Folklore" (1943) went so far as to say that hagiography was despised because of this connection (p. 321). For a brilliant study of hagiographic folklore, see Schmitt, *Le Saint lévrier* (1979); also Le Goff, "Culture ecclésiastique et culture folklorique" (1970).

21. For a discussion of the unwillingness of many critics to admit the presence of folkloric material in "learned" works, see Rosenberg, "Folkloristes et médiévistes" (1979).

22. See Delehaye, *Les Légendes hagiographiques* (1927), p. 70.

knows the pieces and the rules and even (aside from some very minor variations) the outcome."[23] A similar phenomenon exists, I suggest, for hagiography. The reader (or listener) knows perfectly well the outcome of the martyrdom of a St. George or the ascetic life of a St. Paul of Thebes—after all, the hero is a saint, and that fact alone ensures a "happy" ending to the tale. As a result, attention is focussed more on the way the story was told, and on small variations of detail.

Furthermore, the same redundancy and repetitiousness are found in medieval romances. Writing of the Middle English text, Susan Wittig notes: "To even the casual reader, the most striking feature of style . . . is its redundance."[24] She goes on to review various explanations for this situation, ranging from that of oral, formulaic composition to Laura Loomis' theory of bookshop composition and extensive textual borrowing and, more importantly for this study, Edmund Leach's theories about mythic redundance (see below, p. 75). Aspects of all three explanations are valid for hagiography. The traditional explanation for repetitiveness in saint's lives involves the notion of textual borrowing. In some cases this may be the correct reason, but it is not always satisfactory. Oral traditions and mythic redundancy also play their part.

While names, places, and dates may differ in hagiographic accounts, many stories employ a common narrative grammar, a fact that in itself favors accretion, for audience and author alike shared a common horizon of expectation concerning narrative deep structure of saintly behavior. Hagiography, moreover, is not a genre that favors surprise endings or narrative suspense. Furthermore, like the orally composing epic poet who built his story out of established and familiar themes, the hagiographer could (and did) construct a seemingly infinite number of biographies out of a few essential elements, expanding or contracting the basic plot as circumstances required.

    23. Eco, "James Bond" (1966), p. 96: "Le plaisir du lecteur consiste à se trouver plongé dans un jeu dont il connaît les pièces et les règles, et même l'issue à part des variations minimes."
    24. Wittig, *Stylistic and Narrative Structures* (1978), p. 12.

Some of the reasons for the inventiveness of hagiographers are understandable. Frequently there was very little authentic (that is, written) information available about a particular saint. The last great persecution, under Diocletian, probably caused some loss of church records; as a result there are perhaps no more than seventy authentic *Acta* extant that contain historically reliable accounts of martyrdom.[25] For many martyrs, the only "hard" facts the hagiographer had to go on were a name, the fact of martyrdom, and its date; for the rest he had to rely upon oral traditions and his imagination. Of the so-called plagiarism that resulted, G. H. Doble remarks of the hagiographer that "in so acting he is not guilty of a conscious fraud. He is doing his best with an impossible task."[26]

If, on the other hand, the saint in question happened to be an ascetic hermit rather than a martyr, everyone had a general idea of the broad outlines of his life but did not know the particulars. Legends were transferred by analogy: that which was once true is, given similar presuppositions, true today.[27] Moreover, the shared structure, the common narrative grammar, fostered a kind of "plagiarism." The borrowing of motifs or anecdotes is most common between tales of the same type. A few themes are common to both martyrs' *passiones* and the *vitae* of the desert saints (for example, the merciful beast), but many more are genre specific.

For whatever reason, hagiography, with certain notable exceptions, has not enjoyed great favor in recent times. Hagiographic texts have been studied by the Bollandists for religious and theological issues and examined by historians for source material. As a subject for literary investigation, they have largely been ignored. Peter Dembowski has written of Old French literature that "hagi-

25. Lot, *The End of the Ancient World,* p. 162. Lot's generalizations, however, are not always reliable. The destruction under Diocletian may have been less widespread. See Augustine's newly discovered letter 29, ed. J. Divjak, *Corpus Scriptorum Ecclesiasticorum Latinorum* 88 (Vienna, 1981) 137–38; F. E. Consolino, "Modeli di santità femminile nelle più antiche passioni romane," *Augustinianum* 24 (1984): 83–113; Clare Stancliffe, "Red, White and Blue Martyrdom," *Ireland in Early Medieval Europe: Studies in Memory of Kathleen Hughes,* ed. D. Whitelock (Cambridge University Press, 1982): 21–46. [I owe these references to Peter Brown—Ed.]
26. "Hagiography and Folklore," p. 324.
27. Günther, "Psicologia della leggenda" (1976), p. 78.

ography . . . is important and the study of that genre has been un-justifiably neglected."[28] His words are even truer for documents from the late antique period.

Curiously, there has been equal neglect from students of myth. Joseph Campbell, for example, devotes a brief section of *The Hero with a Thousand Faces* to "The Hero as Saint" (pp. 354–56) and makes other passing references to saintly heroes, but he does not explore the subject in depth. Yet the lives of the saints who are central to this study, the desert hermits, conform to the paradigms he proposes. It may be that the supposed historical accuracy of these accounts has fostered this omission, for if the lack of authenticity of a particular saint has been demonstrated, then his or her biography has been passed by in silence once the fiction is revealed. One of the most important recent developments in literary scholarship, how-ever, has been the reexaminations of texts in light of findings of structural anthropologists such as Claude Lévi-Strauss and formal-ists such as Vladimir Propp. Such examinations have demonstrated the symbolic structures that lie beneath the surface, even in purely "literary" works. Similarly, in genres traditionally considered non-literary such as historiography and hagiography, such methodolo-gies bear fruit.

My interests are not those of the traditional hagiographer. Like the Bollandists, I am concerned to sift fact from fiction, and my task would be next to impossible without the previous work of such dedicated scholars as Hippolyte Delehaye, Baudouin de Gaiffier, and others. But I am more interested in the fiction than the fact. The rules and requirements of the hagiographic genres are most easily grasped from an examination of the more obviously fictional lives, although details that such accounts throw into high relief can often be paralleled or supplemented from more genuinely biographical works. This study concentrates on the generative narrative matrix that underlies the accounts, and therefore focuses primarily on the more fictive biographies. Such lives, not confined by what "really happened," are free to give expression to what "ought to have hap-

28. Dembowski, "Literary Problems" (1976), p. 117.

pened." They conform more closely to literary or mythic norms of conduct and portray the ideal rather than the actual.

The corpus of hagiographic literature is enormous, and it has been necessary to impose some limits upon the material considered. I have in general restricted my investigation to texts prior to the year 1000, with special emphasis on those accounts dating to the fourth and fifth centuries, although later reworkings can be revealing (St. Onuphrius is a case in point). While I try not to obscure chronology and development, my reading is essentially a synchronic one, as I interpret the different legends as chapters of a single megatext. In addition, although Syrian and Egyptian monasticism were in many ways very different institutions, I have tended to stress the similarities rather than the differences, thereby perhaps obscuring the latter.

Not all saints' lives are the same. *Passiones*, accounts of the martyrs, differ substantially from *vitae*, tales of confessor saints such as the desert hermits. Both tell stories about heroes, but the type of hero and the specific mode his heroic action takes are not identical. While in all cases the ultimate goal is the same, the attainment of the kingdom of heaven, the road taken is a different one. The values encoded alter, and the appeal of the stories may change as well.

For the discussion of the ethos of martyrdom, I have concentrated on two bodies of material: the early passions contained in the *Acta Martyrum Sincera;* and the *passio* of one saint, Vincent of Saragossa, for whom we have three related accounts—the epic *Acta*, the hymn by Prudentius, and the hymn from the Mozarabic liturgy. This wealth of material fosters a sense of reliability and authenticity, but the imprint of the narrative matrix upon the accounts of Vincent is clear.[29]

In considering the non-martyr saints, I have relied primarily upon the texts collected in the *Vitae Patrum*, Book I (*PL* 73). This is essentially an anthology of twenty-seven lives, some of which were translated into Latin before 500 A.D.[30] At first glance, the lives con-

---

29. Ste. Croix, for example, dismisses his *Acta* as no more than a "historical novel"; "Aspects of the 'Great' Persecution" (1954), p. 93.
30. Rosenthal, *The Vitae Patrum* (1936), p. 11. The *vita* of Onuphrius was not

tained in the *Vitae Patrum* offer a bewildering variety. We may read of the well-known and the obscure, of Mary the Egyptian and Onuphrius, of Antony and Macarius. The collection includes Evagrius' translation of the life of Antony and three biographies composed by St. Jerome (the lives of Paul of Thebes, Malchus the captive monk, and Hilarion, which are actually printed in *PL* vol. 21); there are *vitae* of genuinely historic figures such as Pachomius, Ephrem of Syria, and Basil the Great, as well as accounts of Macarius the Roman, whose life has been stigmatized as a "vita fabulosa," a fairy-tale life,[31] and *Barlaam and Josaphat*, a long didactic romance based on the life of the Buddha. In between fall such lives as that of St. Symeon Stylites, supposedly the work of his disciple Antony, which ought, therefore, to be authoritative but which is in fact an apocryphal composition (see below). While most saints in this collection were confessors, a few achieved martyrdom (e.g. Eugenia, Epictetus, and Astion), but their stories differ structurally from the traditional *passio* discussed in chapter 2. These accounts are *vitae* that happen to terminate in martyrdom rather than death by natural causes.

Despite its authoritative status and comparatively early date, many of the stories in the *Vitae Patrum* are rich in the mythic patterns that are the central concern of this study. Of particular importance are the lives of two saints little known today, St. Onuphrius and St. Macarius the Roman. The biography of Macarius has been rightly judged to be fabulous, and its debt to imaginative literature is apparent. The story of Onuphrius is in some respects more complex. This life exists in multiple versions and over the centuries generated the most imaginative fictions. The subject is further complicated by the tentative identification of the Coptic

---

contained in the earliest editions of the *Vitae Patrum;* it was first added in the Nuremburg edition of 1478, although the account is much older (see *PL* 73, 211–22; *AA.SS.*, June III, vol. 23, pp. 16–30 [June 12]). Pope Gelasius in 494 was the first to apply the title *vitae patrum* to the lives written by Jerome, and the entire collection has often been ascribed to Jerome's pen.

31. *AA.SS.*, Oct. X, vol. 58, pp. 563–74 (Oct. 23). See especially the editors' preface, entitled "De Fabuloso S. Macario Romano," section 3, p. 563.

hermit with Osiris, one of whose epithets was Ounnofer, the Good One.[32] This identification is most suggestive in view of the mythic paradigms that, I hypothesize, shape the narratives, but ultimately it remains tenuous.

In addition, I have turned for corroborating material to the works of three writers of monastic biographies: the lives written around 440 A.D. by Theodoret of Cyr to publicize the activities of the Syrian monks, the *Historia Religiosa;* the *Pratum Spirituale* of John Moschus (d. 619); and Palladius' *Historia Lausiaca* (419– 420) which in a Latin translation forms the eighth book of the *Vitae Patrum.*[33] Finally, I have upon occasion included material from the Greek lives collected in the tenth century by Simon Metaphrastes. They are rich and varied. Although later than the other texts, they frequently offer valuable corollary evidence for the nature of the hagiographic genres.

The martyrs were the first heroes of Christianity. Accounts of their lives conform to a pattern of binary opposition in which values are not shaded by absolute. As a result, these tales are structurally simpler than the later stories of the desert hermits. Their strong, positive ethos is well suited to a polarized society of conversion and/or conquest. They have features in common with the later medieval epic, and their appeal, I suggest, increased at a period of great stress and religious confrontation, the Crusades, the very time in which the Old French epic flourished as well.

The martyrs' successors, the monks, fought a different enemy, and the shape of their lives and the narrative structures used to tell them are different. It has frequently been observed that many hagiographic legends are a subspecies of romance. By and large, the accounts of the desert saints form a coherent body of literature. From a synchronic reading of them as individual segments of a megatext, there emerges a coherent hagiographic romance struc-

32. L. Leblois, *Les Bibles et les Initiateurs Religieux* (Paris, 1883), I, 360, n. 302, cited by Saintyves, *Les Saints, successeurs des dieux* (1907), p. 300; see also Neytor, *Les Clefs païennes du christianisme* (1979). Onuphrius' feast, June 12, coincides with the beginning of the flooding of the Nile, an event associated with Osiris.

33. These texts are really a collection of anecdotes, not full narrative *vitae.*

ture. While hagiographic romance resembles, and indeed exploits, traditional romance in a number of ways, it differs in others. In its turn, it exerted influence on later medieval chivalric romance.

Like the more familiar romance heroes, the saintly heroes are questers who travel, usually alone, into an unknown world and there experience suffering and miraculous encounters. But the hagiographic romance is predicated upon the paradox of Christianity: Blessed are the meek for theirs is the Kingdom of Heaven. In hagiography, as elsewhere, the last shall be first. To attain the golden-age life of the terrestrial paradise, the hermit lives and tests himself in the harshest landscape he can fine, the barren desert fastness, and there he gladly suffers.

The treatment of suffering in the hagiographic romances may seem paradoxical. The martyrs' passions should, by rights, be stories of suffering, but these accounts stress instead the relative unimportance of suffering and pain. The hero rises above his torments. The elaborate tortures, which generally fail either to harm the saint or to persuade him to recant, only serve to show the powerlessness of the tyrant and the triumph of the martyr. In the *vitae*, however, the hero suffers, although his pain is often self-inflicted. This fact links hagiographic romances with traditional romance. According to Northrop Frye, the ability to suffer is a romance virtue: "With the rise of the romantic ethos, heroism comes increasingly to be thought of in terms of suffering, endurance, and patience, which can coexist with such [physical] weakness, whatever other kinds of strength it may require."[34] Men need both kinds of heroes, those who are above suffering and are able to face pain and adversity with laughter, and those who suffer and weep, and triumph all the same. The martyr is the first kind of hero and the ascetic the second.

In the chapters that follow, I investigate first the narrative structure of the martyrs' passions, then the *vitae* of the early ascetics. The structure of the former accounts is comparatively simple. The ethos is one of binary and inflexible opposition between Christian and pagan, good and evil. The road followed is, comparatively

34. *The Secular Scripture* (1976), p. 88.

speaking, a straight one. The narrative strategies employed to fabulate the lives of the desert solitaries are more complex. Such accounts are predicated less upon the basic conflict between two religions—an external, social struggle—than on an interior conflict, as the saint flees society in his or her search for perfection. To continue the metaphor of the journey, the road taken is winding. The narrative matrix of the ascetics' lives differ; as a result of its complexity, the greater part of this book is devoted to exploring the way these lives are told. Since the martyrs were chronologically the first saintly heroes, and since their stories are simpler, it is to these that we first turn.

Chapter 2
Hagiographic Epic

The martyrs were the earliest Christian heroes. In a seminal article entitled "Two Types of Opposition and the Structure of Saints' Lives," Charles F. Altman presents a provocative analysis of the plot structures found respectively in the *passio* of the martyr-saint and the *vita* of the confessor. He begins by pointing to two types of contrast common in medieval narratives, *diametrical* opposition such as that between virtue and vice, and *gradational* contrast such as that observable in Gregory the Great's distinction between action and contemplation ("Action is not bad, like vice, it is simply not as good as contemplation").[1] Altman perceives the same two-fold opposition in the plot structures of hagiographic texts.

In the first group are the *passiones*, or legends of the martyr saint; these, like the medieval epic, operate according to the principles of diametric opposition. In the second we have the *vitae*, or biographies of the confessor saints; these grew slowly away from the diametrical configuration of the *passio*, eventually adopting fully the gradational form of romance (p. 1).

The pure *passio* (as distinct from certain later, hybrid accounts such as that of Epictetus and Astion in the *Vitae Patrum*) is a unified narrative depicting a single, heroic action, even though that action may extend over as many as seven years, as in the martyrdom of St. George. It opens with a confrontation scene between saint and

1. "Two Types of Opposition" (1975), p. 1.

tyrant during which the government representative tries to convince the future martyr to recant and sacrifice to the pagan gods. This scene, according to Altman, serves to identify the values represented in the *passio* not with the particular individuals portrayed but with the issues, the religious and moral values that they represent. Between the two sides there can be no middle ground, no mediation. The concluding section of the narrative deals with the support group for both sides, including a deity and a sympathetic audience; the narrator of the *passio* identifies with the martyr's support group and therefore regularly employs the first person plural in his narration instead of the third person singular.

The *vita*, by comparison, presents a gradational view of the universe, in which *good* is opposed to *better* and *worse*. The narrator (often in the first person singular) relates a series of events that are designed primarily to reveal the confessor saint as one set apart from his or her fellows,[2] one better than they are. The saint, especially if an ascetic, generally withdraws from society to pursue his *personal* goal of achieving the perfect religious life. Unlike the martyr's opposition to pagan society, the ascetic's act does not necessarily imply that society is evil or corrupt, only that the eremetic life is "better." This action is one of the individual seeking his own salvation in solitude. Sometimes the saint, having completed his quest, returns to society (p. 6) (although often unwillingly), but frequently he does not.

The description of hagiographic plots formulated by Altman is, as he admits, highly simplified, but it is nonetheless useful.[3] The abstract plot of the passion, moreover, bears a close resemblance to medieval epic, while that of the *vita* is like ancient as well as medieval romance. These conclusions are vital because, I believe, the similarity in narrative structures facilitated the perpetuation of a common ethos and symbolism. The narrative deep structure, the

2. Since most of the desert "fathers," with the obvious exception of St. Mary the Egyptian, were male, I will for simplicity use masculine pronouns, without, however, intending to ignore or belittle the female saints.

3. Olsen in "'De Historiis Sanctorum,'" p. 407, criticizes Altman for ignoring "the many different hagiographic works which belong to neither category." In spite of this limitation, Altman's work is original and valuable.

matrix, both allowed the preservation of archaic symbols (particularly in the *vita*), and allowed those paradigms privileged by hagiographic accounts to be easily assimilated and reused in similar narratives, as well as in closely related medieval genres such as the *chanson de geste* and the chivalric romance (see ch. 8).

THE ETHOS OF MARTYRDOM

The spirit of martyrdom is a social one. Passion literature is a celebration of community, and the values depicted are those of an entire society. Although the accounts describe acts of great personal courage, the purpose is not the glorification of the individual per se but the affirmation of the ideals for which the saint has given his or her life. In the more historic *Acta*, often little or nothing is known of the saint prior to his appearance in the magistrate's court. Even when more material is available (for example, for St. Cyprian of Carthage or Justin Martyr, both of whom left a substantial body of writing),[4] these details are generally excluded from the *passio*. Many accounts provide absolutely no background information other than what emerges during the interrogation. From the *Acta* of the Veteran Julius, for instance, we learn from the saint's own mouth that he enjoyed a blameless soldierly career and had reenlisted as a veteran; we know nothing more.[5] By comparison, the rather meager information provided in the *Acta* of Perpetua and Felicity seems positively lavish:

A number of young catechumens were arrested, Revocatus and his fellow slave Felicitas, Saturninus, and Secundulus, and with them Vibia Perpetua, a newly married woman of good family and upbringing. Her mother and father were still alive and one of her two brothers was a catechumen like herself. She was about twenty-two years old and had an infant son at the breast.[6]

Later accounts generally added material. After the Peace of Con-

---

4. For Justin Martyr (d. ca. 165 A.D.), see Musurillo, *Acts*, (1972), pp. xvii–xx, and for Cyprian, pp. xxx–xxxi. Cyprian's *Acta* are based on official court records; see Delehaye, *Les Légendes hagiographiques* (1927).
5. See Musurillo, *Acts*, pp. 260–63, and see below.
6. Translation from Ibid., pp. 108–109, slightly modified.

stantine ended the days of martyrdom, audiences became more interested in the lives of their heroes prior to the "Baptism by Blood," but in the early passions the background of the saint pales into insignificance. The life in this world was irrelevant in comparison with the passage to that to come.

Nevertheless, even though the martyr disdained this world, he defined himself in social terms, albeit negatively. He was distinguished by his diametrical opposition to pagan culture. The ethos of martyrdom is at once dissociative and integrative since to reject A (paganism) is by definition to embrace B (Christianity). There is no tenable middle ground, no position of compromise. Therefore, the things of this world, or of a prior (possibly pagan) existence, were of no value. What mattered was citizenship in the City of God.

For example, in one of the earliest documents, the anonymous "Epistle to Diognetus," the Christians are described as strangers on earth but citizens of heaven. This relationship, moreover, is expressed in diametric terms:

They reside in their own fatherlands, but as if they were *non-citizens;* they take part in all things as if they were citizens and suffer all things as if they were strangers; every foreign country is a fatherland to them and every fatherland is to them a foreign country . . . They dwell in earth, but they are *citizens* in heaven.[7]

The author of the third version of the *Acta* of Justin Martyr and his companions notes the confraternity of the martyrs:[8]

Now the saints did not have the same native city, for they came from different countries. But the favour of the Spirit bound them together, and taught them to have fraternal thoughts. . . . They confessed that they were Christians . . . and said that their only city was God's, the free city, the heavenly Jerusalem.[9]

They refuse to tell the praetor the names of their earthly cities.

Even the metaphoric and figurative language of the *passiones* stresses the abnegation of personal identity and the compensating

7. Quoted by Ladner, *"Homo Viator"* (1967), p. 236, emphasis added.
8. Recension C, "literary version," which Musurillo dates around 431; Musurillo, *Acts,* p. 57, n. 16.
9. Ibid., p. 55.

sense of community. St. Polycarp is described as being "bound like a noble ram chosen as an oblation from a great flock."[10] When St. Papylus, responding to a question about his family, stated that he had many children, he meant, we are told, "children in the Lord," or "spiritual children."[11] Many martyrs, moreover, went to their deaths together, comforting and exhorting each other. Blandina, one of the many martyrs of Lyons, strove to comfort her fellows, and the hagiographer compared her action to that of a mother encouraging her children.[12] The image is a societal one, the family. Finally, echoing the Pauline metaphor of *militia Christi,* the great hymn of praise, the *Te Deum,* refers to the martyrs as an army: "Te martyrum candidatus laudat exercitus" (The shining army of martyrs praises Thee).[13]

One of the clearest indications of the collective ethos of passion literature is the frequency with which martyrs abandoned their personal names in favor of the generic identification, "Christianus sum." Thus St. Carpus replied to the question, "What is your name?" with the answer: "My first and most distinctive name is Christian, but if you seek to know my name in the world, it is Carpus."[14] Asked "What is your station and what is your name?" the soldier Dasius answered: "I am a soldier by rank. Of my name I shall tell you that I have the distinctive one of Christian; but the name given me by my parents is Dasius."[15] Sanctus, one of the martyrs of Lyons, was more stubborn, responding to all questions with the statement, "I am a Christian."[16] The soldier Maximilian considered his name irrelevant: "Why do you want to know my name? It is not permitted to me to be a soldier because I am a Christian."[17] Finally, in Pamphylia, Conon, a slave of Greek ancestry to judge by

10. Ibid., pp. 12–13.

11. Ibid., pp. 26–27 and 30–31.

12. The reference is specifically to the mother of Maccabbees, 2 Macc. 7:20–23; see Musurillo, *Acts,* pp. 78–79.

13. Cf. Rom. 13:12; 2 Cor. 10:3–8; Eph. 6:10–18; Phil. 2:25; 1 Tim. 1:18; 2 Tim. 2:3–4.

14. Musurillo, *Acts,* p. 22.

15. Ibid., p. 276.

16. Ibid., pp. 68–69.

17. Ibid., p. 244.

his name, claimed Christ's hometown as his own and refused to give his name:

> The prefect said to the martyr: "Tell me, fellow, where are you from? Of what descent are you? What is your name?"
>
> "I am from the city of Nazareth in Galilea," answered Conon, "and my kinship [suggeneia] is with Christ, whose worship I inherited from my forefathers."[18]

In addition, personal identity is obscured by the symbolic interpretation given many names,[19] modeled on Christ's statement to Peter, "Tu es Petrus" (Thou art Peter). In the *Legenda aurea*, for example, a *praesagium nominis*, an *argumentum a nomine* (prophecy from the name or argument from the name) precedes most accounts.[20] Names, then, do not serve to distinguish one saint from another. What the name "Christianus" does is to distinguish one religion from another.[21]

The motif also appears in the legendary account of Epictetus and Astion,[22] one of the two martyr stories contained in the *Vitae Patrum*, where it shows the centrality of the motif to the ethos of martyrdom. Neither this *vita* nor that of another martyr, Eugenia, conforms wholly to the preceding description of passion literature, for both are genuine *vitae*, not *passiones*—that is, while the saints die a martyr's death, this event, far from being the central narrative interest of the story, comprises but one element in a complex tale.

The persecuting magistrate asks the pair: "Quae sunt vocabula

---

18. Ibid., pp. 188–89. Musurillo writes of Conon's response, "It is noteworthy that a man with such a historic Greek name should have come from Nazareth; if he was not originally a slave, he may have been descended from some Greek soldier stationed in Palestine" (p. 189, n.4). It is, I suggest, equally likely that Conon did not come from Nazareth but gave here the geographical equivalent of "Christianus sum."

19. See also Esbroeck, "Le saint comme symbole" (1980), 128–40. "Sanctus," one of the martyrs of Lyons, mentioned above, is a case in point.

20. See Boureau, *Les Formes narratives de la Légende dorée* (1981), p. 209.

21. The detail, moreover, survived in accounts of non-martyr saints; therefore in later versions of the *Vie de saint Alexis*, when asked his name, the saint responds that he is called "Chrestiens" (ms. S, 797, ms. M², 668, 709; ed. Elliott).

22. For the legendary nature of this account, see Delehaye, "Saints de Thrace" (1912), p. 273–74.

vestra, quod genus, seu de quali provincia vos estis oriundi?" (What
are your names, what is your family, and from what province have
you come?). The saints reply in unison: "Nos Christiani sumus,[23] et
de parentibus nati Christianis, atque de Christianorum patria nos
sumus oriundi"[24] (We are Christians, and are born of Christian parents, and we have come from the fatherland of the Christians).
When Conon the slave claimed Nazareth as his hometown, I suspect he was speaking figuratively although I have no proof. In the
case of Astion at least, the statement "born of Christian parents" is
demonstrably false. Although we are told nothing of Epictetus'
background, Astion's wealthy father was described as a "primarius
urbis" (a man of the first rank in the city); his mother was the
daughter of a senator named Julian. Astion fled in secret (see below)
because he feared his pagan father's violent reaction to his becoming a Christian: "Si Christianus effectus fuero, [pater] prae nimia
desperatione, aut spiritu violenter careat, aut in profundum maris
semetipsum praecipitet" (397C; If I became a Christian, [my father]
from an excess of despair would either lose his life violently or
throw himself into the depths of the sea). Astion's parents are converted to Christianity only after their son's death. The motif has become a *topos*, a significant and desirable element in the narration.
The martyrs denied (and were expected to deny) a private and personal identity in order to embrace a public one.

The verb *marturein* is in origin a legal term meaning "to bear witness," "to testify," an act that requires the presence of others before
whom one testifies; the word in its literal sense is meaningless in
solitude. In marked contrast to the private nature of the spiritual
martyrdom of the ascetics, literal martyrdom is unimaginable divorced from its social and political context. It transpires in a wholly
different environment, in the hellenized *polis*, not in the desert
wilderness. If its goal was the attainment of the next world,
its locus was this one. The scene in which the drama of martyrdom
is played out is public: the magistrate's court, the arena, the ex-

23. The refrain "Christiani sumus," (We are Christians), recurs four times in
their response to the tyrant.
24. *PL* 73, 402B.

ecution ground. The texts are dramatic, often recording not only the exchange between martyr and persecutor but the remarks of the onlookers as well, whether hostile pagans or sympathetic Christians.[25]

In this atmosphere of public confrontation, as in other respects, the *passio* reveals its affinities with an epic ethos. The goal of the Homeric warrior, for example, was *kleos aphthiton* (undying glory),[26] but such glory, such good repute, is possible only when men know what the hero has done. It is defined in terms of other— other men's opinion, other men's talk. In a medieval epic such as the *Chanson de Roland*, the hero exhorts his knights to fight well so that men will not make bad songs about them (v. 1014), and the poem itself is a good song. The martyr, to be sure, does not care about men's opinion, only about God's, and yet just as much as an Achilles or a Roland, he too can only act in a socially defined and structured context. Unless the Roman magistrate exists to enter into the dialogue with him, the saint cannot attain martyrdom. His tale cannot be told. He must bear witness to someone before someone. For the audience, however, his publicly-earned glory matters greatly. It is a goal to be aspired to. Martyrdom, therefore, is a cultural artifact—one that in fact challenged the entire fabric of society.

TO SPEAK A MARTYRDOM

In his monograph, *Structure and Sacring: The Systematic Kingdom in Chrétien's Erec et Enide*, Donald Maddox distinguishes between two types of reading:

The reader is simultaneously drawn into and driven beyond the opening segment. If the centripetal attraction is dominant, he will begin to observe a static hierarchy of features analogous to a musical chord. If the centrifugal drive takes over, the chord becomes animated rhythmically and transformed, assuming the dynamic forward sweep of an orchestral score.[27]

25. Musurillo, *Acts*, pp. lii–liii, in the Acts of Phileas, Irenaeus, Apollonius, Carpus and Companions, Pionius.

26. For a discussion of this concept, with a full bibliography, see Nagy, *Comparative Studies* (1974), 229–61, as well as his *The Best of the Achaeans* (1979).

27. Maddox, *Structure and Sacring* (1978), pp. 73–74.

Maddox is here talking about complementary modes of reading, but the terms "centripetal" and "centrifugal" can also be used to describe forms of narrative. Centripetal narrative moves, with very little structural variety, in a straight line toward a single climax; it presents a predictable, almost rigid, and univalent story. The *passio* is such a narrative, as it progresses inevitably to confrontation (sometimes preceded by arrest), followed by torture and death. A postlude is sometimes added with the aftermath of death—miracles, punishment of the wicked. The action pulls into itself all who witness it, even the poet. The role of impartial observer is not a narrative option since the act involves the entire society and polarizes everyone; all witnesses are moved either to greater fury or to compassion and conversion. In *Peristephanon* III, Prudentius gave symbolic expression to this force of polarization as he depicted the impetuous Eulalia bursting into the praetor's court (see below). But whatever the individual circumstances may be, the passion narrative, without reversals, obstacles, or suspense, moves relentlessly to its triumphant conclusion. All roads lead to a known destination—to Rome, whether literally or figuratively, and thence to the Heavenly Jerusalem.

As Altman noted, the climactic center of the *passio* was not the moment of death but the interrogation scene in which tyrant and martyr face each other in public in the courtroom. A common early Latin translation of the Greek *marturein* was *martyrium dicere*, "to speak one's testimony or witnessing to the faith."[28] In the *passiones* direct speech constitutes an act of the first importance.[29] The drama calls for intense physical suffering, but the necessary prelude to physical *agon* is verbal *agon*: the ritual contest prefigures the literal. The hero must triumph in word and in deed.

Direct discourse, moreover, is unambiguous, and it serves as the primary means by which the polarities of the narrative are established. As we shall see, characters whose significant actions do not

28. For example, *Vita Antonii* 46.6.
29. In what follows I am drawing on my articles, "The Power of Discourse" (1982), and "The Martyr as Epic Hero" (1978).

include important speech acts tend in later reworkings to be eliminated from the drama. In addition, direct speech often performs a
function beyond the purely denotative. In the martyr's speech of
defiance and confession of faith during the confrontation scene, the
words are directed beyond the seemingly intended receiver in the
text—exceeding, therefore, their apparent dramatic function—to
the audience at large. Speeches that seem, from the actor's point of
view, designed to persuade or convert are, from the audience's perspective, statements of belief, incapable of alteration and proof
against mediation. On the other hand, discourse that appears to be
purely declarative may be persuasive for the listeners.

In the climactic confrontation scene the tyrant attempts to persuade the saint to recant; the saint defiantly refuses, confesses his
(or her) faith, and assails pagan religion. Then follow torture and
death. The prominence of such scenes probably owes as much to
literary criteria as to historical fact. In the comparatively few "historic" accounts that have survived, this section of the narrative is
usually brief.[30] Compared to later documents, these official *Acta* are
almost wholly devoid of emotion or rhetoric. The confrontation
consists of a few brief interchanges between the accused and the
presiding magistrate. For example, in the *Acta* of the Veteran
Julius, the magistrate Maximus is portrayed as a reasonable man
who unwillingly gives the order for the soldier's execution only after persuasion has failed to move the saint.

Maximus dixit: Suadetur tibi; nam si pro patriae legibus patereris, ha-
beres perpetuam laudem.
Julius respondit: Pro legibus certe haec patior, sed pro divinis. . . .
Maximus dixit: Condolens tibi do consilium ut magis sacrifices et vivas
nobiscum.
Julius respondit: Si vixero vobiscum, mors mihi erit; si in conspectu
domini mortuus fuero, in perpetuum vivo.
Maximus dixit: Audi me et sacrifica, ne te, sicut promisi, occidam.
Julius dixit: Elegi mori ad tempus ut in perpetuo vivam cum sanctis.

30. Probably not more than seventy authentic *passiones* are extant (Lot, *The End
of the Ancient World* [1931], p. 162). There is a good selection of texts in Harnack,
Militia Christi (1905); see also Musurillo, *Acts.*

Sic Maximus praeses dedit sententiam, dicens: Julius, nolens praeceptis regalibus adquiescere, capitalem accipiat sententiam.[31]

(Maximus said: Be persuaded, for if you obey the laws you will gain eternal praise.

Julius replied: Certainly I suffer these things for laws, but for divine ones.

Maximus said: Grieving for you, I advise you that it is better for you to sacrifice and live among us.

Julius replied: If I live among you, it will be death for me; but if I die in the sight of the Lord, I live forever.

Maximus said: Listen to me and sacrifice, lest I kill you as I have promised.

Julius said: I choose timely death so that I may live forever with the saints.

Thus Maximus the presiding magistrate passed sentence, saying: Let Julius, since he is unwilling to abide by the king's instructions, receive the death sentence.)

Although the exchange between saint and magistrate is carefully balanced to stress the opposition between *militia Christi* (military service to Christ) and temporal service, between this world and the next, only the first and last sentences of the document (where the executioner, for example, is described as a "minister diaboli" [servant of the devil]) use emotional language that would not be found in a court transcript.

In later *Acta*, those dating to the fourth and fifth centuries, which Hippolyte Delehaye has christened "epic,"[32] we find a far different situation. The courtroom scene is long and dramatic, its function dialectical. Two facts about the "epic" *Acta* are significant here: they were composed after the Peace of Constantine; and they were largely based on oral traditions, since many Church documents had been destroyed during the persecution of Diocletian.[33] Consequently, for the epic *Acta* there is the possibility of adherence to ideal, as well as to actual, standards of behavior. In these passions, Delehaye distinguished a new emphasis on the miraculous, although miracles

31. Text from Harnack, *Militia Christi* (1905), pp. 120–21.
32. *Les Passions des martyrs et les genres littéraires* (1966), pp. 171 ff.
33. Prudentius comments on this destruction, *Peristephanon* I, 73 ff. For a discussion see Ste. Croix, "Aspects of the 'Great' Persecution" (1954), p. 75.

play a far less important role than they do in the "romanesque" passions such as that of St. George. More important, however, is a new recognition that the martyr is indeed a hero: "The hagiographer makes one understand that the martyr is for the Christian what heroes are for peoples who have founded nations at the cost of their lives."[34]

The triumphant heroism of the martyrs is perhaps most plainly visible in the hymns entitled collectively the *Peristephanon* (*Crowns of Martyrdom*) composed by Aurelius Prudentius Clemens around 405 A.D.[35] The most interesting hymn for our purposes is the fifth, dedicated to St. Vincent of Saragossa, martyred during the reign of Diocletian. Vincent became one of the best-known Spanish martyrs; his adversary, Dacian, provincial governor of Tarragona, acquired great repute as a savage persecutor, a fame he largely owed to his connection with Vincent.[36] The two serve as useful templates for the ideal martyr-hero and the stereotyped tyrant.

Vincent's *Acta* are a good example of an epic passion.[37] Their connection with historical fact, however, is tenuous. Noting that no reliable passion survives from Spain, Ste. Croix has called the *Acta* of Vincent a "historical novel."[38] Jacques Fontaine remarks upon the "démesure" (exaggeration) of popular tales, which is also apparent in Prudentius' hymn in honor of Vincent.[39] The hero is bold and defiant; the tyrant, in marked contrast to Maximus in the account of the Veteran Julius, has been metamorphosed into an inhuman monster—"furore caecus . . . prae ira . . . extra se positus . . .

34. Delehaye, *Les Passions*, p. 172: "L'hagiographe fait comprendre que, pour le chrétien le martyr est ce que sont pour les peuples les héros qui, au prix de leur vie, ont fondé la nationalité."

35. The earliest hymns in honor of the martyrs were written a generation earlier by St. Ambrose. They all consist of thirty-two lines of iambic dimeter.

36. Gaiffier, "*Sub Daciano Praeside*" (1967), pp. 6 ff.

37. *AA.SS.* Jan. III, vol. 3, pp. 6–10 (Jan. 22); *Acta Vincenti.*

38. "Aspects of the 'Great' Persecution," p. 93 (quoting Delehaye, *Les Légendes*, p. 114).

39. "Quelle désinvolture dans l'invention folklorique, mais aussi quelle démesure de conte populaire se manifestent dans une hymne comme la pièce 5 en l'honneur de saint Vincent" (What offhandedness in folkloric invention, but also what exaggeration of the popular tale are revealed in a hymn like number 5, in honor of St. Vincent, "Le mélange des genres," in *Etudes*, p. 772.)

fervens insania"[40] (blind with raging anger . . . outside himself with
wrath . . . seething in madness)—a melodramatic stereotype that
Prudentius not only retained in his hymn but expanded. Vincent replies to Dacian's threats with polemical sermons. There are many
actors in the drama. Vincent's nobly-born parents are named;
Bishop Valerius of Saragossa, whose archdeacon Vincent was, figures prominently; a throng of guards witnesses the miracle of the
blooming potsherds and the appearance of the band of angels in
prison.

In general Prudentius followed the *Acta* closely, but he made a
number of informative alterations and omissions, as he narrowed
the focus of the story and reduced the number of actors involved.
Two principles seem to lie behind this action on the poet's part. The
first was Prudentius' apparent desire to free his hero from all personal and local associations. For example, in the previous hymn,
Peristephanon IV, in honor of the eighteen martyrs of Saragossa,
Prudentius made much of St. Vincent's local connections. In the
fifth hymn, however, he does not mention the saint's origins; there
are, in fact, no geographical references at all in *Peristephanon* V.
This omission alone is somewhat surprising, given Prudentius' de-
served reputation for patriotic Hispanicity and the spirit of local
fervor that frequently pervades hagiography. For Prudentius,
moreover, Vincent would have been a local hero, having been born
at Osca (Huesca), and educated at Caesaraugusta (Saragossa),
where he served as archdeacon, although actually martyred at
Valentia (Valencia). But in this poem Prudentius deemed all such
geographic references undesirable. He also ignored the saint's family, omitting the name of his parents, contained in the *Acta*, as well
as the tradition that Vincent was the nephew of St. Lawrence (the
hero of *Peristephanon* II).

Prudentius isolates Vincent's passion in time and space. Avoiding
all extraneous details and minor characters, he builds his narrative
around the interactions of four mortals—Vincent, Dacian, a single
jailor, and the soldier charged with the disposal of the saint's

40. *Acta Vincenti* (see above, note 37), pp. 7–8.

body—together with the angel who appears dramatically at the center of the poem. Consequently the lines of Prudentius' account stand out in stark relief. Unlike ordinary mortals, Vincent is superior to private and personal concerns,[41] and his drama is thereby universalized. Vincent becomes a hero for all Christendom, not merely for Spain or for Saragossa. *Peristephanon* IV exalts a group of martyrs for their local associations, as does *Peristephanon* VI, dedicated to the martyrs of nearby Tarragona. Placed between these two expressions of regional piety, the fifth hymn celebrates one of Saragossa's martyrs in universal terms.

By removing specific geographic and personal references from the hymn, Prudentius has given it almost epic proportions. The conflict is not the confrontation between two individuals named Vincent and Dacian; it is a figuration of the cosmic conflict between good and evil, new and old.[42] The action occurs not in early fourth-century Caesaraugusta or Valentia but anywhere and everywhere. The passion of the martyr is not only an individual *imitatio Christi*, but it is also an example for all Christians to follow even after the days of literal martyrdom have come to an end, for it is an image of the fight between good and evil that is fought by Christians everywhere.

The second reason for the narrowing of focus in Prudentius' version of Vincent's passion highlights the importance of speech. Those characters who are not called upon to make significant speeches are eliminated from the drama. Discourse becomes the most significant action, the means by which the polar oppositions of the drama are established. Of Prudentius' use of speech, Jacques Fontaine writes: "The importance of the speeches . . . in the poetry of Prudentius is another source of difficulty for the modern reader, especially in the works that the meter itself places under the sign of lyricism."[43] He notes that it is not enough to invoke the speech of

41. A similar desire to isolate the saint may lie behind the frequency with which the more mythic or fictional saints are depicted as only children; see below, ch. 4.
42. For a discussion of this general theme in Prudentius, see Smith, *Prudentius' Psychomachia* (1976), p. 237.
43. Fontaine, "Le mélange," p. 772: "L'importance des discours . . . dans la poésie de Prudence est pour le lecteur moderne une autre source d'inconfort, en par-

Regulus in Horace or to point to the exclamatory nature of Lucan
to explain this phenomenon.

After a brief, hymnal proem, Prudentius plunges into his drama.
He omits the first act, to which the *Acta* devoted an entire chapter,
the arrest of Vincent's immediate superior, Bishop Valerius, and the
subsequent exile of the bishop. His poem begins abruptly with Dacian's first speech interrogating the saint after Valerius' exile. Dacian summarily orders Vincent to obey Roman law and sacrifice. In
the *Acta* the martyr's refusal is preceded by a long profession of
faith; Prudentius' hymn retains this speech but reduces it to its
essentials in order to highlight more dramatically the diametrical
opposition between pagan and Christian.

> "Tibi ista praesint numina,
> tu saxa, tu lignum colas,
> tu mortuorum mortuus
> fias deorum pontifex;
>   "nos lucis auctorem patrem
> eiusque Christum filium,
> qui solus ac uerus deus,
> Datiane, confitebimur."[44]

(33–40)

("Let these be your masters; you may worship stones and wood and become the dead priest of dead gods. We shall confess the Father, the author
of light, and Christ His Son, who is the only and true God, O Dacian.")

The balanced structure of the strophes reflects the binary opposition. The first, with its triple anaphora, stresses the pagan's error;
the second, whose first word is "nos" (we) and whose last is "con-
fitebimur" (confess), states the Christian position. This speech is
not intended to convince Dacian of his folly, nor does it do so. Its
purpose is to remind the audience at the outset of the religious positions embraced by the two antagonists.

---

ticulier dans les pièces que leur mètre même place sous le signe de lyrisme." *Peris-*
tephanon V is in iambic dimeter.

44. All citations of Prudentius are from the edition of Cunningham, *Aurelii*
Prudentii Clementis Carmina (1966).

In the *Acta* Vincent's refusal to sacrifice throws Dacian into a rage, and he immediately orders the infliction of the severest punishments on the martyr. For Prudentius, however, the confrontation between saint and tyrant is the high point of the drama, so he prolongs the scene. Dacian orders Vincent to sacrifice or die. Vincent replies with a thirty-nine line speech of excited defiance, continuing to attack pagan religion (vv. 54–93). It is in this scene (vv. 21–204), 86 percent of which consists of direct discourse, that the inflexible opposition between Christian and pagan is most clearly stated, as both antagonists remain inflexible. Then physical violence replaces verbal, as Dacian hands Vincent over to the torturers. To Dacian's utter frustration, Vincent only smiles at the torments and threatens the pagan governor of Tarragona with hellfire.

> "Exemplar hoc, serpens, tuum est,
> fuligo quem mox sulpuris
> bitumen et mixtum pice
> imo inplicabunt tartaro."
>   His persecutor saucius
> pallet rubescit aestuat
> insana torquens lumina,
> spumasque frendensque egerit.

(197–204)

("This is your example, serpent, whom one day soon sulphurous soot and bitumen and pitch will envelop deep in Hell." Wounded by these words, the persecutor at first turns pale, then red, and in the heat of his passion rolls his maddened eyes, gnashing his teeth and foaming at the mouth.)

With this depiction of Dacian as an insane beast, the first section of the hymn concludes. It has been characterized by the unyielding opposition between the representatives of good and evil; neither side will give an inch. The more terribly the tyrant rages, the more defiant and scornful the martyr becomes. Over three-quarters of this dramatic scene consists of direct speech, as the martyr confesses his faith and challenges the beliefs of his adversary. Now actions replace words. The baptism by blood begins.

The transition between the first and second sections stresses the binary opposition between good and evil.

> Ventum ad palestram gloriae;
> spes certat et crudelitas,
> luctamen anceps conserunt
> hinc martyr illinc carnifex.
>
> (213–16)

(They come together on the athletic field of glory; Hope and Cruelty do battle, and martyr on one side, torturer on the other, they join in the crucial struggle.)

The athletic metaphor (a hagiographic commonplace) stresses the active nature of the saint's role in the ensuing action. It signals the change from verbal to physical *agon*. Of his own accord ("sponte," v. 221), Vincent ascends the pyre, unafraid. He is no passive victim, but a willing, energetic participant in the contest. But more is at stake than the fate of one man: Hope and Cruelty, Good and Evil, are pitted against one another in mortal combat.

Vincent's tortures are described in minute and painful detail for eight lines (vv. 225–32) to emphasize the martyr's heroic indifference to them: "Haec inter inmotus manet / tamquam dolorum nescius"[45] (vv. 233–34; Amid these things he remains unmoved, as if ignorant of the pains). Finally, as a previously unheard-of torment, the saint is thrust into a totally dark dungeon and there made to rest his battered body on the sharp edges of broken potsherds. In prison he is comforted by a band of angels, one of whom addresses him:

> "Exsurge, martyr inclyte,
> exsurge securus tui,
> exsurge et almis coetibus
> noster sodalis addere!"
>
> (285–88)

("Arise, illustrious martyr, arise, confident of yourself, arise, and as our companion join in the propitious throng!")

This is the only speech in the middle section of the poem (vv. 209–

---

45. Some see "inmotus manet" (remains unmoved) as a Vergilian echo, citing *Georg.* II, 294, *Aen.* IV, 449, etc.; see Rodriguez and Guillén, *Obras completas de Aurelio Prudencio* (1950), p. 785. A more immediate parallel is to be found in the description of *Patientia* in the *Psychomachia*, who stands "inmota" (v. 110) before the attack of *Ira*. *Ira* is described in the same terms as the traditional tyrant of the *passiones*.

368), in contrast to the first section, where direct address accounted for the majority of the narrative. Portions that in the *Acta* had been in direct address—for example, the order to imprison the saint in total darkness—have been shifted to indirect speech. As a result the angel's speech rings out in dramatic contrast to the surrounding descriptive passages. The invitation to join the band of angels prior to the Last Judgment is the specific reward for martyrdom, a doctrinal point that the structure of the poem throws into high relief. It is a fitting reflection of the communal ethos of passion narrative.

After Vincent's death, the remainder of the hymn concerns the tyrant's vain attempts to destroy the saint's corpse, attempts foiled by a series of miracles. A crow defends the exposed body from marauders; when the soldier Eumorphio throws it into the sea, weighted by a millstone, it floats to shore. The poem closes with a prayer asking the martyr to pity those venerating his holy day and to intercede with Christ on their behalf.

In Prudentius' drama, direct discourse is unproblematic. There is little gap between interior and exterior, actual (or intended) and apparent meaning. Characters—their speeches and actions—are diametrically opposed, their differences irreconcilable. But here history and the generic expectations of hagiographic narrative are in conflict. In the "historic" *Acta*, some magistrates (for example, Maximus cited above) tried with apparent sincerity to persuade the martyrs to recant. Prudentius, however, is careful that we do not think Dacian anything but dedicated to the cause of evil. The narrator characterizes the tyrant's first speech as mild and flattering:

> Ac uerba primum mollia
> suadendo blande effuderat . . .
>
> (17–18)

(But first he poured out soft words, gently persuading . . .)

These lines, however, are immediately followed by a simile that undercuts the apparent softness of Dacian's words:

> captator ut uitulum lupus
> rapturus adludit prius.
>
> (19–20)

(just as the hunting wolf first plays with the calf it is going to capture.)

The future active participle, "rapturus," excludes any possibility of doubt about Dacian's intentions. He has no genuine desire at all to convince. At best the tone of his first speech might be characterized as matter-of-fact: it is neither particularly soft ("mollia") nor flattering ("blande"). The Roman monarch, says Dacian, has ordered the Christians to sacrifice; the imperatives are peremptory:

> vos, Nazareni, adsistite,
> rudemque ritum spernite.
> Haec saxa quae princeps colit
> placate fumo et victima.
>
> (25–28)

(You Nazarenes, attend; shun your crude rites. Propitiate with smoke and sacrificial victims those stones that the prince worships.)

In a second, more emotional ("commotior," v. 41) speech, Dacian threatens immediate death if the appointed sacrifices are not made, and flattery is nowhere apparent in his speech. Overt threats and orders are his normal mode of discourse, but they are ineffectual, as he fails to frighten or to persuade.

The apparent conflict between the tone of Dacian's speech and the interpretative preface to it (vv. 17–20) is not a sign of failure or lack of artistic control on Prudentius' part. The historical tradition indicated that the opening speeches of the Roman magistrates were often mild; the later hagiographic tradition admitted no stance but that of total commitment. Intention and appearance must coincide. Consequently the simile (vv. 19–20) focusses the reader's attention on the predatory nature of Dacian's verbal play. In verses 17–18, Prudentius bows to expectations aroused by history, in 19–20 he undercuts them.[46]

The world of hagiography as depicted in the passions is black and white. Words mean what they say; what men say corresponds

---

46. Similarly, in the *Acta* of Saint Fides of Agen (whose tormentor is, in violation of history, none other than Dacian), the tyrant first attempts to talk the saint into relenting, but the narrator characterizes him in this instance as "callidissimus simulata tranquillitate" (most clever in his pretended calm) (*AA.SS.* Oct. III, vol. 51, p. 288E, [Oct. 6]). This interpretation of Dacian's behavior is perpetuated in Hildebert of Lavardin's metrical life ("mentem tranquillam simulans" [pretending a calm mind], *AA.SS.* Oct. VIII, vol. 56, p. 827A [Oct. 20]).

to what they do.[47] The saint confesses his faith, then translates words into actions. Thus in *Peristephanon* III as she kicks the pagan idols, Eulalia declares, "pectore et ore deum fateor" (v. 75; With breast and mouth I confess my God). The tyrant cannot carry out his threats, but it is not for the lack of trying. There is, then, no conflict between word and deed. In fact, the hero might be defined in this context as the actor capable of achieving his expressed goals, his opponent as the one who is impotent. The narrator hopes to find himself ultimately aligned with the hero. The concluding lines of the hymn express the hope that the hymnal performance will aid in winning clemency and absolution of sin. Specifically, it is the act of veneration, involving both purity of heart and performance of the hymn, that the narrator poet hopes will obtain him his desired end:[48]

> Si rite sollemnem diem
> ueneramur ore et pectore . . .
> paulisper huc inlabere
> Christi fauorem deferens
>
> (561–62, 565–66)

(If we properly reverence the day of your festival with mouth and heart . . . come down here for a little while, bringing the favor of Christ.)

Prudentius has written the hymn that will provide the means for venerating the saint "ore et pectore" (v. 562), the hymn that provides the possible mediation between sin and salvation. By the end of the poem, the poet-creator, the poet-audience (one of the faithful witnessing the hagiographic drama), and the poet-performer and -worshipper (one of the congregation venerating the saint) have been harmoniously united into a single person, the Christian poet, an active participant in the hagiographic text.[49] For a Christian, the

47. Only villains attempt (unsuccessfully) to lie; cf. Dacian's dissimulation discussed above. In the *Chanson de Roland*, Ganelon tries to misrepresent the truth of Roland's horn-blast; see the discussion of Kay, "Ethics and Heroics in the 'Song of Roland'" (1978), 480–91, esp. n. 21.

48. At the conclusion of several hymns of the *Peristephanon* (e.g. II, III, VI), Prudentius specifically comments on the mediating role of his poetry in obtaining salvation.

49. For the significance of hagiographic performance and its role in validating belief, see Uitti, *Story, Myth, and Celebration* (1973), pp. 25–27.

performance of such a hymn is a significant act, a form of unambiguous discourse. Such speech is capable of effecting mediation, and
the role of mediator between good and evil is played by the text
itself, together with its poet. The poet then will have achieved his
goal, literally aligning himself with the side of the saints and angels.

The Mozarabic liturgy contains a hymn, "Beate Martyr pros-
pera"[50] (Prosper, blessed martyr) which consists of the first half of
Prudentius' poem with only minor alterations; it concludes at line
288 of *Peristephanon* V, after the exultant first strophe of the
angel's speech to the saint, quoted above. Ruth Messenger has suggested that the ensuing portions of Prudentius' hymn were omitted
as "perhaps too prolonged and gruesome to be used as a hymn."[51]
On the contrary, one suspects that the end of the poem is too un-
dramatic, too descriptive and lyrical. The Mozarabic hymn includes
the frightful details of Vincent's torture, details more horrible than
those depicting Dacian's attempts, unsuccessful after all, to des-
ecrate the saint's body. The hymn-writer perceived what the modern scholar has not, that the true climax of the poem occurs at the
angel's speech welcoming Vincent into the heavenly band. The
Mozarabic hymn ends when the significant *action* of the account
has concluded. The scenes that follow the saint's death, with their
attendant miracles, testify to Vincent's sanctity, but they are not integral to the narration of triumphant, active heroism.

The martyr is the one who witnesses (< Gk. *marturein*), in Latin,
moreover, the one who *speaks* his witness (*martyrium dicere*). The
Christian act of bearing witness is active, not passive. The speaker
must be willing to back up the confession of faith with deeds. Vincent voluntarily ascended the pyre. In *Peristephanon* V, Prudentius
limited the cast of characters to those who acted unambiguously in
word and deed. In this respect, moreover, the binary unambiguous
structure of the *passio* resembles the Old French epic. Good and
evil are diametrically opposed. Larry S. Crist has written that the
world of medieval epic "is one in which oppositions are great and

50. *PL* 86, 1074.
51. "Mozarabic Hymns" (1946), p. 157.

exclusive: one is A or X; there are no tenable non-A or non-X categories."[52] We can diagram such a universe using the "semiotic square" elaborated by A. J. Greimas:[53]

positive attitude	S_1----------S_2	positive attitude
towards ideal S_1		towards ideal S_2
$[+]$		$[-]$
negative attitude	$\overline{S_2}$----------$\overline{S_1}$	negative attitude
towards ideal S_2		towards ideal S_1

In such a schematization, S_1----------S_2 represents the axis of contraries (logical opposites), S_1————————$\overline{S_1}$ the axis of contradictories (the affirmation or negation of the term in question), and S_1·········$\overline{S_2}$ indicates implication (the logical consequence of the above relations). Positions, moreover, have moral values attached. The left-hand side of the square represents positively valued ideals (S_1 and, less good, $\overline{S_2}$), while the right-hand values are negative (S_2 and, less bad, $\overline{S_1}$). For hagiography (and medieval epic) we may attach religious labels to these positions:

Christian S_1----------S_2 Pagan
$[+]$ $[-]$
Non-Pagan $\overline{S_2}$----------$\overline{S_1}$ Non-Christian

For medieval epic, following the work of van Nuffel and Crist,[54] we note that the lower two positions of the semiotic squares ($\overline{S_2}$ and $\overline{S_1}$, "Non-Pagan" and "Non-Christian"), constituting the axis of subcontraries, are not tenable on a permanent basis. Allegiances must be unambiguous, not defined by implication. Shifts between the top two positions (S_1 and S_2) are possible (i.e. conversion, apostasy, or treason),[55] and to alter positions a character may move through the

52. "Deep Structures in the *chansons de geste*" (1975), p. 6.
53. Greimas and Rastier, "The Interaction of Semiotic Constraints" (1966), 86–105. For further discussion of this subject in medieval epic and hagiography, see my article, "The Power of Discourse" (1982).
54. Nuffel, "Problèmes de sémiotique interprétative: L'Épopée" (1973); Crist, "Deep structures" (1975). See also Calame, "L'univers cyclopéen de l'Odyssée" (1976).
55. Zumthor, *Essai de poétique médiévale* (1972), p. 326.

bottom positions; he is not, however, allowed to remain there (at $\overline{S}_2$ or $\overline{S}_1$). He either moves up or dies. In the *Chanson de Roland*, for example, Ganelon, whose betrayal of the Christian knights has put him into the "Non-Christian" position, $\overline{S}_1$, is killed. Bramimonde, the Saracen queen who converts to Christianity, ends up at position S_1.

Prudentian hagiography is even more sharply polarized than is medieval epic. The prose *Acta* on which Prudentius relied for his account of Vincent contain a larger cast of characters than does *Peristephanon* V. As noted earlier, the saint's parents are named; Bishop Valerius is an important figure; and there are many jailors and Christian witnesses. Prudentius has eliminated from his poem all characters who take no important action or who might be considered to occupy one of the two lower positions of the semiotic square ($\overline{S}_2$ or $\overline{S}_1$). In the *Acta* Vincent's parents are named only; they *do* nothing. The crowd of Christians listens passively to the saint's deathbed speech; Prudentius omits this scene of passive witness but includes their *act* of preserving relics of the saint.

More significant is the omission of Valerius. The Bishop suffered from a speech impediment, and Vincent was therefore compelled to serve as his spokesman. In suffering the punishment of exile rather than the supreme penalty (and reward) of a martyr's death, Valerius might seem to have slipped down to the "Non-Pagan" position ($\overline{S}_2$). That is, he is not a "Non-Christian" ($\overline{S}_1$) or a Pagan (S_2), but his position has not been affirmed by clear-cut, Christian action. His relationship toward the ideal, Christianity (S_1), is defined by implication and is, potentially at least, problematic. He opposed the (negative) ideal Paganism (S_2) along the axis of contradictories, not contraries.

The polarized world of Prudentian hagiography (like medieval epic) does not admit a stance such as that assigned to Valerius in the *Acta*. Valerius, incapable of effective speech and exiled, neither moves up nor dies. Therefore he has been eliminated from the narrative.

Prudentius' poetic representation of a fully polarized world appears, however, to be a literary rather than a historically accurate interpretation. The more historic accounts of the years of persecution tell of many who occupied "Non-Christian" or "Non-Pagan" positions—those Christians who backslid or managed to escape confrontation, even saints like Paul of Thebes who fled to the desert to avoid persecution, or on the pagan side, those who retained their belief in the old ways but avoided open persecution.[56] Toleration and compromise may be admirable qualities in real life; they are not positively valued in hymns like the *Peristephanon*.

Several other of the *Peristephanon* reveal a similiar emphasis upon heroically unambiguous speech and action. *Peristephanon* II, for instance, opens with a situation potentially parallel to that of Valerius and Vincent; Pope Xystus has been arrested together with his Spanish-born archdeacon, St. Lawrence. Prudentius includes the arrest in his hymn to St. Lawrence; in the first scene of *Peristephanon* II, Prudentius, following St. Ambrose,[57] depicts the martyred Xystus addressing Lawrence from the cross, predicting that Lawrence too will be martyred within three days. The account appears to be at variance with history at this point; Xystus was beheaded, not crucified, but since a victim of the former punishment cannot speak during his execution, the mode of death has been altered.

Peristephanon III, celebrating the martyrdom of twelve-year-old St. Eulalia of Mérida, gives an especially vivid picture of saintly heroism.[58] Eulalia's loving parents attempt to keep their headstrong[59] daughter safe from persecution by hiding her in the country

56. See Frend, *Martyrdom and Persecution* (1965), pp. 409–10. Ste. Croix points out that since almost all our evidence comes from Christians interested in recording martyrdoms, most trials of which we know end in conviction and death; there were, however, some magistrates who went out of their way to be friendly to the Christians, and some potential martyrs were acquitted. See Tertullian *Ad Scapulam* 4, 3–4, cited by Ste. Croix, "Why were the Early Christians Persecuted?" (1963), p. 12.

57. Walpole, *Early Latin Hymns* (1922), pp. 94–100; the same version is followed by the Mozarabic hymn, *PL* 89, 1179.

58. The *Acta* of Eulalia have not survived, and Prudentius' hymn is our earliest record of this saint. For further discussion of Eulalia's violent heroism, see Elliott, "The Martyr as Epic Hero" (1978).

59. Prudentius characterizes her with the adjectives *ferox* (32) and *torva* (103).

away from the city (vv. 36–42), but the future martyr, impatient at delay, slips out one night, and, guided by an angel, seeks out the Roman tribunal:

> Illa perosa quietis opem
> degeneri tolerare mora
> nocte fores sine teste movet
> saeptaque claustra fugax aperit,
> inde per invia carpit iter.
>   Ingreditur pedibus laceris
> per loca senta situ et vepribus
> angelico comitata choro,
> et, licet horrida nox sileat,
> lucis habet tamen illa ducem.
>
> (41–50)

(Hating the aid of calm and hating to endure a cowardly delay, at night she opens the door without a witness and, as a fugitive, makes her way through the enclosing fence and through the trackless land. With torn feet she goes through land filled with briars, accompanied by a chorus of angels; and, although the awful night is silent, she still has a light to guide her.)

Eulalia rushes into the court and impetuously bursts into speech without waiting to be questioned; "uociferans: 'quis furor est?'" (v. 66; shouting out, "What madness is it?").[60]

The emphasis on speech is not wholly to be explained in terms of the importance of preaching in early Christianity (although Prudentius himself testifies eloquently to the need for spreading Christian doctrine in *Peristephanon* XIII, dedicated to St. Cyprian of Carthage, a voluminous writer). Not all the *Peristephanon* feature direct discourse as prominently as the poems under discussion. It is precisely in those hymns that stress most clearly the heroic character of the martyr that speech constitutes such an important act.

In this chapter I have discussed two kinds of hagiographic document—the relatively straightforward, unelaborated texts of early

---

60. In fact the church in the third century discouraged voluntary martyrdom; see Frend, *Martyrdom and Persecution* (1965), p. 415; Nock, *Conversion* (1933), 197–202; Ste. Croix, "Aspects" (1954), 101–3, and, "Why were the Early Christians Persecuted?" (1963), pp. 21–22.

passions such as the *Acta* of the Veteran Julius, and the more complex, artfully crafted work of a skilled poet like Prudentius. In both categories, the narrative structure was comparatively simple, but it is not to be mistaken for a "mere retelling of the facts." Certain conventions, *topoi*, and themes help to determine its structure and emphases, first among which has been the privileging of discourse and a submergence of individual identity into the corporate one of Christian. In the accounts of the desert fathers that follow, we leave poetry for prose, and in some cases we leave literature influenced by classical norms for something more closely resembling folklore. Discourse, while still an important technique in telling a story, loses its critical importance as the means by which the dynamics of the tale are established. In its place we find a series of themes and motifs that, in addition to relating the events of a particular life, serves to carry much of the deeper "meaning" of the tale.

Chapter 3

Hagiographic Romance

With the Peace of Constantine in 313 A.D., the days of literal martyrdom largely came to an end. The successors to the martyrs were the desert fathers,[1] those heroes of self-persecution[2] who fled the cities for the *interior mons*, the mountain in the interior, the uninhabited deserts of Egypt, Syria, and Palestine. But if the goal of these spirtual martyrs was the same as that of their predecessors, the kingdom of heaven, the hermits' methods of attaining it differed radically. Their stories differ from the *passiones* in genre and in narrative structure. The *vita* of the confessor saint stands in the same relationship to the *passio* as romance does to epic.

The enemy is now within[3]—the Devil himself and not his public representative or surrogate, the Roman magistrate. The symbolic

1. The term is ancient; it was first applied to the monks of the Egyptian desert in the fourth and fifth century. Palladius used it in the *Historia Lausiaca*; see Guillaumont, "La conception du désert" (1975), p. 3.

2. For the heroism of ascetic denial, see the definition of "ascéticisme" in the *Vocabulaire* of the Société française de Philosophie (1926), I, 67, as "l'effort héroïque de la volonté qu'on s'impose à soi-même en vue d'acquérir l'énergie morale, la force et la fermeté de caractère" (the heroic effort of will that one imposes on oneself to acquire moral energy, force and firmness of character) quoted in *Dictionnaire de Spiritualité*, I, col. 937.

3. Labriolle has written: "C'était maintenant le combat, non moins âpre, de l'homme contre lui-même, dont il fallait proposer l'exemple à la piété des fidèles. Désormais la vie des saints, leurs travaux, leurs *gestes*, seront l'aliment des âmes religieuses" (Now it was the combat, no less bitter, of man against himself, the example of which had to be offered to the piety of the faithful. Henceforth the life of the saints, their works, their heroic deeds [*gestes*] will be the food of religious souls), Labriolle, *Histoire de la littérature latine chrétienne* (1947), p. 509.

nexus of the drama lies in images of interiority—the saint's secret flight from his family, his surrogate death and burial—not the public ones of confrontation and execution found in the *passio*. In contrast to the urban setting of the drama of martyrdom, the most important acts transpire in the privacy of the desert fastness, witnessed by at most one or two persons. The story reflects its gradational ethos as it relates a journey, and its impetus is centrifugal. To use Donald Maddox's musical analogy, its movement is rhythmical and repetitive.[4] Finally, in comparison with the martyr, as the saint flees the *polis* for the desert he may appear to select a variety of paths, although the variety is more apparent than real. In comparison with the *passio*, such narratives contain elements of detour and suspense.

Although the impact of the desert Fathers upon subsequent generations of heroes—those saints called "confessors" who bore witness to their faith by their lives rather than by their deaths—was in the long run probably even greater than that of the martyrs,[5] the suspicion remained that the martyr was the best saint. Certainly on the surface the story of his passion was more exciting than the details of a life of denial. Physical martyrdom, however, had been possible for only a comparatively few Christians; the importance of the spiritual martyrdom of *askēsis* was that it represented a form of *imitatio Christi* open to all. The requirements for spiritual martyrdom remained constant. In his study, *The Monk and the Martyr*,[6] Malone wrote: "There must be the express desire of martyrdom and to this desire must be joined some sort of suffering patiently borne for the love of God and imitation of Christ and the martyrs." In particular, the preservation of virginity was seen as the equivalent of martyrdom. Jerome's *Life of Malchus the Captive Monk* testifies to this spirit. As he is about to stab himself, Malchus says: "Habet et servata pudicitia suum martyrium. Jaceat insepultus Christi testis in eremo, ipsi mihi ero et persecutor et martyr"[7] (Pre-

---

4. See above, Ch. II, section II.
5. See Lorrie, *Spiritual Terminology* (1955), p. 5.
6. Malone, *The Monk and the Martyr* (1950), p. 44.
7. PL 23, 59A.

served chastity has its own martyrdom. Let the witness of Christ lie unburied in the desert; I shall be for myself both a persecutor and a martyr). Prudentius praised the virgin martyr Agnes for winning a double crown:

> Duplex corona est praestita martyri:
> intactum ab omni crimine virginal,
> mortis deinde gloria liberae.
>
> *(Per.* 14, 7–9)

(A double crown was offered to the martyr: virginity kept free from every crime, and then the glory of a freely chosen death.)

The actual transition from the ideal of physical martyrdom to spiritual—from martyr to monk—had begun prior to Constantine's edict of Milan. The value of the ascetic life had been extensively discussed by Clement of Alexandria (d. ca. 219) and even more importantly, by Origen, who considered the life of *askēsis* a "martyrium cotidianum"[8] (a daily martyrdom).

The most influential biography of a desert father is Athanasius' encomiastic *Life of St. Antony*, written in Greek shortly after the saint's death in 356.[9] Two Latin translations were made of this work within twenty years—the anonymous version shortly after the original Greek, and the better known one of Evagrius before 375. (In this study, Latin citations are from the more literal, and earlier, anonymous version.[10]) In his biography, Athanasius related how Antony's fervent desire for martyrdom caused him to leave his desert solitude and go to Alexandria:[11] "Optabat enim et pro voto

8. Origen's attitudes are discussed by E. Malone, *The Monk and the Martyr* (1950), pp. 14–26.

9. For the date, see Barnard, "The Date of S. Athanasius' *Vita Antonii*" (1974), suggesting late 357 or early 358. See also Brennan, "Dating Athanasius' *Vita Antoni*" (1976).

10. Edited by Bartelink, 1974.

11. There is some doubt about the historicity of Athanasius' account of Antony's trip to Alexandria. As Bartelink notes in his edition, the anonymous translator added the name of Diocletian, the best known of the persecutors, to that of Maximian given by Athanasius, an alteration that changes the date of the persecution (Bartelink, *Vita di Antonio*, [1974], p. 231). A still earlier account may be the text in R. Draguet, *La vie primitive de S. Antoine*, CSCO 418, Script. Syri 184 (Louvain, 1980), which shows Saint Antony going out of his way to be conspicuous at the governor's court. [I owe this reference to Peter Brown—Ed.]

habebat . . . martyrium dicere" (46.6: for he wished and held it as a vow to 'speak a martyrdom' [i.e. be martyred]). When this wish was denied, and the persecution had died down, Antony returned to the desert to practice ascetic renunciation with even greater dedication than before. Athanasius' description of the saint's *askēsis* will serve as a convenient summary of such activities. Antony returned to his solitary abode:

et erat ibi cotidie martyrium dicens conscientiae et certans certaminibus fidei. Etenim amplius studio et fortiori studebatur. Ieiunabat enim semper, vestimentum autem ipsius sacceum autem intrinsecus, extrinsecus autem pellinum. Ad consummationem vitae suae hoc observavit. Neque corpus suum aqua lavit, neque, pedes, neque tetigerunt praeter necessitatem aquam, neque nudum corpus ipsius Antoni aliquis, aliquando vidit, nisi quando post mortem sepeliebatur (47).

(And he was there martyring himself ["martyrium dicens"] in his conscience and struggling in contests of faith. Moreover he was devoting himself to a more harsh asceticism. He always fasted, his inner clothing was sackcloth, his outer a hairshirt. He observed this custom until his death. He never washed his body or his feet, and water never touched his body unnecessarily, nor did anyone ever see Antony's body naked until he was being buried after his death.)

GRADATIONAL STRUCTURES

To depict the *lives* of the saints, as opposed to their deaths, required a different narrative structure. Charles Altman, in the study cited earlier,[12] has noted that in the place of the binary structure common to *passiones* (and medieval epic), the *vitae* utilize a gradational scheme. The motivating thrust of the narrative is not the comparatively static opposition between good and evil, Christian and pagan, but a fluid scale of values that moves from good to better to best. Such a plot, perhaps as a graphic representation of the motion implied by its fundamental ethos, often involves a journey, a quest, as the saint withdraws from the world in search of greater sanctity. Altman remarks upon the similarities between these stories and medieval romance; the parallels with ancient romance are

12. Altman, "Two Types of Opposition," (1975).

striking as well. Indeed, it has become commonplace to refer to the more fantastic saintly biographies as "romances" or "novels," and the label is not entirely unwarranted. This type of plot, moreover, is not a late development (in contrast to the so-called epic passions). In some of the earliest accounts of non-martyr saints the imprint of Greek romance is clearly discernible, since the authors appear to have turned to such tales for structure and incident when they came to fabulate the lives of their Christian heroes.[13] The romance structure is apparent in the *vita* of the saint for whom we have the earliest documentation, Thecla, who will be discussed shortly. Her legend, moreover, achieved extremely wide circulation.

A typical Greek romance is the *Ephesiaca*, composed by Xenophon of Ephesus sometime between the second and fifth centuries A.D.[14] Its plot utilizes a number of themes and motifs that figure prominently in hagiographic romances as well. In this tale, the two teenaged lovers, Habrocomes and Anthia, first catch sight of each other during a religious procession.[15] They are of such surpassing beauty that people think the young man is Eros, the girl Artemis.[16] After their marriage, they set out on a journey during which they are captured by pirates, and their tribulations begin. Everyone who sees them is immediately infatuated. Anthia is eventually sold to merchants, but Habrocomes manages to slip secretly (*lathōn*) away

13. Pavlovskis, "The Life of St. Pelagia" (1976), pp. 138–39, noting the transformation of Greek novelistic themes, considers that the authors' purpose was to provide adherents of the new religion with suitably edifying yet exciting stories to compare in interest with the best of contemporary fiction; she provides a detailed comparison with Xenophon's *Ephesiaca*. For a discussion of the attempts by Merkelbach and Reitzenstein to read the Greek romances as novels of religious initiation, see the long review article of Turcan, "Le roman 'initiatique'" (1963). While the Greek novels may well include "serious" religious elements, they also contain much that cannot be ascribed to such concerns. The resemblances between certain Greek novels and Christian "mystery" may have accounted for the continuing popularity of the former. For an analysis of "*Apollonius of Tyre* as Greek Myth and Christian Mystery," see Pickford (1975). See also Elizabeth Clark, *The Life of Melania the Younger* (New York: Edwin Mellen, 1984): 153–70 on the Life of Melania and Romances.

14. See the edition of Dalmeyda (1926).

15. Pavlovskis, (above, n. 13), notes that the first "meeting" of Pelagia with her confessor, Bishop Nonnus, occurs in a festive context, an episcopal synod.

16. Perhaps this is a variant of the motif of mistaken identity (d¹), prominent in hagiographic romance (see below).

in pursuit. In order to escape an unwelcome marriage, Anthia requests a friendly physician to give her poison. The drug which he gives her in fact only produces a deathlike sleep. Anthia is buried in a tomb, where she awakens. She is then stolen away by grave robbers who break in and find her.[17] Meanwhile Habrocomes attracts the attention of a married woman who murders her husband to be free for him. When he rejects her, she accuses him of the murder, and he is condemned to be crucified. While bound to the cross, Habrocomes protests his innocence, and the god hears his prayer and takes pity on him; a storm overturns the cross. Next Habrocomes is sentenced to the stake, but the waters of the Nile rise, extinguishing the flames, and he is eventually set free. The plot of this involved and repetitious romance is far too complex to summarize here; ultimately, however, after many more adventures the lovers are reunited and presumably live "happily ever after."

An additional episode bears mentioning, for it introduces two motifs important in the accounts of many saints: the wedding-night flight and the disguising of a woman as a man. In his pursuit of Anthia, Habrocomes arrives in Sicily where he meets an old Spartan named Aigialaos, who tells the young hero his life's story. Aigialaos had been in love with a girl, Thelxina, whom he could not marry because she was betrothed to another. On the very night of Thelxina's marriage, the two lovers determined to flee Sparta. Aigialaos cut Thelxina's hair and disguised her as a man, and they made their successful escape.[18]

The early Christian "romances" take a number of forms. The "biography" of Pope Clement I of Rome (fl. 96 A.D.) has been dubbed the "First Christian Novel."[19] Although this work was

17. For further discussion, see below, p. 104, note 5. One might also note the use made of this motif in such romances as *Romeo and Juliet* (with a tragic dénouement), and Chrétien de Troyes' *Cligès*. A useful resource on the history of the false death motif is Henri Hauvette, *La Morte vivante* (Paris: Boivin, 1933).

18. L. Radermacher saw in this episode the origin of the theme in hagiography ("Hippolytos und Thekla," *Akad. Wiss.*, Vienna vol. 182, [1916], cited by Delcourt, "La complexe de Diane" [1958], p. 8, n. 1).

19. The text is in *PG* 1, 1027ff. For discussion, see Lowe, "The First Christian Novel" (1931); Perry, *The ancient Romances* (1967), Appendix I; Quasten, *Patrology* (1950), I. Quasten calls the work "a comprehensive novel for didactic purposes" (p. 59).

given its present form some time after the Council of Nicaea (325 A.D.), its roots extend back as far as the second century, if not earlier, for the author has borrowed the plot of pagan romance to provide a narrative frame into which are inserted the missionary sermons of St. Peter.[20] The work is presented as a first-person narrative relating Clement's search for the meaning of life and for an answer to the question whether there is life after death. Clement tells the story of his early years in response to a question from Peter concerning his parents. The tale contains many elements familiar from Greek romance: Clement's mother fled from Rome with two of her sons (twins) in order to preserve her chastity and was shipwrecked; the children were sold into slavery. After many adventures, the biographical portion of Clement's story concludes with a scene of joyful reunion as a series of wondrous coincidences reunites Clement with his parents and long-lost brothers (hence the title, *Clementine Recognitions*).

Closer to the *Ephesiaca* are the *Acts of Paul and Thecla,* although many motifs are displaced due to the work's religious rather than erotic orientation. This document is the earliest full-fledged hagiographic romance,[21] composed perhaps as early as the last third of the second century.[22] The story opens with a journey. St. Paul is on his way from Antioch to Iconium. As he enters the town, a certain Onesiphorus, having been given a description of the saint, sets out to meet him. When they meet, Onesiphorus remarks that the saint "sometimes . . . seemed like a man, sometimes . . . had the countenance of an angel."[23] The heroine, Thecla, is a perfect romance heroine—seventeen years old and beautiful. She hears Paul preach

20. Quasten, *Patrology*, I, 59.
21. In the *Bibliotheca Sanctorum*, XII, 176, it is called "Un romanzo fantastico." In his edition, *Vie et miracles de sainte Thècle* (1978), p. 36, Dagron called it a "roman à tiroirs tout à fait classique."
22. *Bibliotheca Sanctorum*, XII, 176. For the text, see Dagron, *Vie et miracles.* Thecla is mentioned by Tertullian *(De Bapt.* 17.4, *CSEL* XX, p. 215), and is depicted in the third-century frescoes of a hypogeum not far from S. Paolo Fuori le Mura in Rome, today in the Vatican Museum.
23. *Acts of Paul and Thecla*, trans. Walker, *Apocryphal Gospels* (1870), p. 279. See below, ch. 7, for a discussion of the motif d¹, mistaken or wavering identity.

about virginity and sits in her window, enraptured, watching and listening, refusing to move. Converted by Paul's words, she rejects her fiancé; in anger her mother denounces the girl to the praetor as a Christian, and Thecla is condemned to the stake, but rain miraculously extinguishes the flames.[24] Meanwhile, Paul is fasting in a tomb outside of town, and after her release Thecla joins him there. She wants to cut her hair and follow Paul, but he is at first unwilling, fearing for her virtue. He says: "It is a shameless age, and thou art beautiful. I am afraid lest another temptation come upon thee, worse than the first, and thou not withstand it but be cowardly."[25] Finally, however, he takes Thecla with him to Antioch, where a wealthy Syrian no sooner catches sight of the girl than he covets her. When she rejects him, he delivers her once more to the magistrate, and Thecla is sentenced to the beasts. A lioness licks her feet and defends her in the arena, and she is again released unharmed (an incident to which we shall return in chapter 6.)

Meanwhile Paul, banished from Antioch, has gone to Myra and Thecla follows him, disguised as a man. Then she goes to Seleucia where she lives in a cave for seventy-two years, eating only herbs and water. At the end of her life, certain Greek physicians set out to destroy her, claiming that she is a virgin who served Artemis and had on that account miraculous powers of healing. They plan to rape her but she escapes, entering alive into a rock which opens up for her. The story, however, has two endings, and in the alternative conclusion, she manages somehow to make her way to Rome where she dies ("fell asleep") near her master Paul.

Tomas Hägg has recently noted the abundance of "novelistic motifs" in this tale:[26] jealous rivals, Thecla's spurned fiancé, travel, imprisonment, miraculous escapes from mortal peril, and so forth. Even the erotic element is not wholly obscured. To be sure, it remains sublimated but, as Hägg observes, although Thecla and Paul do not marry, "eyes, gestures, and speech indicate that their rela-

24. Like Habrocomes in the *Ephesiaca*, Thecla is spared twice.
25. Walker, *Apocryphal Gospels*, p. 285.
26. *The Novel in Antiquity* (1983), p. 160.

tionship is not of an exclusively spiritual kind." It recalls the "purely physical manifestations of awakening love in, for instance, the
Ephesiaca."[27]

One of the earliest, and strangest, of the Christian romances
sounds more like a fairy tale than a Greek novel, as it casts Jesus in
the role of dragon-slayer. This text is the Syriac "Hymn of the
Soul," an earlier poem thrust abruptly into the *Apocryphal Acts of
Thomas* composed in the first half of the third century.[28] This hymn,
a first-person narrative, tells of the adventures of a king's son
(Christ) who is sent out of the East, laden with treasure, into Egypt
to bring back a single pearl that lies in the midst of the sea, guarded
by a devouring serpent. If Christ succeeds at this task, he will be
able to put on once again a garment set with gems and become the
heir to the kingdom. He says: "And I came out of the East by a road
difficult and fearful, with two guides. . . . But when I entered into
Egypt, the guides left me . . . and I set forth by the quickest way to
the serpent. . . . And foreasmuch as I was alone I made mine aspect
strange, and appeared as an alien to my people" (vv. 16–23). In
Egypt, however, he eats the food of forgetfulness;[29] eventually he is
miraculously awakened and, remembering his quest, kills the dragon and returns in triumph. This lovely tale, whether intended primarily as allegory or not, contains many themes prominent in
hagiographic (and other) romance: the dangerous journey, the
guides, the disguised hero. The hero commits an error, endures
symbolic death in the form of forgetfulness, and then is pardoned
and resurrected to complete his mission and ascend into Heaven.

Despite these similarities, hagiographic romances also differ substantially from the Greek novels. They celebrate a new kind of hero,
and the object of the saintly quest differs from that of the hero of

27. Dagron remarks that Thecla is depicted naked more often than usual. Dagron, *Vie et Miracles*, p. 26.
28. The text is in James, *Apocryphal New Testament* (1924), pp. 411–15.
29. Under "Themes of Descent" (see below), Frye, *Secular Scripture* (1976), p.
102, points to the prevalence in romances of a break in consciousness, which he calls
"the motif of amnesia." Macarius (see below) "forgets" to make the sign of the cross
and sins. In "The Story of Asdiwal," (1958), pp. 17 and 22, Lévi-Strauss notes the
prominence of forgetfulness in this myth.

erotic romance. Motifs are displaced, and the metamorphosed structure, while still revealing its parentage, forms a new and distinct species. It is the purpose of this study to investigate the narrative transformations made by the new species and to determine the underlying import of the structure of these tales.

THE ROMANCE MODEL

A good example of the generative power of a single structural model is the account of the experiences of the Coptic monk Paphnutius,[30] known either as the *Peregrinatio Paphnutii* or the *Vita Onuphrii (VO)*. In the Ethiopian tradition, Abbâ Nâfer (or Abunâfer [= Onuphrius]) was held to be the first ascetic to live in the desert of upper Egypt.[31] The version summarized below is Surius' Latin translation of the account by Simon Metaphrastes (BHL 6334),[32] with cross references to a Coptic version published by Amélineau.[33]

I. One day a monk named Paphnutius thought to himself that he should go into the inner solitude to see whether there was any other monk dwelling further ("interius") in the desert than he in service of God. He departed secretly and walked for four days into the desert without food, water, or wine, until he came to a wondrous cave ("antrum venerabile"). He spent an hour knocking on the door; finally he went in and saw a hermit sitting there. Touching the

---

30. The name is a common one; in Coptic *Pa-fnu-ti* means "servant of God"; see Joseph-Marie Sauget, *Bibliotheca Sanctorum*, vol. 9, *s.v.* We should not assimilate all the Paphnutii to a single figure (i.e. this Paphnutius is probably not the same as the hero of the legend of Thaïs), as does O'Leary *The Saints of Egypt* (1937), pp. 219–20. For Surius' text, see the edition of Gastaldi (1878).

31. Budge, *Book of Saints* (1929), vol. 4, 1002–3.

32. Laurent Surius was born in Lübeck in 1522 and died in Cologne in 1578. For other versions of Onuphrius' Life see PL 73, 211–22 and *AA.SS.*, Jun. XII, vol. 23, pp. 16–30, (June 12).

33. Amélineau, "Voyage d'un moine égyptien" (1884). The manuscript published by Amélineau is dated 979 A.D., but he ascribes the version to the mid-fourth century. The cult of Saint Onuphrius is attested by the end of the sixth century; see the homily on the saint by Pisenthios, bishop of Qeft, published in a French translation by Crum, "Discours de Pisenthios" (1915–17), and in English by Budge, *Miscellaneous Coptic Texts* (1915).

man's shoulder, he found that it was like wood.[34] The hermit, he discovered, had been dead for a long time, and his clothing fell to dust when touched. Covering the naked body with his own cloak, Paphnutius buried it.

II. Paphnutius continued into the desert and came to a cave ("spelunca") showing traces of human habitation. It was empty, and looking further, Paphnutius found the actual cell. At sunset he observed a herd of cattle coming towards him, and in their midst he saw a naked man covered with long hair. The man at first thought that Paphnutius was a spirit, for he had frequently been tempted by them. In response to Paphnutius' questions, the hairy man told his story:

III. He was once a coenobitic monk from the Thebaid who decided to leave his community, "et solus quiete habitare in monasterio, studens majorem invenire mercedem" (and to live quietly alone in a "monastery," desiring to find a greater reward). He went off by himself and built a small cell, but soon many people flocked to him. The devil, motivated by envy and determined to compass his downfall, entered into the mind of a nun who had joined Timotheus (for that, we later learn, is the hermit's name), and they lived together in sin for six months before Timotheus was overcome with repentance. He made his escape and came to this cave, spring, and palm tree which had nourished him so well that he needed nothing else. When his clothes fell apart, his hair served as covering, and he had lived in this fashion for thirty years.

One day, however, his stomach hurt him so terribly that he could only lie on the ground in pain and pray to God for mercy. Suddenly he saw a splendid figure ("virum insignem") standing before him who asked him the trouble, and Timotheus showed him the place that hurt. Placing his fingers on Timotheus' side, the figure cut it "just like a sword" and took out the liver.[35] He showed Timotheus the liver's wounds; meanwhile Timotheus, not unnaturally, was in great pain. The figure scraped the liver with his hand, put it in a

---

34. In Amélineau's version (p. 169), the arm falls to dust.
35. The liver is traditionally viewed as the seat of the passions.

clean cloth, and replaced it in Timotheus' side: "Then when he had touched my entire body with his blessed hands, the wound in my side closed up, and he said: 'Behold, you are made healthy. Do not sin any more lest you suffer worse, but serve God now and henceforth.' Lo, on that day all my insides were cured and my liver ceased hurting." As proof, Timotheus showed Paphnutius the cloth in which the liver had been wrapped. Paphnutius then asked to remain with the hermit, but Timotheus refused, saying that Paphnutius would be unable to withstand the assaults of the devil. Paphnutius next asked the hermit his name, and Timotheus told him, asking Paphnutius to pray for him.

IV. So Paphnutius set out into the desert once more, "in interiorem solitudinem in via avia" (into deeper solitude, by a pathless route). He had taken with him enough food and water for four days. When this was exhausted he collapsed, then suddenly regained strength and was able to continue for four days more. Overcome then by weakness, he fell to the ground, awaiting death.[36] Suddenly he saw a splendid figure ("virum insignem") approaching who touched his lips "non secus atque medicus scalpellum oculo" (not otherwise than when a doctor touches a scapel to the eye), and Paphnutius found himself able to go on, without food or water, for another four days. When he weakened again, the mysterious figure returned and revived him once more. When Paphnutius had spent seventeen days in this fashion, he espied yet another hairy hermit. At first Paphnutius thought this figure was a murderer.[37]

V. This hermit told Paphnutius his story: his name was Onuphrius,[38] and he had spent sixty[39] years in the wilderness without seeing a living soul prior to Paphnutius' arrival. As a boy he had been a member of a Theban monastic community for one hundred

36. Amélineau's version reads, "I entered into death" (p. 174).

37. Amélineau's version states that his hair covered him like a "pardalis." (p. 174), while Petrus de Natalibus (1493, 1519) says that Paphnutius thought him either a monster or a wild beast.

38. In Surius the name is spelled Honofrius; in Amélineau's Coptic version, it is Benofer.

39. In Amélineau, seven; in the *PL* 73 version, seventy (chap. 15, p. 218). Details such as numbers tend to vary between the two versions. I will cease to note such minor differences hence forth.

brothers, and he had heard there of the exploits in the desert of Elijah and John the Baptist. He had asked his abbot whether the desert dwellers were greater in God's sight ("majores apud Deum") than were coenobitic monks and was told that they were, for coenobitic monks had their fellows to aid them in sickness and danger, while the solitary had no one but himself; there follows a long panegyric of the eremitic life pronounced by the monks. This discourse concludes: "Beatus est ergo qui facit Dei voluntatem super terram. Angeli ministrant ei, et faciunt eum exultare, et ei vires addunt singulis horis, dum est in carne"[40] (Blessed is he who does the will of God on earth. Angels minister to him, and make him exult, and give him strength during every hour that he is on earth). The young Onuphrius was inspired to pursue such a life, and, taking enough bread for four days, one night he left for the desert. As he set out towards the mountains, he saw a light before him which so terrified him that he almost turned back, but a splendid figure ("insignis ille") told him not to fear, that he was an angel who would guide him on his way (i.e. his guardian angel). The angel led him to a wondrous cavern, ("speluncam venerabilem"), in which an old hermit dwelled. The hermit knew Onuphrius' name without being told. He instructed the boy in the anchorite's life, then led him further into the desert to another cave. The two visited each other once a year until the old hermit died, whereupon Onuphrius buried him.

When Onuphrius finished telling his own story, Paphnutius accompanied him back to his cave.[41] Here was a palm tree that furnished the hermit with sufficient food (it provided twelve bunches of dates, one a month). God also sent an angel daily with a little water and food. Noticing that Paphnutius was weak from hunger, Onuphrius urged him to eat the angelic food, and only with difficulty could Paphnutius persuade the hermit to share it with him.

The next morning Paphnutius observed that Onuphrius had changed color, and he was terrified. The saint told him not to fear for God had sent Paphnutius to him so that he might receive burial.

40. Surius, cap. 8, vol. 6, p. 271 (June 12).
41. In Amélineau's Coptic version, a hut (p. 180).

Paphnutius asked for permission to stay on in the desert after Onuphrius' death, but the hermit refused: "Son, you have not come for this task, but God has sent you so that you may recreate (*recreas*) his saints who live in the solitude, and so that you may announce the good odor of their life in the midst of the brethren." Onuphrius then died, and Paphnutius buried him, cutting his own tunic in half to wrap the body, which he placed in a rock hollowed out like a cistern and covered with stones.[42] He then prayed to remain in the place, but an earthquake toppled the palm tree and destroyed the cave, so that Paphnutius recognized it was God's will that he depart.

VI. Once more Paphnutius set forth. He prayed and saw the now-familiar figure.[43] Strengthened, he followed it for four days and came to another cave or cell (both words are used). He went in and shortly thereafter a white-haired hermit, wearing only palm fronds for clothing, entered. This figure greeted Paphnutius with the words: "Tu es frater Paphnutius, qui contexisti corpus sancti patris Honofrii" (You are brother Paphnutius who buried [lit. "covered"] the body of the holy father Onuphrius). The hermit had obtained this knowledge in a dream. Paphnutius was the first man he had seen for sixty years, other than the three brothers who lived with him. These three soon joined them, and suddenly loaves of bread miraculously appeared; normally, they said, the Lord provided four loaves, but on this occasion there were five. Paphnutius asked to remain with the four hermits, but they refused, telling him to go back to Egypt to tell the other brothers what he had seen: "Non est voluntas Dei, ut tu habites in hac solitudine" (It is not God's will that you dwell in this solitude). They also refused to tell him their names.

VII. Paphnutius thereupon set out once again.

42. In a late version of the legend, Onuphrius is buried by two lions who come to aid Paphnutius; Petrus de Natalibus (d. 1400), *Catalogus sanctorum* (1519), Book 5, Ch. 106, f. 102v.

43. The Latin is ambiguous here, but presumably it was the ministering angel: "et vidi virum illum ad me venientem, eo modo, quo vidi ambulans in solitudine. Qui mihi vires addens, ambulat ante me" (And I beheld that man coming toward me, just as I beheld him when I walked in solitude. And he, adding strength to me, walks before me) Surius, p. 274.

FIGURE 1. Paphnutius buries St. Onuphrius.

When I parted from them, I walked for a day through the interior solitude. And when I reached a cave with a spring of water, I sat there to rest a while from the labor of the journey. For the place was inviting for that purpose, as there were many trees about the spring, full of fruit. When I had rested a little, I got up and wandered through the trees, admiring the multitude of their fruit and wondering to myself who had planted the place. For there were many fruits of the following trees—palms, citrus, pomegranates, mulberries, jujubes, and vines, and other, lovely trees bearing fruit whose taste is sweeter than honey. To these were added myrtle, and other kinds of trees in their midst were planted there, giving off a sweet scent. The spring bubbled out and watered all the trees, so that I thought it was God's Paradise.[44]

44. Surius, ed. Gastaldi (1878), p. 276.

While he was admiring this spectacle, Paphnutius observed coming towards him four boys, "hilares et valde speciosos" (cheerful and most handsome), wearing sheepskins. "Erant vero tanta gloria insignes, ut ego existimarem eos esse Angelos, et descendisse de coelo" (They were so distinguished in splendor that I thought that they were angels and had descended from heaven). This impression, however, turned out to be mistaken.

VIII. The boys were four students from Oxyrhynchus[45] who found their way to this "Paradise" guided by a "virum gloria insignem" (man splendid in glory); they too had taken enough food and water for only four days. The heavenly figure entrusted them to the care of an old hermit who lived in the garden. This hermit taught them much, and they lived with him for six years until his death. They ate no other food but the fruit that grew on the trees.[46] (Paphnutius did not ask to stay with the boys). Their names were, they volunteered, Joannes, Andreas, Heraklambon,[47] and Theophilus.

IX. This was Paphnutius' last adventure, and he headed for home, rejoicing that he had been blessed by the holy hermits and by an angel. He came to the abode of two brothers with whom he stayed for ten days. He told them his adventures, and they made a book of them, which was received into the Church.

Repetition is the key to the *Peregrinatio Paphnutii* or the *Vita Onuphrii*. Not only did sections IV–V circulate separately in the version of the *Vita Onuphrii* contained in the *Vitae Patrum*, Book I, but they also occur, in somewhat condensed form, in the *Verba Seniorum*, Book III, where as chapter 12 they purport to relate the life of an unnamed bishop who, fearing torture during the persecutions, sacrificed to the pagan gods and then, overcome by remorse, fled to the desert to do penance for his lapse. The introductory sections of the *Vita Onuphrii*, I–III, comprise chapter 11 of this work, where they are told as the experiences of an anonymous solitary.

---

45. Coptic Pemdjé (p. 186). They greet the traveler as "Brother Paphnutius" without being told his name.
46. In the Coptic version, every Sunday an angel brought them communion (p. 187).
47. In the Coptic, Raklamon (p. 188).

Furthermore, a number of details found in the *Vita Onuphrii* occur elsewhere—for example the miraculously provided ration of bread that increases when a "guest" arrives, which is also found in St. Jerome's *Vita Pauli*.[48] Although such borrowings may be dismissed as signs of the unhistorical, even plagiaristic, nature of many saints' lives, they suggest a more important difference between hagiography and history. Whatever the genealogical relationship between the *Vita Onuphrii* and the *Verba seniorum*, in terms of structure Paphnutius' account, preserved as the *Peregrinatio Paphnutii*, consists, not of nine distinct adventures, but of one tale told nine times.

A very similar narrative pattern lies beneath the surface of a number of lives of desert saints in addition to Onuphrius (e.g. the *Life of Macarius the Roman*, Jerome's *Life of Paul of Thebes*, the *Life of Saint Mary the Egyptian*, and the *Life of Mark the Athenian*.) If the narrative is reduced to its essential structural components, a basic frame or outline emerges. In the following discussion, the major narrative elements, which I have called "themes," are indicated in capital letters.[49] Within each theme, specific "motifs" occur, indicated by lower case letters. If a motif or theme is enclosed in slashes (e.g. /a^1/), that motif is implicitly present in an account (for example, it is implied, but not stated explicitly, that at his death the four boys buried the hermit who had been their instructor). Motifs enclosed in brackets (e.g. [g^1]) occur in a version of the tale other than the one being analyzed (usually in a later version), while letters preceded by a minus sign (e.g. $-b^1$) represent motifs considered to be "present" in the narrative, but with a negative value or "valence," since their absence is specifically noted in the text. A schematic analysis of the overall pattern of themes and motifs found in these lives is as follows:

---

48. There is a problem of dating. If Amélineau's attribution of the Coptic *Vita Onuphrii* to the mid-fourth century is correct, then this little-known legend must be considered Jerome's source, or we must look for an explanation other than textual borrowing, for the accepted date of composition for the *Vita Pauli* is 374–75 (Coleiro, "St. Jerome's Lives," [1957], p. 161).

49. Capitals with apostrophes (e.g. B') indicate that the function is the same but the content different. I am attempting nothing as rigid or as detailed as a Proppian analysis, but there are interesting points of contact with that methodology.

TABLE OF THEMES AND MOTIFS

THEME A: CIRCUMSTANCES PRECEDING DEPARTURE

Motifs may include a description of the hero's prior life (he is probably a *puer-senex*, a youth with the wisdom of an old man), and his reasons for departure, usually marriage (a^1) or the "more" motif (seeking a "more" holy life) (a^2); he or she may depart in secret (a^3); the motivation may be the search for penance (a^4); a particularly common motif in lives of women saints.

THEME B: THE JOURNEY

Typical motifs include provisions, particularly the ability to survive without food or water (b^1); the hero may have unusual guides (b^2); especially animals or angels, and may experience symbolic death (b^3); he or she may be disguised (b^4); a particularly common motif in accounts of female saints.

THEME C: DISCOVERY OF A PLACE

Usually a cave or a cell, which is empty (c^1) or contains a dead body (c^2).

THEME D: ENCOUNTER (DISCOVERY OF A PERSON)

Often distinguished by several departures from normal experience:[50] mistaken identity (d^1); miraculous knowledge of identity (d^2) unusual appearance (d^3); miraculously provided food (d^4); other miracles (d^5); or an uncorrupted body (d^6).

THEME E: THE TALE

The person encountered relates his life's story, which recapitulates the narrative pattern.

THEME F: THE REQUEST

Often denied (f^1); it precipitates the next journey.[51]

---

50. This central episode seems to correspond to Propp's "Lack Liquidated," designation K; *Morphology of the Folktale* (1968), pp. 53–55.

51. This motif parallels Propp's motif D, *ibid.*, pp. 40–43, especially D^3, "A dying or deceased person requests the rendering of a service" (p. 40). The motif does not, however, occur in the same position in the hagiographic accounts.

THEME G: BURIAL

Often with the aid of lions (g^1).

Not all elements need be present at all times. For example, motif A may appear only once or twice; E, F, and G may be omitted, depending on circumstances, but they are present more frequently than one might expect. The narrative order is stable, although not inflexible; for instance, the account of the meeting between Onuphrius and Paphnutius precedes the visit to the saint's cave, but several encounter-motifs (d) occur in their expected place (see below). The pattern, however, is sufficiently consistent to suggest the presence of a single narrative archetype.

Analyzed in detail, the nine adventures of Paphnutius are as follows:

Narrative I (Paphnutius sets out)

A1: DEPARTURE—In secret to find someone "interius meo" (further within than I) (a^2, a^3).

B1: JOURNEY—four days without food or water (b^1).

C1: PLACE—an "antrum venerabile" (wondrous cave) with a dead hermit (c^2).

D1: ENCOUNTER—an uncorrupted body (d^6).

G1: BURIAL

Narrative II (Paphnutius)

B2: JOURNEY—further into the desert.

C2: PLACE—a "spelunca" (cave) (c^1).

D2: ENCOUNTER—the hairy hermit, Timotheus (d^1, d^3).

Narrative III (Timotheus' story)

A3: DEPARTURE—to seek a greater reward ("majorem mercedem") (a^2).

B3: JOURNEY—travels alone.

C3: PLACE—builds a small cell.

D3: ENCOUNTER—the devil corrupts a nun who tempts Timotheus.

B'3: JOURNEY—the second flight, with implicit secret departure /a^3/.

C'3: PLACE—the cave, spring, and palm tree.

F'3: REQUEST—to God for mercy.

D'3: ENCOUNTER—the healing angel.

(*Narrative II*, Paphnutius)

F2: REQUEST—P asks to stay (denied, f^1).

Narrative IV

B4: JOURNEY—"in interiorem solitudinem" (into deeper solitude) without sufficient food or water (b^1); sustained by an angel (b^2); lies on the ground as if dead ("velut mortuus") (b^3).

D4: ENCOUNTER—with the hairy hermit (d^3) whom Paphnutius thinks a murderer (d^1). Onuphrius knows P's name (d^2).

Narrative V (Onuphrius' story)

A5: DEPARTURE—secretly to seek one greater with God ("majorem apud Deum") (a^2, a^3).

B5: JOURNEY—takes only enough food and water for four days (b^1); guided by an angel, "insignis ille" (that splendid one) (b^2).

C5: PLACE—a "speluncam venerabilem" (wondrous cave).

D5: ENCOUNTER—with an old hermit.

/E5/: TALE—The hermit instructs Onuphrius.

G5: BURIAL—Onuphrius buries the hermit.

(*Narrative IV*)

C4: PLACE—Onuphrius and Paphnutius go to Onuphrius' cave, where miraculous food appears (d^4); in the morning Onuphrius' appearance unusual (d^3).

F4: REQUEST—Paphnutius asks to stay (f^1).

G4: BURIAL—Paphnutius buries Onuphrius, with aid of lions in a later version [g^1].

Narrative VI (Paphnutius)

B6: JOURNEY—an angelic guide gives Paphnutius strength (b^2).

C6: PLACE—cave or cell (c^1).

D6: ENCOUNTER—an old hermit and three companions (d^2); rations miraculously increased (d^4).

E6: TALE—they tell Paphnutius the story of their lives.

F6: REQUEST—Paphnutius asks to stay (f^1).

Narrative VII (Paphnutius)

B7: JOURNEY—"per interiorem solitudinem" (through deeper solitude).

C7: PLACE—the garden paradise.

D7: ENCOUNTER—four boys, "tanta gloria insignes" (splendid with such great glory) that Paphnutius thinks them angels (d^1, d^2, d^3, d^4).

E7: TALE

Narrative VIII (the boys' tale)

A8: DEPARTURE—students from Oxyrhynchus.

B8: JOURNEY—travelled with insufficient food (b^1); guided by an angel (b^2).

C8: PLACE—the garden.

D8: ENCOUNTER—an old hermit.

/E8/: TALE—he instructed them.

/F8/: BURIAL—the hermit died and presumably they buried him.

Narrative IX (Paphnutius)

B9: JOURNEY—Paphnutius heads home, rejoicing.

C9: PLACE—the abode of two brothers.

D9: ENCOUNTER—Paphnutius stays with the brothers for ten days.

E9: TALE—Paphnutius tells them his story, which they make into the tale that we have just read.

Although the narrative pattern is consistent, the account is not static. The deeper the traveler goes into the inner solitude, the more the events touch upon the sacred and the miraculous. Paphnutius' first encounter was with a dead hermit; the story reveals a common hagiographical motif, the uncorrupted body,[52] but the episode is presented in a realistic fashion. It is unusual, to say the least, to find still sitting upright the body of someone who has been dead so long that his clothing or his limbs fall to dust when touched, yet the experience is not past belief. The second episode, the encounter with Timotheus, contains a greater miracle, the story of the angelic physician who healed the hermit's ailing liver. On the next stage of the journey, Paphnutius himself is privileged to be succoured by an angel, who gives him the strength to survive in the harsh Egyptian desert without food or water. The most impressive miracles, appropriately enough, concern the titular hero of the story, Onuphrius himself, who was also conducted through the desert by an angel and who has been for years provided miraculously with food. At his death, an earthquake destroys his cave, spring, and palm tree, thereby making manifest God's will. On the first leg of Paphnutius' return trip to civilization, he is still guided by the heavenly figure. When he reaches the paradisiacal garden, he meets not an angel but four students so lovely ("tanta gloria insignes") that he at first thinks they are angels, an event that may be interpreted as a miracle that has been given a rationalized explanation. His final encounter is with the two brothers who are able to make a book of his experiences, a normal enough occurrence from a modern perspective but far more extraordinary in the largely illiterate Coptic culture of the fourth or fifth century A.D. (This final episode suggests that Paphnutius himself may have been illiterate.)

Other lives of desert saints conform to the same basic narrative pattern and utilize the same motifs. The legend of St. Macarius the Roman[53] has a similar structure. Briefly, this *vita* takes the form of a first-person narrative told by Theophilus, one of three monks who

---

52. The uncorrupted body has always been a sign of divine favor; it occurs in pagan as well as Christian literature, in Homer's *Iliad*, for example, and Quintus Curtius relates the same phenomenon of the body of Alexander (see Saintyves, *En marge de la légende dorée* [1930], ch. 8 and Appendix II). According to Kurtz, "From St. Antony to St. Guthlac" (1926), p. 131, St. Jerome first introduced this folk motif into hagiographic literature with his account of the uncorrupted corpse of St. Hilarion (Kurtz makes no reference to the legend of Paphnutius).

53. *Vitae Patrum* I, *PL* 73, 415–26; *BHG* 1004, 1005, *BHL* 5104.

FIGURE 2. St. Macarius the Roman and his lions.

decides to walk to the place where the earth meets the sky (for detailed discussions of this plot, see below, pp. 122–24). After many adventures and close brushes with death, they come to a beautiful cave inhabited by the saint and his two pet lions. He tells them his story: a Roman citizen, he fled the city during his wedding and made his way to this spot, twenty miles from Paradise. While he was living in his cave, the devil tempted him by assuming the form of his abandoned bride, and Macarius succumbed. To atone for this sin, Macarius spent three years buried up to his neck. The three monks then return to the civilized world to tell their experiences.

VITA MACARII ROMANI

Narrative I (The Three Monks)

A1: DEPARTURE—they slip out secretly (a^3).

B1: JOURNEY—they have many adventures, including long periods without food or water (b^1); they enjoy the services of two animal guides (b^2); they are imprisoned and left to die (b^3).

C1: PLACE—they arrive "ad speluncam honorabilem" (at a beautiful cave) (c^1).

D1: ENCOUNTER—suddenly they see a hairy hermit approach (d^3).

E1: TALE

Narrative II (Macarius)

A2: DEPARTURE—Macarius departs secretly during his wedding (a^1, a^3).

B2: JOURNEY—Macarius enjoys the aid of two angelic and two animal guides (b^2); lack of food (b^1).

C2: PLACE—he finds a cave in which there is a dead lioness (c^2) and her two cubs, whom he raises on leaves (d^4, miraculous feeding).

G2: BURIAL—he buries the lioness.

C'2: PLACE—outside his cave Macarius finds articles of woman's clothing.

D'2: ENCOUNTER—the demonic bride (d^1).

E'2: TALE

Narrative III (The Bride)

A3: DEPARTURE—the bride departs from her wedding (a^1, a^3).

B3: JOURNEY—without, she says, the aid of any guide ($-b^2$).

C3: PLACE—Macarius takes her inside his cave where she seduces him in his sleep and disappears.

Narrative II (Macarius)

F'2: REQUEST—Macarius devoutly prays for Christ's pardon.

G'2: BURIAL—he is buried for three years up to his neck by his lions (g¹).

Narrative I (The Three Monks)

F1: REQUEST—in the form of a question, as Macarius asks if they are strong enough to stay (f¹); they elect to leave.

Narrative IV (The Three Monks)

B4: JOURNEY—recapitulates the motif of the inward journey; Macarius' lions serve as guides (b²).

C4: PLACE—they return to their monastery.

E4: TALE—they relate their adventures.

The basic components of this narrative are the very ones that made up Paphnutius' account, although there is more displacement. In the "bride's" tale, the guide-motif is present but with a negative valence since its absence is noted (−b²). The demon-bride's lack of a guide was a bad omen; she is the negative image of Macarius (see below), and lacked the divine guidance which he and the others enjoyed. (For further discussion of the bride's tale, see below, pp. 86 and 92–98.)

The same narrative pattern underlies one of the best-known of the tales of the desert hermits, St. Jerome's Life of Paul of Thebes, although the structural matrix differs in one important respect. This account is told in chronological order by an omniscient narrator rather than having the titular saint, Paul, tell his life's story to the questing hero, Antony. In a later retelling of the story, to which we shall have occasion to return, the account slips into the first person, as if Antony himself were telling his adventures, a change that makes the story conform more closely to the underlying prototype.

VITA PAULI

Narrative I (Paul)

A1: DEPARTURE—Paul seeks the desert to escape denunciation as a Christian, /a³/.

B1: JOURNEY—he flees through the desert; in a later version, he stops in a tomb [b³] and is transported by an angel [b²].

C1: PLACE—the wonderful cave, spring, and palm tree (c¹).

Narrative II (Antony)

A2: DEPARTURE—It is revealed to Antony in a vision that deep in the desert there lives someone much holier than he, whom he ought to visit (a²).

B2: JOURNEY—strange creatures guide him (b²).

C2: PLACE—he finds Paul's cave (its occupancy is unusual).

D2: ENCOUNTER—Paul, a hairy hermit⁵⁴ (d³), at first is unwilling to admit Antony. When he does, food is miraculously provided (d⁴). Paul says he is dying. (Knowledge of death is a common form of miraculous knowledge [d⁵].)

F2: REQUEST—Antony asks to accompany Paul in death [f⁵].)

F'2: REQUEST—Paul asks Antony to go for a *pallium* (cloak) to wrap his body in; Paul's knowledge of the existence of this garment is miraculous.

Narrative III

B3: JOURNEY—Antony goes to his monastery for the *pallium* and returns (b¹).

C3: PLACE—Antony finds Paul dead in his cave (c²).

/D3/: ENCOUNTER—at first Antony thinks Paul is alive, for he is kneeling in prayer, his arms uplifted. Antony sees angels escorting Paul's soul to heaven⁵⁵ (d⁵).

G3: BURIAL—Antony buries the body with the aid of two lions (g¹).

The story of the adventures of Zosimas, discoverer of St. Mary the Egyptian, fits the pattern as well.⁵⁶ The account in the *Vitae*

54. In the prologue he is described as "subterraneo specu crinitum calcaneo tenus hominem" (*PL* 23, 18) (a man living in an underground cavern, covered with hair down to his heels).

55. This appears to be the first appearance of this common motif in Christian legend; Saintyves cites it as a pagan theme taken over by the Christians (*En marge*, [1930], p. 127).

56. Gallais analyzes the version of Mary the Egyptian contained in the "Miracles

Patrum[57] opens with a description of Zosimas' unblemished monastic life (A1), which culminates in his desire to leave this sheltered existence to find, he says, someone "prior me in actibus" (before me in his (holy) works [a²]). His journey (B1) is in two stages, first to a monastery on the banks of the Jordan, and then further into the desert. There, after a twenty-day walk, he is praying, looking eastward,[58] when he sees a figure (D1) that he thinks is a spirit, "phantasiam alicujus spiritus" (d¹). This figure, naked and blackened by the sun (d³), is St. Mary the Egyptian. She miraculously knows Zosimas' name (d²). Their encounters are marked by miracles, as he once sees her levitated in prayer (d⁵). She tells him her story (E1), a narrative that includes the traditional motifs of long periods spent without food or water (b¹); her flight had been motivated by a desire to do penance for the lascivious life she had led (a⁴). She asks him to return the following year (F1), bringing her communion. He complies; on his third visit to the desert (Narrative IV), he finds her dead body lying on the ground (c²), with the request that he bury her (F4) written beside her, a miracle since Mary was illiterate. The date reveals that she died a year earlier (d⁶). A lion aids Zosimas in burying the body (G4, g¹).

A final example concerns a saint of little fame, Mark the Athenian (also known as Mark of Termaqa). The account starts out sounding more like a traditional monastic anecdote of the sort found in the *Verba Seniorum* than an obviously fictitious tale such as the legend of Macarius the Roman, but although there are no grave-digging lions in this tale, it conforms very closely to the same paradigm as the better known and more obviously fictional accounts. As Serapion, the questing hero, nears Mark's magic mountain, his experiences become wilder and wilder, and reveal their roots in myth and folktale.

Mark the Athenian, a hermit in the Libyan desert, was presumed

de Nostre Dame" in terms of Propp's formulation, Lack Liquidated; "Remarques sur la structure" (1974), p. 124, n. 19.

57. Book I, *PL* 73, 673–90; the Greek life by Sophronius, Patriarch of Jerusalem, is in *PG* 87, iii, 3697–726.

58. Macarius also appeared coming from the east, as will the Redeemer at the Last Judgment.

to have lived in the fourth century, according to the introduction to his *vita* in the *Acta Sanctorum*.[59] The legend comes complete with a pedigree designed to vouch for its authenticity, for it purports to be a first-person account related by one Abbot Serapion to his disciples who are in turn responsible for the tale's dissemination: "Narravit nobis Abbas Serapion in eremo interiori Aegypti, sic dicens: Cum dormirem aliquando. . ." (779C; Abba Serapion told us in the desert of inner Egypt, saying: "When I was once asleep . . ."). In a dream Serapion hears the Abba Joannes talking to two ascetics; they are speaking of Serapion and of a hermit, Mark the Athenian, who is 130 years old and has lived in the desert for 95 years. Serapion wakes up with an intense wish to visit the holy hermit. To this end, he goes to Alexandria to find out from merchants how to get to the mountain called Thrace where Mark lived; the trip to Alexandria normally takes twelve days but Mark covers the distance in five. The merchants tell him the journey overland to the mountain would require thirty days; putting water in a flask (no mention is made of food), Serapion sets out. After twenty days the water runs out, and unable to find either food or drink in the barren desert, he falls to the ground as if dead, ("velut mortuus" [b^3, surrogate death]). Suddenly he sees the two ascetics of his dream; they tell him to get up and follow them (/b^2/, miraculous guides). They show him the roots of a tree which he can eat, and doing so he feels refreshed (b^1). They point out the way he should go and suddenly vanish from sight (an event that confirms their miraculous nature). Serapion comes to a mountain with a lake at its summit, the home of Mark the Athenian.

After wandering around the top of the mountain for seven days, Serapion one night observes angels visiting the holy hermit and telling Mark that they have brought the Abba Serapion to him (more proof of the miraculous nature of his guides). Serapion and Mark meet, and the hermit recounts his life story. Mark knows Serapion's name since the angels told it to him (d^2).

Mark was an Athenian who had studied philosophy, and at his

59. *AA.SS.* March III, vol. 9, pp. 775–78 (29 March). The legend may go back to the fourth or fifth century (Williams, *Oriental Affinities* [1927], II, 60).

parents' death had decided that since the world gave him no benefits he would renounce it. He had lived in the desert for ninety-five years without seeing man or beast, but he had engaged in many fights with devils. After thirty years, God suddenly caused his hair to grow, covering his nakedness (d^3), and angels brought him spiritual food (d^4). He tells Serapion of his visions, among which were vistas of Paradise and the tree of life.

Dawn breaks and Serapion observed that Mark's entire body is covered with hair "like a wild beast's" (d^3). That evening, when they enter the cave, a table and two chairs miraculously appear, and many good things to eat—two fish, fresh bread, olives, dates, and honey-sweet water. Mark comments, "You see how God loves his servants. He usually sends one fish but today there are two" (d^4). Another miracle marks the encounter of the two holy men. Mark demonstrates the power of faith to move mountains (Matt. 17:19), as his mountain moves from its place and returns (d^5). He repeats the story of God's causing his hair to grow, but this time adds a significant detail: once his hair grew, the demons lost their power to hurt him.[60]

Mark tells Serapion that his death is imminent and asks the latter to bury him (F, the request). He adds that he is to be buried as he is, naked but for his hair, and that after his death Serapion is to block the door to the cave and depart (an implicit denial of the request to remain, /f[1]/). Serapion asks to accompany the hermit wherever his journey should lead him, but Mark denies this request (f^1), and foretells that Serapion will return home by a different route from the one he followed coming. The saint then dies; Serapion buries him (G), blocks the cave's door, and descends the mountain. At the bottom he is at once joined by the two "brothers." Suddenly he finds himself back in Abba Joannes' church and realizes that he has been magically transported there by the two wonder-working ascetics.

60. For the sanctity of hair as "soul-power" or strength, see Hopkins, *Origin and Evolution of Religion* (1924), pp. 115–28; also Firth, *Symbols* (1973), ch. 8, "Hair as Private Asset and Public Symbol," esp. pp. 283–87; Leach, "Magical Hair" (1967).

The similarities between the fabulous account of the travels of Serapion and Jerome's life of Paul of Thebes are striking;[61] all we appear to lack are the two lions. Indeed, the customary explanation for the obvious similarity between many lives of the desert fathers is to attribute this phenomenon precisely to the influence exerted by Jerome's very popular *Vita Pauli*,[62] perhaps the earliest extant version of the now familiar tale of the desert saint on the eve of his death discovered by a pious traveler. Tales like that of Mark the Athenian, as Paul Peeters has commented, "are adaptations, scarcely veiled, of the type created by the story of Paul of Thebes."[63] Of Paphnutius' tale of Onuphrius, Peeters writes:

This Paphnutius had read the life of St. Paul of Thebes; he remembered it a little too well, and sought inspiration from still other sources. The turn of his account, the marvelous alternating regularly with danger met with a gay heart, the rectilinear succession of the climactic reversals, and the symmetry of the formulas that introduce them—in short the whole anecdotal framework—overpoweringly recalls the manner of Eastern story-tellers. One could call it a Christian page of the *Thousand and One Nights*.[64]

For many hagiographic legends, the theory of literal (and literary) borrowing is no doubt correct. For example, as Hippolyte Delehaye has shown, the account of St. Theoctista of Lesbos is nothing more than an adaptation of the extremely popular legend of St. Mary the Egyptian.[65] For other accounts, however, the situation is perhaps more complex. Peeters notes the differences as well as the similarities between the *Vita Pauli* and the *Vita Onuphrii* and

61. See the article on the saint by Sauget in *Bibliotheca Sanctorum*, vol. 8, s.v., 701–3.
62. See Oldfather, *Studies in the Text Tradition of St. Jerome's Vitae Patrum* (1943).
63. "Des accomodations à peine dissimulées du type créé par l'histoire de S. Paul de Thèbes." In a review of B. Turaiev, "Légende copt-ethiopienne" (1907), p. 126.
64. In a review of Francesco Maria Esteves Pereia, *Vida de santo Abunafre* (1906), p. 204: "Ce Paphnuce avait lu la vie de S. Paul de Thèbes; il s'en souvenait un peu trop et cherchait son inspiration à d'autres sources encore. La tour de son récit, le merveilleux qui alterne régulièrement avec le danger affronté de gaîté de coeur, la succession rectiligne des péripéties et la symétrie des formules qui les introduisent, bref tout le cadre anecdotique . . . rappelle invinciblement la manière des conteurs orientaux. On dirait d'une page chrétienne des *Mille et une Nuits*."
65. "Un groupe de récits 'utiles à l'âme'" (a group of stories "useful for the soul") (1934), pp. 199–200.

ascribes them to Paphnutius' reliance upon "still other sources." This scholar is, I think, far closer to the truth when he observes the resemblance with popular tales of the Near East than he is in postulating the direct influence of the Life of Paul of Thebes on the early versions of the Life of Onuphrius (on those versions, for example, prior to the inclusion of the detail of burial by lions). Indeed, in terms of plot structure, Jerome's *Vita Pauli* is somewhat anomalous; the other lives have more in common with each other than they do with their putative model.

The *Vita Pauli* resembles the other *vitae* in the motifs it includes (secret flight, miraculous sustenance, deathbed encounter, burial) but not in the order in which these details are presented. This tale is the only one to employ a purely chronological order of narration, beginning (as Aristotle recommends) at the beginning, with the departure of the young Paul for the desert, and then switching the narrative focus from this saint to relate the experiences of the traveler, Antony, who comes to visit Paul. All other stories begin with the traveler (indeed, he is the narrator), and the events that lead up to the discovery of the desert saint are described from the point of view of this character; then, in the form of a tale-within-a-tale the life of the saint is depicted, as he tells his story to the visitor. This alteration in the structure of the *Vita Pauli* might seem like a minor one, but it is, I think, of paramount importance. It changes the narrative from a single, sharply-focused tale of a quest, in which the quester, moreover, may originally have been the primary hero,[66] to a bi-partite, logical structure, which in this respect more closely resembles historical writing than romance. It is precisely the sort of transformation that might have occurred when a traditional narrative form (cf. Peeters' reference to "Eastern fairy-tales") was reworked by a well-educated, sophisticated theologian. The logic of Jerome's tale is temporal, not structural. For this influential life, I suggest, Jerome may have adapted a popular tale and utilized

66. Paphnutius, therefore, may have been the genuine hero of the *Peregrinatio Paphnutii*, not Onuphrius. In certain later Old French versions of the Life of St. Mary Egyptian, this episode becomes merely a secondary incident in what is really the story of Zosimas; Rudder, "La Vie de sainte Marie" (1982), p. 41.

motifs already hallowed by tradition before he took them over.[67] Jerome's great personal authority gave an *imprimatur* to the form, but the form would not have been so frequently reused, the motifs so often "borrowed," had not the basic pattern already been familiar and, moreover, been felt to be significant. The desert saints, like the martyrs before them, were heroes, and their experiences were to be fabulated according to pre-existing norms for describing the adventures of heroes. Those motifs that were in some way particularly important were reused time and time again in these lives. By isolating and analyzing them, we may be able to discover an aspect of the "meaning" of that tale that has been obscured by more traditional modes of analysis.

Of the plot structure of traditional myth Joseph Campbell writes: "The standard path of the mythological adventure of the hero is a magnification of the formula represented in the rites of passage: *separation—initiation—return*: which might be named the nuclear unit of the monomyth."[68] We find this basic monomyth exemplified in the lives of the desert solitaries. The essential plot of these legends is a journey, a quest. The hero goes forth, finds a person who imparts knowledge (the story of his life) and who then usually dies.[69] Although the traveler would like to remain in the enchanted spot, he may not do so but must return to the world with his acquired knowledge.

Narrating the life of the desert solitary poses a serious problem,

67. Even in Jerome's own day there was doubt about the historicity of Paul of Thebes. Delehaye, noting the fabulous details such as the raven who brings bread and the grave-digging lions, believes that Jerome's purpose was to write an "edifying romance," a "roman d'édification"; he holds, however, that Jerome himself believed in his hero's existence ("La personalité historique de S. Paul de Thèbes" [1926], p. 64). Coleiro thinks the story historical: "St. Jerome's Lives of the Hermits" (1957) p. 163.

68. *The Hero* (1949), p. 30. For rites of passage, see below, ch. 7.

69. Williams (*Oriental Affinities*, II, 60), positing a possible gnostic influence, notes that for the Gnostics what mattered was the ascent of the soul, and for this a witness (the traveler) was especially important.

Such double tales appear to belong to folk narrative. Kemp Malone ("Rose and Cypress" [1928]) notes the popularity of the compound form in Urdu and Persian tales: "The frame-story is the tale of a quest. The quester finally reaches the one man who can enlighten him, and forces this man to tell his own story" (p. 416). See also Todorov, *Poétique de la prose* (1978), p. 40.

for unless the author adopts the stance of the anonymous, omniscient narrator (as in *Barlaam and Josaphat*, for example), there is no way for the experiences of these saints to become known to the world except for a traveler to return to civilization, bearing the tale. The traditional view of these tales has been to regard the embedded narrative, the "Life of Paul," or the "Life of Onuphrius," as the most important episode and to consider the surrounding material as "narrative frame," and therefore as material of secondary importance, which may be (and which usually is) omitted from consideration. Yet in terms of narrative structure, the inner tale cannot exist without the outer. Without the account of Paphnutius' adventures, we would never know of Onuphrius.[70]

The accounts of the three monks who find Macarius and of Paphnutius are told in the first-person, a narrative stratagem that lends them authority,[71] but the device of the embedded tale adds more than expediency or credibility to the discourse. The complex, double structure allows the author to widen his perspective and embrace a larger universe; his story may now include a greater variety of experiences. The outer tale may serve as foil to the inner[72] (e.g. the martyr tales with which St. Jerome prefaced the life of Paul of Thebes), or, in cases where the two stories echo one another, the doubling reinforces and generalizes the ideas expressed.

Charles Williams complained of the episodes in the *Peregrinatio Paphnutii* that follow the encounters with Timotheus and Onuphrius (sections VI–IX) that they form a "dull appendix to the other two accounts."[73] From a purely hagiographic point of view,

70. It is noteworthy that, with a minor exception in the account of St. Mary the Egyptian, the tales of the desert ascetics exclude a possibility utilized in later stories, the deathbed letter (e.g. St. Alexis; see Boureau, *Les Formes narratives* [1981], p. 64). The lack of letters suggests a primarily illiterate society.

71. Hagiography favors first-person narration. Several third-person accounts, moreover, tend to slip into the first person: e.g. the Life of Paul of Thebes ascribed to Athanasius contained in an Arabic synaxary (*CSCO*, vol. 78, ser. III, vol. 18, p. 463); also St. Theopista in the same volume, p. 35; and the *Protevangelium of James*, 18, in Walker, ed., *Apocryphal Gospels*, Ante-Nicene Christian Library, vol. 16, p. 11. In ancient fiction the first-person narrator was used only for the wildest accounts, e.g. the works of Lucian and Apuleius. See Söder, *Die apokryphen Apostelgeschichten* (1932), p. 211 ff.

72. For foil narrative in romance, see Frye, *Secular Scripture* (1976).

73. *Oriental Affinities*, II, 60.

perhaps this verdict is correct, since on his return journey Paphnutius meets no saints as spectacular as Timotheus and Onuphrius. Yet in addition to answering the question, "Did anything happen on the way home?" the final four episodes, whether a "dull appendix" or not, are important precisely because of their lack of originality (hence the impression of dullness). They replicate the narrative pattern of the earlier episodes. The theories of Edmund Leach concerning the "redundancy" of myth are valid here.[74] Citing J. Schniewind's definition of myth as "the expression of unobservable realities in terms of observable phenomena" (p. 7), Leach uses the concept of redundancy derived from information theory, where a high level of redundancy makes it easy to correct errors introduced by noise (interference), to explain the repetitive nature of myth. Leach writes:

Now in the mind of the believer, myth does indeed convey messages which are the Word of God. To such a man the redundancy of myth is a very reassuring fact. Any particular myth in isolation is like a coded message badly snarled up with noisy interference. Even the most confident devotee might feel a little uncertain as to what precisely is being said. But, as a result of redundancy, the believer can feel that, even when the details vary, each alternative version of a myth confirms his understanding and reinforces the essential meaning of all the others (p. 9).

This, then, is why Paphnutius has nine structurally identical adventures. The importance of the motif of symbolic death, for example, is reinforced by repetition, and the audience's perception of its value is underlined by its appearance in other, structurally similar, tales.

The technique is perfectly adapted to reflect a gradational ethos—Zosimas is holy but Mary is holier; the coenobitic monks are *fortes* (strong) but a desert solitary like Onuphrius is *fortior* (stronger). Finally, it is the more mythic of the *vitae* that form the core tales of the double narratives; these are the stories whose plot structures reflect most clearly the ideological constructs that underlie the narrative and that are set in the most symbolic landscape. The heroes of such tales are no longer really a part of this world,

74. *Genesis as Myth* (1969), pp. 7–23.

having already experienced symbolic death and rebirth into the next. But the questing hero, as narrator, mediates between the saint and the world, bringing back the story to the Christian community where it can be an inspiration to others.

In "The Story of Asdiwal," a study whose influence on the much of the subsequent discussion will be clear, Claude Lévi-Strauss remarked after analyzing the myth: "Having separated out the codes, we have analyzed the structure of the message. It remains to decipher the meaning" (p. 21). I have demonstrated the existence of an underlying structure in a group of hagiographic legends. In the pages that follow, I investigate the implications of certain of the most common motifs and themes. I will concentrate in particular on the following: the childhood of the hero; three motifs of departure—the "more" motif (a^2), secret departure (a^3), and marriage (a^1); motifs of descent, symbolic death, and burial; the two journey motifs, food (b^1) and guides (b^2); and finally, mistaken identity (d^1) and its allomorph, miraculous knowledge of identity (d^2).

Chapter 4

The Saint Sets Forth: Motifs of Departure

THE CHILDHOOD OF THE HERO

From birth, or even before, the saintly hero of legend, like his secular counterpart, is often marked as a man or woman set apart, extraordinary. Many historic monks came from simple origins. Antony, for example, was the son of small landowners, and probably illiterate.[1] St. Simeon Stylites was the son of farmers and tended the family's sheep. But legend paints a different picture of many saintly heroes.

We are all familiar with the origins of fairy-tale heroes:

Once upon a time there was a king and a queen and every day they said, "O, if only we had a child!" But they never had one.[2]

Lord Raglan, noting the repeated pattern in many accounts of the childhood of the mythical hero, offers the following description:

The hero's mother is a royal virgin; . . . his father is a king, but the circumstances of his conception are unusual, . . . and at birth an attempt is made, usually by his father or maternal grandfather, to kill him, but he is spirited away, and . . . reared by foster parents in a far country.[3]

---

1. This point, however, is controversial; see Meredith, "Asceticism," (1976), p. 311.
2. *Grimm's Fairy Tales*, "Sleeping Beauty," cited by Lüthi, *Once Upon a Time* (1976), p. 22.
3. Raglan, *The Hero* (1956), p. 174.

Among the saintly heroes under consideration here, only the accounts of Jesus (particularly as related in the apocryphal gospels) and later versions of the Life of St. Onuphrius conform closely to this archetype. The early lives of Onuphrius include no details about him prior to his joining a coenobitic monastic community, but in subsequent accounts, he becomes the son of the King of Persia or Egypt.[4] The devil (a displaced evil-father figure), disguised as a pilgrim, persuades the king that his son is the result of an adulterous union, and in an attempt to prove the veracity of the charge, the baby is thrown into a fire, from which he escapes unscathed. Later the baby is suckled by a doe[5] who remains with the child for three years, and he is raised not by his own family but by a community of monks.

Accounts of other saints' childhoods conform to a somewhat different archetype. The child is usually from a noble family,[6] and he or she is nearly always an only child and almost invariably a *puer* or *puella senex* (boy or girl with the wisdom of old age).[7] That the hero should so consistently be an only child[8] is perhaps surprising. It certainly goes against the norm in an era of high infant mortality when more than one child was necessary to ensure the inheritance.[9] One of the most awkward problems for orthodox Christianity concerns the status of those referred to in the Gospels

4. For the son of the King of Egypt, see Boneta y la Plana, *Vidas de Santos y Venerables Varones de la Religión* (1680); the son of the King of Persia, see Raoli, *Vita di Sant' Honofrio Heremita* (1705). The frescoes painted by Giuseppe Cesari, the "Cavaliere d'Arpino" (1568–1640), and others at the church of Sant' Onofrio on the Janiculum in Rome depict the saint as son of the King of Persia.

5. A variant of motif b^1, reminiscent of the tale of Rome's founding heroes, Romulus and Remus.

6. A theme that heightens the contrast of the saintly humility of the *servus Dei* (St. Alexis is a good instance); see Boureau, *Les Formes narratives* (1981), p. 198, and for the importance of nobility in local cults, Vauchez, "Beata stirps" (1977), 397–99.

7. See Curtius, *European Literature and the Latin Middle Ages* (1963), pp. 98–101; also Carp, "*Puer-senex*" (1980).

8. Not only were Mary and Jesus only children, but so too were Abraham, Astion, Maria Meretrix, Euphrasia, Euphrosyne, Onuphrius, Alexis, Josaphat, Eusebia, Christina, Eleutherius, Barbara, Nicholas, and many others.

9. Reliable population figures for the period in question are, to be sure, difficult to come by.

as Jesus' brothers. In the case of the Virgin Birth, the necessity for Jesus to lack siblings is apparent,[10] but there is no obvious reason (except for *imitatio Christi*, not as strong motive as it was to become in later centuries), why so many other saints should be said to be only children. Among the saints whose biographies are contained in the *Vitae Patrum*, Book I, only Antony, Pachomius, Paul of Thebes, and Eugenia are exceptions. Paul has a sister in Jerome's account and a brother in a later Arabic retelling, while Eugenia has two brothers. The case of St. Simeon Stylites (d. 459), a historic figure for whom more than one biography survives, is instructive here as elsewhere. In the Syriac account, generally regarded as historical, the saint has a brother,[11] but in the more fictional *vita* written some years after the saint's death and circulated as the work of Simeon's disciple Antony, there is no mention of the brother.[12] Antony's version conforms more closely to the archetype.

The authors of these hagiographic accounts, then, appear to have limited voluntarily the narrative possibilities open to them. The story of Paul of Thebes shows the way such a detail could have been developed, as the sister (or brother) could act as a foil to the ideal of Christian conduct that the saint embodies (compare, for example, the use Sophocles made of the sisters of Electra and Antigone). In Jerome's account, the husband of Paul's sister threatens to betray his young Christian brother-in-law to the pagan authorities, an act that motivates Paul's flight for the desert. In the version of the life contained in an Arabic synaxary[13] (a collection of saints' legends), presumably written after the threat of martyrdom had lost some of its immediacy, Paul has a brother whose greed contrasts with the saint's relinquishment of worldly goods in order to attain the greater treasure laid up in the heavenly Jerusalem.[14]

If the saint's birth is interpreted as a miracle (as frequently is the

10. The necessity applies, of course, only to *Maria semper virgo*.
11. See Festugière, *Antioche païenne* (1959), pp. 357–58.
12. Antony's version is in *PL* 73, 325–34, *Vitae patrum*, Bk. 1.
13. CSCO, vol. 78, *Scriptores Arabici*, ser. III, vol. 18, p. 458.
14. The doubled hero or heroine, one good and one bad, is common in romance; see Frye, *Secular Scripture* (1976), pp. 142ff.

case), and if it is, like that of such biblical figures as Isaac, Samuel, and John the Baptist, the result of fervent prayer (e.g. Euphrosyne and, later, Alexis), then it is not remarkable that the child has no brothers or sisters. Sleeping Beauty was also an only child, born after many years to a childless couple. But in other cases the frequency with which this detail occurs exceeds expectation. It serves to set the hero apart from normal human experience.[15] It also distinguishes him from the hero of folktale (often the youngest of three brothers or sisters—e.g. Joseph, Psyche, Cinderella)[16] but aligns him with the hero of classical myth, for the great Greek heroes—Achilles, Odysseus, Telemachus, Ajax, Theseus, Perseus, and of course Oedipus—are only children.[17] Of the major heroes Heracles alone violates this norm. For both pagan and Christian narrative, the detail emphasizes the uniqueness and the difference of the hero. His nature is special, not to be shared with uterine siblings. In the case of the Christian hero, moreover, particularly the males, the detail reinforces the magnitude of the rejection when the hero refuses to marry and continue the family and its property. Alexis' father in particular complains at length about his son's betrayal of his responsibilities to the community.[18]

By and large, the classical Greeks were not much interested in the childhood of their heroes. Except for Achilles, only Heracles is credited with an infantile exploit as, still in his cradle, he strangles the threatening snakes. In hagiography, the topos of the *puer (puella) senex* is a common one.[19] In the *Protevangelium of James*, for ex-

15. Moreover, the more obviously fictional the biography, the greater the likelihood that the saint will be an only child; Saints Christina, Barbara, Nicholas, and Eleutherius were all only children.

16. See Bettelheim, *The Uses of Enchantment* (1977), pp. 105–6, for a discussion of the role of sibling rivalry in fairytales.

17. Heiserman notes that Jason was not traditionally an only son but that Apollonius Rhodius makes him one in his romance epic, *The Argonautica* (*The Novel* [1977]). Those heroes who have siblings often come to grief for that very reason (e.g. Eteocles and Polynices, Paris and Hector).

18. *La Vie de saint Alexis* (ms. L, ed. Storey) (1968), vv. 401–5.

19. See Curtius, *European Literature* (1963), 98–101; Festugière, "Lieux communs littéraires," (1960), pp. 137–39; For precocious infant behavior, see the folklore motif, popular in hagiography, of the infant who, usually to free its mother from an unjust suspicion of adultery, names its father; Canart, "Le nouveau-né qui dénonce son père," (1966).

ample, the Virgin Mary is able to walk at the age of six months,[20] while in the *Gospel of Pseudo-Matthew*, at the age of three she is said to be as wise as if she were thirty.[21] In the same source, the baby Jesus is able to stand and to talk during the flight into Egypt.[22] Saint Eugenia, one of the women saints whose Life is found in the *Vitae Patrum*,[23] was a splendid student; educated in both Greek and Latin, she possessed a photographic memory. (Examples of saints who were *pueri* or *puellae senes* could be multiplied indefinitely.) Once again, the detail serves to underscore the difference between the saint and ordinary people. From the very beginning, the saint is marked as someone special.

THE BREAK WITH THE PAST

In common with more traditional romances, most hagiographic romances involve a change of scene (witness the prominence of theme B, the Journey, found in all tales analyzed here). Very few saints, it seems, were able to remain at home and attain sanctity.[24] St. Jerome enthusiastically sang the praises of a Roman girl, Asella, who in the metropolis lived the solitary life as if she were in the desert, who "enclosed by the constriction of a single cell enjoyed the expanse of Paradise."[25] But Asella was the exception that proved the rule; the others had to leave home. For many, "leaving home" may have been a more traumatic experience than it is today. The society was firmly structured. "If there was ever a society

20. Ante-Nicene Christian Library, vol. 16, *Apocryphal Gospels, Acts, and Revelations*, trans. Walker (1870), section 6, p. 4. The *Protevangelium* probably goes back to the middle of the second century and may have been written in Egypt; in its present form, it dates to the fourth century (see Quasten, *Patrology* [1950], I, 121).

21. *Apocryphal Gospels* (above, n. 20), ch. 6, p. 23.

22. Ibid., chapter 18, pp. 35–36.

23. *PL* 73, 605–20.

24. The importance of departure, of a radical break with the past, has roots in reality. Monod concludes that many religious conversions followed journeys abroad. Change of place brought about a change of life. He cites the examples, among others, of Saul converted on the road to Damascus (Acts 9:3, 22:6) and Augustine at Milan, and notes that Luther's conversion in 1513 at Wittenberg was preceded by a trip to Rome in 1510. He writes that Abraham, "le père des croyants, est essentiellement un voyageur, un pèlerin" (Abraham, father of the faithful, is esentially a traveler, a pilgrim) "Le voyage, le déracinement de l'individu" (1936), p. 386.

25. *Epistle* 24b, to Marcella (*PL* 22, 427–28).

which suffered from a permanent ache of 'center' and 'periphery,' it was the Roman Empire."[26] We may surmise that what held good for the institution, about which Brown writes above, also was true for the individual.

The frequently-cited scriptural precedent for this significant action was the injunction in Matt. 19:29, "And every one that hath forsaken houses, or brethren, or sisters, or father, or mother, or wife, or children, or lands, for my name's sake, shall receive an hundredfold, and shall inherit everlasting life." But in hagiographic romance, when the hero journeys to a new place, he has not only left behind the familiar but has also made a significant move in terms of spatial codes. While picturesque descriptions such as those encountered in the *Vita Macarii* (see below) may have been included largely for their entertainment value,[27] they also have spiritual meaning. The city and the desert, inner and outer, enclosed and unenclosed spaces, are all symbolic loca as well as geographic designations.

Many of the saints who abandoned their homes were forced to flee in order to escape an unwelcome marriage.[28] Others set forth for reasons that more closely resemble those of traditional romance heroes, in search either of a woman or of knowledge (and to the extent that the woman functions as a sapiential or *anima* figure, the two quests may coincide). The implication, then, is that to attain sanctity the hero has to test himself not by walking the familiar paths at home but by seeking out "new roads of salvation." For a very few, such as Asella, a cell in busy Rome sufficed; for most the desert, the *interior mons*, to quote Athanasius' *Life* of St. Antony (51.1), was the place of spiritual adventure.

26. Peter Brown "Saint as Exemplar" (1983), p. 9.
27. For the popularity of pious travel literature, see Casson, *Travel in the Ancient World*, esp. ch. 19, "To the Holy Lands," and *DACL*, "Pèlerinages aux lieux saints." For pagan culture, an equivalent was provided by the immensely popular Alexander romance of Pseudo-Callisthenes, an anonymous Greek text composed sometime before the fourth century A.D., in which Alexander is credited with having reached the Ganges. It is full of accounts of terrifying adventures and tales of wonderful beasts.
28. Macarius the Roman, Abraham, Eugenia, Euphraxia, Eusebia Hospita, Malchus, and Euphrosyne, to name only a few whose names figure prominently in the *Vitae Patrum* or in Symeon Metaphrastes.

In Arthurian romances or in the fairy tales analyzed by Vladimir Propp,[29] the event that stimulates the hero to leave home or court is usually the arrival of a stranger. Calogrenant's tale of his adventure at the fountain inspires Yvain to depart; the Green Knight's challenge is the motivation for Gawain's journey. In the account of Paul and Thecla, the girl falls in love with Paul when she sees him first arriving at Inconium from Antioch.

By contrast, in hagiographic romance the stimulus more often comes from within—from within society (the threat of marriage) or from within the saint himself. Many saints, inspired by an inner prompting, a desire, a vision, set forth for the desert. For such questers the thematic word used to describe the process that compelled them to seek a change of scene is *cogitatio*. Theophilus, who wanted to walk to the edge of the world, said: "Tunc mihi misero Theophilo venit in mentem *cogitatio*" (*PL* 73, 415C; then the thought came into the mind of wretched Theophilus). Antony set out to find Paul of Thebes because "Haec in mentem eius *cogitatio* incidit" (*PL* 23, 22B; This thought occurred in his mind). Paphnutius decided to visit the desert because "*cogitavi* in corde meo" (*PL* 73, 211A; I thought in my heart). Since he was "pulsatus . . . a quibusdam *cogitationibus*" (*PL* 73, 674A; driven by certain thoughts), Zosimas journeyed to find a new source of inspiration. It may be that this motif is merely a displacement of the "more" motif found in later romance, that is the arrival of an outsider, in so far as the thought comes to the thinker from "outside." Yet the direction of the displacement, from event to thought, is significant. It is a sign of the greater internalization of the narrative, and it emphasizes the purely personal nature of the quest. The desert saint is a self-motivated hero.

THE "MORE" MOTIF (A²)

The impulse, the *cogitatio* that sends the hero off into the desert in many cases takes a specific form, as the traveler abandons home

29. Propp, *Morphology of the Folktale* (1968), p. 27, discusses the arrival of a new person, "who can be termed the *villain*," whose role is to disturb the peace.

or community to seek a *better* way of life or to find someone better, more holy, than himself. "Better," moreover, is equated with "farther": the saint is not found in these tales to be the occupant of the cell next door. The "more" motif appears, for example, three times in the *Peregrinatio Paphnutii*: Paphnutius left his monastic community for the desert to see if there was anyone living further in than himself ("interius meo"); Timotheus set forth desiring to find a greater reward ("majorem mercedem"); Onuphrius went off inspired by tales of those solitaries stronger ("fortiores") than the coenobitic monks. In Jerome's *Vita Pauli*, Antony traveled to find Paul whom a vision had told him was more holy than he.[30] Zosimas left his monastery to discover the one ahead of him in acts ("prior me in actibus").

The "more" motif is present in patristic literature from the earliest times.[31] The desert not only became the testing ground and the locus for spiritual combat but in itself it represented a better place than the city. Origen wrote that John the Baptist, fleeing the tumult of the cities, went to the desert where "the air was purer, the heavens more open, and God nearer" (*familiarior*).[32] In an article studying the folkloric elements in early hagiographic literature, Fes-

30. The historical value of the *Vita Pauli* is moot, but Rousseau suggests that the work is not "pure fiction," and specifically he singles out Antony's dream that someone more perfect that himself lived further into the desert as a detail that "rings true." It may not have occurred to Antony but, according to Rousseau, it was typical of the anxieties of the Egyptian ascetics (*Ascetics, Authority, and the Church* [1978], pp. 133–34).

31. It is perhaps an allomorph of a tale-type that can be documented from the earliest texts, and that is popular in patristic literature. Gerould christened the tale "The Hermit and the Saint," and noted that the oldest variant occurs in the *Mahābhārata*; he considers the *Vita Pauli* a variant of the type ("The Hermit and the Saint," [1905], p. 537). Nor is the motif limited to hagiography; it is common in fairy tales. To give one example from medieval historical writing, Etienne de Bourbon writes of the troubadour (or so it is usually assumed), Duke William IX of Aquitaine: "Audivi quod quidam comes Pictaviensis experiri voluit qui status esset in hominibus delicacior; et cum transfigurasset habitum suum, et diversos status hominum expertus fuisset rediit ad pristinum statum" (I have heard that a certain count of Poitiers wished to discover what was the more refined condition among men; and after he had changed his dress and tried out different conditions of men, ... he returned to his ancient condition). Cited by Martín de Riquer, *Los Trovadores: Historia literaria y textos*, vol. 1 (Barcelona: Planetas 1975) p. 133.

32. "Homilies on Luke," *PG* 13, 1827D (only the Latin text is given).

tugière noted the presence of an agonistic element in both the *Historia Monachorum* and the folklore of Delphi, and he cited numerous examples of consultations of the Delphic oracle to determine who was the most pious or the most happy.[33] But whatever the origin of this motif, its importance for the *Vitae Patrum* is paramount. It is a manifestation, in structural form, of the gradational ethos that underlies these stories. The *passiones* narrate tales of unmediated opposition between good and evil, right and wrong. Although the forces of evil are present in the lives of the desert fathers, the account is not, at the level of deep structure, *about* this conflict. The hermit may indeed do battle with demons (Antony is here the classic example), but in the stories under consideration, this element of the plot is surprisingly minor. More important is the account of the process by which a good man becomes better, by which a holy man draws closer to God. The "more" motif is a visible representation of this difference in narrative concern.

SECRET FLIGHT (A³)

Of the various stylized narrative motifs that make up the typical *vita* of the desert saint, that of secret flight is the most common. It is, indeed, a popular element of most romances. In the *Ephesiaca*, for example, Habrocomes slipped away secretly (*lathōn*) to find Anthia (*Eph.* II. 12.2). This motif most clearly sums up the generic difference between the martyr's *passio* and the confessor's *vita*. The *passio* is a centripetal narrative, and all action converges inward towards a single, climactic act: in *Peristephanon* III, Eulalia runs from concealment in the country into the public spectacle of the magistrate's court. The *vitae* under consideration here are apparently centrifugal in movement, as the saint flees from the social center outwards to the lonely desert. The secrecy of his departure emphasizes the purely personal, individual nature of the hero's journey. He travels alone, denied the comforting presence of a human guide, of a Vergil, and leaves behind all artifacts of civilization—the

33. "Lieux communs littéraires" (1960), p. 144.

bonds of family life, friends, possessions—for all are impedimenta on the journey to salvation.[34]

In many cases there was a good reason for the saint's flight from civilization to be secret. Paul of Thebes, for instance, fled to the mountains to escape being betrayed by his brother-in-law to the pagan authorities.[35] A far more frequent motive for flight was the desire to escape an unwelcome marriage.[36] In St. Jerome's Life of St. Malchus, a tale in praise of the virgin life, the saint told his biographer: "This one fact serves to illustrate with what great threats my father and with what great blandishments my mother pursued their goal that I betray my chastity—I fled both home and parents" (PL 23, 56B). The saintly Abraham of Qiduna was also threatened by marriage. Symeon Metaphrastes, expanding the *vita* ascribed to St. Ephrem of Syria in the *Vitae Patrum*, painted a vivid picture of the dilemma Abraham faced: whether to accede to "his mother's prayers and his father's orders" and marry, or to flee. Finally, "he accepted the yoke of matrimony because he knew that it was one of the Lord's precepts to obey father and mother" (PG 115, 45C). On the seventh day of the ceremonies, however, his heart was suddenly illuminated and he escaped (48B; see below). Macarius of Rome, forced to marry against his will, also made his escape during the wedding festivities (PL 73, 422B).[37] Though initially unwilling to disobey her father, St. Euphrosyne eventually left home "occulte" (secretly), disguised as a monk, to escape marriage (PL 73, 645B).[38]

34. The young Buddha Gautama Sakyamuni also set out in secret on his journey to enlightenment: see Campbell, *The Hero* (1949), p. 31.

35. Flight is not a common motif in the *passiones*; indeed, the heroic martyrs are more often depicted as resisting the urging of their families to flee and escape punishment (for example, *Peristephanon* III). In the legend of the Seven Sleepers of Ephesus (PG 115, 427–48), the heroes retired to their cave only to seek a respite before showing up for martyrdom; the hagiographer takes pains that this behavior should not be interpreted as cowardice.

36. The motif of flight from an unwelcome marriage or suitor is present in most Greek romances. Moreover, the saint's fears of parental displeasure were no doubt well founded. The twelfth-century biography of St. Christina of Markyate (ed. Talbot, 1959), offers a detailed picture of the unpleasant consequences that might befall one bold enough to defy openly his or her parents' wishes in this matter.

37. The parallel with the life of St. Alexis has been noted; see Gaiffier, "Intactam Sponsam Relinquens" (1947). He gives twenty-one instances of spouses abandoned.

38. In addition, Euphraxia, mother of St. Euphrasia, slipped away from Rome, *principe nesciente* (without the Emperor knowing), to avoid an unwelcome suitor

Although many parents may have been displeased at their child's preference for a religious rather than a secular life, the frequency of this theme suggests that it is a literary as well as an actual event. There were, at least at other periods, alternative courses of action. To give one example, the biography of St. Licinius, written by Marbod of Rennes,[39] shows us a saint able to overcome parental objections. Licinius was a *puer-senex* with a strong vocation, but since he was a relative of Clothar, he was compelled to lead the active life of a knight rather than the contemplative existence he desired. He was betrothed against his will but ("mirabile dictu!") his bride was struck with leprosy. Yet another marriage was proposed, but Licinius succeeded in persuading his parents to allow him to remain celibate, and eventually he became a monk, a bishop, and a saint. The option of persuasion, however, does not appear to have been available to the more legendary figures.

Even without the explicit threat of marriage, fear of parental displeasure at the child's choice of the religious life might also enforce secret flight. Astion, the only child of a wealthy pagan family, persuaded his mentor to sail away with him to Scythia where they were unknown. The boy feared, if his resolution to pursue a religious life were known, "ne immaculatam conscientiam meam per suas lacrymas polluat pater"[40] (lest my father pollute my unstained conscience with his tears). Astion was right concerning the violence of his parents' reactions. The account of his flight is followed by a lengthy chapter devoted to the passionate, and highly rhetorical, *planctus* (lament) uttered by his parents who feel that their lives, both personal and social, have come to naught with the loss of their son. Another beloved son, St. John Calybite (one of the precursors of the Alexis legend),[41] wished to accompany a monk to Jerusalem but knew that his mother would try by her tears to prevent him

---

(*PL* 73, 626C). The secret departure is all the more striking here as the Emperor is the Christian ruler, Theodosius, who has the role of spiritual father and, in contrast to his match-making wife, fully approves Euphraxia's decision to remain celibate (4, 626C).

39. *PL* 171, 1493–1504.

40. *PL* 73, 397D. Astion's use of "immaculatam" and "polluat" suggests his fear of sexual defilement.

41. Stebbins, "Les origines de la légende de saint Alexis" (1973), pp. 502 ff.

from going; therefore he urged the monk that they should "leave quietly so that no one knows" (*PG* 114, 572A). Finally, young St. Benedict slipped secretly away from his nurse to go to the "desert" of Subiaco (*PL* 66, 127–28C).

In contrast to these figures fleeing a secular mode of existence, there is no apparent reason why a monk should have to sneak away from his monastery. Athanasius' very influential Life of Antony, for example, does not record any secret departures for this frequent visitor to the desert. In Jerome's Life of Malchus, the abbot objected to the saint's leaving the monastery after his parents' death in order to settle their estate on the grounds that this act demonstrated too great a concern for worldly goods; in spite of his abbot's explicit disapproval, Malchus left openly.

Two biographies of St. Simeon Stylites the Elder show the way the motif of secret flight becomes an almost obligatory element in the narrative.[42] The first *vita* is that by Theodoret, Bishop of Cyr (b. 395 A.D.), which comprises chapter 26 of the *Historia Religiosa*. This *vita* was written around 440, some nineteen years before Simeon's death in 459. Theodoret knew the saint, and his biography is generally regarded by hagiographers as reliable.[43] It lacks the flamboyant miracle stories that color the pages of the later account ascribed to Antony. The second life, also originally composed in Greek and contained in the *Vitae Patrum*, purports to be the work of a disciple of Simeon named Antony, but this version, for all its vaunted authenticity, conflicts in significant ways with Theodoret's biography.[44] Paul Peeters has concluded that Antony's account was written in the early years of the sixth century, probably at Constantinople where there were claimed to be relics of the saint. Peeters writes: "Unfortunately we cannot grant [Antony's life] any kind of authority. The Greek Life is the work of a hagiographer without any direct knowledge of the country, the setting, or the local

42. For Simeon, see Delehaye, *Les Saints stylites* (1923); also Peeters, "S. Syméon Stylite et ses premiers biographes" (1943), p. 32; Festugière, *Antioche païenne*.

43. Delehaye, *Les Saints stylites*, pp. VI–X.

44. In questions of numbers, for example; see Peeters, "S. Syméon" (1943).

tradition."[45] For our purposes, however, it is its very lack of historical authenticity that recommends Antony's tale. Not limited by actual fact, or even by probability,[46] Antony's mythopoeic fiction is free to depict the ideal behavior of his saintly hero.

Simeon's biography contains three accounts of departure. The first occurs when the thirteen-year-old saint leaves his family to join a monastic community. This leave-taking is not described; if the saint's family objects, we are not told.[47] The treatment of the second and third departures is more revealing. Having alienated the monastic community by the rigor and seemingly antisocial nature of his ascetic practices,[48] Simeon is asked by the abbot to leave. Theodoret describes this departure with a simple participle devoid of descriptive modification (*PG* 82, 1469A). Because of popular outcry, however, the monks bring the saint back to the monastery, whence he eventually goes off a second time. Once again, Theodoret's account merely notes the fact: "he went away to the village of Telanissos" (1469B).

Antony's biography gives a slightly different account of these two events. Since the abbot had asked Simeon to leave, there was no reason for secrecy, yet the saint stole away: "exivit . . . nullo sciente" (*PL* 73, 327; he went out, unbeknownst to anyone). The second departure was also secret: "egressus occulte" (328A; he left secretly). These small alterations, found in a work written some time after the event although pretending to the authority of an eye-witness account, suggest that the secret flight has become a desirable and significant element in the narrative.

Other monks also displayed a preference for secret flight, regardless of necessity. The three monks who determined to walk to the

45. Ibid., pp. 43, 47: "Nous avons le regret de ne pouvoir lui reconnaître aucune espèce d'autorité. . . . La Vie grecque est l'oeuvre d'un hagiographe sans aucune connaissance directe du pays, du milieu et de la tradition locale."

46. It is Antony who purveys the popular legend of the blinded dragon healed by the saint, *PL* 73, 330AB.

47. In a version composed in Syriac, they are already dead; see Festugière, *Antioche païenne*, pp. 358–70, for the Syriac life.

48. He so mortified his flesh by wrapping chains around his body that the wound stank and was filled with worms (*PL* 73, 326C).

edge of the world left their community in the evening after vespers: "Caeteris quiescentibus *clam* monasterio egressi sumus" (*PL* 73, 415D; while the others were resting, we secretly left the monastery). Paphnutius, struck one day by desire to seek out the holy men of the desert, left quietly: "Unde factum est ut *tacitus* iter arriperem" (*PL* 73, 211A; whence it came about that I silently went on my way). Onuphrius stole away from his monastery in the dead of night: "*nocte silenti* concitus surrexi" (214D; awakened in the silent night, I got up). On the eighth day of her repetence, Pelagia abandoned the entourage of Bishop Nonnus, her confessor, and went alone to Jerusalem: "surgens nocte, *nobis ignorantibus*" (*PL* 73, 669C; arising at night, unknown to us). Finally, Symeon Metaphrastes tells the story of Cyriacus; the son of pious parents, the youthful saint had already been made a lector in the church by his uncle, the Bishop of Corinth. One day Cyriacus conceived the desire to visit the Holy Land and immediately put his plan into action, slipping "silently" out of church (*PG* 115, 921C). For these pious travelers, there is no obvious reason for secrecy. They need not have feared parental tears or anger. Their monastic brethren would, one assumes, have understood their motives for leaving the community and would have supported their endeavor. Why, then, did they consistently depart in secret?

For the ancients, man was by nature, as Aristotle wrote, a social creature,[49] a "political" animal—city-dweller and family member. It was man's aptitude for social organization, as well as the ability to speak, that lay at the root of his sociability, and that set him apart from the beasts. But not the desert saint. He is the direct antithesis of the ideal citizen of classical antiquity.[50] The anchorite, the saint who journeys into the desert, is basically a "loner," isolated from a

---

49. Aristotle, *Politics* I. 1253a2–7. Augustine opened *De Bono Conjugali* with the words: "Quoniam unusquisque homo humani generis pars est, et sociale quiddam est humana natura, magnumque habet et naturale bonum, vim quoque amicitiae," (*PL* 40, 373; because each and every man is part of the human race and because human nature is a social entity and possesses a good that is both great and natural, the capacity for friendship . . .).

50. Browning, "The 'Low Level' Saint's Life" (1980), p. 127.

larger social context,[51] even though his peers, whether parents or
monastic brethren, desire his presence and often seek either to keep
him with them or to join him in the solitude.[52] Of such figures,
Robert Browning has written: "The holy man does not depend on
his family to define his position in society. He is alone in his confrontation with metaphysical sources."[53] In the *Pratum Spirituale*,
John Moschus reports the saying of the Abbot Olympius: "Wherever you sit, say constantly, 'I am a stranger.'"[54]

By and large, the journey into the desert is a solitary one.[55] The
saint departs in secret, usually at night when the rest of the world is
asleep[56] (freedom from the normal need for sleep is yet another
characteristic that sets him apart from ordinary men). A nocturnal
departure not only prevents men from keeping the saint from
leaving; it also insures that no one tries to accompany the voyager.
But in addition to fulfilling such practical needs, the secret journey
assumes a symbolic significance in these tales. It points to the private nature of the journey. In traveling alone to the interior of the
desert, the empty uninhabited regions of the mountains, the saint is
exploring an inner and an outer landscape. In both environments
there are battles to be fought and obstacles to be overcome. The
journey is at once real and symbolic.[57]

51. Brown, "The Rise and Function of the Holy Man" (1971), p. 91, writes of
the social significance of asceticism that it is "a long drawn out, solemn ritual of
dissociation—of becoming the total stranger."
52. In the *Peregrinatio Paphnutii* Timotheus refers to the monks (and nuns) who
joined him in his first desert retreat.
53. "The 'Low Level' Saint's Life," p. 121.
54. *PG* 87, iii, 2861B. For a discussion of the social role played by hermits precisely because they were strangers, see Brown, "Rise and Function," p. 91.
55. Exceptions to solitary travel are the three monks who found Macarius the
Roman, and Epictetus and Astion. The latter, however, were also martyrs, and their
legend may share some of the communal ethos of passion literature (it is, moreover,
pure fiction.)
    In the world of the fifth and sixth centuries depicted in the *vitae*, solitary travel
was dangerous. Jerome's *Life* of Malchus the Captive Monk, captured by a bedouin
tribe while traveling, gives a vivid picture of the risks of travel in the ancient world.
56. The night-time departure is a motif of descent (see below).
57. Concerning the symbolic nature of these accounts, Festugière has written:
"Ce qui est essentiellement une lutte contre le *moi* y devient une lutte contre les

THE FLIGHT FROM MARRIAGE (A¹):
LÉVI-STRAUSS IN THE DESERT

The motif of the secret departure serves as a sharply focused and dramatic emblem of the anchorite's total rejection of and alienation from his society—from his biological family and even from his surrogate family, the monastic community. The most common reason for secret flight is impending marriage. Two of the *vitae*—those of Macarius the Roman and Abraham of Qiduna—depict the saint not merely fleeing from the threat of marriage but running away from the very midst of the wedding festivities. The choice of this particular moment appears to be an implausible (or at least an impractical) one; if a saint is going to wait until after the ceremony to rebel against his parent's will, it would seem that a midnight escape like that of St. Alexis would provide a better chance of success than one from a crowded room in broad daylight. But the flight from the wedding feast can be viewed as symbolic of the saint's entire rejection, summing up and encapsulating the full oppositional range between saint and society. The saint is fleeing not just marriage but the world.

If we examine these accounts sentence by sentence, phrase by phrase, noting not only what the saint rejected but also what he embraced, we find a consistent pattern. In terms of structural codes, every detail in these narratives of flight represents a cultural artifact or cluster of artifacts that the saint rejects but that has its corresponding opposite manifestation in the natural world of eremitic life. In many cases the anchorite's "nature" is an artificial construct (the pursuit of virginity is not genuinely "natural"), but it is nonetheless diametrically opposed to the highly structured and codified social world he was fleeing.

The account of Macarius' flight is as follows:

Cum autem pueriles excessissem annos, me renuente ac nolente, pater meus desponsavit mihi uxorem, diemque statuit nuptiarum. Interea thalamo

---

démons" (*Les Moines d'Orient* [1961], pp. 34–35; What is essentially a struggle against the self becomes a struggle against demons).

adornato, cum jam frequentia populi fuisset invitata, et sponsa sedente, pater meus hilarior effectus, cunctos invitatos hortatur ad voluptatem convivii. Omnibus autem, qui aderant, jocis ac saltationibus intentis, furtim
exivi.[58]

(When, however, I had outgrown boyhood years, my father betrothed me
to a wife, much against my will, and he fixed the wedding day. Then, when
the bridal chamber was decorated, and the throng of wedding guests was
thick, and the bride seated, my father became more jovial and urged all the
guests to the enjoyment of the banquet. While all who were present were
intent upon the games and dancing, I stealthily departed.)

There are two versions of Abraham's departure, that attributed
to St. Ephrem of Syria found in the *Vitae Patrum* (*PL* 73, 281–92),
and a fuller, tenth-century account given by Simeon Metaphrastes
(*PG* 115, 43–78).[59] First, St. Ephrem:

Cumque memorati parentes ejus tempus nuptiarum propinquabile
judicarent, compellebant eum matrimonii vinculis obligari. Sed cum haec
ille primo renueret, postmodum molestiam eorum jugem sedulamque non
ferens pudoris verecundia superatus, acquiescere perurgetur. Cum itaque,
celebratis nuptiis, sponsa die septimo in thalamo resideret, repente quasi
lux quaedam in corde ejus divina gratia refulsit, quam veluti ducem quem-
dam sui voti inveniens, illico exsiluit (283AB).

(And when his aforementioned parents judged that the time of his wedding was near, they tried to compel him to be bound by the chains of matrimony. But although he at first resisted, being later unable to endure their
continuous and persistent vexation, conquered by the modesty of shame,
he hastened to agree. And so when the wedding had been celebrated and
the bride on the seventh day was sitting in the wedding chamber, suddenly
like a flash of light divine grace shone in his heart. Finding it as the guide
for his prayer, he at once ran forth.)

Symeon Metaphrastes' expansion of the account of Abraham's
flight from his marriage is particularly revealing (45D–48A). It is
the seventh day of the wedding:

---

58. *PL* 73, 422B.
59. *BHG* 5–8, *BHO* 16–17, *BHL* 12–13, 12a–e. Legend places Abraham in the
sixth century, and it is generally admitted that both the Greek and Syriac *Acta* are
apocryphal; see Wilmart, "Les rédactions latines de la vie d'Abraham ermite"
(1938), p. 223, n. 3.

Ἐκάθητο μὲν γὰρ μετὰ τῆς νύμφης μάλα λαμπρὸς ὁ Ἀβράμιος, ὡς
νυμφίος ἀληθῶς ἐπὶ τοῦ παστοῦ αὐτοῦ. θορύβου δὲ καὶ κρότου τὸν οἶκον,
ὡς εἰκὸς, κατεχόντων, καὶ περὶ τὴν τράπεζαν πάντων καὶ τοὺς
δαιτυμόνας ἀσχολουμένων, ὁ κρυπτὸς τῆς σωτηρίας ἡμῶν ἐραστὴς ὁ
νοητὸς τῶν ψυχῶν νυμφαγωγός τε καὶ νυμφίος Χριστὸς ὅσαι δηλονότι
καὶ τῶν ἐκείνου νυμφώνων ἄξιαι, ἀκτῖνά τινα γλυκεῖαν τῆς ἀνωτάτω
περὶ αὐτὸν ἐκείνης καὶ ἀπορρήτου λαμπρότητος ἠρέμα πως ἐπαφεὶς τῆι
παστάδι φῶς οἷον ἐπαγαγόντι καὶ ἥδιστον τὰς Ἀβραμίου περιηύγαζεν
ὄψεις, μετακαλῶν οἱονεὶ πρὸς ἑαυτὸν καὶ διὰ τοῦ φωτὸς αὐτὸν
ἐφελκόμενος. ἤρα γὰρ τοῦ κάλλους περιφανῶς τῆς ἐκείνου ψυχῆς καὶ
κρείττοσιν εἰσοικίσασθαι τοῦτον παρὰ πολὺ καὶ παστάσι καὶ θαλάμοις
ἐβούλετο.
    . . . οὐκέτι οὔτε σῖτα οὔτε ποτὸν αἱρεῖσθαι ἤθελεν. . . . (ἑστιάσεως)
λυθείσης καὶ οἴκαδε τῶν δαιτυμόνων ἑκάστου ἀφικομένων, ὑπέξεισι
ἡσύχωι ποδὶ τοῦ οἴκου, μηδέ τωι ἄλλωι ὅτι μὴ μόνωι τῶι καλοῦντι Θεῶι
βλεπόμενος.

(In the bridal chamber itself Abraham, most resplendent, sat with the bride
as being in truth the bridegroom. But while the shouting and festive noise
filled the house, as is to be expected, and while everyone was busy with the
table and with the banqueters, Christ, who is the hidden lover of our salvation, perceptible to the mind, and of our souls the spiritual bridegroom and
escort of the bride—that is, of all those souls worthy of His bridal chambers—silently sent down to the chamber a sweet ray of that highest and
ineffable brightness that surrounds Him, as to one who attracted it, and
most sweetly illuminated the eyes of Abraham, as if summoning him to
Himself and drawing him by means of the light. For Christ most clearly
loved the beauty of Abraham's soul, and He wished to make him dwell in
rooms and chambers far better than those [on earth]. . . .
    Then no longer did [Abraham] wish to take either food or drink. When
the feasting was over and the guests departed each to his own home, he
crept out of the house on quiet foot, nor was he seen by any one save by
God alone Who called him.)

Macarius' so-called "biography" has been judged a complete
fiction. The account of his flight, consequently, may most clearly
reveal the structural archetype, and will serve as the basic text (indicated by the abbreviation *VM*), supplemented, where necessary, by
the Greek and Latin versions of the *vita* of Abraham (*VAb*).

CUM AUTEM PUERILES EXCESSISSEM ANNOS, ME RENUENTE AC
NOLENTE, PATER MEUS DESPONSAVIT MIHI UXOREM, DIEMQUE

STATUIT NUPTIARUM (*VM*) (When, however I had outgrown boyhood years, my father betrothed me to a wife, much against my
will, and he fixed the wedding day.)

Code	Opposition
Age	child/adult
Social	child/parent
	self/other
Sexual	chastity/marriage

The crisis comes with adulthood and sexual maturity. A wedding
represents not just the union of man and woman; it is in many ways
the best symbol of man's civilized state, for man alone, in opposition to the beasts, undergoes (or is supposed to undergo) the ritual
sanction of the marriage ceremony before coupling sexually to produce legitimate offspring.[60] It is the ultimate *rite de passage* between
childhood and adulthood; the married individual is considered to
be fully assimilated into the society and, it is assumed, is thereby
pledged to perpetuate its values as well as the race. But not the desert saint. The saint's life in the desert involves a total rejection of the
values of culture in favor of a life lived in accord with the dictates of
nature. The saint's rejection of sexuality might seem to violate the
scheme, but for the orthodox Christian, sex was not part of the
natural innocence that he sought: "Eve was a virgin in Paradise,"
wrote St. Jerome.[61]

CUMQUE MEMORATI PARENTES EJUS TEMPUS NUPTIARUM PRO-
PINQUABILE JUDICARENT, COMPELLEBANT EUM MATRIMONII
VINCULIS OBLIGARI (*VAb*) (And when his aforementioned parents
judged that the time of his wedding was near, they tried to compel
him to be bound by the chains of matrimony.)

Code	Opposition
Social	child/parent
Ethical	free will/compulsion

60. See Elena Cassin, "Le Semblable et le différant" (1975), pp. 117–20, on En-
kidu and Gilgamesh.
61. *Ep.* 22, *PL* 22, 406. For further discussion of virginity, see ch. 6.

For Abraham, marriage is an unwelcome chain. Similarly St. Ambrose wrote,[62] "Primo ipsum conjugium vinculum est" (First of all, marriage itself is a chain), and claimed that one who is married "nec liberum sui habere arbitrium" (does not have his will free). With marriage, the individual is no longer free but socialized. His destiny is irrevocably linked with that of another. This bonding to worldly concerns, indeed, formed the nucleus of one of the clerical objections to marriage, for the married person might find himself or herself putting concern for spouse above concern for God:[63] "Qui sine uxore est, cogitat ea quae sunt Domini, quomodo placeat Domino; qui autem matrimonio junctus est, cogitat ea quae sunt mundi, quomodo placeat uxori" (I Cor. 8:32; He who is without a wife thinks about those things which are of the Lord, how he may please the Lord; he, however, who is joined in matrimony thinks about those things which are of the world, how he may please his wife). For both Macarius and Abraham, the marriage conflict dramatically highlighted the opposition between father and son (*VM*: "me renuente ac nolente, pater . . . ," [my father, much against my will]; *VAb*: "parentes . . . compellebant eum," [his parents compelled him]), an opposition that is echoed again and again in the saints' lives.[64] From the parents' point of view, the child is obligated to do what they have done—carry on the family line and produce grandchildren who will ensure the continuity of property rights.[65]

62. *Exhortatio Virginitatis, PL* 16, 342C.

63. See Gregory of Nyssa, *On Virginity*, esp. XI.2; also Guillaumont, "Monachisme et éthique judéo-chrétienne" (1972). Evagrius, writing for desert solitaries, maintained that the goal was to be *amērimnon* "without care"; "Bases of Monastic Life," *PG* 40, 1253B.

64. Browning, "The 'Low Level' Saint's Life," p. 21, remarks: "It is striking that no [male] saint has much to do with his father," and he speculates whether this is a reflection of Oedipal jealousy or of the tension between generations, which marked a society better equipped for the transmission rather than the creation of wealth.

65. On family estates, see the above reference to Browning's essay. In the eleventh-century version of the Old French *Vie de saint Alexis* (ms. *L*, ed. Storey), the father laments:

> O filz, cui erent mes granz ereditez
> Mes larges terres dunt jo aveie asez,
> Mes granz paleis de Rome la citét?

(401–3)

(O son, where will my great inheritances go, my broad lands that I possess in abundance, my great palaces of the city of Rome?)

The saint, on the other hand, is diametrically opposed to all such material and social interests. His mind is fixed on the kingdom to come. Of this concern his dedication to chastity, with the total rejection of the intrinsic values of society which it implies, is the fitting manifestation.

INTEREA THALAMO ADORNATO (*VM*) (Then, when the bridal chamber was decorated)

Code	Opposition
Habitation	cave/house
	simplicity/splendor

The marriage chamber is adorned; the hermit's habitation is notable for its total lack of decoration and of any provision for the creature comforts.[66] Most often, indeed, it is not even made by human hands, let alone ornamented. Macarius lives in a cave, and only its cleanliness distinguishes it from the lair of beasts.[67] Abraham spends the first twelve years following his flight from marriage barricaded in an abandoned cell outside of town. Spatially, Macarius' abode is opposed to normal human practice, since a cave is cut into the earth, not built on top of it. It is a natural structure, not a human fabrication. The implication, then, is that its inhabitant belongs to the natural, not to the civilized, world. Appropriately enough, Macarius shares his lair with two lions who are tame to him, but until he has a word with them, fierce to those from the world outside.

66. On avoiding *ornatus* (comfort, decoration, elegance, embellishment) Jerome wrote: "qui virtutibus pollet, ornatus est. . . . Sunt enim quidam ignorantes mensuram suam, et tantae stoliditatis ac vecordiae, ut et in motu et in incessu, et in habitu, et in sermone communi, risum spectantibus praebeant: et quasi intelligentes quid sit ornatus, comunt se vestibus et munditiis corporis, et lautioris mensae epulas parant: cum omnis istiusmodi ornatus et cultus sordibus foedior sit" (*Ep.* 69, *PL* 22, 662; He who is strong in virtues is already decked out. . . . There are certain ones, ignorant of their due measure, and of such folly and madness, that in their movement and walk and dress and everyday conversation they are a laughing stock to those who behold them; and, as if they know what ornament [*ornatus*] is, they dress themselves elaborately with clothing and bodily elegance, and they set out banquets of rich table: when in truth ornament and cultivation of that sort are fouler than filth).

67. The three monks remark: "Munditia haec non est, nisi de manu hominis" (*PL* 73, 420D; This cleanliness is surely from the hand of man.)

Ἐκάθητο μὲν γὰρ μετὰ τῆς νύμφης μάλα λαμπρὸς ὁ ᾿Αβράμιος
(Abraham, most resplendent, sat with the bride.)

Code	Opposition
Dress	neglect/care
	nudity/clothing

With reference to adornment the Greek life by Symeon Meta-phrastes adds an important detail, since it refers to the personal appearance of the saint. Abraham sits next to his bride (see ET SPONSA SEDENTE, below), splendidly attired or gleaming ("mala lampros"). The desert hermit rejects utterly all splendor of garb and of person. In the civilized world, dress is an important signifier of social status, and differences are many; in the desert there is little variety. The hermit does not even wear clothing fabricated in customary ways, but prefers garments made of date-palm fronds, shaggy animal skins, or none at all.

The hermit's rejection of the customary dress-code represents a greater rebellion against society than we, accustomed to considerable latitude in these matters by such movements as the hippies, are likely to realize. Even in our permissive society, however, hippy dress often provoked violent anger in more conservative segments of society. Furthermore, from about 300 A.D. on, a change in garb had occurred in the Greco-Roman world. The Late Antique society tolerated far less nudity than did the classical society.[68] As yet a further sign of the antisocial nature of the hermit's behavior with regard to clothing, we may note that Ephrem's biography of Abraham maintains that in the fifty years of his ascetic life he never once changed his hair shirt (292C).

When the three monks first caught sight of Macarius, they noted his unkempt appearance: "his eyes were not visible because his eyebrows covered them, the nails of his hands and feet were very long, and his beard and hair surrounded his entire body, . . . the skin of his face was like a turtle's" (421B). The figure of the hairy hermit was a common one.[69] In his book, *Symbols*, Raymond Firth

68. Marrou, *Décadence* (1977), pp. 15–20.
69. See below, and Williams, *The Oriental Affinities of the Legend of the Hairy Anchorite* (1925, 1927).

notes that in general wearing long hair is equivalent to being out-side society.[70] The use of clothing to cover the body instead of the natural hair distinguishes man from beast. The saint has here allied himself with the beasts, and with man before the Fall who did not need artificial coverings for his body. But since he in fact lives after Adam's sin, the hermit may not go wholly uncovered (or not in the presence of others); Mary the Egyptian borrowed Zosimas' cloak before she would talk to him; Athanasius reported of Antony that the sight of his own naked body embarrassed that saint.[71] But in general, the hermit's clothing comes from nature, not from the city.

CUM JAM FREQUENTIA POPULI FUISSET INVITATA (*VM*) (When the throng of wedding guests was thick)

Code	Opposition
Social	one/many

The chamber is thronged with people; the hermit lives alone (cf. the etymology of "monk" from *monachos*, solitary). Abraham lived for twelve years enclosed in a cell. Macarius took a further step away from the social world of men, for he lived beyond the boundary of the known world in harmony with beasts—with only two lions for company.

ET SPONSA SEDENTE (*VM*) (And the bride seated)
Ἐκάθητο . . . Ἀβράμιος, ὡς ἀληθῶς ἐπὶ τοῦ παστοῦ (In the bridal chamber itself Abraham sat, as being in truth the bridegroom)

Code	Opposition
Sexual	male/female
	chastity/sexuality

The Greek text here stresses the potential sexuality of the situa-tion. The principle of temptation is female.[72] The hermit entirely

70. *Symbols*, p. 262. Hair is also intimately connected with sex; see Leach, "Magic Hair," p. 82.

71. Athanasius, *Vita Antonii*, ch. 47. St. Jerome's Latin version de-emphasizes this feeling. In the *Life of Plotinus*, I, Porphyry related that the sage was ashamed that he had a body. This malaise, however, concerns the very fact of corporeality, of inhabiting a human body, whereas Antony's malaise is sexual embarrassment at his body.

72. See Campbell, *The Hero* (1949), pp. 120–26.

avoids the company of women (Simeon Stylites the Elder did not permit himself the sight even of his mother).[73] The one time Macarius forgot to fortify himself against the machinations of the devil and sat next to a woman, he was seduced in his sleep by the diabolic image of his deserted bride, for which involuntary sin he did penance by being buried in the ground up to his neck for three years.

PATER MEUS HILARIOR EFFECTUS (*VM*) (My father became more jovial.)

Code	Opposition
emotional	sorrow/joy

The monk's characteristic activities are the opposite of hilarity, as he spends his days in prayer and weeping.[74] Macarius greeted the three monks with tears ("Tunc ipse cum lacrymis ad nos exorsus est," 421B). The sexual encounter with the demonic bride also left him in tears (424D), and his lions were moved to grief by his sin and fled: "fugisse scilicet leones, cum luctu nimio ac dolore" (424D; to be sure his lions fled with great sorrow and grief).

CUNCTOS INVITATOS HORTATUR AD VOLUPTATEM CONVIVII (*VM*) (He urged all the guests to the enjoyment of the banquet.)

Code	Opposition
Social	*apatheia/voluptas*
	one/many
Dietary	raw/cooked

The anchorite flees all bodily *voluptas* as corrupting. He also lives alone (or in the company of beasts, not men). The pleasures of the banquet are presumably elaborately prepared foods and wine, as well as entertainment such as singers and dancers (see the next

<hr/>

73. *PL* 73, 329B (Antony's version).

74. In Evagrius' Latin translation of the *Vita Antonii*, the saint's passivity is depicted: "Nunquam hilaritate nimia resolutus in risum est, nunquam recordatione peccati tristitia ora contraxit" (*PL* 73, 134B; Never did he relax into laughter with too great cheerfulness; never did he gloomily draw tight his countenance in the recollection of sin). Symeon Metaphrastes gives an elaborate description of the tears of St. Ephrem (*PG* 114,1253).

item). The customary diet of the hermit consisted of bread, water, and raw vegetables (see ch. 6), and St. Jerome drew an explicit connection between the consumption of meat, cooked food, and wine, and sexual appetite.[75] When the three monks met Macarius, the only entertainment they might be said to have shared consisted of a vespers service followed by a simple meal of acorns, herbs, roots, and water, eaten in silence (422A).

OMNIBUS AUTEM, QUI ADERANT, JOCIS AC SALTATIONIBUS IN-
TENTIS, FURTIM EXIVI (*VM*) (While all who were present were intent on games and dancing, I stealthily departed.)

Code	Opposition
Social	one/many
	self/other
Moral	virtue/vice

Macarius fled while everyone else was absorbed by the feats of the acrobats and dancers. No better symbols for the seductive charms of culture could be found than professional entertainers. These figures were secular by definition, opposed in the eyes of the Church to religious occupations—the very figure of vanity. Dancing was particularly suspect.[76]

The flight, then, encompasses a greater symbolic range than its literal interpretation might imply. More than preservation of chastity is involved. The marriage festivity contains in microcosm all that the saint is fleeing—not only sexuality, but civilization. Moreover, Roman civilization of the period has been described as a

---

75. *Epistle* 79, *PL* 22, 729.

76. To give only two examples from St. Ambrose: "Deliciarum comes et luxuriae ludibrium est lasciva saltatio" (*Ep.* 58, *PL* 16, 1179B; Lascivious dancing is the companion of soft delights and the plaything of luxury); "Debet igitur bene consciae mentis esse laetitia, non inconditis comessationibus, non nuptialibus excitata symphoniis; ibi enim intuta verecundia, illecebra suspecta est, ubi comes deliciarum est extrema saltatio. Ab hac virgines Dei procul esse desidero" (*De Virginibus*, Lib. III, Ch. V, *PL* 16, 227B; Joyfulness should be the property of a mind in good conscience, not excited by disorderly revels or by the music played at wedding feasts; for there, when unbridled dancing is the companion of delights, modesty is unprotected, and there is the suspicion of licentiousness. From this I wish the virgins of God to be far removed).

"splendid theatre."[77] Such is the pageantry-oriented world the saint flees on his wedding night. The full opposition between nature and culture is symbolically depicted in this dramatic scene, a fact that suggests one reason why the theme of the saint's flight from the wedding ceremony remained such a popular one in hagiographic legend.

77. MacCormack, *Art and Ceremony* (1981), p. 9, quoting "splendid theatre" from Edward Gibbon, *History of the Decline and Fall of the Roman Empire*, ed. J. B. Bury, chap. 17, vol. 2, p. 170.

Chapter 5

The Downward Journey

In his study of the structure of romance, *The Secular Scripture*, Northrop Frye notes two types of spatial movement, which he discusses under the rubrics "The Bottomless Dream: Themes of Descent," and "Quis Hic Locus? Themes of Ascent."[1] Each of these directional movements is subdivided: there are two descents, the first from heaven to earth, the second from earth to the underworld; under "Themes of Ascent" come the narrative motifs that reverse these movements.

For every Christian romance, the first descent, Adam's Fall, is the given condition against which the rest of the action is played out, and whether it is specifically mentioned or not, its presence is always felt, shaping and defining the action. All hagiographic accounts, whether *passiones* or *vitae*, are ultimately tales of ascent, but, paradoxically, in the lives of the desert fathers the actual narrative is primarily concerned with Frye's downward journey. The stories tell of motion, change, the quest into the unknown. The downward direction of this journey is often a metaphoric paradox, since the movement may be geographically "up," up a mountain, up into the higher desert. Not all tombs are built below ground. But, as we shall see, the symbolism surrounding this journey is one of darkness and descent. Then, after the hero goes out into the unknown, an encounter occurs, generally accompanied by a miracle, and the hero returns or reascends. In the saintly quest, the hero

1. *Secular Scripture* (1976), pp. 97 ff. and 129 ff.

penetrates a perilous landscape (the *interior mons;* the inner space of the urban brothel), and commonly experiences a form of symbolic death and burial before his final ascent. Usually in these tales, the saint ascends to heaven while others return to civilization, bearing his story, and occasionally his relics.[2] The motion is paradoxical because every step on the downward journey brings the saint closer to Paradise.

SYMBOLIC DEATH (B³) AND BURIAL (G)

The narrative of the journey into the perilous desert may of itself function as a theme of descent into death. The saints discussed here all survived their encounter with the desert, but others were not so fortunate. Eusebius quotes a letter of Dionysius, Bishop of Alexandria, to Fabian, Bishop of Antioch, describing the hardships endured by those who fled, as Paul of Thebes is supposed to have done, into the wilderness to escape the harsh persecution of Decius in 249:

What need is there to speak of the multitude of those who wandered in deserts and mountains,[3] and perished by hunger and thirst and frost and diseases and robbers and wild beasts? Those who survived this are witnesses (*martures*) to their election and victory.[4]

In many cases, even for the survivors, the first stop on the journey was the grave. After disposing of his worldly goods, Antony spent twenty years shut up in a tomb (*VA*, ch. 14). Abraham, like Macarius, fled from marriage to burial, but in his case the juxtaposition of the two events was immediate.[5] Two miles from town he found an

---

2. Altman, "Two Types of Opposition," p. 6.
3. Eusebius' language here is formulaic; he echoes Heb. 11:38.
4. *Hist. Eccles.* 6. 42.2; trans. Oulton, slightly altered.
5. The theme of false burial may serve to initiate the journey in Greek romance. For example, in Chariton's *Romance of Chaereas and Callirhoë*, the heroine, Callirhoë, kicked in the stomach by her jealous husband, falls in a faint. She is thought to be dead (*nekras eikōn*, I.5, [the image of a corpse]) and she is buried. She regains consciousness in the tomb, from which she is "rescued" by grave robbers, who determine to sell her at a profit. When her husband learns the truth, he sets off in pursuit. Cf. also the false death ("Scheintod") of the heroine in Achilles Tatius, *Clitophon and Leucippe* 3.15 and 5.7.

abandoned cell into which he barricaded himself: "he blocked the door to the cell, and shutting himself within, he left a very tiny hole of a window through which on the appointed day he received food."[6] Here he dwelled isolated from the distractions of the world for twelve years (284A). Macarius spent three years buried up to his neck in penance for the sin he committed in his sleep. Abraham's form of "burial" is more typical of monastic practice than is Macarius', although a parallel to the latter does exist. Before St. Simeon Stylites the Elder chose to isolate himself from the world by ascending his column, he descended below ground. After he was asked to leave his monastery because of his seemingly antisocial practices (his putrefied flesh stank so badly that no one could endure to stand next to him), he took refuge in an abandoned well.[7] Later he lived for three years in a small, tomb-like enclosure at Telannisos.[8] According to the Syriac life, completed in 479, only fifteen years after the saint's death, Simeon also spent two years buried up to the chest in the monastery garden.[9]

In the version of the life of Paul of Thebes contained in an Arabic synaxary written long after the Roman persecution of Christians ended, the story has a new beginning. Now the young hero no longer flees from the threat of persecution; he is the younger of two brothers, and at their father's death the elder brother tries to take all of their inheritance for himself. Paul not unnaturally objects, and they go to seek an impartial judge. On their way, however, they observe the funeral of a rich man; and, learning that the dead man will not obtain the kingdom of heaven, Paul is convinced of the futility of earthly riches and tells his brother to go home. When they reach home, Paul suddenly vanishes from sight.

But Paul, going out a little way from the western part of the city, found a tomb in which he spent three days, pouring forth prayers and tears to God;

6. *PL* 73, 283D. Symeon Metaphrastes' more detailed account specifies that Abraham's diet was restricted to bread and water (*PG* 115, 49A).

7. Antony, *PL* 73, 327A; Theodoret, *PG* 82, iii, 1468. According to Theodoret he stayed there for five days, according to Antony for seven, while the Syriac life says that he was there for all of Lent.

8. Today Deir Sem'an; see Festugière, *Antioche païenne* (1959), p. 313.

9. Ibid., p. 358.

then on his fourth day in the tomb, God sent His angel to him, who transferred Paul to the East and put him down near a spring of water. When the
angel ascended into Heaven, Saint Anbā Paul found a cave of wild beasts
into which he entered.[10]

In this account two traditional motifs of descent occur—death and
burial (twice over, in the account of the rich man's funeral and
Paul's tomb), and the angelic guide (b²).

Examples of monks dwelling in small, dark, airless spaces
(whether actual tombs or not)[11] are not confined to legendary figures like Macarius and Paul of Thebes. According to Athanasius,
Antony's first place of withdrawal was a tomb (*Vita Antonii*, 8–9).
In the *Historia Religiosa* Theodoret tells of Zeno (ch. 12) who gave
up life in a palace for a tomb where he lived without a bed, lamp,
fire, or any other comfort. Marcianus (ch. 3) built himself a hut so
small that he could neither stand up straight nor stretch out while
lying down.[12] Palladius relates the story of a young girl who shut
herself up in a tomb for ten years to avoid tempting her suitors
(*Historia Lausiaca,* ch. 5). Many of these early tomb-dwellers,
moreover, were Egyptians. According to Guillaumont, "the desert
was not only the sterile land, but the region of tombs, the domain of
death."[13] To go into its wilds was to enter the kingdom of the
dead.[14]

Frye points to confinement in a restricted space as a form of

10. *CSCO*, "Synaxarium Alexandrinum," vol. 78, p. 460. Since I do not read
Arabic, I cite from the modern CSCO Latin translated version which accompanies
the text.
11. See Festugière, *Antioche païenne*, pp. 296–98. He speaks of the inhabitants
of these cramped quarters as being "dead to the world" (p. 298). In "The 'Low
Level' Saint's Life," Browning cites the example, from a slightly later period, of Aly-
pios, and in the tenth century, the Bulgarian St. John of Rila who lived in a hollow
tree that resembled a coffin.
12. Paralleled, perhaps, by the practice of wearing chains so that it was impossible to stand upright—a purely Syrian phenomenon of which the Egyptian monks
disapproved; see Festugière, *Antioche païenne*, p. 293.
13. Guillaumont, "La conception du désert" (1975) p. 11. Athanasius, in his
biography of Antony, perfectly illustrated this Egyptian attitude towards the desert.
14. The Coptic word *toou* means both "mountain" and "desert," and may often
mean "cemetery" as well, since in accordance with ancient tradition, the dead were
buried in the desert; see the Bohairic life of Pachomius, in Veilleux, *Pachomian
Koinonia*, I, 269, n. 3.

descent.[15] That it is a surrogate form of death can be seen most clearly in the life of St. Theodore of Sykeon (first half of the seventh century).[16] The teen-aged saint first excavated a dark hole (*spēlaion skoteinon*) under the altar of a church where he lived from Epiphany to Palm Sunday, nourished only by fruit and vegetables (ch. 16). Later, desiring to imitate John the Baptist, he went into the mountains and dug a small cave where he lived for two years, his whereabouts known only to one companion who brought him food. When he was eventually found, he looked like a corpse; he was barely conscious, his body was full of worms, and the bones showed through his skin; his stench was that of death. Theodore's contemporaries, far from finding such behavior pathological, considered him a second Job; he was immediately ordained as a subdeacon and shortly thereafter as a priest, and his sanctity was considered past doubt. At this time Theodore was eighteen (chs. 20–21).

The ascetic's symbolic burial prefigured rebirth, for the dark, confining cell was also a womb, as is apparent from the account of Marcianus (*Historia Religiosa*, ch. 3) who could neither lie down nor stand up in his cramped cell but had to remain curled in a fetal position. The womb-cell is a total environment. Food entered through a small hole, and was usually administered by only one person. Although the accounts usually fail to mention the subject for reasons of decorum, no provision seems to have been made for the removal of waste. In Hroswitha's play, *Paphnutius*, the repentant prostitute, Thaïs, finds herself disconcerted by this fact, but when asked whether she finds the prospect of hellfire less appalling, withdraws her objection.[17] She emerges from her cell, purified and radiant, ready for immediate entry into heaven. Athanasius, too,

15. *Secular Scripture*, p. 114; as an example, Frye cites Daniel in the lions' den, for which he notes that the experience of Anthia shut up with two mastiffs provides a parallel; *Ephesiasca*, IV, vi.

16. For a partial translation in English of the life of this saint, see Dawes and Baynes, trans., *Three Byzantine Saints* (1948). Festugière published the Greek life with a French translation, *Subsidia Hagiographica* 48 (1970). For discussion, see Browning, " 'Low Level' Saint's Life."

17. The detail also occurs in a Greek life dating to the eleventh century; see Kuehne, *A Study of the Thaïs Legend* (1922), p. 25.

noted that Antony ended his long confinement in the tomb in better physical shape than when he entered (*Vita Antonii*, ch. 14).

Being buried alive or lying on the ground "velut mortuus" (as if dead), both obvious forms of symbolic death, are transparently motifs of descent. Frequently, however, the theme of burial occurs in a displaced form, as the quester arrives just in time to bury someone else.[18] Antony buries Paul of Thebes before returning to the world. Zosimas buries Mary the Egyptian. Onuphrius buries the unnamed hermit he met in the desert, and Paphnutius buries Onuphrius as well as the dead anchorite he found in a cave. The most interesting displacement, however, transpires in the story of Macarius the Roman who, upon reaching the cave that will be his home, finds a dead lioness there whom he buries, an event that the saint interpreted as miraculous:

. . . prospexi duos leonis catulos jacentes, mater autem illorum juxta illos mortua jacebat. Quam ego foras ejiciens, sepelivi, et Dominum collaudans, glorificavi, qui tanta in me mirabilia fecit, et de tam gravibus angustiis liberavit, ipsos autem leunculos, frondes arborum decerpens ac illis porrigens, ut proprios enutrivi filios (*PL* 73, 423D).

(I saw two lion cubs lying there, and their mother dead beside them. I threw her outside and buried her, and praising God, I glorified Him who had performed such great miracles on my account and had liberated me from such dangerous straits. Plucking leaves from the trees, I offered them to the cubs and nurtured them like my own sons.)

While it would, no doubt, feel "miraculous" to come upon a splendid cave and discover conveniently dead the former inhabitant, a nursing lioness who would normally have been savage in defense of her home and family, and while reasons of sanitation might suggest burial as the only sensible method for disposing of the corpse, hagiographic accounts are not generally notable for their concern for verisimilitude or hygiene. As in Onuphrius' burial of the hermit, the story suggests that the saint is ready in some way either to re-

18. See, for example, the story in the *Apothegmata* (*PL* 73, 1008, ch. 9), of the two hermits who find a female hermit on her deathbed. This story, however, remains an anecdote, and is not developed into part of a larger pattern, as are the tales analyzed here.

FIGURE 3. St. Antony, helped by two lions, buries St. Paul of Thebes.

place the buried person (or animal) or to carry on the important task of relating the saint's story to the world and permitting the latter, therefore, to fulfill the vital task of serving as an exemplar to society.[19] Macarius' own "burial," moreover, is effected by the very two lions whom he raised "ut proprios filios" (as his own sons). The desert saints are not generally known for their nurturing qualities, and the deed has symbolic overtones. Rejecting marriage (and the procreation of his own children), Macarius has left the world of men behind; he is dead to that environment. He has joined the realm of the beasts where his sons are lions.

Numerous myths, folktales, and romances tell of symbolic death

19. For importance of exemplars and the "culture of paideia", see P. Brown, "The Saint as Exemplar" (1983).

and resurrection—a descent to the underworld,[20] a miraculous sleep. In a number of legends of the desert saints, after the hero has successfully escaped the world of culture he must experience a form of death, burial, and rebirth prior to his ultimate attainment of transcendent purity. This emblematic death prefigures his real death and resurrection into Paradise, but even more it serves as a *rite de passage*, a purificatory ritual in which the saint sheds his cultural existence in preparation for his new way of life. It marks or confirms his step across the division between the cooked and the raw.

In no account is the symbolic function of this act more apparent than in the legend of Macarius, as the event mirrors and ultimately negates through burial and rebirth that other *rite de passage* from which he fled, marriage. When the "substitute bride" (the devil) suddenly appears in the desert, Macarius relives his wedding experience but does not flee. Marriage is a ritual marking assimilation and conformity; death separates irrevocably. Macarius' ritual death through his initial journey from marriage to the desert denotes the saint's triumphant alienation from the world, and his worthiness of heaven.

According to the story of his life that Macarius tells the three monks, after he had been living for two years in peace with his lions, the devil succeeded in compassing his fall into sin. Emerging one day from his cave into the hot midday sun, Macarius suddenly noticed a woman's veil lying on the ground beside him: "tunc subito subtile fasciolum et oculis delectabile juxta me in terra positum aspexi" (423D–424A; Then suddenly I saw a delicate veil, delightful to my eyes, lying on the ground before me).[21] Forgetting to for-

20. Cassin, for example, interpreted Daniel's night-time descent into the lions' den as a descent into Sheol ("Daniel dans la 'fosse' aux lions" [1951], p. 161).

21. St. Jerome mentioned the *fasciolum*, (veil), only to exclude it explicitly as an item of monastic garb (*Ep. 2, De Vita Clericorum:* "Crebra munuscula, et sudariola et fasciolas, vestes ori applicitas, et oblatos ac degustatos cibos, blandasque et dulces litterulas sanctus amor non habet [Frequent gifts, and handkerchiefs and veils, garments held up to the face, and preferred and tasted foods, and cozening, sweet little notes—these are not the possessions of holy love]). It is then an artifact highly symbolic of refinement and civilization, all of which the saint has rejected. It belongs to the sexual or erotic code.

tify himself by making the sign of the cross,[22] he brought this delightful artifact of sex and culture into his cave. The next morning he found a pair of woman's shoes in the same place; again neglecting to cross himself, he took these in as well. On the third day, he discovered the devil in the shape of a beautiful woman, richly garbed, standing by the door ("diabolum in decore vel specie mulieris, vestibus pretiosis indutae," 424A).[23] Once more forgetting to make the ritual sign, he asked her who she was. Weeping, she spun him a tale that closely replicated his own history:

Ego miserrima, o pater sanctissime, filia sum viri Romani; quae [sic] cum me invitam ac nolentem desponsasset juveni cuidam nobilissimo Romano, ac dies nuptiarum venirent, et thalamam ac convivium ordinarent, inter nuptias ipsas sponsus meus disparuit. Cumque turbati omnes, huc illucque inquirendo, turbarentur, ego gavisa effecta, clam exii; et nocte eadem iter arripiens. . . . (424B).

(Oh most holy father, I am the most wretched daughter of a Roman citizen; my father betrothed me, very much against my will, to a certain very noble Roman youth. When the day of the wedding had arrived, and the room and the party were set in order, from the midst of the wedding festivities my husband disappeared. While all were in confusion, looking for him hither and yon, I secretly departed, very happy; and that same night setting forth. . . .)

Believing that the woman was indeed his abandoned bride, Macarius also wept, and led her into his cave where he seated her beside him and gave her a supper of acorns. They spent the evening in conversation (she was presumably the first human he had seen in two years).

Then came his fall:

Tunc coepi quasi de labore nimio somno gravari; at illa manibus suis mea omnia membra mulcendo palpavit, et eo amplius somno gravatus sum.

---

22. For the importance of forgetfulness, see above, p. 100. Antony insisted particularly on the power of the sign of the cross to chase away demons (*Vita Antonii*, ch. 13).

23. See figure 4, from the Campo Santo in Pisa. This marvelous fourteenth-century fresco, attributed to the "Master of the Triumph of Death," depicts the diabolic bride at the door of the hermit's cave; "she" is a beautiful woman, dressed in late medieval traveling costume, but out from under "her" skirt extends a chicken-like claw foot.

FIGURE 4. The devil, disguised as a lady pilgrim, tempts a monk at his cave
(St. Macarius). Note the revealing claw foot (see note 23).

Quid morer? miser ego, qui antea nunquam cum femina peccare consensi, in somnis me peccatum perpetrasse cognovi (424C).

(Then I began to grow heavy with sleep as if from excessive labor, and she with her hands stroked carressingly all my limbs, and I grew even heavier with sleep. Why should I delay? Poor me, who never before consented to sin with a woman, I knew that I had committed a sin in my sleep.)

When he awakened, the woman had disappeared. Overcome by remorse, Macarius rushed from his cave in tears, and his lions, when they learned of his crime ("delictum"), fled from him with great grief. Through God's mercy, however, the lions returned, and they all went into the cave where the animals dug a deep hole. Macarius entered it as far as his neck and ordered them to bury him.[24] He spent three years buried like this; a great rain storm opened up a hole in the roof of his cave above his head which admitted enough light and water for grass to grow around him, and, freeing his hands, he was able to feed himself. After three years the lions returned, and seeing the light around his head, dug him up. He emerged, "toto corpore sanus," and felt himself purified ("virtutem pristinam in me sentiens," 425A). He fell to his knees, for forty days and forty nights praying to God in thanksgiving. When he at last reentered his cave, he was welcomed by a vision of Christ.

There are a number of notable features about this wondrous tale of temptation and fall, repentance and purification, one of the most remarkable of which is the way the narrative of the demonic bride doubles Macarius' own history. The verbal parallels between her situation and his are striking.

MACARIUS (422B)	THE "BRIDE" (424B)
Lineage	
filius viri Romani (son of a Roman gentleman)	filia sum viri Romani (I am the daughter of a Roman gentleman)

24. The form of punishment, being buried alive, recalls that of Vestal Virgins who had broken their vow of chastity (they were actually immured; see the long description in Plutarch, *Numa*, 10).

FIGURE 5. The monk drives the disguised female pilgrim from his cave (St. Macarius).

Betrothal

me renuente ac nolente (as I refused and was unwilling)   invitam ac nolentem (reluctant and unwilling)

Flight

furtim exivi (secretly I departed)   clam exii (in secret I departed)

No explanation is offered for the girl's unwillingness to be married, nor for her joy ("gavisa effecta") at her husband's departure. Like Macarius, she left Rome in stealth. Macarius asked no questions: why should he question one whose story was his own? He forgot the ritual protection of the sign of the cross. He took her into his cave, and once again found himself seated next to a beautiful woman, with all that act implies in terms of spatial and social codes. He had stepped through the looking glass.

As an example of a tale of descent below the earth, Frye discusses the myth of Narcissus: "The reflecting pool is a mirror, and disappearing into one's own mirror image, or entering a world of reversed or reduced dimensions, is a central symbol of descent."[25] The woman is in many ways Macarius' mirror image, his feminine reflection or Jungian shadow (the phrase *viri Romani* is identically predicated to *filius*—son—and *filia*—daughter—in their respective narratives). The result of sterile, narcissistic love is death; the boy Narcissus wastes away and leaves behind no trace but the homonymous flower. Macarius falls into a strange stupor and in his sleep breaks his vow of chastity. Sleep too is a motif of descent, and the saint twice uses a word connoting heaviness, being weighed down (*gravari, gravatus*), to describe it. After he awakes, Macarius expiates in corresponding spatial terms his fall from grace in both the inner and outer world. He descends into the grave.

In addition, Macarius' tale manifests both types of Frye's ascent narrative—that from the lower world to this one and from this one to the next. Discussing Dante's ascent to Eden at the end of *Purgatorio*, Frye notes in *Secular Scripture* that Dante is moving towards a self-recognition scene:

That is, he finds and becomes his real self as it would have been if Adam had not fallen and man's original identity had been preserved. . . . Self-recognition, or attaining one's original identity, reverses all the Narcissus and twin and doppelganger themes that occur in the descent (p. 152).

When Macarius is unburied after three years, mysteriously he is not weakened but restored by his confinement: "toto corpore sanus, virtutem pristinam in me sentiens" (whole in my entire body, feeling in myself my virtue of old). Perhaps better than any other Latin word, *pristinus* (of old, ancient) serves to exemplify his spiritual condition, for it denotes not only priority in time (from *prius*) but also superiority in condition. Macarius has been reborn into the

25. *Secular Scripture*, p. 108.

pristine condition he enjoyed before his fall. He has triumphed over the world, the devil, and himself. When he returns to his cave, he enjoys the grace of a celestial visit, as he sees Christ. The second ascent is Christ's, as he returns to heaven (*ascendebat*). It prefigures Macarius' future, triumphal ascent.

UNUSUAL GUIDES (B²)

Given the rigors of the desert, a natural question concerning the desert solitaries might have been: "But how did he find his way across the unmapped wilderness?" In the *Vita Antonii*, Athanasius provides a realistic answer; the saint is guided by a tribe of Saracens (ch. 49). Jerome depicts Malchus' attempt, in vain as it turned out, to seek safety in numbers by joining a large party of travelers.[26] In the more fabulous accounts, however, the saint is usually aided by miraculous guides, either animals or angels.[27] In the *Vita Pauli* Antony has two guides in the desert. He first meets a hippocentaur who holds out his right hand to indicate the desired road and then vanishes; it is not clear, says Jerome, whether this creature was sent by the devil (*PL* 23, 23A). Later, not knowing where to turn, Antony sees a she-wolf, panting with thirst, making her way to a mountain; following her, he finds Paul's cave. Jerome here seems to have utilized the motif of the animal or miraculous guide but to have provided a naturalistic explanation for the phenomenon.

No such rationalizing occurs in the *Vita Macarii*. The three monks are aided in their trek by a dove and a roaring stag, and are guided on the first part of their homeward journey by Macarius' two lions. Macarius himself has not two but four miraculous guides on his trip: first an old man, who turns out in fact to be the Archangel Raphael, shows him the way; then a wild ass;[28] than a

26. *PL* 23, 57C.
27. Campbell (*The Hero*, pp. 69–77) gives many examples of "supernatural aid" enjoyed by heroes.
28. The *onager*, or wild ass, was a type of the monk; see the very popular definition of Eucherius of Lyons, "*Onager, eremita, vel qui remoti a turbis popularibus versantur*" (Wild ass, hermit, or those who spend their time far from the crowds of the people), *Formulae* 4 (CSEL 31, 26); also Cassian, *Collatio*, 18 (*PL* 49, 1101B–1102A).

stag who approaches him "veluti animal domesticum" (like a tame animal); and finally a dragon who, when challenged says he has been sent by Raphael and then changes himself into a young man.[29] Serapion is revived and directed on his journey in search of Mark the Athenian by two figures whom he takes for monks but who are in reality angels.[30]

A biblical romance that follows the classic "bride-winning" plots and that includes a clear example of the theme of descent is the *Book of Tobit*.[31] On a journey in which he defeats the devil to win a bride, Tobias is accompanied by a dog and an angel, the Archangel Raphael disguised as a "juvenem splendidum" (5:5; radiant youth). Macarius' account, indeed, may refer to the story of Tobias. The young man who has guided Tobias safely through his adventures reveals his identity and says: "Ego enim sum Raphael angelus" (12:15; I am the angel Raphael); Macarius' guide identifies himself in the same words (in the Latin translation of the original Greek: "Ego enim sum angelus Raphael"; *PL* 73, 422D).[32] In another

29. A later but seemingly independent parallel for Macarius' helpful dragon may be found in medieval romance: the Old French *Chevalier du Papegau*, and the Middle High German *Wîgâlois*, both of which are presumed to go back to a common but lost Old French romance. In these two tales a beast of miraculous appearance guides the hero to a beautiful tree, then transforms itself into a man clad all in white who explains that he is the soul of a slain king; see A. C. Brown, "The Knight of the Lion" (1905), p. 699.

30. The *Synaxarium Alexandrinum*, CSCO, vol. 78, p. 26, states of St. Agathus the Stylite that he sought the desert, "Et apparuit ei angelus Domini specie monachi, iterque cum eo per desertum fecit, quoad eum ad coenobium sancti patris Macarii magni deduxit" (And there appeared to him an angel of the Lord in the likeness of a monk, and he made a journey with him through the desert until he led him to the cell of the holy father, the great Macarius).

31. See Frye, *Secular Scripture*, p. 115.

32. Onuphrius' unnamed angel closely parallels the words of Macarius' angel, saying: "Noli pavescere, ego enim sum Dei angelus, tibi ad custodiendum ab ortu tuo providentia divina destinatus, ut jubente Deo tecum manerem, et te in hanc eremum ducerem" (*PL* 73, 215A; Be not afraid, for I am an angel of the Lord, assigned by divine providence to guard you from your birth, that I might remain with you as God orders, and that I might lead you into this desert). Cf. Raphael in the *Vita Macarii*: "Noli turbari, dilectissime, ego enim sum angelus Raphael, in adjutorium tibi missus, qui te huc perduxi praecepto Altissimi" (*PL* 73, 422D; Be not disturbed, dearest friend, for I am the angel Raphael, sent to aid you, I who have led you here by the command of the Highest One). "Ego enim sum Raphael angelus, unus ex septem, qui adstamus ante Dominum . . . Pax vobiscum, nolite timere" (Tob. 12:15–17; For I am the angel Raphael, one of the Seven who stand before the Lord . . . Peace be

apocryphal book of the Bible, Raphael serves as Enoch's guide to Sheol,[33] explaining to the traveler the meaning of what he is seeing, and later elucidating the meaning of the tree of wisdom when Enoch reached Paradise (32:6).

The customary role of the angel in Christian legend, as elsewhere, is that of *psychopompos*, leading the souls to heaven.[34] In the *Passion of Perpetua and Felicity* (203 A.D.), the martyr Saturus related a vision of being carried east by four angels into a wondrous garden filled with rose bushes and all kinds of flowers.[35] So too Gregory of Nyssa's account of the death of his sister Macrina describes the dying woman repeating the prayer: "Place beside me an angel of light, to lead me by the hand. . . ."[36] Belief in guardian angels was also widespread. Gregory Thaumaturge fell back on this concept to explain his feelings about discovering Origen and his circle: "For a long time, that angelic presence has nourished me, has formed me, and led me by the hand."[37] Onuphrius was escorted through the desert by an angel. Paphnutius, too, in the quest that ultimately led him to Onuphrius, was revived when he lay on the ground "velut mortuus" (as if dead) by a wondrous figure:

Extemplo quoque coelesti solatus adjutorio, assistere mihi vidi virum, gloria mirabilem, splendore terribilem, pulchritudine laudabilem, magnitudine procerum, aspectu praeclarum (*PL* 73, 211B).

(Suddenly comforted by heavenly assistance, I saw standing near me a man, marvelous in glory, terrible in splendor, praiseworthy in beauty, tall in height, outstanding in aspect.)

Touching Paphnutius' hands and lips, this figure restored him to

---

with you; be not afraid). "Etenim cum essem vobiscum, per voluntatem Dei eram" (For when I was with you, I was with you through the will of God, 12:18).

33. The realm of the dead, Enoch, 22:3. Sheol was located in the far west and was not underground; see Charles, *The Apocrypha and Pseudepigrapha of the Old Testament* (1913; rpt. 1964), Vol. 2.

34. See Rush, *Death and Burial* (1941), pp. 36–43; for pagan precedents, Saintyves, *En Marge de la légende dorée* (1930), pp. 127–28.

35. Musurillo, *Acts*, ch. 11, pp. 118–21.

36. *Vita Macrina* (PG 46, 984D), cited by Brown, *Cult of Saints* (1981), p. 53.

37. "Speech of Thanksgiving and Praise of Origen" (*PG* 10, 1064A), quoted by Brown, *Cult of Saints*, p. 67.

life. Macarius was guided on his journey by the Archangel Raphael, but significantly his demonic bride stated that she made her way halfway across the world without any guide (*PL* 73, 424B). "She" did not enjoy divine guidance.

DISGUISE (B⁴)

Most *vitae* end with the saint's death and burial, but in a number of accounts this event signals more than the end of the hero's earthly career. Particularly in tales of women saints, it serves as a moment of recognition; it is, therefore, doubly an ascent theme, for the saint mounts to heaven and the world gains knowledge. The motif of disguise (b⁴) is especially common in accounts of women, many of whom flee home clothed as men, a strategem for which there were good practical reasons in that it made pursuit more difficult and also protected the heroine from unwelcome sexual advances.[38] In some cases the woman abandons the disguise after she reached safety (e.g. Thecla), but others continue as men until their deaths. Euphrosyne, for instance, lives for thirty-eight years as a monk named Smaragdus; only when she knows death is imminent does she reveal her true identity to her father who for years has been coming to "Brother Smaragdus" for consolation over the loss of his beloved daughter (*PL* 73, 649–52). Marina, who has been disguised as "Brother Marinus," is only discovered to have been a woman when the monks wash her body for burial (*PL* 73, 693–94). Exactly the same story is told of Pelagia.[39] Finally, although Zosimas knows the history of Mary the Egyptian, he does not know her name until he finds her body with the injunction written beside it: "Sepeli, abba Zosima, miserae Mariae corpusculum" (*PL* 73, 688B; bury, Abba Zosimas, the little body of poor Mary), together with the exact date of her death.

38. Delcourt, "La complexe de Diane" (1958), examines the stories of sixteen saints as well as the case of Joan of Arc and a mystic named Antoinette Bourignon (d. 1616). See also Patlagean, "L'histoire de la femme déguisée en moine" (1976).

39. In "The Life of St. Pelagia" (1976), p. 146, Pavlovskis notes that changing names is a form of disguise; "Pelagia" was the saint's original name, but during her sinful existence she was known as "Margarito"; she was, however, baptized as "Pelagia."

In these accounts of death and recognition, words for knowing such as *cognoscere* are common, the very words prominent at the beginning of the quest when the traveler "thought" to himself that he should set forth. Only at the death of Pelagia do the monks "know" (*cognoverunt*) that she was a woman (*PL* 73, 670D). The abbot of Marina's monastery laments at her death, "Ego non *cognovi* in veritate sanctam conversationem tuam" (*PL* 73, 694A; In truth I did not know your holy way of life). Zosimas rejoices that Mary has taught (*didicit*) him her name (*PL* 73, 688C). At the death of Euphrosyne-Smaragdus, a monk is dumbfounded, "Cognoscens *tam mirabilem causam*" (*PL* 73, 650D; knowing such a miraculous event). This vocabulary suggests that disguise also is a motif of descent, a step on the downward journey that will ultimately lead to ascent, recognition, knowledge, conversion, union with Christ. Disguise is yet another form of surrogate or displaced death in which the hero, having shed an old identity, assumes an interim one prior to the final moment of revelation with which comes the integration of past and present.[40] Metamorphosis is a common theme of descent;[41] disguise is a displacement or rationalization of that theme. In the hagiographic metamorphoses, women "become" men; men "mother" lions; monks "become" knights.[42]

THE JOURNEY'S GOAL

The definitive action of romance is the quest. Indeed, one of the appeals of the genre, then as now, must have been the glimpses it affords of exotic lands and places. These descriptions, moreover, are often rich with symbols and motifs of descent, for the symbolic directions of the questing hero, despite all his aspirations toward heaven, is downward. The immensely popular *Romance of Alexander the Great*, written in Alexandria by "Pseudo-Callisthenes" prior to the fourth century A.D., provides a good example of a descent story within the context of a pagan romance roughly contem-

40. See ch. 7 on the saint as a liminal hero.
41. Frye, *Secular Scripture*, p. 105.
42. See below for Abraham's "rescue" of his niece, Maria.

Figure 6. The devil, disguised as an elderly pilgrim,
tempts a monk in his cell.

porary with the desert fathers.[43] Alexander has traveled all the way to India where he has just succeeded in defeating the giant King Poros, who stood five cubits to Alexander's three. The conquering hero then pays a visit to the wise and peace-loving gymnosophists who dwell in subterranean realms "under huts and in caves," and asks them a series of penetrating questions such as, "Which is more powerful, death or life?" "What is a king?" "To whom can we not lie, but must speak truly?" This dialogue is initiated by the following exchange:

[Alexander] asked one of them, "Do you not have graves?" And he replied: "This place we live in is my grave. I shall lie here in the earth and bury myself in the sleep of those who dwell under the earth. For, in dying, I shall dwell in eternal sleep."[44]

After leaving the gymnosophists and their talk of death and dying, Alexander "[undergoes] many hardships in passing through impenetrable and untrodden places" (p. 123). Soon afterward he visits a garden of prophecy where he receives an oracle concerning his imminent death at the hands of his own men. In this account, themes of descent—travel to the unknown, life in caves, knowledge of death, and death itself—are prominent and inextricably intertwined.

The *Vita Macarii* (*PL* 73, 415–28) is pious travel literature filled with themes of descent. The quest of the three monks was for knowledge, for a demonstration of the "mirabilia et misericordiae Domini" (miracles and mercies of the Lord). Thus far we have largely considered Macarius' story and ignored the role of the three travelers, but their adventures, which comprise more than half the total narrative,[45] merit careful attention as well.

The narrator, Theophilus, recounts that one day he was sitting on the banks of the river Euphrates (rivers are potent symbols of change, as seen by their prominence in rituals such as baptism),

43. All citations of the Alexander-romance are from the fifth-century Armenian version, translated by Wolohojian (1969) because the Greek text is fragmentary at this crucial point. For a translation of the Greek, Pseudo-Callisthenes, *The Life of Alexander of Macedon*, trans. Haight (1955).
44. Ch. 223, p. 121.
45. Chs. 1–14 and 23–24 in the *Patrologia Latina* text.

when the thought came to him that he would like to spend the rest of his days walking until he came to the place where the earth and sky join. His fellow monks, Sergius and Hyginus, determined to accompany him, and that very night they stole out of their monastery and, rather surprisingly in view of their avowed goal, headed west to Jerusalem.[46] There they toured all the important holy places—the church of the Anastasis on Golgotha, the Mount of Olives, Bethlehem, and then retraced their steps eastward, visiting the shrines of several martyrs along the way. They passed through Persia to India. Throughout this journey, Theophilus provides a detailed account of the number of days necessary for each stage of the journey, thereby lending an air of guidebook verisimilitude to his wondrous tale.

The account is filled with descriptions of spectacular scenery and miraculous escapes from man and beast (many of which are plainly forms of symbolic death). In India, for example, they are surrounded by a hostile band of three thousand Ethiopians[47] who throw the travelers into prison without food or water; miraculously our heroes, sustained by prayer, are able to survive for eighty days without food (b[1]). Liberated at last, they pass on to greater marvels:

> Post haec autem devenimus in montes altissimos terribilesque, ubi sol non intrat, nec arbor nec herba crescunt;[48] ibi ergo serpentes innumerabiles, et dracones et aspides, sed et basiliscos, et viperas, et unicornes,[49] et bubalos vidimus multos; alias quoque bestias mortiferas multas, et venenosa animalia, quorum nomina vel naturam penitus ignoramus. Dextera igitur Dei nos protegente, illaesi pertransivimus illa; sed et sibilos draconum et serpentium per viginti continuos dies in auribus habuimus, et non nisi aures obturantes illos ferre quivimus (ch. VII, PL 73, 417CD)

46. In the Christian tradition, Jerusalem was the *omphalos gēs*, the center of the world. The route of the three goes from the place of change (the river) to the center, then to the edge of world, and back again.
47. Strabo, the first-century A.D. Greek geographer, noted the resemblance between India and Ethiopia (*Geography* 15. 1. 25), and noted that the people in the south of India resemble the Ethiopians in color. For the confusion between India and Ethiopia, and the location of Paradise in India, see Le Goff, "L'Occident médiéval et l'océan indien" (1970), pp. 291, 295.
48. The death-imagery of this sterile landscape is apparent.
49. Strabo attests to belief in the presence of unicorns in India (*Geography* 15. 1. 56), and in the next chapter to the existence of pygmies.

(After this we came to extremely high and terrible mountains on which the sun did not shine nor any tree or grass grow. There we saw innumerable serpents and dragons and asps, and especially basilisks and vipers, and unicorns and many wild cows, as well as many other deadly creatures and venomous animals of whose name or nature we were completely ignorant. But the right hand of God protected us and we passed unharmed through this region, but we had the hissing of dragons and serpents in our ears for twenty days in a row and were able to endure it only by blocking our ears.)

Eventually they reach a place where they observe the varied tortures of sinners, then come to the fields of the blessed, a region of unsurpassable charm.[50] At last they find the cave of Macarius who is dwelling twenty miles from Paradise. After he tells them his story, they return to the world to share their wonderful experiences with their brethren: "per ordinem quae vidimus et audivimus mirabilia et misericordias Domini, sed et vitam et conversationem beatissimi Macari illis enarravimus" (PL 73, 426D; We described to them in order the marvels we had seen and the mercies of God, and especially the life and character of the blessed Macarius).

Their return journey, moreover, recapitulated the inward trip with a ritual thoroughness. Theophilus noted that their travel home was without incident ("sine angustia aliqua nostram ambulavimus viam," [but without any danger we went on our way]); but he mentioned in turn each of the places they passed on the way in: from India to Persia to the marvelous plain called Assia where St. Mercurius slew the Apostate Julian,[51] to Ktesiphon (Kitissedum), not far from Babylon, and so forth across the Tigris to Jerusalem, where they prayed once again at the holy shrines before at last turning eastward again to their monastery in Mesopotamia. The journey

50. Purgatory, a later invention, is omitted; see Le Goff, La Naissance du Purgatoire (1981).

51. According to legend, Mercurius, martyred under Decius and Valerian (253–260 A.D.), slew Julian. The Apostate emperor died in 363, struck by a spear. It was unclear whose hand was responsible for the actual blow, and Sozomen (Hist. Eccl. 6. 1–2) knew a tradition asserting that divine vengeance was responsible (PG 67, 1293–94). For the legend associating St. Mercurius with the deed, see Delehaye, Les Légendes grecques des saints militaires (1909) pp. 96–101. The earliest reference to this tale seems to be a Syriac romance about Julian composed between 502 and 532; See Hoffmann, Julianos der Abtrünnige, Syrische Erzählung (Kiel, 1887), cited by Delehaye, p. 98, n. 1.

has a sense of ritual completeness to it, a sense of order and purpose. They have come to the end of a divine mission.

Like Theophilus, Paphnutius is moved by the desire for pious travel: "One day, while I, Paphnutius, was sitting quietly by myself, I thought in my heart that I should seek the desert and all the places of the holy monks . . ." (PL 73, 211A). Paphnutius' journey illustrates a different form of the symbolic death-motif, not confinement in prison or a visit to the underworld, but a brush with death from hunger in the harsh desert and a miraculous salvation (the ability to survive for long periods without food [b^1] is a common motif to which we shall return). Paphnutius takes only enough food for four days (in the barren Egyptian desert, an act seemingly tantamount to suicide), and when it is gone he collapses. But he is then illuminated by divine grace, and "mors imminens ablata est" (imminent death was taken away). He goes on for another four days and collapses again: "humo prostratus jacui velut mortuus" (PL, 73, 211B: prostrate on the ground I lay there as if dead). A miraculous, radiant figure appears to him and touches his hand and lips. Restored, Paphnutius is able to continue his journey without food until he finds St. Onuphrius who has lived alone in the desert for sixty or seventy years.

Onuphrius' history in many ways duplicates Paphnutius'. He too had been a coenobitic monk, and he had heard from his brethren the story of Elijah who through abstinence was privileged not to know the pain of death. Onuphrius was inspired to imitate the harsher life of the desert and one night slipped away, taking little food with him; an angel appeared to him and guided him on his way.

In the story of Zosimas' travels, the quest for knowledge is explicit. One day Zosimas thought to himself, "Is there no monk on earth who can teach me something new? . . . Is there nowhere to be found among those who live in solitude a man who is ahead of me (*prior me*) in deeds?" Then a figure appeared to him and said: "Oh Zosimas, you have striven well, insofar as it is possible for a man, and have led a good monastic life. But no one among men is perfect. . . . So that you may know how many are the roads to salvation, go

forth from your land and your kind, and the house of your father
..." (*PL* 73, 674AB). The search took Zosimas beyond the confines of his known world and exposed him to greater trials than he
had hitherto experienced. The gradational structure of the *vita* of
the questing saint is here apparent. Zosimas was holy but he sought
one "prior me in actibus." He has fought well but there are "aliae
viae salutis" (other roads of salvation). What he eventually finds in
the desert is both a woman and knowledge; he finds St. Mary the
Egyptian.

SEEKING THE WOMAN

A second type of quest narrative is, as in more familiar romances,
the search for a woman.[52] The plots of these accounts conform
more closely to traditional narrative patterns, although elements
are often reflected as mirror images with polarities reversed or are
"displaced" (a displaced element is transposed from one motif,
character, event, or stage of the story to another).[53] The woman
sought is not a virginal bride but a whore. At the conclusion of the
quest, the pattern in which the heroine joyfully surrenders her
much-defended virginity (or chastity, in the case of married
heroines such as Anthia in Xenophon's *Ephesiaca*) to the hero on
the final page of the story[54] is replaced by a renunciation of sexual
activity for a life of virtuous chastity and penance. The tale of the
quest for the woman also reverses the spatial codes normal to
hagiographic romance, as the hero "descends" from the purity of
monastic life to the locus of sin, the city, and then returns again to
his cell. Moreover, in the double tales of the quest for knowledge,
the principal hero has been considered to be the saint whose life
forms the subject of the inner tale, while the actual quester,
although an important figure and often a saint himself (Antony,
Zosimas, and occasionally, Paphnutius[55]), is reduced to playing the

52. Beatie, "Patterns of Myth in Medieval Narrative" (1971).
53. On romance displacement, see Frye, *Secular Scripture*, pp. 37–39.
54. Ibid. pp. 72ff.
55. Petrus de Natalibus considered Paphnutius a saint.

seemingly secondary role of transmitter of information. In accounts of the quest for the woman, the hero is the seeker (e.g. the account of Abraham and his niece, Maria). Finally, in these tales, the hero sets forth in disguise (b⁴).[56]

There are four lives of repentant prostitutes in the *Vitae Patrum*, those of Pelagia, Mary the Egyptian, Maria Meretrix, and Thaïs. The latter two are really doublets, and since the account of Maria is much fuller in the *Vitae Patrum* than is that of Thaïs,[58] I shall concentrate here on this saint.

The Life of Maria Meretrix forms the final chapters of the *Vita Abrahae*, although it is printed separately in volume 73 of the *Patrologia Latina* (651–60). Maria, the hermit's niece,[59] has lived in sanctity with her uncle for twenty years until she is courted by a sinful monk and at last slips out of her cell one night to meet him and loses her virginity. Maria is immediately stung by remorse, and her lament is strongly colored with images of descent. She interprets her fall as death, crying aloud:

Ego . . . jam me ex hoc *mortuam* sentio. . . . Ubi *abscondar?* . . . aut in quam *foveam* memetipsam *praecipitem?* . . . Non audeo jam coelum aspicere, cum apud Deum et homines me *mortuam* esse cognoscam. . . . Melius est ergo mihi abire in aliam patriam, ubi nullus est qui me possit agnoscere, eo quod semel jam *mortua* sim (653D–654A, emphasis added).

(I feel myself dead because of this deed. Where shall I hide myself, into what hole can I throw myself? I do not dare to regard heaven since I know that I am dead to God and men. It is better that I go away into some other country where there is no one who can recognize me, especially since I am already dead.)

56. Barlaam also assumed a disguise to seek out Josaphat.

57. I keep the Latin form of the name here to avoid confusion with Mary the Egyptian. On Pelagia see Dronke, *Women Writers of the Middle Ages* (1984), pp. 1–16.

58. The brief account of this sinner occupies only two columns in the *Patrologia Latina* (73, 661–62); the Paphnutius who saved Thaïs is probably not the same as the hero of the *Peregrinatio Paphnutii*. Indeed, her original savior may have been named Serapion; Kuehne, *A Study of the Thaïs Legend*, pp. 12–13. Hrothswitha dramatized the lives of both Maria and Thaïs.

59. Abraham is Maria's mother's brother, a relationship invested in many primitive societies with particular significance; see Turner, *Dramas, Fields, Metaphors* (1974), p. 235.

Maria's fall was revealed to Abraham in a dream in which descent imagery is again prominent:

Vidit namque draconem terribilem atque immanem, aspectuque ipso foetidissimum, et in fortitudine sibilantem; quasi exeuntem de quodam loco, et usque ad cellulam suam venientem, et reperisse ibi columbam, atque glutisse eam, et rursus in suam foveam remeasse (654B).

(For he saw a terrible great dragon, most repulsive in appearance, and hissing in strength; it seemed as if it was going out of some place and coming to his little cell, and there it found a dove and swallowed her, and then returned to its lair.)

Two days later Abraham had another dream in which the dragon returned; realizing that the dove was still alive in the monster's belly, the saint stretched out his hand and drew her forth.[60]

Two years later Abraham succeeded in learning Maria's whereabouts; he borrowed a soldier's garb[61] and horse, concealed his face with a floppy hat, and went after her. The knight literally sets forth. The hagiographer, St. Ephrem, makes explicit the military nature of this quest:

Venite igitur, admiramini, dilectissimi fratres, hunc secundum Abraham. Primus quidem Abraham egressus ad praelium regum, percutiensque eos, Loth nepotem suum reduxit: hic vero secundus Abraham contra diabolum profectus est ad bellum, ut eo devicto, neptem suam cum *majori* triumpho revocaret (655B, emphasis added).

(Come, therefore, dearest brothers, and let us admire this second Abraham. For the first Abraham went out to the battle of kings and, striking them, led his nephew Lot home: this second Abraham set forth against the devil, so that, having defeated him he might recall his niece with a *greater* triumph.)

Abraham finds Maria in a brothel and arranges to dine with her. There follows a scene of considerable sexual titillation, as the disguised saint plays the role of aging lecher almost to the last. The scene contains all the elements of a traditional seduction:[62]

60. Here the dragon of popular legend who preys on innocent maidens has been displaced to a dream-image, but it remains nonetheless an integral part of the tale.
61. The Paphnutius who rescued Thaïs from sin set forth clothed "habitu seculari" (*PL* 73, 661A; in worldly dress).
62. Scenes like this one tend to substantiate the suspicion that one of the functions of hagiography was to provide entertainment, and that a good deal of disguised salaciousness slips through under the cloak of edification.

Residentibus itaque eis atque bibentibus, coepit cum ea vir mirabilis ludere. Quae consurgens, complexa cervicem ejus, osculis demulcebat. . . . Igitur postquam epulati sunt, provocabat eum puella ad cubandum, ut in cubiculum introierent. At ille: Eamus, inquit, Cumque introisset, cernit lectum in sublime stratum, in quo statim resedit alacriter (655D–656C).

(While they were sitting and drinking, that marvelous man began to toy with her. She got up, threw her arms around his neck, and began to caress him with kisses. . . . Later, after they dined, the girl continued inviting him to bed so that they should enter the bedroom. And he responded, "Very well, let us go." When he went inside, he saw the bed piled high with covers, and he quickly sat down on it.)

Here St. Ephrem interrupted his narrative with a rhetorical apostrophe in praise of his hero who endured sitting upon such a bed instead of his own humble mat, who ate meat and drank wine—all to save a lost soul. Yet in spite of this pious outburst to remind the audience that the hero is only acting and that his deeds are in diametrical opposition to his inclinations and his normal life, the traditional themes of romance are fully operative here: the sexually provocative situation; the danger of the hero's fall; and, because of the hero's disguise, even the threat of incest.[63] These themes are displaced from reality to pretense but remain a vital part of the narrative all the same.

The drama moves yet closer to the sexual brink. One can almost imagine the monastic audience following with bated breath to see how long the deception will go on, how close Abraham will have to come to sin.[64] Maria wants to take off Abraham's shoes, thereby initiating the process of undressing. Abraham tells her to bar the door first, then takes her hand "quasi qui putaretur osculari eam" (657A; like one who thought to kiss her). Finally the moment has come. Weeping, he sweeps off his hat and cries: "Filia mea Maria, non me agnoscis?" (657A; My daughter, Maria, do you not recognize me?). With recognition, the ascent pattern begins. They set out to return to Abraham's cell at daybreak, in direct contrast to Maria's flight, which, like most voyages of descent, commenced at

63. For the obsessive concern with incest in romance (e.g. *Apollonius of Tyre*), see Frye, *Secular Scripture*, p. 44.
64. The tales of Timotheus and Macarius contain accounts of actual sin.

night. When they reach the cell, Abraham shuts his niece in what, significantly, had been *his* room, the inner cell, where Maria lives in solitary penance for ten years until Abraham's death. In place of the transcendent happiness at the conclusion of more traditional romances, Maria enjoys the heights of remorse, as she endures "vigiliis arctissimis" (the most severe vigils) and hopes for mercy with "spe firmissima" (with firmest hope).

St. Ephrem's exploitation of a horizon of expectation set up by secular romances is clear in this account. The hero sets out as a disguised knight (militem) on horseback to rescue a beautiful woman who has been living "quasi in ventre atrocissimi draconis" (as if in the belly of the most terrible dragon). He is placed in a situation redolent of sexual temptation but, although he appears to come near to the brink, he does not fall. Salvation is effected through a last-minute recognition scene, and the couple lives, from the hagiographer's point of view, happily ever after. Their days of journeying and adventures are over.

Chapter 6

The Ascent: Paradise Regained

After the downward journey, whether literal or symbolic, is completed, the ascent that will ultimately lead to heaven begins. It is not an easy road to travel, and the means that the saints of the desert took to earn their right to final bliss were rigorous and even, from some points of view, perverse.

Many explanations have been offered for the form of life espoused by such saints as Macarius, Abraham, and Onuphrius—ranging from a desire to escape a corrupt world and devote their entire lives to God, to charges of extreme masochism.[1] That this renunciation of the world was seen by contemporaries primarily as a form of *imitatio Christi* is evident from many texts. To give only one example, Antony was inspired to pursue the monastic life by hearing Matt. 19:21 read aloud in church: "Si vis perfectus esse, vade, vende omnia tua et da pauperibus, et veni, sequere me, et habebis thesaurum in caelis"[2] (If you wish to be perfect, go, sell all your possessions and give them to the poor, and come, and follow me, and you will have your treasure in heaven). The problem of explanation, however, remains. Herbert Musurillo, in a study of ascetic fasting, writes:

One of the difficulties in the history of Christian asceticism is to discover any principle of growth and unity, a particular fact or text which might

1. See Janet, *De l'angoisse à l'extase* (1926), and Penido, "Une théorie pathologique de l'ascétisme" (1932).
2. *Vita Antonii*, PG 26, 841, ch. 2.

explain why it developed as it did. Granted that the supernatural unity with Christ, in this world as in the next, was the ultimate goal of this asceticism, how, when all is said, can the practice of self-inflicted pain, particularly by fasting and abstinence, have any connection with it?[3]

This study does not attempt to answer Musurillo's question of how pain led to holiness, nor is it concerned with the sources of this belief;[4] it does examine the way tales of ascetic renunciation are told, tracing the development of one form of these legends.

The structural oppositions manifest in the accounts of Macarius and Abraham suggest that their imitation took a specific direction. The story of Macarius and the three monks is purely legendary, but as a mythopoeic fiction it is free to give literal (in this case geographic) expression to the metaphor that also underlies other accounts. Macarius categorically rejects the world, but his flight is simultaneously a negative and a positive act. Structually, his renunciation involves social, ethical, biological (sexual), habitational, dietary, and spatial codes. If the opposite of culture is nature (however defined), in every case Macarius places himself in unequivocal opposition to all manifestations of culture and opts for a life seemingly lived in accord with the dictates of nature. In point of fact, his lifestyle is not "natural," for it is decidedly unnatural to forgo eating, but this account is not concerned with biological nature but with a spiritual reinterpretation of it. The viewpoint is so dominated by the necessary rejection of culture that the practitioners of asceticism go to an "unnatural" extreme. It suggests that the simple binary opposition between nature and culture must now be redefined. The desert saints sought a third pole, superior to either culture or actual nature, although its physical location was in the latter. They sought a repression of physical nature and the exalta-

---

3. Musurillo, "The Problem of Ascetical Fasting" (1956), p. 55.
4. On this subject, see *inter alia* Dodds, *Pagan and Christian in an Age of Anxiety* (1965), for a psychological (Freudian) analysis of the sources of asceticism. Writing of the sense of alienation from their society felt by Christians in predominantly pagan cultures, Dodds suggested that there were two results: philanthropy, and an introjection of hostile feeling leading to physical acts of self-punishment (pp. 27–28). Vööbus attributes extreme asceticism to the strong influence of Manichean doctrine and anti-bodily dualism (*History of Asceticism* [1958], pp. 21 ff.).

tion of a spiritual one. They sought, in short, the paradisiacal nature lost by Adam at the Fall.[5]

In Macarius' narrative, the use made of the spatial code is perhaps the most revealing. Having fled the society of Rome, the saint travels through a marvelous landscape and experiences symbolic death and spiritual rebirth. Then, together with two lions, he lives in a cave as near to Paradise as man still clothed in mortal flesh may come. Such fantasies evoke, as A. J. Festugière suggests, the Lost Paradise, "the miraculous time when man existed in friendship with the beasts."[6] The object of this solitary quest is to atone for Adam's sin by living in imitation of the new Adam,[7] and thereby to regain the lost Golden Age of Eden.

Macarius certainly finds Paradise,[8] but what of the others? Neither the Old Testament nor the New gives any clue to the fate of Eden after the Fall, but that it existed somewhere was almost universally believed.[9] We have seen the prominence given in these narratives to the discovery of a place (Theme C). In several accounts, the place takes on a paradisiacal coloring or symbolism. The clearest example, after Macarius, is the eighth adventure of Paphnutius in the *Peregrinatio* where he comes to the lovely garden filled with every kind of tree imaginable: "Ille quoque fons ex se scatens, et omnes illas arbores irrigans, adeo ut existimarem eum esse Dei paradisum"[10] (The spring was flowing out from there and watering all the trees, so that I thought it was the Paradise of God). This *locus amoenus* was inhabited by four boys whose beauty made them resemble angels. Few desert travelers, however, were as fortunate as Paphnutius in finding edenic gardens. The classic resi-

5. On this point see Flusin (1983), *Miracle et histoire*, pp. 104, 125–26.
6. *Les Moines d'orient* (1961), p. 57: "On songe au temps merveilleux où l'homme était en amitié avec les bêtes. On songe au Paradis Perdu."
7. See Methodius, *Symposium, Thecla's hymn*, 21ff., cited by Rush, "Death as Spiritual Marriage" (1972), pp. 99–100.
8. Macarius' legend had an influence on medieval cartographers; Graf, *Miti, leggende, e superstizione* (1892), I, 86, reports that the map of Andrea Bianco placed beside the terrestrial paradise a little church labeled *ospitium macorii*.
9. Boas, *Essay on Primitivism*, (1948), p. 154; Morino, "Ritorno" (1952). The exceptions were those commentators such as Philo and Origen for whom the significance of Paradise was purely allegorical.
10. Surius (1878), p. 276.

FIGURE 7. A desert monk at work, plaiting a basket of leaves.

dence of the desert saint was a cave located beside a spring and a palm tree: Paul of Thebes lived in such a place; so did Timotheus and Onuphrius. While shelter, food, and water are all necessary to sustain life, there are signs of a miracle in these stories, for the hagiographer explicitly mentions that the palms of Timotheus and Onuphrius produce, not seasonally as do palms in nature, but throughout the year, bearing one bunch of fruit each month. The date palm with twelve bunches of fruit comes from the Tree of Life of Rev. 22:2, "which bare twelve manner of fruits, and yielded her fruit every month."

Springs and palms are imbued with sacredness in Semitic belief.[11] There is some reason to identify the date palm with the tree of life of Genesis, for the oldest part of the Ethiopian *Book of Enoch* (ch. 24) relates how Enoch visited Paradise and found the date palm growing there.[12] The Koranic version of the birth of Jesus also attests to a belief in the sacral nature of this tree; according to Mohammed, when the time approached for the birth of her son, Mary withdrew to a palm tree and was miraculously nourished by dates produced out of season (Sura 19:23, 25).[13]

The account of Mark the Athenian is also rich with symbols of Paradise. Although accounts of the terrestrial Paradise in the Christian tradition most often picture it as a garden, a common variant in near-eastern mythology places Paradise on the top of a mountain whose summit is occupied by a lake.[14] Serapion finds the hairy hermit living on the summit of a mountain by the edge of a lake where he is fed by angels and has been honored by visions of Paradise and of the Tree of Life. In the hermit's cave, the saint and his visitor enjoy a miraculously provided feast of fish, fresh bread,

11. See Barton, *A Sketch of Semitic Origins* (1902), pp. 86, 88. They were associated with Ishtar, the mother goddess of the ancient Semites.

12. The *Book of Enoch* is dated before 170 B.C.; see Barton, *A Sketch*, p. 89. See also E. O. James, "The Tree of Life" (1968), p. 242.

13. Barton, *A Sketch*, p. 89. Mohammed's source for this story probably came in part from Arabic Christians. See also the legend of Leto and the birth of Apollo on Delos: *The Homeric Hymn to Apollo*, lines 25–126, especially 117–18.

14. For a survey of this tradition, see Ringbom, *Paradisus Terrestris* (1958). Ringbom wants to identify the Iranian holy city of Shiz, discovered in 1937 by A. U. Pope, with the original inspiration of the Paradise myth.

olives, dates, and honey-sweet water—a marked and significant change from the normally sparse diet of the desert dwellers, the majority of whom are strict vegetarians who eschew even the use of fire to soften their harsh existence. This surprisingly lavish and un-ascetic feast that Serapion and Mark enjoy calls to mind the images of plenitude that often accompany paradisiacal reveries. Serapion, moreover, is not allowed to remain in this wonderful place after the saint's death. Whether or not Serapion has found the earthly Para-dise, the spot, like the dwelling place of Onuphrius, is tabu, and may only be visited by ordinary persons under special circum-stances and in the presence of a guide, just as it can only be found with divine assistance.

Thus far we have been concerned largely with legendary accounts such as the lives of Macarius the Roman, Onuphrius, and Mark the Athenian. Yet the same themes and motifs prominent in these accounts can be found as well, if transposed or somewhat modified, in the more historical biographies of ascetic saints. The symbols that underlie the quests for sanctity of the historic anchorites are easier to perceive in the legendary accounts because there they have been given mythic status and appear in the narrative as dramatic incidents, but an examination of patristic sources reveals the extent to which these same concerns were the preoccupation of all.

From one point of view, Paradise is the goal of every Christian. Cyprian writes:

> Who therefore does not strive with all his strength to attain such lustre that he may become the friend of God, that he may immediately rejoice with Christ. . . . If it is a source of glory to worldly soldiers to return trium-phantly to their homeland, having conquered the enemy, how much more powerful and great a victory is it, having defeated the devil, to return in triumph to Paradise whence the sinner Adam was thrown out.[15]

But the desert hermits' search has a more specific quality to it; they made manifest the universal inner and spiritual quest in outward and symbolic ways. Chitty notes than when Antony emerged from a twenty-year period of seclusion in a dark and tomb-like fort, his

15. *Ad Fortunatam de Martyrio, PL* 4, 702A.

comrades marveled to find him unchanged, and indeed even purified by this experience (*Vita Antoni*, ch. 14). Antony's perfection was seen as "the return to man's *natural* condition. This is the constant teaching of East Christian ascetics. Their aim is the recovery of Adam's condition before the Fall. That is accepted as man's true nature, man's fallen condition being *para phusin*," contrary to nature.[16]

The desert was the place for man to recapture his lost nature. In his lyrical praise of the desert Eucherius, Bishop of Lyons, wrote in 449:

Hic interioris hominis pratum et voluptas, hic incultum desertum, illic mira amoenitate jucundum est; eademque corporis est eremus, animae paradisus.[17]

(Here is the meadow and delight of the interior man, here the uncultivated land, there a "pleasance" of wonderful charm; the desert is the same for the body as Paradise is for the soul.)

Three characteristic practices unite the seekers of "paradise for the soul" in the desert.[18] These are (1) arduous fasting coupled with other forms of mortification of the flesh and denial of all forms of creature comfort; (2) virginity; and (3) power over beasts, particularly lions. These categories are related, and patristic texts connect all three with the quest for Paradise. In terms of structural codes, the pole embraced by the hermit reveals a consistent and total rejection of civilization (cooked), and a concomitant pursuit of the life they regarded as consistent with *phusis*, nature (raw), spiritually defined.

FOOD AND SEX

Macarius flees the "voluptatem convivii" (pleasure of the banquet); he offers his three guests a frugal meal of uncooked vegetables and water. For Origen (*Homilies on Luke*), the dichotomy between culture and nature is vital; it is important that John the

---

16. Chitty, *The Desert a City* (1962), p. 4.
17. PL 50, 710B.
18. Meredith, "Asceticism" (1976), pp. 316ff.

Baptist was nurtured in the desert on *wild* honey ("mel silvestre").[19] Many texts make explicit the opposition between nature and culture reflected in the nourishment of the saint. The desert hermits are vegetarians. In the Romano-Byzantine world, eating meat was linked to life in urban society, and this was one of the reasons for banning it in ascetic regimes.[20] Throughout the accounts of the desert fathers, historic as well as legendary, tales of prodigious fasting are legion,[21] and even the more restrained biographers (e.g. Athanasius in the *Vita Antonii*) feel obliged to include a description of their heroes' meager diet.[22] In common with many hermits, Antony's staples were bread, salt, and water,[23] a regimen known as "xerophagy" (eating dry), in contrast to those who included moistened legumes or other greens.[24] All monks rejected highly prepared or processed foods, particularly meat[25] (which men eat cooked, not raw as do the beasts), and, except in cases of illness, wine. But the real athletes among the fasters went still further and did not eat bread or other food prepared with fire.[26] This diet, in patent opposition to the usual practices of culture, was known as "omophagy" (eating raw).[27] Onuphrius, for example, lived for sixty or seventy

19. *PG* 13, 1828A; the Greek text is lacking.

20. Patlagean, "Ancienne hagiographie" (1968), p. 114.

21. Cf. Simeon Stylites' unequaled (and nearly fatal) forty-day fast in imitation of Christ's similar fast in the wilderness. Total veracity, however, is questionable: the saint's water, which supposedly did not change level, would have evaporated in the dry desert climate. The detail does not occur in Antony's biography of this saint.

22. For Antony's diet, see *Vita Antonii*, Ch. 7.

23. A diet that, if rigidly adhered to, should have led to scurvy.

24. *Xērophagia* is defined by St. Epiphanius, *PG* 42, 828C, as eating bread, water, and salt at evening time.

25. According to Tertullian, *De Jejunio* 4, not only were Adam and Eve vegetarians, but so were all their descendants until the time of Noah, when God abrogated the restriction against eating meat (Gen. 9). Jesus was a confirmed vegetarian; see Vööbus, *A History of Asceticism* (1958), p. 15, n. 36.

26. In the *Historia Religiosa*, ch. 1, Theodoret relates the habits of Jacob: Τῶν γὰρ ἀγρίων δένδρων τοὺς αὐτοφυεῖς συλλέγων καρποὺς, καὶ τῶν βοτανῶν τὰς ἐδωδίμους καὶ λαχανώδεις, ἐκ τούτων ἐδίδου τῶι σώματι τὰ εἰς τὸ ζῆιν ἀποχρῶντα, τὴν τοῦ πυρὸς παραιτούμενος χρείαν. (*PG* 82, iii, 1293D; Gathering the natural fruits of the wild trees and edible herbs and grasses, from these he gave to his body what sufficed for life, and he rejected the use of fire.)

27. For the Greeks *ōmophagia* was characteristic of carnivorous animals like lions (*Iliad* 5.782, 11.479, 16.157) and savage men (Strabo, *Geography*; 15.1.47; Porphyry, *De Abstinentia* 1.13).

years in the desert on herbs and fruit in the place of bread (*PL* 73, 213A). In his much-quoted letter to Eustochium, St. Jerome wrote: "Monachi aqua frigida utantur, et coctum aliquid accepisse, luxuria sit"[28] (Let monks use cold water, and let it be a luxury to accept anything cooked). To give up fire is to give up the first artifact of culture. In *Myths of the Origin of Fire*, Sir James Frazer reflected on the psychological importance of fire, discussing myths of the lack or loss of it:

Some peoples, without dwelling on the other hardships of the Fireless Age, single out the necessity of warming their food in the sun as if it were the sorest to bear of the privations which the want of fire entailed on the community. The insistence on this particular hardship suggests that the craving for hot food is a natural instinct of the human organism, for which physiological causes may probably be assigned by science.[29]

In the *Historia Religiosa* Theodoret described a number of omophages among the Syrian monks. The first biography is that of Jacob of Nisibis (d. ca. 338) who gathered the fruit of wild trees that grew of their own accord, and who explicitly rejected the use of fire.[30] Simeon Priscus (ch. 6) ate only plants. Macedonius (ch. 13) refused bread and vegetables, and consumed only bruised barley moistened with water. Abraames (ch. 17) by his diet of raw vegetables "showed that the crafts (technas) of the baker and the cook were superfluous" (1424B). Arthur Vööbus wrote of such stellar Syrian ascetics: "These monks abandoned their communities and civilization and lived a life which reduced them to the state of wild animals. They lived with animals, ate grass with them, and perched on the rocks like birds."[31] Palladius' *Historia Lausiaca* also contains stories of omophages: Macarius of Alexandria (18.1), having heard that some monks ate for forty days without benefit of fire, deter-

28. *Epistle* 22, *PL* 22, 398.
29. *Myths of the Origin of Fire* (1930), p. 203. It is interesting to note that Judeo-Christian mythology does not include a myth about the origin of fire.
30. PG 82, iii, 1293D, cited above, note 26. It is, however, significant that Theodoret only ascribed the practice of omophagy to monks who were no longer alive. Peeters, "La Légende de S. Jacques" (1920), pp. 285ff., denies any historic value to Theodoret's account of Jacob. See also Vööbus, *History of Asceticism*, pp. 141ff.
31. *History of Asceticism*, p. 152.

mined to eat only raw food for seven years;[32] Poseidonius (36.1) ate only wild dates and herbs; Philoromus (45.1) wore chains and ate no bread or anything cooked by fire. Some hermits lived without benefit of fire although they would consume bread (Ammonius, 11.4), but still others explicitly rejected the use of fire even for light (*Historia Religiosa*, ch. 11, Romanus; ch. 12, Zeno).

Most omophages' housing was "raw" as well; like Macarius, they lived in caves. Theodoret's encomium of the monk Julian (*Historia Religiosa*, ch. 2) relates that the hermit lived in a cave not wrought by human hands (οὐ χειροποίητον[1305C]), which he thought finer than palaces made of gleaming gold or silver. Simeon Priscus, a plant-eater, was also a cave-dweller. The pursuit of the raw can go no further. Those who reject fire and bread and dwell in caves have returned to the state of primitive man or of animals. A monk like Jacob (*Historia Religiosa*, ch. 1), eating only fruits produced spontaneously, has totally relinquished civilization and become a food gatherer, not a cultivator of fields. He has tried to return to that Golden Age when beneficent nature, *sponte sua*, provided man with all his needs. Adam gathered the fruit of all trees but one, and he did not need to till the soil, nor Eve to spin, until after their expulsion from Paradise.[33] Novatian wrote in the third century that "the first food of man was the produce and fruit of trees alone. For the use of bread was introduced later by man's guilt, the very position of his body in gathering grain indicating the state of his conscience."[34]

In some of the fathers, fasting was interpreted specifically as an atonement for Adam's fall.[35] The precise nature of original sin could be variously interpreted,[36] but gluttony was a leading candidate.

32. On the competitive tendencies of some hermits, see Festugière, "Le problème littéraire" (1955).

33. For the debate whether Adam did any work in Paradise, see Boas, *Essays on Primitivism* (1948) p. 33.

34. *De Cibis Judaicis*, ch. 2. Cited by Boas (above, note 33), p. 26. Also Marguerite Harl, "La prise de conscience de la nudité d'Adam," Studia Patristica 7, *Texte und Untersuchungen* 92 (Berlin, 1966).

35. Chrysostom, *De compunctione ad Demetrium* 10, represented all ascetics as mourning the loss of heaven (*PG* 47, 409).

36. In *Essays on Primitivism* Boas wrote of St. Ambrose that he, "like so many other theological moralists, has at least two opinions" (p. 43).

Jerome wrote: "Primus de paradiso homo, ventri magis obediens, quam Deo, in hanc lacrymarum dejectus est vallem"[37] (The first man, more obedient to his belly than to God, was ejected from Paradise into this vale of tears). In *De octo spiritus malitiis* (On the Eight Evils of the Spirit), "Gula" (Gluttony) is the first vice discussed by the Abbot Nilus: "It was the desire for food that spawned disobedience: it was the pleasure of taste that drove us from Paradise."[38] Tertullian claimed that all abstinence from food had as its aim the expiation of original sin ("primordiale iam delictum expiaretur").[39] St. Ambrose maintained that gluttony cost man Paradise but fasting regained it.[40] Citing Eve's first statement in Gen.: 3:13, "Serpens persuasit mihi, et manducavi" (The serpent persuaded me and I ate), he wrote: "Itaque gula de paradiso regnantem expulit, abstinentia ad paradisum revocavit errantem"[41] (As gluttony expelled the one who ruled from Paradise, so abstinence has recalled the one who has gone astray to Paradise). Moreover, according to Ambrose, those who need neither food nor drink are equal to the angels; in Paradise Adam lived the angelic life.[42]

In addition, the church fathers often drew a specific connection between fasting and chastity. John Cassian (d. 435) maintained that fasting was necessary to repress desire,[43] a position for which there is indeed some physiological basis as biological studies of human starvation have documented a reduction in interest in sex due to

37. *Epistle* 22, PL 22, 400.
38. PG 79, 1145B.
39. *De Jejunio adversus psychicos* III. 4: CCSL 2, 1260. This statement occurred in a treatise on fasting; in remarks on patience (*De patientia*), he interpreted Adam and Eve's sin as impatience. See Church, "Sex and Salvation in Tertullian" (1975), pp. 86–87. The *De Jejunio* is a controversial treatise written during Tertullian's Montanist period.
40. In the *Liber de Elia et Jejunio* (PL 14, 700B), Ambrose connected fasting with creation; there was no eating until the sixth day.
41. PL 14, 700D. There are other examples of the "Adam-motif": "we fast now because Adam did not" (e.g. Gregory Nazianzen, *Orat.* 45, 28, PG 36, 662C). See Musurillo, "The Problem of Ascetical Fasting," pp. 23–24. St. Irenaeus connected Christ's forty-day fast in the wilderness with Adam's sin (*Contra Haereses*, Bk. V, PG 7, 1180B).
42. *Liber de Paradiso*, PL 14, 311B.
43. *De Coenobiorum Instit.*, "De spiritu gastrimargiae," PL 49, 224.

decreased hormonal function.[44] But for the more detailed connections drawn between diet and carnal appetite, the reasoning of the fathers owed more to ethics than to biology. St. Jerome was, as usual, one of the more outspoken. Quoting Rom.: 14:21, "Bonum est vinum non bibere, et carnem non manducare" (It is good not to drink wine and not to eat flesh), he enjoined, "Let them eat flesh who serve flesh,"[45] and maintained that wine, meat, and cooked vegetables encouraged sexual appetite, quoting Terence in support: "Sine Cerere et Libero friget Venus"[46] (*Eunuchus* 732; Venus grows cold without Ceres and Bacchus). He described the effects of such "poisons" in rhetorically flamboyant terms: "Non Aetnaei ignes, non Vulcania tellus, non Vesevus et Olympus tantis ardoribus aestuant, ut juveniles medullae vino plenae, et dapibus inflammatae"[47] (The fires of Aetna, the land of Vulcan, Vesuvius, and Olympus do not burn with such flames as do the hearts of youths filled with wine and inflamed by banquets). St. Mary the Egyptian lived for seventeen years in the desert on two half-loaves of bread and on grass because, as she explained to Zosimas, if she ate anything it inflamed her appetite.[48]

Much has been written about the Christian emphasis upon virginity;[49] for our purposes, two points are particularly relevant. Milton's sensuously beautiful vision of innocent sex in the Garden of Eden was not shared by the early fathers. According to Jerome, "Eve was a virgin in Paradise."[50] Tertullian held that it was a virgin whom the serpent tempted: "In virginem enim adhuc Evam irrep-

---

44. *The Biology of Human Starvation*, ed. Ancel Keys et al. (Minneapolis: University of Minnesota, 1950), cited by Musurillo, "The Problem of Ascetical Fasting," p. 2.

45. *Epistle* 79, PL 22, 729.

46. PL 22, 554. The phrase is proverbial.

47. PL 22, 554.

48. PG 87, iii, 3717C.

49. There is a good summary of attitudes in general in Noonan, *Contraception* (1965). For the Egyptian monks, see Resch, *La doctrine ascétique des premiers maîtres égyptiens* (1931); Resch maintained that for a long time virginity was the only quality that set these first monks apart from the rest of the community (p. 1). See also E. Malone, *The Monk and the Martyr* (1950), pp. 59–60.

50. *Epistle* 22, 102; PL 22, 406. In *Adversus Jovinianum*, I.4 (PL 23, 225A), Jerome referred to Adam and Eve as "immaculate virgins."

serat verbum aedificatorium mortis" (Into Eve, still a virgin, crept the word in which dwelt death). The earth too, not yet plowed or sown, was virgin: "Virgo erat adhuc terra nondum opere compressa, nondum sementi subacta."[51] The command, "Increase and multiply" (Gen.: 1:28), seems not to have included Adam and Eve, at least not interpreted literally.[52] In *De Genesi contra Manichaeos*, St. Augustine maintained that this text ought to be interpreted *spiritualiter*: after the fall, what had been a spiritual increase was converted to "carnal fecundity" ("in carnalem fecunditatem post peccatum conversa est creditur"). Before it, Adam and Eve "filled the earth with the spiritual offspring of intellectual and immortal joys" (spiritualis fetus intelligibilium et immortalium gaudiorum replens terram).[53]

Second, according to Tertullian, only martyrs enjoyed the grace of immediate entry into Paradise prior to the Last Judgment: "Nemo enim peregrinatus a corpore, statim immoratur penes Dominum, nisi ex martyrii praerogativa; paradiso, scilicet, non inferis deversurus"[54] (Except for the privilege accorded martyrdom, no one departing the body dwells at once with the Lord—to inhabit Paradise, not Hell). The authority for this belief cited by Tertullian was the vision of the martyr St. Perpetua; in the saint's vision of Paradise, she saw only martyrs.[55] After the Peace of Constantine,

---

51. *Liber de carne Christi*, PL 2, 827BC. In the *De anima* he connected eating the forbidden fruit with sexual maturity.

52. In the Letter to Eustochium (*Epistle* 22, PL 22, 406), Jerome wrote: "'crescite et multiplicamini,' hoc expletur edictum post paradisum et nuditatem, et ficus folia, auspicantia pruriginem nuptiarum" ("Increase and multiply": by this is fulfilled the decree after Paradise and [awareness of] nakedness and after the [putting on of] fig leaves that forebode sexual desire in marriage.)

53. PL 34, 187; see also *De Genesi ad litteram*, Bk. IX, ch. 4–8, cols 395–98. In the *City of God* he maintained that the immaculate conception would have been possible for Adam and Eve in Paradise had they not been evicted (*De Civ. Dei*, XIV, 26). Augustine's position, however, was not consistent over the years, and in the course of his life he changed his mind toward an increasing acknowledgment of the sexual side of marriage.

54. Tertullian, *De resurrectione carnis*, PL 2, 903A.

55. Tertullian, *De anima*, 55 (PL 2, 789B). For the text of this vision, properly that of St. Saturus, see Musurillo, *Acts of the Christian Martyrs* (1972), pp. 118–23. For a discussion of its symbolism, see Musurillo, *Symbolism and the Christian Imagination* (1962), pp. 47–50.

the opportunities for physical martyrdom were largely eliminated, but virginity was considered to be a form of spiritual martyrdom. Indeed, the connection between ascetic renunciation (especially virginity) and martyrdom appears as early as Clement of Alexandria (d. 215), who wrote: "If one renounces everything while alive, one truly carries one's cross."[56] St. Ambrose maintained: "non enim ideo laudabilis virginitas, quia et in martyribus reperitur, sed quia ipsa martyres faciat"[57] (Virginity is not praiseworthy because it is found in martyrs but because it makes martyrs). St. Jerome concurred: "Habet et servata pudicitia martyrium suum"[58] (Preserved chastity has its own martyrdom).

THE PEACEABLE KINGDOM

The final characteristic that marks the saint out as different from ordinary men is his rapport with animals. In Jerome's *Life of Paul of Thebes*, Antony asks: "Why do you who receive beasts keep out men?"[59] In this respect the saint's behavior does not accord with specifically Christian scripture. While the hermits shared with the Jews the story of creation, the New Testament is remarkably silent about relations between man and animals, and according to Bosquet, in comparison with Judaism and especially with Islam, Christianity concerns itself very little with animals.[60] We have here, then, a revealing dichotomy between official doctrine and legend. Of the popularity of such legends there is little doubt. Even those who know little of hagiography are familiar with St. Francis preaching to the birds or speaking to "brother wolf." In portraits of St. Jerome, including those that depict the saint indoors in his study, a lion is his almost constant companion. Indeed, it is the "King of the Beasts" who is most frequently associated with the desert fathers,

---

56. *Stromata* VII. 12, 79 in *PG* 9. 509C; see Viller, "Le martyre et l'ascèse" (1925), p. 106.
57. *De virginibus* I.3, *PL* 16, 191B.
58. *Epistle* 130. 5; *CSEL* 56, 180.
59. *PL* 23, 25A.
60. "Des animaux" (1958).

and it is on this animal that the present section focuses, although the saints' relationships with all animals are informative.[61]

The association of the desert fathers with the lion probably owes something to New Testament iconography where this animal is the emblem of St. Mark.[62] The symbols of the four evangelists are derived from Ezekiel's vision of the four faces (Ezek. 10:14), where he saw the faces of a man, a lion, a cow, and an eagle. The assignment of these four emblems to the evangelists was suggested by the opening lines of the respective books. As Gregory the Great, for example, explained, the first words of the *Gospel of Mark* are: "Vox clamantis in deserto, 'Parate viam Domini'" (Mark 1:3; A voice crying in the desert; prepare the way for the Lord), and since the lion is, *par excellence*, the symbol of the desert, "Mark is rightly designated by a lion."[63] Gregory went on to explain the allegorical significance of the lion: "The lion is said to sleep with open eyes because in the death which He has from His humanity our Savior could sleep, but immortal from His divinity, He remains on guard" (815B). "The lion is a mighty beast, as is written, 'The lion is the strongest of beasts; he fears the attack of none'" (Prov. 30:30; 815C). "The just man, like the confident lion, will be without fear" (Prov. 28:1; 815D). In an allegorical interpretation of the tetramorph, the lion represents resurrection.

For many people, however, the most obvious connection between saints and animals is a negative one, as the word "martyr" conjures up an image of countless Christians being thrown to the

61. For a discussion of the symbolic role of animals in miracle stories, see Patlagean, "Ancienne hagiographie byzantine" (1968), p. 116; of the saints' power over beasts, she writes: "La plupart du temps cette puissance s'exerce symboliquement sur les lions."

62. This association may have facilitated the transferral of the story of Gerasimus' lion (see below) to the better known St. Jerome. According to Künstle (*Ikonographie der Heiligen*, p. 299ff.), the Four Latin Fathers were paralleled with the Four Evangelists, and the four evangelical symbols were associated with them from early times. Thus Mark was associated with Jerome. Since Jerome was known to have spent time in the desert, the lion was an even more apposite symbol for him.

63. PL 76, 815A; *Homilies on Ezekiel*, Bk. II, Homily IV. See also Alcuin (*dubia*), PL 101, 1133; Rabanus Maurus, PL 111, 71D.

lions.[64] The words of Tertullian depicting the pagan populace's tendency to turn the Christians into scapegoats seem indelibly imprinted on the imagination (particularly on that of makers of such cinematic spectacles as *The Last Days of Pompeii*):

The pagans suppose that the Christians are the cause of every public disaster. If the Tiber overflows or the Nile does not, if there is a drought or an earthquake, a famine or a pestilence, at once the cry goes up, "*The Christians to the lions.*"[65]

One of a series of slides of the Colosseum on sale to tourists all over Rome, including the Vatican, is entitled "Il Colosseo—Martirio di Christiani" (the Colosseum—place of Christian martyrs); it depicts in the foreground a large lion, while in the background a group of Christians kneel in prayer. Yet the viewer ought to hesitate before drawing the seemingly inevitable conclusion that the lion is going to eat the martyrs—at least, if we may judge by the texts collected in the three volumes of Symeon Metaphrastes, *Patrologia Graeca* 114–16, or those in the 540 folio pages of the *Acta Martyrum Sincera* (*AMS*). Statistically, it is far more likely that the beast is going to run up to the saints, fall in reverence before them, and lick their feet. *Damnatio ad bestias* did occur, but the way this event was represented by both the hagiographers and their artists differs from the exuberant bloodthirstiness of later era's representations of the deed.

In the two hagiographic compilations mentioned above, only St. Ignatius, martyred under Trajan, is unambiguously reported to have been eaten by a lion (or another beast), and the saint himself prayed for this form of death.[66] In three other *Acta* we read of martyrs dying as a consequence of being subjected to wild animals, but all three contain as well accounts of saints' being spared by the beasts. Unnamed saints (not Roman citizens) from among the mar-

---

64. In 1981, a guide at the catacombs of St. Calixtus on the Appian Way, explaining the small size of some of the tombs, maintained, "Dalla bocca di leone si salva poco" (From the lion's mouth little is saved.)

65. Tertullian, *Apology*, 40.2 (emphasis added).

66. *AMS*, p. 10; *PG* 114, 1286B. Tertullian, *Ad Martyres*, Ch. V (*PL* 1, 626B) does include *bestias* among the torments to which the martyrs were subjected, and he claims that the bites and scars which they received seemed beautiful.

tyrs of Lyons were killed, but Blandina escaped unscathed from her encounter.[67] In the *Passion of Perpetua and Felicitas*, Saturus eventually died, just as he had predicted, from a single bite of a leopard, but he survived several previous episodes: the boar to which he was being bound killed the gladiator who was to tie on the saint, while Saturus was only dragged; the bear with whom he was supposed to fight refused to leave its cage. Perpetua herself was tossed by a "ferocissima vacca" (very savage cow) but not seriously injured.[68] St. Euphemia died (miraculously?) as the result of a "harmless" nibble from a bear, but unspecified *bestiae* previously had refused to harm her, and four lions and two bears approached her "caute simul et reverenter" (carefully and reverently at the same time) and kissed her feet in kindly manner ("humane").[69]

Of these accounts, at least those of Saints Ignatius, Perpetua, and Felicitas and of the martyrs of Lyons are generally regarded as historically accurate. No doubt the animals were unpredictable, as likely to turn on their keepers as on their intended victims, especially when wild with hunger. In his chronicle of those martyred under Diocletian, Eusebius wrote that in Palestine he himself had witnessed occasions on which the beasts did not touch the bodies of the saints or "dare" to approach them, but turned instead on the pagans who were inciting them.[70] In the early or more restrained accounts, the hagiographers were ready enough to ascribe the animals' behavior to divine providence,[71] but they did not otherwise elaborate. In the passage of Eusebius cited above, only in the word "dare" do we have an emotional interpretation of the event. In the *Passio Perpetuae*, the reason given for Saturus' escape from the bear was the animal's unwillingness to leave its cage. Other

67. AMS, p. 57; see also p. 59.
68. AMS, pp. 87–88; Musurillo, *Acts* (1972), p. 126.
69. I quote from the Latin. PG 115, 731C–732C, εὐλαβῶς ἅμα καὶ πεφεισμένως; ἀνθρωπικῶς.
70. Eusebius, *Ecclesiastical History*, 8.7.2. The incident recurs in the accounts of St. Trophimus (PG 115, 749–50A), and St. Christinia (AA.SS July V, vol. 32, p. 527F [Feb. 4]).
71. Eusebius wrote of seeing bears and lions draw back just as they were about to bite a young martyr and "by a divine and mysterious power I cannot explain, their mouths were muzzled, so to speak" (*Ecclesiastical History*, 8.7.4).

accounts are less restrained, and as the episode is repeated in *passio* after *passio*, the language used becomes more vivid; the animals progress from merely sparing the saints to worshiping them, and the Hand of God is far more visible in the action. The detail, then, becomes a motif, an event that assumes a deeper significance, a symbolic coloring.

The first female martyr is considered to be St. Thecla,[72] who was not only spared but even protected by a lioness who first bowed at the girl's feet and then gave up her own life in defense of the saint:

And this excellent lioness showed clearly the impetuosity and the wrath of a lioness, but, when she approached, she made one rather think of a serving maid [therapainis].[73] And not only did she not touch the holy and sacred body, but she crouched at the feet of the virgin and assured her of her protection against the other wild animals. . . . It was already a miracle that the lioness did not touch Thecla; it was an even greater one that she even protected her, for the beasts are always beasts and have the nature that they have; it is God who then transforms them as he wishes, retaining in them their instincts, and makes them gentle and kind with regard to the saints when they remain cruel and fierce towards other people.[74]

According to St. Ambrose, Thecla's virginity was the reason she was spared.[75] But Thecla was not alone in her fortunate relationship with lions. Daria, a converted vestal virgin, when she was condemned to a brothel as a punishment for her Christian beliefs, was defended by a lion who had escaped from the amphitheater. He knocked down a man who had entered the saint's room with evil intent, and then looked at the saint "as if asking her what he should do." Telling the animal not to harm the man, Daria turned to her would-be assailant and said, "Behold, the ferocity of the lion, on hearing the name of Christ, reverences God, and you, a rational man, are engaged in great crimes. . . ."[76] According to a poem

72. Thecla did not die but was nevertheless counted as a martyr because she was forced to submit to the punishments inflicted on martyrs.

73. One wonders whether there is a pun here on *thēr*, beast of prey, particularly the lion (see Liddell and Scott, *Greek Lexicon, s.v.*).

74. *Vie et miracles de sainte Thècle* (1978), ed. Dagron, pp. 245–47; this paragraph is not included in the version of Symeon Metaphrastes.

75. *De virginibus*, II. 3 in *PL* 16, 211C.

76. *AA.SS.* Oct. XI, vol. 59, p. 482B (Oct. 25).

ascribed to Pope Damasus, the lion was sent by God for the specific purpose of defending Daria's virginity.[77]

In the many stories of saints defended by the beasts sent to kill them, a common detail is that the animal licks the soles of the saint's feet healingly,[78] or sometimes, in a healing fashion, his wounds.[79] Perhaps the nicest story concerns St. Anicetus, martyred under Diocletian. With a rare touch of verisimilitude the account of this saint testifies to his fear, and to a lion's compassion:

> An extremely large lion was sent against St. Anicetus, so that the saint was drenched with sweat from fear at the roaring of the monster (belua). Seeing this, the lion with his right paw and his tongue wiped the sweat from his face as though with a sponge.[80]

The metaphorical language used to describe the compassionate lions and bears displays a certain sameness, yet behind the clichés lies a consistent vision of the significance of the animals' actions. All terms of comparison, with varying degrees of explicitness, point to a reversal of codes, a change of nature. Paradoxically the animals (*bestia, belua*) refuse to act in accord with their "bestial" natures, while man is degraded and becomes worse than beast. The passion of Saints Carpus, Papylus, and their companions states of a bear that it "not only did nothing harmful nor acted savagely [agreste, agrion], nor, in a word, did anything bestial [beluinam, *thēriōdes*], but fell before their feet and embraced them in a friendly fashion [amice, *philikōs*]."[81] St. Thecla's protecting lioness called to mind a serving maid. The adjective applied to the bear's tongue that licked St. Panteleemon was "friendly toward man." This same account, moreover, makes plain the contrast in behavior between man and

77. *PL* 74, 529A.

78. E.g. Saints Clement of Ancyra; Paulinus, Marcellus and companions; Terentius and companions; Eleutherius. So pervasive, indeed, did this detail become that the *Synaxarium Alexandrinum* describes a lion licking Daniel's feet, although the bible contains no such incident; it does, however, occur as early as 337 A.D. in the homily of the Syriac father Aphraat (see below, p. 153).

79. St. Panteleemon (*PG* 115, 469–70BC); Sts. Probus, Tarachus, Andronicus, et al. (*AMS* p. 392; *PG* 115, 1077–78CD).

80. *AA.SS.* August II, vol. 36, p. 708A (Aug. 12). The sweat of St. Mamas was licked off by a leopard (*PG* 115, 574A).

81. *PG* 115, 123–24C.

beast, as the hagiographer wrote: "Then one could see something very new and delightful—men indeed transformed into the savagery of wild animals, while the animals seemed as if gifted with reason and could be believed to have human kindness."[82] Man's inhumanity to man is balanced by the compassion of savage creatures who recognize and reverence what the seemingly more rational humans do not, the majesty of God revealed in His saints. They remember what man has forgotten.

The most frequent term of comparison for the wild animals is the lamb—the fierce beast grows as gentle as this traditional emblem of mildness in the presence of the saints[83]—but two extended similes are more revealing. The lions sent to attack Clement of Ancyra and his companions looked upon the saints with gentle, kindly eyes and joyfully licked their feet, then leapt upon them in a "gentle" fashion, acting "not otherwise than dogs often do to their masters who have returned after a long absence."[84] Similarly a lion wept at the sight of Saint Eleutherius "like a father who sees his son after a long time."[85] What these comparisons have in common is the theme of memory; they depict joyful reunions. The identical motif is found in a pagan version of the same incident, as Aelian (b. 170 A.D.) told the popular story of Androcles and his lion to illustrate the proposition that animals possess the faculty of memory.[86] The animals remember a good state and forget an evil one. Symeon Metaphrastes describes the bear who licked the wounds of St. Probus and his companions as "forgetful of its wild nature" and the one who spared St. Trophimus as "forgetful of nature and hunger."[87]

82. PG 115, 469–70BC. The motif of the bestial judge became a *locus communis*; see Eusebius, *Liber de martyribus Palestinae*.
83. Marcellus, *AA.SS.* August VI, vol. 40, p. 15A (Aug. 27); Paulinus, *AA.SS.* July III, vol. 30, p. 258AB (July 12); Probus, *PG* 115, 1079–80A; Eleutherius, *AA.SS.* April II, vol. 11, p. 528E (April 18); Tarachus, *AMS*, p. 392.
84. *PG* 114, 853–54D. A similar detail finds its way into the Jewish tradition about Daniel. L. Ginzberg ("Daniel," *The Jewish Encyclopedia*, vol. 4, p. 428, cited by Hartman and Di Lella, *The Book of Daniel*, 1978, p. 24) records that the lions greeted Daniel "as faithful dogs receive their returning master."
85. *AA.SS.* April II, vol. 11, p. 529A (April 18).
86. Aelian, *On Animals* (1959), VII, 48.
87. *PG* 115, 747D.

In a study of the iconography of martyrdom in Africa, Salomonson notes a similar change in atmosphere occurring around 300 A.D.[88] The images lose the details of painful realism that characterized them before this time. For example, a plate illustrating a scene of *damnatio* shows the victim, a young girl, tied to the stake and approached by an enormous bear.[89] The bear puts its paws on the girl's shoulders but turns it head away. Amid the considerable body of folklore, pagan and Christian, that surrounds the arena, there is Aelian's version of the Androcles story. Tacitus and Pliny give similar accounts of beasts refusing to kill.[90]

The miracle of the merciful beast is a subset of a larger category of miracles in which the tyrant is unable to harm the saint by any means other than decapitation.[91] This type of miracle occurs so frequently that examples are unnecessary. It always serves to illustrate the impotence of evil, the power of God. The miracles involving compassionate beasts have, however, an added significance, for they contain a suggestion of the theme of recognition and reunion, as well as being a visible manifestation of God's power to alter nature for those He loves.[92] There is in the tales a hint of remembrance of the days when savage beasts had a different nature and did not harm men, a nostalgia for Paradise before the Fall.

The biblical precedent for dominion over lions is the story of Daniel who twice survived unscathed in the lions' den (Dan. 6 and 14).[93] The second time that Daniel underwent this ordeal,[94] he was shut in for seven days, and the beasts were starved beforehand so that they would be very hungry; nevertheless they spared the prophet, who claimed that he was unharmed because of the justness

88. Salomonson, *Voluptatem* (1979), p. 47.

89. Ibid. plate 39, p. 48, from a private collection.

90. Tacitus, *Histories* II.61 and Pliny, *Natural History*, VIII. 56.

91. For a discussion of this form of death, see Gaiffier, "Le glaive dans les passions des martyres," in *Recherches d'Hagiographie Latine* (1971), pp. 70 ff.

92. This latter meaning is explicit in Metaphrastes' account of the martyrdom of Sergius and Bacchus, *PG* 115, 1024A.

93. Chapter 14 of the Vulgate is not contained in the King James' Version, which ends with the Hebrew text at chapter 12. After their escape from the beasts, St. Clement of Ancyra and his companions offer prayers of thanksgiving to God: "You who were wholly with us, you who are the God of Daniel" (*PG* 114, 855A).

94. Cassin, "Daniel dans la 'fosse' aux lions" (1951), p. 152.

of his cause: God sent an angel, "et conclusit ora leonum, et non nocuerunt mihi, quia coram eo justitia inventa est" (Dan. 14:22; And he shut the mouths of the lions and they did not harm me because before Him justice was found). When, however, Daniel's accusers were thrown to the lions, they were devoured immediately. The story of Daniel's miraculous rescue belongs to the class of martyr tales in which the hero is willing to suffer death for his faith but is spared (as was Thecla), and the persecutors are punished.[95]

The tale was one of the most popular in early Christianity as an image of liberation and a symbol of the resurrection. There are no fewer than forty frescoes in the Roman catacombs of Daniel in the lions' den, the earliest, in the Catacomb of Domitilla, dating to the end of the first century A.D.[96] Daniel claimed innocence and purity as the reasons for his escape.[97] The early Fathers, however, connected Daniel's safety with his fasting, not mentioned in the Vulgate.

Daniel, vir desideriorum, trium hebdomadarum jejunio leones quoque docuit jejunare, missus in lacum, in adamantis rigorem, abstinentiae soliditate membra duratus non patuit vulneri. Sic eum constrinxerant jejunia, ut in ejus corpore ferarum morsibus locus esse non posset. Clausa tenebant leones ora, quae abstinentiae propheticae sanctitas comprimebat. . . . Jejunia ora obstruxit leonum.[98]

(Daniel, a man most dearly beloved, by a fast of three weeks taught lions too to fast; sent to the lake, he was hardened in his limbs to the hardness of steel; by the firmness of his fasting he was invulnerable. Fasts so compacted

95. Hartman, Book of Daniel (1978), p. 196.
96. See H. Leclerc, "Daniel," DACL, IV, cols. 224–27. Daniel in lacu leonum became almost de rigueur for the opening initial of the Book of Daniel in illuminated manuscripts. The illustrator of the Bible of Roda (10th or 11th century; ms. Paris, Bibliothèque Nationale, Fonds Latin, 6 [3]), a work whose illustrations have a remarkable penchant for scenes of violence, depicted both of Daniel's encounters with lions, showing the prophet first in lacu and then the lions swallowing the malefactors who had falsely accused Daniel (fols. 66r and 66v). A thirteenth-century bible (Paris, Bibl. nat. Lat. 22, fol. 304v) depicts a fine variant of the stock theme. Daniel is depicted not merely surrounded by lions, as is customary, but with his arms affectionately around the necks of two of the beasts. Salomonson, Voluptatem, has a lengthy discussion of the African material from an earlier era.
97. See Cassin, "Daniel dans la 'fosse' aux lions," pp. 147ff., for a long discussion of the meaning of "purity" in Aramaic.
98. St. Ambrose, Liber de Elia et jejunio, PL 14, 704B. St. Basil the Great echoed the sentiment that fasting (nēsteia) closed the lions' mouths (PG 31, 173C).

him that his body offered no place for the biting of wild beasts. The lions
held closed the jaws that the holiness of the prophet's abstinence fastened.
. . . Fasting blocked the lions' jaws.)

According to John Damascene, Daniel was saved because of his
chastity,[99] a view similar to Ambrose's assessment of the reason for
Thecla's salvation.

In the stories of non-martyr saints' power over animals, there is a
progression from the natural to the miraculous, from instances
where the beast, as in passion literature, refuses to harm the saint
(what we might characterize as negative assistance, where the animal witholds or restrains its natural violence), to those cases where
he performs a positive service. As early as 337 A.D. such details
have become a part of the Daniel legend. The Syriac father Aphraat
(died ca. 345 A.D.) composed a homily in which he recounted
Daniel's adventure in the lions' den; not only do the beasts in this
version refrain from eating the hero, but they kiss his feet and
actively assist him:

Daniel prayed, and his prayer shut the mouths of the voracious lions. . . .
The lions also stretched out their paws and caught Daniel so that he did not
hit the ground. They embraced him with their paws and kissed his feet. . . .
When Daniel wanted to lie down and go to sleep, the lions stretched themselves out so that he could sleep on their backs and not on the ground.[100]

Stories of the beasts' refusal to harm find their way into even the
more sober accounts. Athanasius in the *Vita Antonii* relates an
anecdote demonstrating this saint's control of wild creatures. When
Antony was living alone in the desert, the animals who came for
water damaged his crops; the saint, displeased, took one aside and
asked the reason. Thereafter he had no more trouble, "and the
fierce beasts, as it is written in Job, were peaceful with him."[101] In

99. *De fide orthodoxa* IV, 24, in *PG* 94, 1210A.
100. Translated for the first time from the Syriac by Di Lella in Hartman and Di
Lella, *The Book of Daniel* (1978) p. 22.
101. *Vita Antonii* 51.5; cf. Job 5:3. Of Antony's pact with the animals, Chitty
writes: "Already we have the picture, constant throughout our monastic documents,
of a relationship with animals which marks the recovery of the condition of Adam
before the Fall" (*The Desert a City*, p. 16).
Antony, like a number of other saints who cohabited peacefully with beasts, was
Egyptian. Te Velde notes that in the traditions of ancient Egypt, man was not the

the *Vita Malchi* the saint told Jerome how he and his wife were
saved from their pagan pursuers when a lioness burst from a cave in
which they were hiding and killed their enemies, but did not harm
them. The *Verba Seniorum* contains a story about a lion who, roaring and gnashing his teeth, made it plain that he did not wish to
share his cave with a passing hermit. The hermit said to him: "Why
are you upset? There is room enough for you and me. If you don't
like it, get up and leave." The lion left.[102] In the *Pratum Spirituale*
we read of another solitary who, whenever he found a lion's den,
would sleep there unharmed.[103]

A popular variant of the motif, "the beast who refuses to harm"
might be called "the grateful beast,"[104] for a number of stories tell of
an animal who, in gratitude for being healed by the saint, not only
does him no harm but even performs a service.[105] The best known
instance of this motif, and indeed one of the best known of all
hagiographic legends, is the story of St. Jerome and his lion, and in
consequence the animal becomes an almost obligatory element of
this saint's iconography. The tale, however, is a late addition to
Jerome's *vita*, occurring only in the third life printed in the *Patrologia Latina*, which probably dates to the end of the eleventh century
(*PL* 22, 210ff.; BHL 3870).[106] The story appears to have originated

---

lord but the partner of the animals; see "A Few Remarks" (1980). According to
Mackean, *Christian Monasticism in Egypt* (1920), p. 137, animal stories are characteristic of the accounts of Egyptian monks.

102. *Verba Seniorum* VI.2.15; *PL* 73, 1003.

103. *PG* 87, iii, 2865A.

104. A folk motif; see Thompson, *Motif Index* (1955), B 350 (many examples);
for the long career of the "grateful lion" in medieval literature, see below, ch. 8.

105. For a Proppian analysis of grateful-lion stories, see F. Amy de la Bretèque,
"L'épine enlevée de la patte du lion" (1980).

106. See Vaccari, "Le antiche vite di S. Girolamo" (1920). Vaccari noted that the
appearance of a lion on the banks of the Jordan (the location of St. Gerasimus'
monastery) was not improbable since they were found there during the Crusades,
but that the animals had disappeared from the mountains of Judea, the location of
Jerome's monastery, before the end of Jewish antiquity. The last reliable mention of
a lion in Judea is in Amos 3:10, 5:19, written in the eighth century B.C.; see Tristram, *The Fauna and Flora of Palestine* (1884). Erasmus criticized the story on the
grounds that it was a fable unworthy of so great a man (Waddell, *Beasts and Saints*
[1934], p. xii). On Jerome and the Lion, see Rice Jr., *St. Jerome in the Renaissance*
(1985) pp. 32–83.

in hagiographic literature with a saint of a similar name, St. Gerasimus (d. 475),[107] as told by John Moschus in the *Pratum Spirituale*,
chapter 107.[108] The transferral of the tale to the more popular
Jerome was presumably facilitated by the similarity of the names in
Latin.[109]

Like Jerome's lion, that of Gerasimus turned up one day with a
thorn in its paw. After the saint removed the thorn, the lion was
unwilling to leave Gerasimus but followed him about "like a loving
disciple." The saint fed his beast on bread and soaked legumes and
set him to guard the monastery's donkey. One day, however, when
the lion had wandered away, a passing camel driver stole the donkey. The lion was accused of having eaten his charge and was given
the donkey's work to do as a punishment. Some time later the thief
returned to the country; the lion recognized the donkey, frightened
away the thief, and brought the donkey back to the monastery. As a
reward the brothers named the lion Jordan. Some five years later
Gerasimus died, and "by divine providence" the lion happened to
be away from the monastery at the time. When he returned, Jordan
looked everywhere for his master. The brothers told him of the
saint's death and urged him to come to dinner, but the animal, roaring in grief, refused to eat and continued his search. Finally the
brothers took him out to the saint's grave. In sorrow Jordan beat
his head on the ground and died of grief on top of the tomb. To this
touching tale of loyalty, John Moschus added an explicit moral:
"This event occurred not because the lion had a rational soul, but
because God wished to glorify those who glorify Him, in both life
and death, and also to show us what subjection the beasts had to

107. For the confusion due to the similarity of names, see Aigrain, *L'Hagiographie* (1953), p. 173.
108. *PG* 87, iii, 2965–70. The story is not necessarily historical in the accounts
of Gerasimus. According to Vacarri, *Le antiche vite* (1920), the lion stories in the life
of Gerasimus published by Papadopulos Kerameus (1897) and in that attributed to
Cyril of Scythopolis, are certainly interpolations (p. 13).
109. Vaccari, *Le antiche vite*, (p. 13) noted that the confusion is only possible in
Latin, not Greek, since *Gerasimos* does not resemble *Hierōnymos*. The transferral of
the story probably occurred in Rome. Réau, *Iconographie* de l'art *chrétien* (1958),
III, 741, suggests that the transfer of Gerasimus' lion to Jerome was facilitated by the
identification of the four doctors of the Church with the four evangelists; Jerome
was identified with Mark, whose emblem is a lion.

the first man before he disobeyed the command, and before he was cast out from the earthly Paradise" (*PG* 87, iii, 2969B).

The lion episode is the only event in Gerasimus' life that John Moschus related. St. Gerasimus was popular and other writers provided additional information about him; for example, from the life of St. Euthymius told by Symeon Metaphrastes (*PG* 114, 673A), we learn of the holy father's extremely strict regime: when certain brothers asked Gerasimus to permit them the use of warm water, cooked food, and lamp light to read by, he told them that they had better depart for he would never in his life condone such behavior in anchorites. The composite picture of Gerasimus shows a strict omophage, living a life without fire in any form, being served miraculously by a lion who, in his turn, is willing to reverse the natural dietary code, abstaining from meat (the donkey), and living on bread and vegetables.

Cyril of Scythopolis (524–?) was another biographer with a taste for lion stories;[110] in two of his accounts the theme of innocence emerges plainly. Cyril's *vita* of St. Sabas contains several lion episodes, one of which closely parallels the account of St. Gerasimus and his lion.[111] Like Gerasimus, Sabas also removed a thorn from the paw of a wounded lion, and in gratitude the beast remained with the saint. Sabas had a servant named Flavius and a donkey. Whenever Flavius was away on business, the lion guarded the donkey. One day, however, Flavius fell into the sin of *luxuria*; that day the lion ate the donkey. St. Euthymius also possessed great power over animals; in his life of this saint (written ca. 577), Cyril offered the following explanation for it:

In addition to other graces that the holy Euthymius possessed, he also received from God that of sustaining no harm from the carnivorous and poisonous creatures with whom he lived all the time. One who is initiated in the Holy Scriptures will not doubt this fact, knowing full well that when

110. For Cyril, see Festugière, *Les Moines* (1961), p. 54. Cyril is generally well regarded and held to be one of the best Greek hagiographers, according to Irénée Hausherr, (*Dict. du spiritualité*, II, 2689).

111. Translated into French by Festugière, *Les Moines*, "La Vie de St. Sabas," III. 2, p. 65.

God lives and resides in a man, all beings are subject to him as they were to Adam before he transgressed God's commandment.[112]

According to the *vita* of Euthymius in Symeon Metaphrastes, Euthymius was an only child, the result of a miraculous birth, a *puer-senex* who, thinking monastic life an impediment to virtue, left the city in secret for the desert.[113] He was also a vegetarian.

Antony's fictitious biography of St. Simeon Stylites the Elder contains an apparent variant on the fable of the lion with a wounded paw, as this saint heals not a lion but a dragon with a stake in its eye.[114] The grateful monster remained for a long period of time in reverence of the saint and then departed, harming no one. This story is unusual for, according to Beryl Rowland: "Most dragons are not amenable to either physical or spiritual enlightenment."[115]

Two of the most charming tales of animals grateful for a saint's healing powers involve, not lions (animals often considered sympathetic, even when terrible), but an animal with a poor reputation, the hyena. The better known of the two is told by Palladius (*Historia Lausiaca*, 57.4–58.2) about St. Macarius the Egyptian (not to be confused with his Roman homonym). Once when the saint was praying in his cave, so the story goes, he was approached by a mother hyena who began to nibble on his toes to attract his attention. She then took him gently by the tunic and led him to her lair next door where she showed him her babies, who were blind. The saint prayed over them and restored their sight, and in gratitude the mother brought him the skin of a large sheep, which the saint accepted, but he made her promise to stop killing sheep.[116] (Hyenas,

---

112. Translated into French in *Ibid*. III. 1, p. 77.

113. *PG* 114, 606A.

114. *PL* 73, 330AB.

115. *Animals with Human Faces* (1974), p. 69. The reader may be surprised at the paucity of dragons in this study. A victory over a dragon in a hagiographic legend is usually interpreted as a defeat of heresy (Le Goff, "Culture ecclésiastique [1970]). A dragon is not attested in the stories about St. George before the twelfth century (J. B. Aufhauser, *Das Drachenwunder des heiligen Georg* [Leipzig, 1911], p. 237).

116. The tale is not in Rufinus, *Historia Monachorum*; Waddell translates from the French translation published by Amélineau of a Coptic version, *Histoire des*

like dogs and felines, are born blind, a fact that casts some doubt on the miraculous nature of Macarius' cure.) The second tale, found in the *Synaxarium Alexandrinum*, concerns a solitary named Anbā Hūb. One day this hermit was seated in his cave in prayer. A hyena gave birth to a lame cub and brought it to him, laying it at his feet and indicating that she wanted his help. The holy man touched the cub's feet and healed it, "whereupon the mother, rejoicing greatly, began to lick the feet of Saint Anbā Hūb." The cub was able to follow his mother home. The Synaxary explains the meaning of the episode:

Moreover, God brought all these things to pass to enhance the glory of His saints. And thus one may discover even what sentiments and decorous feelings the wild beasts, however fierce they may be, experience and follow. In the case of Daniel they revealed a wonderful and unheard-of love, such that they first put aside their savage nature, and then, muzzled by a holy miracle, they turned to licking the soles of the saint's feet.[117]

Parallels for the story of an animal grateful for being healed exist in pagan literature as well. The best known today is the story of Androcles and his lion, made popular by George Bernard Shaw and ultimately derived from the account of Claudius Aelianus, discussed above.[118] There exist a number of Oriental fables with the same motif, including grateful elephants and tigers who express their thankfulness to the hermit who has healed them by bringing him food and treasure.[119] The frequency with which the detail of a wounded foot appears[120] suggests that we may be dealing with allo-

---

Monastères de la Basse-Egypte (1894), p. 233 ff. In Palladius, the hyena brings her cubs to Macarius (*PG* 34 1060C).

117. *CSCO*, vol. 78, *Scriptores Arabici*, vol. 18, I, 127. The story is told on the same day that Abū Nafr (Onuphrius) is honored.

118. Aelian, however, remained altogether unknown in the Occident throughout the Middle Ages; see Krappe, "St. Patrick and the Snakes" (1947), p. 329.

119. See Johnston, "The Episode of Yvain, the Lion, and the Serpent" (1907), 161–62. Cosquin ("Contes populaires lorrains," [1881], pp. 141–42) thought that the theme of the grateful animal was Indian and revealed the influence of Buddhist thought.

120. A similar story is told of a St. Aventinus, a sixth-century presbyter in Gaul, who healed the wounded paw of a bear; *AA.SS.* Feb. I, vol. 4, p. 479 ff (Feb. 4). This hagiographic legend, however, may well be modeled on the better-known stories; it does testify to the popularity of the tale.

morphs of a single story. Furthermore, the grateful animal usually repays his benefactor by performing a helpful service. What man, in the figure of the saintly hermit, has to offer the animals in these tales is healing; in return the animals offer food, protection, and, in the oriental fables, wealth.[121]

Animals may also proffer help spontaneously, without being grateful for anything. The helpful beast is a frequent character in fairy tales: ants aid Psyche in *Cupid and Psyche*, while birds help Cinderella sort lentils from ashes in *Grimm's Fairy Tales* (no. 21— Aschenputtel). A common motif of descent, discussed above, was the presence of unusual guides (b^2), either angels (in which case the significance of the motif—the direct assistance of God—is apparent) or animals. A roaring stag and a dove guided the three monks to Macarius the Roman on their inward journey, and Macarius' two lions assisted them on the return trip. St. Antony was aided in his quest for Paul of Thebes by a hippocentaur and a she-wolf.[122] Here the animals' function as a helper is explicit.[123] These creatures are depicted not as refusing to fulfill a natural function (kill), or as repaying a debt, but as voluntarily performing a service for the saint.[124] In contrast to Dante's human guide in the *Divine Comedy*, the saint is generally denied (or refuses) help on the human plane, but he may be granted it from above (an angel) or from below (animals). Such tales, moreover, are not confined to obviously legendary accounts such as that of Macarius. One of Theodoret's subjects in the *Historia religiosa* is Simeon Priscus, an omophage and cave-dweller.[125] Of this saint Theodoret wrote: "By his labor

121. The animal as provider of treasure is perhaps a motif originally belonging to the narrative matrix of the traditional descent tale. Since the only treasure the hermit seeks is spiritual, its direct employment in the western, religious stories is inappropriate.

122. The episode with the wolf is treated purely naturally, not as a miraculous event, but the detail fulfills the same function whether or not it is considered a miracle.

123. In Propp's analysis (*Morphology*, p. 124), the helper or "donor" (D) is magical or gives a magical agent. Aid does not come to the hero in a natural fashion. In the hagiographic accounts, the magical becomes the miraculous.

124. The "guiding beast" is a common folklore motif; see Krappe, "Guiding Animals" (1942).

125. *Historia religiosa*, ch. 6, PG 82, iii, 1357–60.

[*ponos*] Symeon acquired such a treasury of heavenly grace that he controlled the most cruel and ferocious beasts" (1357C). He lived in the company of two lions. One day a party of Jewish merchants lost their way in the desert during a sand storm; finding Simeon's cave, they asked the hermit (who resembled an animal himself, being dirty and dressed in skins), to guide them to the road. At this moment the lions returned home, looking not like fierce beasts but like tame, domesticated animals. In compliance with the saint's orders, they led the merchants back to safety. Aware of possible scepticism concerning this account, Theodoret protested: "Let no one think this story to be fictional [*mythōdes*]." First, he was quick to point out that the witnesses to this miracle were hostile, since they were Jewish, and on that account even more reliable. Second, Theodoret claimed as his authority for the tale that he was told it "by the great Jacob who said he was there when the Jews told the story to the holy Maro" (1360A). The story, then, comes with a pedigree of sanctity ("great Jacob," "holy Maro") designed to dispel doubt.

Another category of miracle in which helpful animals appear prominently is as providers of food, not, since most of the saints were strict vegetarians, as animals usually "provide" food—by being eaten—but by actually bringing nourishment to them. We have already mentioned the service of Androcles' lion in this respect. As with the refusal to harm, this motif is a subset of a larger complex of miracles involving the theme of nourishment. The theme has two manifestations in hagiographic accounts—either the saint is able to survive for prodigious lengths of time without food or water,[126] or they are miraculously provided for him.[127] Both man-

---

126. The forty-day fasts in the wilderness of Elijah, Moses, and Christ, are frequently adduced parallels, which, among the more historic saints, only Simeon Stylites the Elder attempted to imitate. Among the legendary accounts, we may read of St. Mamas, a martyr whose romantic biography displays many traditional motifs (he was an only child, born in prison; beasts refused to harm him). He spent forty days in prison without food or water and was celebrated as a second Moses (*PG* 115, 565 ff.). The three monks claimed that they spent eighty days in prison without food or water, and Mary the Egyptian lived for seventeen years on two half loaves of bread and grass.

127. There are pagan parallels to these legends; Porphyry (*Vita Pythagorae*, ch.

ifestations suggest a hero who differs from normal men in respect to the basic necessities of life and express a nostalgia for a way of life in which one did not have to worry about physical sustenance. They represent a longing for the *angelikos bios* of Paradise[128] or for the womb.

Perhaps the best-known instance of an animal's bringing food is the crow who for years had been supplying Paul of Thebes with a half loaf of bread but, when Antony arrived, brought a full loaf. This episode has an obvious ancestor in the account of Elijah fed by a raven (I Kings 17:6). When Eleutherius was in prison, a dove brought him food, and the saint adduced as a parallel for this act the feeding of Elijah "in the desert" and Daniel "among the lions."[129]

The motif of miraculous feeding has two allomorphs in the tales under consideration here, b^1 and d^4. In both of these motifs, as well as in the related journey motif of unusual guides, b^2, the role of adjuvant is shared between angels and animals. Angels both guide and sustain Macarius, Paphnutius, Onuphrius, and Serapion on their respective journeys into the desert. When Paphnutius discovers Onuphrius, he observes bread and water mysteriously being provided for them, an event that happens again when he visits the four hermits.

The motif of angelic nurture goes back to our oldest documents. According to Mark 1:13, during Christ's forty-day sojourn in the desert, "He was with the beasts and angels ministered to him." The fourth-century Bodmer papyrus of the *Protevangelium of James* re-

---

34, claims that Pythagoras was nourished on *alimon* "that which takes away hunger" prepared from mallows and asphodel, mixed with poppy seed, sesame, barley, chick peas, and other ingredients (Augustus Nauck, ed., *Porphyrii Opuscula Selecta*, 2d ed., [Leipzig: Teubner, 1886] p. 35). The miraculous provision (or discovery) of water is a commonplace; it is one of the miracles of the infant Jesus in the *Gospel of Pseudo-Matthew*; see also the *Vita Antonii*, ch. 54.

128. Angels neither eat nor sleep; cf. St. Ambrose, *Liber de Paradiso, PL* 14, 294C: "quia qui non bibunt, neque manducant, erunt sicut angeli in caelo" (for since they neither drink nor eat they will be as the angels in heaven). Arbesmann, "Fasting" (1949–50), p. 3, writes of the vision of an ideal world where man would be able to live without any earthly food.

129. *AA.SS.* April II, vol. 11, p. 528D (April 18) (*in deserto, inter leones*).

counts that the Virgin Mary lived as a child in the Temple and received nourishment from the hand of an angel.[130] The motif enjoyed the widest popularity. Rufinus' *Historia Monachorum* (X.25) contains the story of a monk named Copres who claimed to have been transported bodily to paradise where he spent five weeks, during which time a figure (presumably an angel) brought him food and water and then disappeared. The importance of the motif of miraculous feeding is confirmed by its seemingly unnecessary inclusion in the highly romantic *Acta* of St. Christina, an only child shut up in a tower by her father. An angel appears to her, and suddenly bread miraculously appears, whereupon Christina thanks this divine messenger, saying that she has touched no bread for twelve days. The hagiographer offers no explanation for this event, and we have no reason to believe that her father was starving her, but the detail's importance seems to call for its inclusion in this legendary account whether or not the plot necessitates it. The appearance of angels to comfort imprisoned saints is a commonplace of hagiographic narrative (St. Vincent of Saragossa, to give only one example from many), but most frequently the aid they bring is spiritual rather than material, perhaps in keeping with their spiritual nature. Material comfort is more often supplied by members of the animal kingdom.

Monastic histories show a considerable penchant for tales of animals aiding saints in other ways, which range from the merely improbable to the patently fabulous.[131] In the *Historia Monachorum* of Rufinus we may read of the blessed Ammon who, after thieves stole his bread, acquired dragons (or snakes) to serve as watchdogs, or of the Abbot Helenus who asked wild asses to help him carry his burdens and was ferried across a river by a crocodile,[132] as was St. Pachomius, according to his biography in the

130. Strycher, *La Forme plus ancienne du Protévangile de Jacques* (1961), p. 100; also Kassel, "*Acta Pauli*" (1960).

131. For a collection of translations of these tales, see Waddell, *Beasts and Saints* (1934).

132. Rufinus, *Hist. Mon., PL* 21, ch. 8, col. 421 (Ammon); ch. 11, col. 430 (Helenus). Cf. Palladius, *PG* 34, 1159, ch. 59.

Vitae Patrum.[133] According to the first-person account by Cyril of
Scythopolis, St. Cyriacus (d. 556), a disciple of two renowned lion-
tamers, Saints Gerasimus and Euthymius, had a lion who protected
his few vegetables from the depredations of wild goats and human
robbers. Cyril relates that as he was coming to visit Cyriacus in the
company of Abbot Joannes, a huge lion appeared on the road.
Cyril, not unnaturally, was terrified, but Joannes reassured him,
telling him that the lion would guide them to the holy father.[134] The
Dialogues of Gregory the Great also contain two tales of helpful
beasts: an unnamed monk employs a serpent to defend his vegetable garden from a thief (I.3), while in III.15 Gregory tells the
touching story of a lonely monk named Florentius who prayed to
God to send him a companion. Going out of his hut he found a bear
who became the guardian of his sheep until jealous monks slew the
beast.[135]

Lion stories are told even about Jesus, and in them the traditional
motifs are present. According to the *Gospel of Pseudo-Matthew*,
first dragons and then lions and "pards" adored the Holy Family on
the Flight into Egypt and served them as guides (b^2): "Similiter
leones et pardi adorabant eum et comitabantur cum eis in deserto;
quocumque Maria et Joseph ibant, antecedebant eos, ostendentes
viam, et inclinantes capita sua adorabant Jesum"[136] (Similarly, lions
and leopards adored him and accompanied them in the desert;
wherever Mary and Joseph went, they preceded them and showed
them the way and, bowing down their heads, adored Jesus). The
same work contains another anecdote, even more revealing, about
the eight-year-old Jesus. In a cave on the road from Jericho to the
Jordan, a lioness had given birth, and no one dared to go there.
When the boy Jesus entered the cave, however, the lions ran to him

133. *PL* 73, 241C. In the Bohairic life (Veilleux, *Pachomian Koinonia*, (1980), p.
43), a more probable version is given, as Pachomius refuses to take fright when a
crocodile appears in the river and splashes water in its face, bidding it go away,
which it does.
134. *AA.SS.* Sept. VIII, vol. 48, p. 156 (Sept. 29).
135. *Dia.* I.3: *PL* 77, 163B–165A; *Dia.* III.15: *PL* 77, 251–52.
136. Michel, ed., *Protévangile de Jacques*, (1924), I, 144.

and adored him. The child sat down, and the cubs ran about his feet and played with him, while the adult lions, with lowered heads, stood at a distance, "fawning on him with their tails." When Jesus left the cave, accompanied by the lions, he said: "How much better than you are the beasts, who recognize their Lord and glorify Him, while you men, who are made in the image and likeness of God, ignore Him. The beasts know me and grow gentle; men see me and know me not" (p. 146). These stories contain the traditional motifs of animal guides, animals who recognize innocence and sanctity, and the concomitant lack of recognition on the part of men.

The most interesting of the purely voluntary, spontaneous services performed by lions is burial. Jerome seems to have established this motif in his biography of Paul of Thebes; where he got it is another question, to which we shall return. The motif is "imitated" or reused in the account of Mary the Egyptian, although one lion was enough, apparently, to bury a woman. It recurs in a late version of the legend of Onuphrius[137] and is a prominent feature of the fabulous life of Macarius.

In all these lion stories there is a double miracle, or a double, and seemingly contradictory, movement between codes. Simeon gives orders to his lions, an act that recalls Gen. 1:28 where God gave Adam dominion over the beasts.[138] St. Ambrose writes of this primal state:

Videbatur nihil elephantis creatura habere robustius, nihil tam terribile vel procerum, nihil tam ferum quam leones vel tigrides sunt; et haec serviunt

137. Petrus de Natalibus, *Catalogus*, V., ch. 106, f. 102v.
138. In patristic texts the animals in this context are usually allegorized as the passions. In the *De hominis structura oratio*, I (*PG* 30, 36C), ascribed, probably incorrectly, to St. Basil, the animals represent the vices of anger, madness, deceit, and so forth (for the authorship of this work, see Quasten, *Patrology* III [1960], 216; and E. Amand, "Les états de texte des homélies pseudo-basiliennes sur la création de l'homme" [*Revue Bénédictine* 59 (1949), 3–54]). St. Augustine, "De Genesi contra manichaeos," ch. 20, "Bestiis dominari per allegoriam," considered that animals were dominated by the force of man's "intellectus"; they were to be understood "spiritualiter" as "omnes affectiones et motus animi" (all the feelings and movements of the mind) which man dominates "per temperantiam et modestiam" (by self-restraint and moderation) (*PL* 34, 188A).

homini, et naturam suam humana institutione deponunt. Obliviscitur quod nata sunt.[139]

(No creature seems to have a stronger nature than the elephant, none are so terrible and large, none so fierce as lions and tigers; and yet these serve men and put aside their nature at man's disposal. They forget the nature that they were born with.)

Simeon gains his dominion from his toil (*ponos*), but when toil was Adam's lot after the Fall, he lost command over the animals, and they became his foes. The role of *ponos* here seems paradoxical, for the toil that earns Simeon his return to the primitive state is usually viewed as an attribute of culture. Hesiod, for one, in the *Works and Days* pictures men in the Golden Age living "without toil [*ponos*] and grief," gathering the fruits that the earth provided spontaneously (vv. 113, 118). But Simeon's toil is spiritual, and like Macarius he has become a second Adam, reborn to innocence and friendship with animals.[140]

At first glance, the lions might seem to have reversed the spatial movement of the hermits, moving from nature to culture, serving man in the capacity of domesticated animals. Simeon's beasts enter his cave, wagging their tails and giving indications of their servitude.[141] The wild lion who digs the grave of St. Mary the Egyptian returns to the desert "like a domesticated creature," or, in the Latin version of Paul the Deacon, like its traditional victim, the sheep (quasi ovis mansueta).[142] The lioness who defends Thecla is compared to a serving maid. But it is more correct to see in these animals' behavior a movement paralleling the saints', for they have abandoned their post-lapsarian nature and returned to their original state, "forgetting the nature they were born with" (obliviscitur quod nata sunt), as St. Ambrose writes. Their return to paradise is most obvious in the dietary code. Macarius nurtures his lion cubs on leaves; Gerasimus' animal rejects donkey meat and eats bread

139. Hexaemeron VI.6; *PL* 14, 255B.
140. See Chitty, *The Desert a City*, quoted above, n. 101, concerning Antony's pact with the animals.
141. *PG* 82, iii, 1360A.
142. *PG* 87, iii, 3725: ὡς πρόβατον; *PL* 73, 690A.

and vegetables instead. According to St. Basil, in Paradise lions and other carnivores ate only the fruits that Nature provided.[143] Lions, moreover, do not normally live with other animals; they are also nocturnal.[144] The lions who, in contradiction to nature live peaceably with the anchorites, are also active by day, a fact made explicit in the *Vita Macarii* where the animals "go outside by day" (per diem foras ambulantes).

Power over lions is not limited to Christian saints. Ignace Goldziher cites a catalogue of twenty typical miracles performed by Islamic saints, of which number five reads: "The savage beasts grow mild in their presence and submit to their will." He notes that biographies often depicted the hero riding on the backs of lions, the "dogs of Allah."[145]

The lion is a potent, bi-valent symbol, evoking both good and evil, and the roots of this symbolism extend far back into eastern (semitic) and Egyptian belief. His conquest is the appropriate symbolic action for the monk. While the specific origins of the Daniel legend are a matter for dispute,[146] the story of a god who closes the mouth of a lion or some other ferocious beast about to devour an innocent victim is an ancient part of the oriental religious repertory.[147] The symbolism of the lion is complex. He stands both for the power of evil and, as the "king of beasts," for God's might.[148] He is a symbol of the resurrection. His use as a solar symbol is due to his tawny color as well as to his savage nature. His positive aspects seem related to this symbolism: justice, courage, power, magnanimity, pity, and royalty.[149] Elena Cassin writes: "The lion is, in a sense, the symbol of everything that does not obey man, of sav-

143. Also in Pseudo-Basil; *De hominis structura oratio* II, PG 30, 45A.

144. For lions living apart, see St. Ambrose, *Hexaemeron* VI, ch. 3; PL 14, 247A. St. Basil, *Hexaemeron* 9. 3; PG 29, 192C, describes the lion as a savage and "monastic" beast.

145. "Le culte des saints chez les musulmans" (1880 rpt. 1971).

146. Cassin, "Daniel dans la 'fosse' aux lions", pp. 131ff.

147. Ibid. p. 145; she gives examples from Babylonia.

148. Originally in Europe (Italy and Germany) it was the wolf, not the lion, who was king of the beasts. Only in comparatively recent times did the Hellenes adopt the notion of the lion as king from Assyria and Persia; Maury, *Croyances* (1863), p. 214.

149. See Igarashi-Takeshita, "Les lions dans la sculpture romane" (1980), 45ff.

age, non-socialized nature, thicket and desert."[150] In the Christian tradition, the devil may be depicted as a roaring lion (1 Pet. 5:8), but the animal is also the instrument of divine vengeance in both the Near Eastern and Hebrew traditions.[151] In Apoc. 5:5 he represents Christ.[152] It is his savage nature that makes him the appropriate executioner of divine will, and that, therefore, makes the one who controls him "like to the gods." His image consequently is depicted at the limits of the socialized world, on the gates at Susa, for example, or at Mycenae. Power over lions, in the Hebrew, Christian, and Arab traditions, is the "touchstone of sanctity and purity."[153]

Such then, is the meaning of the stories about the saints and lions. The wild beasts, savage with evil-doers, perceive and respect the innocence and purity of the saint. The hermit, in his turn, rejecting the civilized life of the *polis*, and experiencing a symbolic death and burial, reascends into the desert paradise where he lives in peace with beasts. He has earned this reward by ascetic fasting and virginity. Such saints have, in this respect as in others, recovered the lost dream of an existence led in harmony with the environment. The Peaceable Kingdom is theirs, paradise regained.

Habitabit lupus cum agno, et pardus cum haedo accubabit: vitulus et leo, et ovis simul morabuntur, et puer parvulus minabit eos. (Isa. 11:6)

(The wolf also shall dwell with the lamb, and the leopard shall lie down with the kid; and the calf and the young lion and the fatling together; and a little child shall lead them.)

150. "Le lion est, dans un sens, le symbole de tout ce qui n'obéit pas à l'homme, de nature sauvage et non-socialisée, brousse et désert" (Cassin, p. 156).

151. Heidel, *Epic of Gilgamesh,* tablet XI, 182 (1963); 1 Kings 17:24; 2 Kings 17:25–27; in the *Apocryphal Acts of Thomas,* a wine-pourer who struck Thomas was killed by a lion when he went to a fountain to draw water (*Apocryphal Gospels,* trans. Walker, p. 393).

152. A thirteenth-century manuscript (Paris, Bibliothèque Nationale, Fonds Latin, 8865, fol. 43r) depicts the lion as the *agnus Dei,* carrying the cross; in the same manuscript the lion is shown as the executioner of vengeance, as the four horsemen of the Apocalypse, wielding swords, are portrayed riding on lions, and the lions are biting people (fol. 37r).

153. Cassin, p. 160.

Chapter 7

The Saint as Liminal Hero

Nothing makes plainer the distance between classical Greek thought and the ethos of early Christian legends, whatever the debt of the latter to the former, than the affinity between saints and animals. Homer has Achilles tell Hector: ὡς οὐκ ἔστι λέουσι καὶ ἀνδράσιν / ὅρκια πιστά (*Iliad* 22:262; There are no trustworthy oaths between lions and men). For the Greeks, man and beast were incontrovertibly different. Animals were "other"; they existed for man's benefit, and it was a "just law" of nature that man should use them as he saw fit, as beasts of burden and means of transportation, as sources of food and sacrificial victims.[1] For the Greeks, eating the cooked meat of animals killed in the ritual of sacrifice separated them from beasts. Animals, including herbivores, ate their food raw, and the opponents of vegetarianism used the argument that for man to give up eating the cooked flesh of animals would be to risk leading a bestial life.[2] If a man became an animal, as in the myths of metamorphosis, this state was a punishment, usually for sexual transgression (e.g. Actaeon, Callisto, Tereus, Atalanta, and Hippomenes). According to Aristotle's well-known definition of man as a "political" animal, a creature of the *polis*, the city, the solitary man must be either "a beast or a god,"[3] and behind such a

1. Aristotle, *Politics* I. 1256b7–26; for discussion see Detienne, "Between Beasts and Gods" (1981), p. 218. See also Vidal-Naquet, "Bêtes, hommes et dieux chez les Grecs," pp. 129–42, especially 130–32.
2. Porphyry, *De Abstinentia* I.6. See Detienne (above n. 1), p. 219.
3. *Politics* I. 1253a2–7.

168

statement lurked the idea that both non-human states were perilous, encountered only at risk. The beast-men such as the centaurs,
although occasionally helpful to man (e.g. Achilles' tutor, Chiron),
generally were lust-ridden and dangerous (e.g. Nessus).

With Aristotle's formulation the desert anchorite might have
agreed whole-heartedly, but for him it was the civilized state that
was dangerous.[4] The purity he sought was to be found in the desert
solitude, away from the corrupting world of men, the pollution,
moral and physical, of the cities. His mythology, unlike the Greeks',
contained an account of the origins of animals that paralleled, and
indeed preceded, his own. God created first the beasts and then man
to whom He gave dominion over the animals. We have seen how
often the moralizing comments added to stories of saints and animals point to man as having become worse—harder, more cruel, less
reverent—than the irrational beasts. If man may be thought of as
existing midway between the beasts and the angels, the hermit left
men's cities and went to join the animals in order to earn the right
to live the *angelikos bios*.[5] For the classical Greek the ritualization
of killing in sacrifice marked the difference between God and man;
for the Christian saint not death but the special powers acquired in
life, such as miraculous healing, marked an existence that approached the divine.

There is no doubting the popularity of such figures as Paul of
Thebes, Macarius, Onuphrius, or Mary the Egyptian[6]—the hairy
hermits, the holy beast-men and -women of the desert.[7] Such heroes

4. Resch, "La Doctrine ascétique" (1931), p. 31, writes that for the Egyptian
monks the world was one of three great sources of sin; the other two were the devil
and one's own concupiscence.

5. Peter Brown, however, has pointed out that historically this free-floating ideal
was a Syrian one; such a life was not physically possible in the extremely harsh Egyptian desert ("The Rise and Function of the Holy Man" [1971], p. 82).

6. Onuphrius, together with St. John Chrysostom, was the most popular type of
hairy anchorite in the East; see Réau, *Iconographie de l'art chrétien* (1958), III,
1009. St. Mary the Egyptian was the most popular saint of all those in the *Vitae
Patrum*; Bate, "La vie de sainte Marie l'Egyptienne" (1916–17).

7. The list of hairy hermits given by Williams (*Oriental Affinities*) is completed
by Peeters in his review of Williams appearing in *AB* 47 (1929), 138–41. Williams
notes a general tendency throughout the East for "the solitary beast-man to coalesce
with the holy man, the religious recluse" (I, 25).

represent a direct antithesis to the cultural ideals of classical anti-quity. The ideal society has become rural not urban, the "good life" is to be sought in the desert, not in the *oikoumenē*, the inhabited world that for classical man was all that mattered.[8] The goals of the ascetic life were alienation and separation—total estrangement from the values of the classical and urban past,[9] and the animal-like hermit attained it to a superlative degree. He (or she) looked like an animal and lived its life. Like the beasts, hair was his only bodily covering; the hermit ate animals' food—grass—and lived in anim-als' lairs, often sharing them with the original inhabitants. Such a life was one of peaceful coexistence, even of membership in the animal family: Macarius, we recall, raised his lion cubs "as his own sons," (ut proprios filios). Furthermore, according to St. Ephrem, the animals of the desert offered a paradigm for the life of complete freedom to which the solitary hermit must aspire, fleeing the com-pany of men.[10] John Chrysostom, in his treatise answering those who oppose the monastic life, writes, that in living closer to nature in the desert, the monk "is healthy in body like the wild animals."[11] This attitude transforms the desert from the sterile place of death and desolation to the locus, par excellence, of purity. It simulta-neously transforms nature: the animals have been changed from harmful monsters, types of the devil, to friends and even to models. The saint, however, whatever he may do, does not want to become an animal but to live the *angelikos bios*. The animals, then, are sym-bols, the desert but a stage in a journey.

The importance of the theme of the journey is apparent in the more mythic accounts such as those of Onuphrius and Paphnutius and of Macarius the Roman. The saint's ultimate goal is Paradise, but the road leading to it is often a difficult one (remember the

8. Browning, "The 'Low Level' Saint's Life" (1980), p. 127.
9. Chronologically, the rise of the holy man coincides with the erosion of classi-cal institutions (P. Brown, "Rise and Function").
10. *Sermo de monachis* 3, cited in Penco, "Il simbolismo animalesco nella letter-atura monastica" (1964).
11. *Adversus Oppugnatores eorum qui Vitam Monasticam Inducunt, PG* 47, 338.

adventures of the three monks). Of such quests, Mircea Eliade writes:

The road is arduous, fraught with perils, because it is, in fact, a rite of the passage from the profane to the sacred, from the ephemeral and illusory to reality and eternity, from death to life, from man to the divinity.[12]

Another approach to mythic structures also refers to rites of passage. Campbell compares what he calls the "nuclear unit of the monomyth" to the tripartite structure of rites of passage (see below), and finds evidence for this pattern in all hero myths.[13] The ritual paradigm has an even more specific relevance for the life of the desert ascetic, and the symbolism of initiation is elaborated in detail. In archaic cultures fasting is almost always linked to rites of renewal and initiation.[14] The saint's life of *askēsis* is a ritual preparation for the life to come in paradise. The existence of the saint in the desert is therefore liminal, transitional. This hero is a marginal figure, his story pervaded with symbols of marginality.

Rites de passage are ritualized responses to a change in status—in identity—and they surround with symbols the transition between, for example, childhood and adulthood, between non-membership and membership in the community. Such rites are almost always regarded as those of status-elevation.[15] They involve a negation of many features of preliminal social structure and an affirmation of another order of things or relations.[16] In his classic study of *rites de passage*, Arnold van Gennep distinguishes three phases in the ritual: separation, margin or *limen*, and aggregation.[17] In separation the individual is detached from an earlier fixed point in the social structure. For those belonging to the rigidly codified society of Late Antiquity, separation must have been particularly traumatic. During the liminal phase, the characteristics of the subject are ambi-

12. Eliade, *Cosmos and History* (1954), p. 18.
13. *The Hero*, p. 30.
14. *Dictionnaire de Spiritualité*, s.v. "Jeûne," 1165.
15. Turner, *The Ritual Process* (1969), pp. 157–58).
16. Ibid., p. 196.
17. See Turner, *Ritual Process*, p. 80, which draws on van Gennep, *The Rites of Passage* (1909; rpt. 1960).

guous, as he passes through a cultural realm that has few or none of the attributes of either his past or future conditions. With aggregation he returns once again to a relatively stable state.

Liminality is frequently likened to death, to being in the womb, or to being in the wilderness.[18] In general, the rites associated with liminality take place outside the everyday world, outside the *polis*, often in forests or caves.[19] The liminars (those in liminal states) may be represented as possessing nothing, and they may wear only a strip of clothing or go naked. Their behavior is usually passive or humble, and among themselves they are egalitarian, secular distinctions of rank and status tending to disappear.[20] Liminal phenomena offer a blend of lowliness and sacredness. Finally, liminars usually practice sexual continence, since sexuality is seen as belonging to social structure, and is not, therefore, a part of the unstructured "nature" of liminality.[21]

Liminality is a condition or state where opposites meet, where some negatives become positive. This fact is of utmost importance for the accounts of the desert saints, where one may oberve the frequent coalescence of man's two opposites, angels and animals, as they fulfill the same functions—guides and food-providers, protectors, and even *psychopompoi*. In liminality there is abundant reference to beasts, birds, and vegetation. Of this state, Victor Turner writes that "when man ceases to be a master and becomes the equal or fellow of man, he also ceases to be the master and becomes the equal or fellow of nonhuman beings." He goes on to note that "theranthropic figures combining animal with human characteristics abound in liminal situations," as do humans with animal characteristics. "Even angels may be regarded in this way—as ornithanthropic figures—messengers betwixt and between absolute and relative reality."[22]

For such liminal situations, the desert provided an admirable literal and metaphoric location. It offered a nexus of powerful but

18. *Ritual Process*, p. 81.   21. Ibid., p. 90.
19. Ibid., p. 196.   22. Ibid., pp. 252–53.
20. Ibid., p. 81.

often contradictory symbols:[23] the place of death in which grows
the tree of life, the date-palm, inhabited by angels and demons and
by the lion, symbol of both Christ and the devil. The life of the true
solitary in the wilderness represents a complete rejection of the
structures and institutions of the *polis* (coenobitic monasticism involved structure, but its opposition to secular life was almost as
dramatic as that of the anchorite). The monk endures the hardship
of the desert to merit admission into a different, and far better,
order of things.

There is scriptural precedent for this view of the desert as a liminal space, "betwixt and between," where miracles could happen.
Of *limina*, thresholds, Edmund Leach writes:

Thresholds, both physical and social, are a focus of taboo for the same
reason that, in the Bible, inspired sacred persons, who converse face to face
with God, or who, in themselves, have attributes which are partly those of
mortal man and partly those of immortal God, almost always experience
their inspiration in a "betwixt and between" locality, described as "in the
wilderness," which is neither fully in This World nor in The Other.[24]

Moses is given the law by God while he is isolated on Mt. Sinai
(Exod. 19–20). The miracle of Christ's feeding of the five thousand,
one of the few miracles reported by all four Evangelists, occurs in
"a desert place apart" (Matt. 14:13).[25]

André Droogers, applying Turner's studies of marginal situations
to his own anthropological research in Africa, has listed the following set of oppositions symbolic of liminality: nature versus culture;
traveling and provisional lodging versus the sedentary life; non-
violence versus violence; solidarity—Turner's fundamental concept
of *communitas*—versus hierarchy; isolation and seclusion versus
life in the heart of society; hardship and ordeal versus comfort; dirt
versus cleanliness; poverty and begging versus wealth; fasting versus eating.[26] For many he notes an additional category, shaving the

23. See Guillaumont, "La concéption du désert" (1975).
24. Leach and Aycock, *Structuralist Interpretations* (1983), p. 16.
25. Ibid., p. 103.
26. Droogers, "Symbols of Marginality" (1980).

head. If we modify this characteristic to "uncommon treatment of the hair," the hairy hermit fits perfectly. As Droogers points out, each symbolic state is an inversion of the normal, the generally accepted. He then goes on to analyze the lives of a series of religious leaders: Jesus, Waldes, William Booth (founder of the Salvation Army), Kimbongu (a Zaire prophet), Buddha, Mohammed, and finally someone not properly speaking a "religious" leader, Karl Marx. He finds the biographies of these leaders pervaded by symbols of marginality. For example, an association with nature, the open air, gardens, parks, occurs in all cases except that of Karl Marx. All showed an affinity for wandering or travel, for isolation and seclusion, for poverty, hardship, and ordeal. All, moreover, had contact with marginal people and counted marginals among their followers, and all manifested strained relations with the establishment.

The desert solitaries conform admirably to these symbolic categories. They rejected the life of the city for one lived in the *interior mons*, the desert solitude. They journeyed away from civilization into the wilderness where they dwelt in caves or rude huts. Rejecting violence, they lived in peace with the animals. They welcomed temporary visitors unless they found their celebrity a deterrent to ascetic life, and they eventually formed communities (coenobitic monasticism), where the traditional distinctions based on wealth and kinship were obliterated and members addressed each other as "brother."[27] They categorically relinquished wealth and hierarchy; begging enters into the accounts of later manifestations of the ascetic ideal such as the *Life of Saint Alexis*.[28] The ascetic totally rejected any form of creature comfort such as baths, clean clothes, haircuts, and the like, and the most strict refused any use of fire. As for association with other marginals, stories of repentant prostitutes are common (Mary Magdalen, Mary the Egyptian, Maria Meretrix, Thais), and such persons are doubly marginal, being both women and prostitutes. John the Baptist, a frequently invoked forerunner

27. Turner, *Ritual Process*, p. 97.
28. Gieysztor, "La légende de saint Alexis en occident" (1974).

of the anchorites, is one of Droogers' examples of a marginal. All the biographies discussed by Droogers show strained relationships with the establishment. Our tales do not reveal this characteristic explicitly, but the frequency of the motif of secret flight implies a certain resistance in society to the hermit's proposed course of action. The saint's secret flight from marriage in particular displays an open antipathy to accepted cultural norms. The hermits, moreover, were regarded as outsiders, strangers,[29] as *akathistoi*, rootless men.[30] They obstinately owed nothing to society.[31]

The fact that the lives of the desert dwellers narrate a form of *rite de passage* helps to explain the prominence of certain themes and motifs. The theme of the encounter (D) is central to all but the briefest of anecdotes. On the surface there is no apparent reason for the obligatory and educational nature of this episode; but in almost every case the desert traveler, after a form of symbolic death, meets an older hermit who has dwelt in the desert for a long time and shares with the neophyte the wisdom he has gained. To give only one example, Onuphrius meets an old man who teaches him about the life of desert *askēsis*. This obligatory father figure who passes on experiential wisdom is a form of initiator, an older initiate who guides and educates the liminar. The sacral nature of this task is indicated by the number of motifs that separate this encounter from normal experience, for example the many miracles that punctuate the narrative of this meeting.

One of the major forms of liminality is death. In initiation rites, the biological order of birth and death is paradoxically reversed as

---

29. Cf. the Abbot Olympius' advice that the monk constantly repeat the phrase "I am a stranger" (*PG* 87, iii, 2861). In the eyes of some ascetics, the *xenos monachos*, the wanderer, possessed greater virtue than did the more settled, the *entopioi* (Rousseau, *Ascetics, Authority, and the Church* [1978], p. 43). The life of Onuphrius exemplifies, and indeed gives explicit voice, to such an ideal. See also the discussion of *xeneteia* in Guillaumont, "Dépaysment."

30. Rousseau (above, n. 29), p. 43.

31. See Peter Brown, "The Rise and Function," p. 91, on the significance of becoming a stranger. Brown notes, moreover, that this "stranger" is not to be confused with the miracle-worker, the "divine man," *theios anēr*, of late Antiquity. In the *Life of St. Alexis*, the saint's flight from Edessa (or Alsis in some Old French versions) is due to the fact that his anonymous status as a stranger is threatened.

"one dies to become a little child."[32] The old identity must be shed before the new one is assumed. In chapter 5, "The Downward Journey," we examined the many forms of symbolic death that the saint encountered. Indeed, death is one of the most consistent elements in a genre that goes under the general rubric of *vita*. Death is an overdetermined topic, its symbols redundant. Actual death is present in the theme of burial (G) and its attendant miraculous motif, burial by lions (g), but nearly every other part of the journey has a death-related motif associated with it. On the journey the traveler may fall to the ground "as if dead" (b^3, Onuphrius, Serapion). The first stop (C) may be a tomb (the Apostle Paul in the *Acts of Paul and Thecla*, Antony, Abraham, Paul of Thebes in the Arabic version), a prison (the three monks), or other enclosed space symbolic of death. The traveler may find a dead body (c^2; Paphnutius, Macarius, Zosimas), which may be uncorrupted (d^6; Paphnutius, Zosimas), pointing to the fact that the meeting was purposeful, not coincidental. The request (F) is often for burial (Paul of Thebes, Onuphrius, Mark the Athenian, Mary the Egyptian).

Symbolic death leaves the voyager's identity in question, and identity is one of the most important, and common, motifs of the theme of encounter. There are two allomorphs: mistaken identity (d^1) and its opposite but structurally equal manifestation, miraculous knowledge of identity (d^2). In the liminal state, identity is not easy for an observer to determine since the liminar is stripped of the customary and easily interpreted emblems of hierarchical status such as dress, ornament, attendants, and so forth. More important, identity in this condition is wavering and in flux. In the tales of the desert fathers, it is either misinterpreted or, if it is correctly ascertained, the knowledge has come to the identifier mysteriously, through a dream-vision or from some other miraculous source.

Types of mistaken identity fall into two categories, both significant in terms of liminality. The person misidentified is thought either to be an animal or a marginal such as a criminal. In the *Peregrinatio Paphnutii*, Timotheus thought that Paphnutius was an

32. Turner, *Dramas, Fields, Metaphors* (1974), p. 273.

evil spirit. On first seeing Onuphrius, Paphnutius compared him to a leopard in the Coptic version; in other accounts, to a brigand or a murderer; in Petrus de Natalibus to a monster or a wild beast. Zosimas took Mary the Egyptian for a ghostly apparition ("phantasium alicujus spiritus"). Monastic histories contain similar details. In Theodoret, Simeon Priscus resembled a shaggy beast (/d^1/); Acepsimus was mistaken for a wolf;[33] Benedict was thought to be a beast.[34] Cassian related that the Abbot Paphnutius (not to be confused with Onuphrius' Paphnutius) was called "bubalus," a wild cow,[35] while the long hair of the Syrian monks, according to St. Ephrem, made them look like eagles.[36] The *Verba Seniorum* (VI. 3, 3) relates an anecdote about Macarius the Egyptian (d. ca. 390), told in the first person. Macarius had gone alone into the desert and there found a little lake with an island.[37] Animals came to drink from the lake, and among them he observed two naked hermits whom he mistook for spirits. He conversed with them and when he asked to share their life, they told him that he was not yet ready for "initiation" into the solitary life. Another anecdote in the same collection (10), tells of a solitary who saw a naked man in the desert, feeding on grass like a beast; this hermit could not endure the scent of man and fled when approached (in the Coptic version of this tale, he traveled with the beasts).[38]

Yet another form of mistaken identity is disguise, a voluntarily assumed false identity (b), discussed above. This generally popular motif is confined in the hagiographic romances to tales involving women,[39] as either a woman flees home in disguise or a crusading monk like Abraham sets off in disguise to rescue the fallen woman.

33. Theodoret, *Historia Religiosa*, chs. 6 and 15, *PG* 82, iii, 1361C and 1416A, respectively.

34. Gregory the Great, *Dialogi*, II. 1, *PL* 66, 131A.

35. *PL* 49, 559AB.

36. *Opera selecta*, p. 120, cited by Vööbus, *History of Asceticism*, p. 152.

37. Reitzenstein (*Historia Monachorum* [1916], p. 177) suggests that the island in the middle of a lake located in the Egyptian desert is to be identified with paradise.

38. Amélineau, *Voyage*, p. 193.

39. Patlagean notes that the motif of the disguised woman disappears from Byzantine hagiographic accounts composed after the ninth century; "L'histoire de la femme déguisée" (1976), p. 597.

The life of the desert saint was one long *rite de passage* in preparation for the ultimate ascent into heaven. Many of the stories of
these heroes, however, are double, consisting of an inner and an
outer tale. In these, the narrator reenacts the same ritual pattern of
separation (often including symbolic death), marginality, and reassimilation as he returns from the desert to society, inspired by the
tale he has to tell. To use Turner's terminology, he has left a Familiar Place, journeyed to a Far Place, and returned once more to the
Familiar,[40] but he has in some ways been changed for the better. In
short, he has gone on pilgrimage.

The Turners have amply documented the liminal characteristics
of pilgrimage.[41] It involves spatial marginality, the sense of *communitas* felt by the participants, and the obliteration or minimaliza-
tion of differences in status among the pilgrims. Pilgrims also go
to places where theophany has occurred. The three monks, like Macarius before them, traveled close to the spot where God appeared
to the first man. Macarius was there blessed by a vision of Christ.
Other pilgrim narrators—Antony, Zosimas, and Paphnutius—were
favored with visions of sanctity, and bring the tale of these visions
back with them.

The third and final stage of the classic *rite de passage* is aggregation or assimilation: the liminar is brought back into his society in a
new, and generally enhanced, status. Our saints did not, in general,
return from the desert, although the traveler (Paphnutius, Zosimas,
the three monks) brought back their story and perhaps relics (as in
the story of Paul of Thebes, where Antony returned with Paul's
tunic). Many of the historical saints, interestingly, did not finish out
their lives in the desert. Jerome, for all his glowing praise of the desert environment, only spent several months in the desert of Chalcis
in Syria before returning to Antioch (he wrote his *Vita Pauli* during

40. *Dramas, Fields, Metaphors* (1979), p. 195.
41. Turner and Turner, *Image and Pilgrimage* (1978), p. 18, write: ". . . there is
undoubtedly an initiatory quality in pilgrimage. A pilgrim is an initiand, entering
into a new, deeper level of existence than he has known in his accustomed milieu."
See also Maddox, "Pilgrimage Narrative and Meaning" (1973).

this sojourn).[42] Gregory Nazianzen regarded the desert life as incompatible with study and therefore as only a preliminary step on the road to perfection.[43] Yet however long they stayed, these visitors to the wilderness returned changed. The concluding sections of their tales testify to their sense of illumination and joy as they return from the desert to the world of men.

In the scheme outlined by van Gennep, the *rite de passage* consists of three stages: separation, margin, and aggregation. The tripartite pattern applies also to the voyage of the ordinary human soul, if it is not that of a sinner condemned permanently to hell. Life on earth may be viewed as the margin, the liminal state, a temporary condition that, if successfully completed, earns someone the right, after the separation of death, to be assimilated among the saints and angels in heaven. As a narrative, the story of such a soul, of Everyman, must concentrate on the movement from life to death. (The emphasis is different, of course, in vision narratives of later date, such as *St. Patrick's Purgatory* or the visions of the Monk of Eynsham or of Dante, in which the traveler is privileged to return to life to tell what he saw). In the epic passions of the martyrs, the narrative depicts at length the drama of separation—the arrest (an optional element), and trial and death (obligatory elements). Margin is omitted, since these saints have by the very manner of their death earned direct entry into heaven. Possibly the scene of martyrdom itself constitutes the marginal space, the point of passage between the kingdom of men and the kingdom of God. The *vita* of the desert saint may include details of separation such as the reasons for departure (the "more" motif and the threat of impending marriage), but it focuses its dramatic interest on the second stage, the life of liminality in the desert.

The final stage, assimilation into heaven, may be actually de-

---

42. Guillaumont, "Conception du désert," p. 10. For Jerome's romantic view, see his letter (14) written in 376 to Heliodorus: "O heremus familiari Deo gaudens!" (ch. 10; O desert, rejoicing in God as an everyday companion).

43. This was the general view of the Cappadocian monks; see Guillaumont, "Conception du désert."

scribed. The questing hero-saint—St. Antony, for example—may observe the soul of a Paul of Thebes being taken up into heaven. Or the scene may be assumed, and not depicted, since the hero in question is, after all, a saint. For the questing hero-saint himself, the final stage closely parallels the initiate's reassimilation into society, in so far as he too has the fixed responsibility of sharing his knowledge with others. Thus the story of Paphnutius' quest concludes with the preservation of his experiences in written form, as he meets the two brothers who make a book about them and place it in the church.[44] The adventure is over; it remains now to monumentalize it, and to pass it on to others. Adventure has become scripture.

Although few accounts are as explicit about their genesis as is that of Paphnutius, the same implicit thesis underlies them all. As the saint is assimilated into heaven, the tale of his heroism must be assimilated into society. In the search for the means to tell the world about the hermit's valor, hagiographers, consciously or not, utilize pre-existing archetypes. They are telling us about "heroes" of a very specific and very special sort, but heroes none the less. They do not worry that narrators before them have used the same motifs and details, nor are they concerned about repetitions within their own stories. The reiteration of familiar events gives the tales both plausibility and immediate intelligibility. Accounts of the martyrs freely borrow details from one another, to be sure, but the imprint of a shared narrative deep structure is more apparent in the lives of the desert solitaries. The borrowings here from ancient romance are palpable. The universality of the romance plot enables the hagiographic romance to reach out to common anxieties and aspirations—the thirst for knowledge, the quest into the unknown to answer questions of identity, the search for lost innocence and harmony with the environment—and to use them in the service of its own special form of heroic narrative, the life of the desert saint. These motifs have not lost their appeal, even for the romancers of today.

44. Several Greek novels end with the depositing in temple archives of the account of the lovers' adventures; Hägg, *Novel in Antiquity* (1983), p. 119.

Chapter 8

The Road's End:
Postscripta

We appear to have reached the end of the road. The hero, whether martyr or hermit, has safely attained his or her goal, the terrestrial or celestial paradise. But the nature of the ideal hero changes with time. In *Anatomy of Criticism*, Northrop Frye claims that the romance mode comes as near as literature can to depicting wish-fulfillment dreams.[1] Hence heroes change from the handsome ephebe and beautiful maiden of Greek Romance to the spiritual martyr, the ascetic, and thence to the chivalric knight of medieval courtly romance, and finally to the child-hero of many modern romances. The structural paradigms underlying such narratives display rather less variety.

In chapter 2, following Charles Altman, we distinguished between the accounts of two types of saints—martyrs and hermits—on the basis of narrative structure. In addition, *passiones* and *vitae* were seen to differ with regard to the apparently centripetal or centrifugal nature of the narrative. The dramatic action of the martyr transpired in a public, usually urban, environment, while that of the hermit, by definition, occurred in the wilderness. Yet ultimately both narratives seek a center—paradise—although the paths followed to attain that goal are distinct. All these saintly heroes, and many others as well, have sought (to paraphrase Mircea Eliade,

---

1. *Anatomy of Criticism* (1957), p. 186.

cited in the previous chapter) that difficult road which leads from the profane to the sacred, from the transitory and illusory to the real and the eternal.

Here I would like to sketch out the apparent survival and utilization, whether conscious or unconscious, of some themes that have figured prominently in the preceding chapters. In many cases I suspect that the authors of these later works drew upon a common stock of narrative themes rather than intentionally recalling hagiographic accounts, but their use in the *passiones* and *vitae* lent them a certain authority.

To deal adequately with the influence of hagiography upon later literature would require a book itself. I have limited my examination primarily to five medieval texts and two modern ones. For epic, I examine *La Chanson de Roland*, *Le Couronnement de Louis*, and the *Poema de mio Cid*; for romance, Chrétien de Troyes' *Chevalier au Lion* and the anonymous *La Queste del saint Graal*. The first modern work is C. S. Lewis' *Narnia Chronicles*, which, in view of the author's piety and erudition, can be assumed to make conscious use of the motifs and themes hallowed in hagiographic literature. The second one is Joseph Kessel's *Le Lion*. The great popularity of these works testifies to the continuation of certain powerful wish-fulfillment dreams, especially those involving lions. I do not consider explicitly those works whose debt to hagiographic sources is obvious—the vernacular lives of the saints, an epic like *Ami et Amile*, or a romance such as *Guillaume d'Angleterre* (directly related to the legend of St. Eustache) ascribed to Chrétien, or among modern works a novel such as Anatole France's *Thaïs*. In such texts the importance of hagiographic legends is apparent; in other works, it is more subtle and less well known.

HAGIOGRAPHY AND EPIC: THE POWER
OF DISCOURSE

In his article on the structure of saints' lives Charles Altman notes the similarity between the martyr's *passio* and the Old French *chanson de geste*. Both are binary in structure and admit no mediation:

in the words of the *Chanson de Roland*, "Pagans are wrong and Christians right" (1015, ed. Whitehead). The martyr's passion and the medieval epic celebrate a similar ethos. Both highlight communal values and ideals. As a result, it is not surprising to find an assimilation of the crusading hero, willing to die in defense of Christianity and granted absolution for that act, to the heroic martyr.

While the ethos of the *Chanson de Roland*, for example, is not to be explained by a wholesale evocation of Christian values, Roland does die a Christian martyr. Before the battle at Rencesvals, Archbishop Turpin exhorts the soldiers to confess and pray for God's mercy; those who die will, he promised, be holy martyrs (1134–35). After Roland's death, the poem depicts the hero receiving the specific reward for martyrdom, immediate entry into heaven prior to the Last Judgment, as the cherubim and archangels escort his soul to Paradise (2393–96). His death is a vindication, not a tragic defeat.[2] Similarly, in the *Chançun de Willame*, Vivien exhorts his men, saying that St. Stephen and the other martyrs are no better than those of them who will die "for God" in the ensuing battle at Archamp (544–47). In view of this crusading spirit and the treatment of his death in the epic, it was inevitable that a cult of St. Roland should emerge. In the church of St. Romanus at Blaye the sarcophagus of the hero, together with those of Oliver, Turpin and the others, was displayed and venerated. The twelfth-century pilgrim's guide to the Camino de Santiago, which forms the fifth book of the *Codex Calixtinus*, describes the burial place of Roland and his companions, making reference to the body of "beati Rotolandi martyris."[3] In the *Pseudo-Turpin Chronicle* (Book IV of the *Codex Calixtinus*), Roland is called "Xpisti martir."[4]

2. It is, however, a defeat in the clerical *Pseudo-Turpin Chronicle*, where the disaster is viewed as a punishment for the Franks' immoral behavior. In *Le Motif du repentir* (1967), p. 137, Payen signals a change in attitude towards the "defeat" from the eleventh to the twelfth century: "Le désastre de Roncevaux est une épreuve providentielle mais ce n'est pas un châtiment, et l'on ne saurait trop déplorer qu'il soit si vite apparu tel au public du XIIe siècle."

3. Vielliard, *Le Guide du Pèlerin* (1938), p. 78.

4. Burger, "La légende de Roncevaux" (1948–49), pp. 437–38. I do not subscribe to Burger's hypothesis that a Latin poem, a *Passio beati Rotolandi*, lies behind the *Chanson de Roland*.

Some of the assimilation between epic hero and martyr may have been the result of the conscious efforts of the Church to propagandize for the Crusades. Other shared features, however, may owe their origin to more subtle factors. Contemporary theorists have introduced two concepts that help to clarify the relationship between the martyrs' passions and the medieval epic: "horizon of expectation" (Jauss, Nichols),[5] and "vraisemblance" (Todorov).[6] In this discussion, I am not suggesting that the jongleur necessarily "imitated" hagiographic narrative, if by "imitation" we understand the sort of conscious poetic cross-reference that, for example, we admit when we say that a classical poet such as Vergil "imitated" Homer.[7] But passion narratives were familiar to all, whether from reading or performing Latin hymns such as those of Prudentius,[8] from hearing vernacular poems such as the *Vie de saint Léger* or the *Canczon de sancta Fides*, or from listening to sermons, preached in the vernacular from the ninth century on. These well-known stories set up a particular horizon of expectation in poet and audience alike with respect to proper heroic behavior and to the proper function of themes such as the role of discourse, prominent, as we have seen, in passion literature. The depiction of the Christian hero finds its norms in literary, not historical, realities. These norms in turn are determined by the "supra-reality" of *vraisemblance*, of which Todorov writes: "One can speak of the *vraisemblance* of a work in so far as it attempts to make us believe that it conforms to reality and not to its own laws. In other words, the *vraisemblable* is the mask which conceals the text's own laws and which we are supposed to take for a relation with reality."[9] Citing this statement of

5. Jauss, "Littérature médiévale et théorie des genres" (1970) and "Literary History as a Challenge to Literary Theory" (1970–71); Nichols, "A Poetics of Historicism?" (1977).

6. "Introduction," *Le Vraisemblable* (1968).

7. Indeed, I wrote a thesis to prove the contrary. See Elliott, "Saints and Heroes" (1977).

8. Peebles, *The Poet Prudentius* (1951), p. 81, points out that at least nine of the *Peristephanon* (including both III and V) attained some liturgical use in Spain. The Mozarabic liturgy was not replaced by the Roman rite in that country until the closing years of the eleventh century (Messenger, "Mozarabic Hymns" [1946], p. 149).

9. Quoted by Nichols, "A Poetics of Historicism?" p. 97.

Todorov, Nichols adds: "*Vraisemblance* belongs, by this definition, to the same kind of internal structure as 'poetic language.' However, it differs from the latter in pointing outward, beyond the text, to other texts and objects in the world" (p. 97). The "laws," the narrative deep structure, of hagiography have extended "outward" to influence the "laws" of medieval epic composition. Both genres, in the case of heroic discourse, reveal similar conceptions of the *vraisemblable*.

In the late antique period, a common expression for martyrdom was *martyrium dicere*, "to speak a witness." Much of that speech was angry. Saint Eulalia, for example, burst into the courtroom, yelled at the Roman praetor, spat in his face as he was trying to reason with her,[10] and kicked the pagan idols *(Peristephanon* III, 126–30). Prudentius qualified her by such adjectives as "torua" (103; stern) and "ferox" (ingeniique ferox / turbida frangere bella parat [32–33; fierce in nature, she is prepared to burst into turbulent warfare]). Similarly, the heroes of the *chansons de geste* are angry, impetuous, argumentative. Much of the narrative of the epics takes the form of direct speech, the most dramatic way to re-create an event. But the uses of discourse are varied, their significance exceeding a desire for vivid mimesis. Audience and poet alike expected their heroes to bear witness to their faith in word as well as deed. Words, moreover, come first.

Of the speeches in the epics, Michel-André Bossy has written:

Two types of verbal encounter shape the hero's career in the early *chansons de geste*: (1) the battlefield confrontation in which the hero insults his enemies and praises the violence he has or will inflict on them; (2) the council-scene confrontation in which the plain binary opposition between Christian society and its pagan antithesis unfolds into a contradiction within society itself.[11]

Bossy notes that discourse in the second instance, unlike the speeches on the battlefield or in the martyr's *passio*, is problematic.

---

10. This conduct, which does not conform with romantic notions of appropriate feminine conduct, has scandalized critics; for further discussion, see Elliott, "The Martyr as Epic Hero" (1978), pp. 127–29.

11. Bossy, "Heroes and the Power of Words" (1980), p. 243.

In the council-scene confrontations, appearance and reality do not coincide. In battle, however, there is no ambiguity.

One important subspecies of battlefield confrontation may reveal a debt to norms of *vraisemblance* and horizons of expectation derived from hagiography, not from history. Although in the press of battle there was probably little opportunity for long prayers and debates, let alone for hearing the enemy's reply, such interchanges are stock epic incidents. In the martyr's trial, however, verbal encounters did occur, even if the historical documents suggest that the interrogations actually took a form simpler than that presented in the *Acta* or in hymns like the *Peristephanon*. Occasionally we find an epic hero on the battlefield appearing to assume a role more appropriate to the martyr than to the warrior, as he turns preacher, expounding religious doctrine and engaging in theological debates with his pagan adversary prior to combat (e.g. the argument between Guillaume and Corsolt that prefaces the first battle in the *Couronnement de Louis*, and the theological debates in the *Pseudo-Turpin Chronicle* between Charlemagne and Agolant, Roland and the giant Ferragut).[12]

Before turning to epic texts, it is useful to consider a work intermediate between Latin hagiography and vernacular epic, the Provençal *Canczon de sancta Fides*, composed around 1060. In defiance of history, the tormenter of the young martyr is none other than Dacian, who has become, largely thanks to his association with Vincent of Saragossa, the torturer *par excellence*. Much of this *passio* takes the form of direct discourse; in particular, the saint has several speeches in which she boldly defies her persecutor. Dacian threatens her with the fire that burnt Saint Lawrence (289–90). In reply Fides utters her *credo* in the form of a prayer:[13]

12. *Le Couronnement de Louis*, in Lepage, *Les Rédactions* (1978), 836 ff.; Pseudo-Turpin, *The Pseudo-Turpin* (1973) ed. Smyser, chs. 15 and 21.

13. Text from Thomas, *La Chanson de Sainte Foi* (1974), 301–11. There is no real parallel for this prayer in the *vita*. There the only prayer is brief, uttered *before* the saint voluntarily presents herself to Dacian. She does not rehearse the creed but prays for support ("adesto nunc famulae tuae, et praebe ori meo sermonem acceptabilem, quem in conspectu tyranni hujus respondeam" (*AA.SS* Oct. III, vol. 51, p. 288DE [Oct. 6]: Be present now to Thy servant and grant to my mouth acceptable speech which I may answer in the presence of this tyrant).

Deus, nostre Donz, lo glorios,
De totas res es poderos.
Del Cel czai deissended per nos
E fez dess homen molt ginnos;
Guerilz malaves els lebros,
Baptismenz ded en l'agua jos.
Pres fol seus corps, lo precios;
Judeu l'aucidrun enveios.
Destruiss Enfern, lo tenebros;
Los seus en traiss, qe connog pros.
Aqel volri' aver espos.

(God our Lord, the glorious one, of everything is He master. From heaven He descended here for our sake, and made Himself into a superior man; He cured the leprous and gave baptisms in the lowly water. His precious body was taken; the envious Jews killed Him. He destroyed shadowy Hell, taking out His own people, for which I count Him valiant. This one I want to have for my bridegroom.)

The martyr's confession of faith rehearses Christ's history, concluding not with the Resurrection but with the Harrowing of Hell, as Christ is depicted as a valiant warrior ("pros," 310), destroying the forces of evil. The speech is not primarily designed to convert Dacian or even to win God's mercy, although the latter is admittedly an important goal; its function is to restate the polarities of the drama at a climactic moment, reminding the audience once again of the ideological basis of the conflict.[14]

In the *Couronnement de Louis*, there are two instances of discourse that demonstrate a horizon of expectation concerning the role of heroic speech that has possibly been created by familiarity with the martyrs' *passiones*. Prior to his fight with Corsolt, Guillaume dismounts and speaks a long "epic prayer" (699–793),[15] which resembles that of St. Fides in the prominent position afforded the Harrowing of Hell, for Guillaume concludes with the Harrowing, which he places after the Ressurrection.[16]

14. For an interpretation of this scene in terms of speech act theory, see Elliott, "Power of Discourse (1982), p. 53.

15. Cf. Labande, "Le 'Credo' épique" (1955), and De Caluwé, "La prière épique" (1976). Critics have failed to note that St. Fides' prayer is the earliest example of the type.

16. Citations are from the edition of Lepage, *Les Rédactions* (1978).

Et au tierz jor surrexis comme Dex.
Droit en enfer fu vo chemins tornez;
Toz voz amis en eüstes gité,
Qui longuement i avoient esté.
Si com c'est voirs, beaus rois de majesté,
Deffent mon cors, que ne soie afolé,
Que doi combatre encontre cel malfé.

(783–89)

(And on the third day you rose like God. Straight to Hell your path led; all your friends, who had been there for a long time you liberated. If this is true, fair king of majesty, defend my body lest it be harmed, since I must fight against this evildoer.)

Such rearrangement of scriptural chronology is, indeed, typical of epic prayers,[17] particularly at their conclusion. A similar alteration occurs in Aude's prayer prior to the combat between Roland and Olivier in *Girart de Vienne* (5710ff.). In the *Poema de mio Cid* (330–65), Ximena inserts references to Old Testament figures into her recital of Christ's life. Like Guillaume, she concludes with the Harrowing of Hell.

The Harrowing is a climactic event used to mark an important juncture in the narration. For Donald Maddox and Sara Sturm-Maddox, the event prefigures the courage of Guillaume who must defeat a demonic adversary before liberating the faithful captives of the Saracens.[18] Antoinette Saly, in her study of the theme of Christ's descent into Hell, traces the rearrangement back to the popular "Gospel of Nicodemus." It is at this point in the sacred story that the binary opposition between good and evil becomes both visible and martial.

Et cum haec ad inuicem loquerentur Satan princeps et Inferus, facta est uox ut tonitruum et spiritalis clamor: "Tollite portas, principes, uestras, et eleuamini porte aeternales, et introibit Rex Gloriae." Haec autem audiens Inferus dixit ad Satan principem: "Recede a me, exi de meis sedibus foras, si *potens es praeliator, pugnare* cum Rege Gloriae."[19]

17. Saly, "Le Thème de la descente aux enfers" (1969), II, 47–63. In Prudentius, *Cathemerinon* IX, the narration of the Harrowing precedes that of Christ's death.
18. "Le Chevalier à l'oraison" (1978), p. 614.
19. Kim, *The Gospel of Nicodemus* (1973), 21.1, emphasis added.

(And while Prince Satan and Hell [Inferus] were saying these things to each other, a sound as of thunders and a spiritual clamor were heard: "Take away your doors, you princes, and be raised up, ye everlasting doors, and the King of Glory will come in." Hearing these things, Inferus said to Prince Satan: "Go away from me, get out of my seats, *if you are a mighty warrior, to fight* with the King of Glory.")

It also marks the intrusion of the romance "theme of descent" into a seemingly epic narrative.

During the actual battle with Corsolt, Guillaume pronounces a second prayer in which chronology is again disordered; after mentioning Christ's resurrection, Guillaume reflects on the Last Judgment, and he concludes this prayer with reference to a mélange of saints and Old Testament heroes, ending with Moses (977–1029). Chronology has been altered in these epic prayers to highlight particular biblical events that have special appropriateness as models or paradigms for the careers of both martyrs and epic heroes.[20] The Last Judgment was the most significant event in any Christian's spiritual life; the scene was dramatically displayed on the tympanon of many Romanesque churches. The Harrowing of Hell prefigures this moment as Christ assaults the Devil's stronghold and releases His friends from their prison. But all Christians, except for the saints, especially the martyrs, and those heroes who died in battle against the infidel, must await the Day of Judgment for their deliverance. Some of Prudentius' hymns in honor of martyrs (e.g. *Peristephanon* II and IV) conclude with specific prayers to the martyrs to intercede on that dreadful *dies irae*. An evocation of the Harrowing of Hell reminds the faithful of Christ's heroic mercy toward his allies (cf. *Sancta Fides*, "los seus" [his own people]; *Couronnement de Louis*, "voz amis" [your friends]), and encourages them to hope. Moses, known for his violent opposition to pagan superstition, prefigures the martyr diametrically opposed to paganism.

The devil, vanquished by Christ in the Harrowing of Hell, is the enemy of every Christian. Like the martyr, the epic hero must con-

---

20. G. Raynaud de Lage, "L'Inspiration" (1972), suggests that the prototype of the "epic prayer" is ultimately a text close to the religious "climate" of the *chansons de geste*, the biblical account of the exploits of the Maccabees.

quer his adversary in word as well as deed. After Guillaume's first prayer, the devil-like Corsolt, "hideus comme aversier" (508; ugly as the Adversary, cf. 677), asks Guillaume to whom "he has so long been talking" (797–98). When Guillaume tells him, Corsolt replies that Guillaume is a fool if he thinks that his God will help him, and a spirited theological debate is under way. The issue is whether God concerns himself in an active fashion with the destiny of mankind. The opposition is absolute. Corsolt cries out, "Crestïenté est *tot* foloiement"[21] (845; Christianity is *totally* folly). Guillaume wins the battle, although he loses a piece of his nose.[22]

The debate between Roland and another giant, Ferragut, in the *Pseudo-Turpin Chronicle* is even more expressly concerned with theology, as Ferragut questions the triune nature of the Trinity, which seems to him a logical impossibility. In his rebuttal, Roland emphasizes the significance for all Christians of the Last Judgment. In combat the question of God's intervention in human affairs is raised, as Roland cries out, "Oh Jesus, son of the blessed Virgin Mary, help me!"[23] He then fatally wounds Ferragut who in turn screams, "Mafumet, Mafumet, help me for I am dying." The pagan's plea goes unanswered.

For Roland and Guillaume to turn theologian is perhaps surprising. Like all medieval epic warriors, both heroes are good Christians, but they appear to be men of action rather than of speech. Although Guillaume, whose legend is conflated with that of St. William of Aniane, eventually makes a pious end, and Roland dies a martyr's death at Rencesvals, both heroes seem more at home with the sword than the book. Guillaume in particular makes a strange cleric (in the parodic *Mariage Guillaume I* [130–37], we discover that this hero cannot even read!). He is a Hercules figure—an oversized, gluttonous, impetuous soldier, not averse to using fists if he

21. On this scene Frappier comments: "Corsolt avait engagé la controverse en théologien"; *Les Chansons de geste du cycle de Guillaume d'Orange* (1976) II, 126.
22. For further discussion, see Nichols, "Sign as (Hi)story" (1980).
23. I quote here from the Old Catalan translation since both speeches are there given as direct discourse (Pseudo-Turpin, *Història de Carles Maynes* [1960] ed. Riquer, p. 82). In the Latin text published by Smyser, Roland's cry is not quoted directly.

does not have a sword handy. Yet it is important for both epic
heroes to take verbal as well as physical action against the enemy.

A final epic example may seem to have more in common with
romance, for it involves power over a lion, but this theme is common to both *passio* and *vita*. In the opening of the third *cantar* of
the *Cid*, while the hero sleeps, a lion gets loose (canto 112):

> saliós de la red e desatós león.
> En grant miedo se vieron por medio de la cort;
> enbraçcan los mantos los del Campeador,
> e çercan el escaño, e fincan sobre so señor.
> Ferrant Gonçalvez, ifant de Carrión,
> non vido allí dos alçasse, nin cámara abierta nin torre;
> metiós sol esçaño, tanto ovo el pavor.
> ....
>
> Mio Çid fincó el cobdo, en pie se levantó,
> el manto trae al cuello, e adelinó pora' león;
> el león quando lo vío, assí envergonçó,
> ante mio Çid la cabeça premió e el rostro fincó.
> Mio Çid don Rodrigo al cuello lo tomó,
> e liévalo adestrando, en la red le metió.
> A maravilla lo han quantos que i son.
>
> (2282–87, 2296–2302)

(The lion broke from his cage and stalked abroad.
Great terror ran through the court;
the Campeador's men seize their cloaks
and stand over the bench, to protect their lord.
Fernando González, Heir of Carrión,
could find nowhere to hide, no room nor tower was open;
he hid under the bench, so great was his terror.
....

My Cid rose to his elbow, got to his feet,
with his cloak on his shoulders walked toward the lion;
the lion, when he saw him, was so filled with shame,
before My Cid he bowed his head and put his face down.
My Cid Don Rodrigo took him by the neck,
led him as with a halter and put him in his cage.
And all marveled, as many as were there.[24])

24. Text and translation from Merwin, *Poem of the Cid* (1959), pp. 202–4.

It is generally agreed that this episode serves to exalt the epic hero by showing his dominion over the wild beast, and, at the same time, its makes apparent the base cowardice of his opponent, the villa-nous Infante of Carrión.[25] C. Bandera Gómez saw reflected in the lion the eternal vigilance of the Cid, in whom he sees a Christ figure.[26] In contrast, David Hook sees the "mood" of the incident in the *Poema de mio Cid* as "resolutely secular"; for Hook, the point of the beast-episode is simply to present the hero as a superman.[27] While I would not go so far as to make the Cid into a Christ-like figure, one does not have to look so high for religious exemplars behind the Cid's lion-taming act.

The closest parallel is the account of Daria, the vestal virgin con-demned to a brothel for her faith. A lion who escaped from the are-na defended her against a would-be lover; with the wicked he was fierce, but obedient to the command of the saint (see above, p. 148). There is, as we have observed, a long tradition that lions spare the innocent and the pure. In the lion's docility before the Cid we are to see, I suggest, not only a scene demonstrating the hero's bravery and the craven behavior of his enemy but also a sign of the Cid's virtue and the righteousness of his cause. He had to earn the lion's respect, and did so. The act is interpreted by all as a "maravilla." Merwin's translation of "maravilla" ("A maravilla lo han") as "all marvelled" obscures the religious connotation, "miracle," which is attached to *maravilla*.

HAGIOGRAPHY AND ROMANCE

Just as the plots of the hagiographic romances are more complex than accounts of the passions, so too the subject of their influence reveals a labyrinthine complexity. The role of the hermit in later medieval literature would necessitate a book-length study of its own. I would like to note here the great rise in the number of her-

25. Hook, "Some Observations upon the Episode of the Cid's Lion" (1976), p. 553.

26. El 'Poema de mio Cid', pp. 175–79.

27. Hook, p. 555. For further discussion, see Spitzer, "Le lion arbitre moral" (1938); Henry, "Sur l'épisode du lion" (1939).

mits at the end of the eleventh and the beginning of the twelfth century.[28] This phenomenon no doubt helped to account for the popularity of stories about the medieval hermits' predecessors, and in turn gave currency and authority to the narrative structures of such tales. Two further points about these late medieval hermits in literature are relevant here. First, hermits are privileged mediators; they talk to angels and participate in divine omniscience. Second, they are at the very center of parapsychological phenomena.[29]

I shall focus here on two topics that emerged as particularly significant in the legends of the desert fathers previously discussed, the role of animals and the concept of liminal space. Both served to some extent to distinguish these tales from similar accounts. The "helpful beast" is the only motif common to both *passio* and *vita*, but animals appear in the latter tales in a wider range of roles than they do in the former. In the *vitae*, as in romance, the action for the most part transpires in a "special" place—in an unfamiliar, and often somewhat magical landscape, whereas the *passio* is located in a public, urban environment familiar to all.

Animals

Stories about helpful animals are not limited to accounts of saints but are frequent in many kinds of tales. The popularity, however, of stories about saints and animals was immense and gave rise to numerous imitations, not all of which need to have been conscious borrowings. From the point of view of narrative incident, the underlying pattern that determined how one fabulated the life of a hero, whether saint or not, contained elements that favored the inclusion of animals. In general we may conclude that the significance of the detail was to indicate that the hero in some way or other enjoyed divine blessing. The friendship and assistance of wild beasts were a privilege enjoyed only by those worthy of it. Moreover, whatever the source, the possibility of an allegorical or symbolic in-

---

28. See Bourgain, *La Chaire française au XIIe siècle* (1879), pp. 140ff.; also Colliot, "Aspects de l'ermite" (1979); Le Goff, *La Civilisation de l'Occident médiéval* (1964), p. 66.
29. Colliot, "Aspects de l'ermite," pp. 175–77.

terpretation encouraged the continued use of the motif. Montalembert, writing of St. Columba and the beasts, saw in these tales a symbol of the struggle of the monks of the early Middle Ages "for liberation from the savage forces of nature and from the still more savage barbarism of men."[30] Jean Bichon offers a different interpretation:

If one considers the totality of hagiographic literature, one is struck first of all by the important place of the animal. The animal is in some way the privileged representative of creation outside of man. The power of the saint, and through the saint the power of God, become manifest by contact with the animal with a clearness and fullness that are almost unique. The animal plays the role of "developing" sanctity (in the photographic sense).[31]

I have suggested that, as well as being an indicator of sanctity, the animals were a token of a nostalgia for the Golden Age of Eden. I shall return to the topic of the quest for a lost, happier state.

As we have seen, in almost all saints' legends, the animal was kind, helpful, friendly (the martyrdom of St. Ignatius is the only outstanding exception). The lion, moreover, enjoyed pride of place in stories about saints and animals. Here are two examples of lions in secular literary works. First, *Iliad* 20, 163–75:

>   . . . From the other
> side the son of Peleus rose like a lion against him,
> the baleful beast, when men have been straining to kill him, the country
> all in the hunt, and he at the first pays them no attention
> but goes on his way, only when some one of the impetuous young men
> has hit him with the spear he whirls, jaws open, over his teeth foam
> breaks out, and in the depth of his chest the powerful heart groans;

---

30. "À livrer aux forces sauvages de la nature et à la barbarie encore plus sauvage des hommes": Charles F. R. Montalembert, *Les Moines d'Occident* (Paris, 1860), II, 427, cited by Saintyves, "Le Thème des animaux sauvages" (1934), p. 58.

31. *L'Animal dans la littérature française* (1976), I, 147: "Si l'on considère l'ensemble de la littérature hagiographique, on est frappé, en premier lieu, par l'importance de la place qu'y occupe l'animal, Il est, en quelque sorte, le réprésentant priviliégé de la création en dehors de l'homme; la puissance du saint, et, à travers le saint, la puissance de Dieu se manifeste au contacte de l'animal avec une netteté et une ampleur presque uniques; l'animal joue le rôle d'un révélateur (au sens photographique) de la saintété."

he lashes his own ribs with his tail and the flanks on both sides
as he rouses himself to fury for the fight, eyes glaring,
and hurls himself straight onward on the chance of killing some one
of the men, or else being killed himself in the first onrush.
So the proud heart and fighting fury stirred on Achilleus
to go forward . . . .[32]

Now another account of a lion wounded by a man:

> Mes il li covient une piece
> tranchier de la coe au lïon
> por la teste au serpant felon
> qui par la coe le tenoit;
>
> ....
>
> Quant le lÿon delivré ot,
> si cuida qu'il li covenist
> conbatre, et que sus li venist;
> mes il ne le sa pansa onques.
> Oez que fist li lÿons donques,
> con fist que preuz et deboneire,
> com il li comança a feire
> sanblant que a lui se randoit,
> que ses piez joinz li estandoit
> et vers terre encline sa chiere;
> si s'estut sor ses piez derriere
> et puis si se ragenoilloit,
> et tote sa face moilloit
> de lermes, par humilité.[33]

(But he had to cut off a piece of the lion's tail to get at the serpent's head,
which held the lion by the tail. . . . When he had set the lion free, he supposed that he would have to fight with him, and that the lion would come
at him; but the lion was not minded so. Just hear now what the lion did! He
acted nobly and as one well-bred; for he began to make it evident that he
yielded himself to him, by standing upon his two hind-feet and bowing his
face to the earth, with his fore-feet joined and stretched out toward him.
Then he fell on his knees again, and all his face was wet with the tears of
humility.[34])

32. Translated by Richmond Lattimore (1950).
33. *Le Chevalier au Lion*, ll. 3378–81, 3384–97, ed. Roques (1974).
34. Translated by Comfort, *Arthurian Romances* (1914), p. 224.

In the *Iliad* the beast is fury personified.[35] In the second text, Chrétien de Troyes' *Chevalier au Lion*, the animal becomes Yvain's faithful and humble vassal ("piez joinz" [3392; with his forefeet joined]).

Clearly something has transpired to alter the view of lions. In the Homeric epics, and in many images of lions in Greek art,[36] what is essential is the animal's basic ferocity and the inherent antagonism between man and beast. The lion is at the same time the adversary of the hero and symbolic of him. According to Annie Schnapp-Gourbeillon, "the animal is a reflection, a validating agent, the mirror in which the hero sees himself in his confrontation with life, that is to say, with war."[37] There is, furthermore, something strange and unnatural about those wild beasts who live tamely with Circe; they signify her menacing magical powers rather than the presence of divine favor.[38] In the two thousand years separating the two texts quoted above, lions had been eradicated from Europe and much of Asia Minor.[39] Lacking first-hand knowledge of these animals, the medieval authors relied instead on literary models.[40] Legends of the saints, I suggest, were one of the vehicles for the transmission of this new view of lions in specific, and of beasts in general. With the Judeo-Christian tradition, a new paradigm for man's relation with the animals emerged, and the literary sources for the transmission of this new model were often the tales of the adventures of new heroes, the Christian saints. Such accounts gave rise to a new horizon of expectation concerning heroic behavior. Instead of being by

35. For lions in Homer, see Schnapp-Gourbeillon, *Lions, héros, masques* (1981).
36. For example, the ferocious lions of Cybele on the Siphnian treasury at Delphi or the many representations on vases of Heracles and the lion of Nemea.
37. Schnapp-Gourbeillon, p. 195: "L'animal est un reflet, un faire-valoir, le miroir dans lequel le héros se regarde affronter la vie, c'est-à-dire la guerre." See also p. 56.
38. Schnapp-Gourbeillon, p. 202.
39. There were lions in Macedonia in 480 B.C. when Xerxes marched through (Herodotus, 7.125–26); Dio Chrysostom states that they were eradicated by his time (ca. 120 A.D.) (*Oratio* 21.1).
40. For example, the English author of the *Life of St. Giles* mingles animals from European forests and eastern deserts in his account of this hermit who lived in Languedoc; Bichon, *L'Animal* (1976), p. 106.

definition the one who fights the lion, the hero now became the one who befriends the "King of the Beasts," and is aided by him.

The lion enjoyed a considerable popularity in medieval literature.[41] The lion that accompanied Chrétien's Yvain is probably the best known instance, but he is not alone. The *Gesta Romanorum* contain a story about a grateful lion (number 104). A knight removes a thorn from the paw of a lion and is later spared by the same beast when he is thrown into a pit with the animal.[42] A popular crusade legend recounts the experiences of one Golfier de Lastours,[43] a knight who went on the first Crusade. Golfier one day chanced to free a lion from a serpent, and in gratitude the lion became his companion. When the knight left for home, forsaking the lion on the shore, the beast swam after the vessel until he drowned from exhaustion.[44]

There have been many attempts to explain the origin of Yvain's loyal companion, and most critics have looked to Celtic folklore.[45] Here there is at least one obvious objection: Foerster holds that since the lion is not an inhabitant of Celtic forest, the animal cannot be part of the original tale.[46] This is, of course, true, although legends are not always scrupulous regarders of geographical probability; the legend of the Crusader's lion was supposed to have taken place on the banks of the Jordan at a time when the beast had

41. The lion's literary favor is paralleled in art. In the mid-eleventh century vegetable motifs in sculpture appear to give way to animal ones, and among the beasts the number of lions is remarkable; see Igurashi-Takeshita, "Les lions dans la sculpture romane" (1980), pp. 38, 45.

42. *Gesta Romanorum*, trans. Swan and Hooper (1876), pp. 180–81.

43. The earliest record of the association of a grateful lion with Golfier is to be found in the *Chronicle* of Jaufré de Vigeois, finished in 1184; the legend, however, was known earlier; see Brodeur, "The Grateful Lion" (1924), p. 486, n. 5. See also Thomas, "Le roman de Goufier" (1905), and Tubach, *Index Exemplorum* (1969), 3057; Tubach lists many examples. Alexander Neckham (b. 1157), in *De Naturis Rerum*, tells a similar, although not identical, story about an unnamed *miles* (Brodeur, pp. 495–96).

44. Jaufré de Vigeois, quoted by Brodeur, p. 494.

45. A. Brown, "Knight of the Lion" (1905). There is a long bibliography on this subject. Johnston, "The Episode of Yvain" (1907) lists a considerable number of oriental tales paralleling the account of Androcles. See also Chotzen, "Le Lion d'Owein" (1932–33). For a further summary of attitudes, see Frappier, *Etude sur Yvain* (1969), pp. 108–111.

46. Foerster, *Yvain* (1902), p. xxvi.

wholly disappeared from Palestine.[47] Such realistic considerations, then, meant less to the consumers and propagators of legend than they do to modern scholars.

Jean Frappier felt that the tradition of Androcles, "renewed and embellished by the chivalric spirit of the Middle Ages," was enough to explain most of the thematic elements in Chrétien's lion story.[48] But while Androcles might be the source of such inventions, the tale was morally neutral. If anything, it revealed more about the lion than about the man (Aelian told it to illustrate the premise that animals possessed the faculty of memory). The accounts of Jerome's lion, or of the many other hagiographic lions, were imbued with an explicit moral and symbolic significance. To the best of my knowledge, only Maurice Wilmotte[49] has seriously considered the possibility that hagiography was the source of Chrétien's tale, and he has been without followers, perhaps because of the generally uncritical nature of much of his work (to cite only one instance, he believed that the story about Jerome went back to the fourth century, rather than to the eleventh).[50] The popularity of such tales (manuscript illuminations depicting Jerome's grateful lion are very common)[51] imparted an added resonance to tales of lion companions.

The precise value and role of the lion in *Yvain* is debatable. For Frappier the lion confirms Yvain's moral superiority (p. 212), as the animal is a sign of chivalric perfection. In the mystical order, he

47. Maury, *Croyances et legendes* (1863), p. 217; lions, moreover, are not strong swimmers but the legend of the Crusader's lion nonetheless enjoyed wide currency; on lions as poor swimmers, see Maury, p. 199.

48. Frappier, *Etude sur Yvain*, p. 109. He thinks the story of the lion's attempted suicide is imitated from Ovid's tale of Pyramus and Thisbe (*Metamorphoses* 4, 55–166).

49. *De l'origine du roman en France* (1923), pp. 16–17.

50. It is, however, a sign of the temper of the times that the legend becomes attached to Jerome only about a hundred years before Chrétien's work, testimony to the continuing interest in this type of tale.

51. See Ring, "St. Jerome Extracting the Thorn" (1945). This article, however, discusses paintings rather than manuscript illuminations. The image was particularly popular from the fourteenth century on; Ring states that from the fourteenth to the sixteenth century, with the exception of the Holy Family and St. John, Jerome was perhaps the most frequently represented saint in art (p. 190).

is an allegorical figure of Christ the savior; in the secular world, he is an allegorical figure of the perfect knight—the allegorical doublet of the hero himself, an "Yvain exemplaire." Frappier writes: "The meeting of Yvain and the lion is, then, far more than a marvelous anecdote and a device of story-telling. . . . It is an 'adventure' in the highest sense of the word, a sign of election, good fortune or a challenge of fate."[52] Frappier has here put his finger on something important. The presence of the lion is not a meaningless event; rather, it is, in Frappier's terms, "a sign of election."

The event transpires in the very center of the tale (3344ff.; the poem is 6808 lines in all), after Yvain regains consciousness and sanity in the forest (after he is, in fact, "reborn" or "resurrected"). In the "dame" who conveniently, if somewhat unexpectedly, shows up with the box of magic ointment that restores Yvain (2884ff.), we may perhaps see a transformation of the mysterious figures who appear to the questing hermits, for example to Paphnutius, and restore them when they have fallen to the ground "velut mortuus" (as if dead). There is much emphasis upon the wonder that surrounds the encounter ("mes de ce se mervoille tote" [2906; but of this he marvels greatly]; "et si s'an mervoille" [2909; and this one marvels]). The clothing that the woman and her damsels bring for the naked Yvain appears to him to have been miraculously provided:

> Devant lui voit la robe nueve,
> si se mervoille a desmesure.
>
> (3020–21)

(Before him he sees the new garment, and he marvels exceedingly).

Compare the motif of miraculous provisioning in the saints' lives, motif d[4].

Chrétien emphasizes that the lion is, and remains, savage by nature (cf. 3416–19, 3442–44). Yet this lion "lies down beside him (Yvain) as gently as does a lamb" (qui ausi dolcemant se gist / lez lui

---

52. *Etude Sur Yvain*, p. 213: "La rencontre d'Yvain et du lion est donc beaucoup plus qu'une anecdote merveilleuse et qu'un ressort de l'affabulation. . . . elle est une 'aventure' au sens le plus élevé du mot, un signe d'élection, une chance ou un défi du destin."

com uns aigniax feïst 4005–6). Therefore there is no possibility that the hero happened to encounter a tame lion; it is his action that has won the beast's affection and loyalty. Yvain's acquisition of the beast is a sign of his progressive redemption, and the lion disappears from the story precisely at the moment when Yvain has regained *mesure*.[53]

Other tales have lions whose debt to hagiography is even plainer. Not surprisingly, *La Queste del saint Graal*[54] shows considerable influence of hagiographic legend. This middle volume of the "Pseudo-Map" cycle is generally acknowledged to be influenced by Cistercian mysticism, and its author was clearly familiar with hagiographic literature. For example, Joseph of Arimathea and his sons are able to survive for forty days in prison without food or water since they have the Grail with them (p. 84)—motif b[1], miraculous feeding; compare the adventures of the three monks who found Macarius the Roman. Like many monks, Perceval is tempted by the devil in the shape of a woman (p. 91). The clearest parallel, however, occurs in Perceval's adventure on the island.

On an island, Perceval sees a serpent carrying a lion cub in its mouth followed by an adult lion, "crying and roaring" (criant et braiant p. 94). He decides to aid the lion against the snake "because [the lion] is a more natural beast and of more gentle degree than the serpent" (por ce que est naturelx beste et de plus gentil ordre que li serpenz).[55] In return for the rescue of its cub, the adult lion makes manifest its gratitude, and after taking its baby home it returns to spend the night with Perceval, and serves as his pillow. Perceval considers it a "mout bele aventure" (a very fine adventure) that "Our Lord" had sent him a lion to be his companion (p. 95). In his sleep, Perceval has a dream in which he sees two women, one riding

---

53. Haidu, *Lion-Queue-Coupée* (1972), pp. 63–64.
54. Ed. Pauphilet (rpt. 1980).
55. Aelian tells the story of a man who aided an eagle against a snake because the serpent is evil, whereas the eagle is a minister of Zeus and belongs to a higher order: *De Natura Animalium* 17:37 (cf. George Devereux, "The Structure of Tragedy and the Structure of the Psyche in Aristotle's *Poetics*," in Charles Hanly and Morris Lazerowitz, eds., *Psychoanalysis and Philosophy* [New York: International Universities Press, 1970], p. 68).

on a lion and the other a serpent. Ultimately he discovers their meaning; the younger one, riding on the lion, represents "the new law," Christianity ("la nouvelle loi," p. 101). The connection here with Christian allegory is plain. What is important, however, is that the *right* course of action is validated or symbolized by the presence of lions.

Other motifs familiar from hagiography abound. People miraculously know each other's names (pp. 100, 105, motif d^2). Perceval, Galahad, and Bors come upon a white deer guarded by four lions. They follow the deer to a hermitage (guiding beast, motif b^2), whereupon it is metamorphosed into a human figure and the lions turn into the four winged emblems of the Evangelists and fly off to heaven (pp. 234–35).

Many of the motifs common to hagiography and medieval romance are prominent in folklore—the guiding beast, for example—and not all of them need have a single source.[56] In some cases, the guiding animal was in fact a divinity in disguise. At Boiai, for instance, Artemis sent the founders in search of a new settlement by following a hare; the hare, a lunar animal throughout the world's mythology, was Artemis in disguise.[57] This usage has relevance for the hagiographic motif, as the presence of the animal here makes manifest the god's favor. Macarius' demonic bride, by contrast, found him without the aid of any guide. In medieval epic, the deer enjoys a privileged position as a guide. From our point of view, what is significant here is the explicitly providential nature of the animal guide. In all but one of the epics considered by Jeanne Baroin in her study of "Le cerf épique," the animals show up immediately after the hero's prayer for divine assistance.[58] The lion in

56. Krappe, "Guiding Animals" (1942); he notes that a large group of guiding-animal tales may be aetiological in nature (e.g., the Macedonian community of Aigai reputed to have been founded by Archelaus who followed a goat [*aix*], p. 228). In medieval literature, *La Mule sans frein*, the *Papagay*, *Wîgâlois*, and *Kulhwch and Olwen* contain accounts of guiding beasts. In eastern literature, in *The Thousand and One Nights*, the "Tale of the Vizier's Daughter" has a guiding lion.

57. Pausanias, III.22.12; see the discussion of Krappe, "Guiding Animals," p. 229.

58. Baroin, "A propos du cerf épique" (1980), p. 7. In the exception, the *Chanson des Saisnes*, the stag who shows Charlemagne where the river may be crossed

Le Chevalier au lion is not properly a guide, although he is a most helpful beast; he catches a deer for Yvain—motif d.

Whether or not the lion is properly a psychopomp, I do suggest that his prominence in hagiographic legend made him an appropriate guide and helper in chivalric romance. The lion as a guide to the other world does appear in an old Celtic tale, the "Wooing of Emer," and there are other instances of beasts who guide to the other world in similar legends.[59] In a discussion of a pious story in which a mule guides a young man to the "au-delà," Giuseppi Gatto speculates that this tale represents the christianization of a pagan legend, and that the paradisiacal region visited by the young man was in the original version the land of the dead.[60]

In a few cases, it may be possible to assign a more specific origin and function to an animal motif. The most original use of lions in the hagiographic accounts is as grave diggers, a motif (g^1) that makes its first appearance in Jerome's life of Paul of Thebes and recurs in the accounts of Mary the Egyptian and Macarius the Roman. The detail appealed greatly to later medieval hagiographers. It occurs in a late version of the life of Onuphrius. In his retelling of the life of Mary the Egyptian, Rutebeuf found the detail sympathetic. His lion displays a degree of anthropomorphic cooperation that falls only a little short of the friendly Mrs. Beaver in C. S. Lewis' children's fantasy, *The Lion, the Witch, and the Wardrobe*, who operates a sewing machine. According to Rutebeuf, Zosimas claimed that after finding the dead body of the saint, he would have rejoiced greatly if he had had someone to help him bury her body:[61]

> Adonc n'i a demoré guere
> Que il vit venir un lyon.
> Moult en fu esbahiz li hon;

---

was chased by dogs. The king, however, does consider the beast to have been sent by God (ed. Michel, Slatkine Reprints, 1969, vol. II, 35–36).

59. A. Brown, "Knight of the Lion," pp. 688–95.

60. Gatto, "Le Voyage au Paradis" (1979).

61. Rutebeuf, *La Vie de ste. Marie l'Egyptienne*, in *Oeuvres complètes*, ed. Faral and Bastin (1977), vol. 2.

Més il vit si humble la beste
Sanz samblant de fere moleste,
Bien sot que Diex li ot tramis.

(1208–13)

(Thereupon he had hardly waited at all before he saw a lion approach. The man was much astonished, but he saw that the beast was so humble, without showing a sign of doing harm, that he knew well that God had sent him.)

Addressing the beast as "Biaus douz amis" (1214; beautiful sweet friend), Zosimas requests his aid. "The gallant beast" ("la beste debonere," 1220) promptly excavates "a grave great and deep for this fair and elegant lady" (grant et parfonde / Por cele dame nete et monde, 1225–26).

Quant la fosse fu bien chevee,
Li sainz hermites l'a levee
A ses main par devers la teste,
Et par les piez la prist la beste:
En la fosse l'ont il dui mise
Et bien couverte a grant devise.

(1227–32)

(When the grave was well finished, the holy hermit raised her up, her head in his hands, and the beast took her by the feet; the two of them put her in the grave and covered her carefully.)

The popularity of the motif of grave-digging lions is apparent; its origin is more obscure. The lion is, as we have seen, a multivalent symbol, emblem of the sun, of royalty, of justice, but also a sign of destruction and the devil. He was perhaps a demon of death among the ancient Semitic peoples.[62] A victory over a lion is therefore a victory over death itself. He is associated with the desert. Paul was a Coptic saint, and it is tempting to speculate upon the possible influence of Egyptian mythology or folklore on his legend.

---

62. Chotzen, "Le Lion d'Owein," citing Rudolf Zenker, *Yvainstudien*, Halle 1921, p. 254, n. 4. Peter Brown kindly pointed out to me (letter of May 20, 1984) that "Ialabaoth, the Gnostic demiurge, is lion-headed, and that means, quite frankly, very mean—tearing, devouring, untrammeled and destructive, blind, nonhuman instinct."

From the earliest times there has been a lion-divinity, a lion-king. This is a universal phenomenon, not limited to Egypt.[63] The image of man between two lions is one of the oldest icons, going back to remote times (for instance, on Akkadian seals). It is, I suggest, an image capable of a variety of interpretations and significances. The lion can destroy the man, or the man may tame the lion. What is interesting about the lion-symbolism is that hagiography seems to have tended to minimize the negative side of this lore. Daniel in the "lions' den" is shown in the earliest depictions standing in prayer between two lions. Paul of Thebes and Macarius the Roman were both buried by two lions. The double lions whose statues were found as guardians of temple gateways were themselves assimilated to their gates. As the door to the temple became identified with the other world, so the lions became the guardians of the other world.[64] The lion, then, could be a psychopomp and messenger between the two worlds.[65] Furthermore, the lion's native habitat is that space "betwixt and between," the desert—the place where miracles happen. Few if any medieval romances transpire in genuine deserts, but as the locus of adventure the medieval authors substituted for the desert the principal uninhabited territory of the medieval world, the opposite of the *polis*—the forest, or a deserted island.

Liminality

One of the most significant contributions of hagiographic romance was the enshrining of the concept of liminal space. Adventures rarely happen when one is securely ensconced between four

---

63. Wit, *Le Rôle et sens du lion* (1951), pp. 461–62.
64. Ibid., p. 464; see also p. 72.
65. The lion's allomorph, the cat, is known in myth and folklore as a psychopomp, perhaps because of its reputation for never getting lost. In the Finnish epic, the *Kalevala*, the cat is a psychopomp, and, more important here, Tutankhamen was led to the underworld by a black cat; Dale-Green, *Cult of the Cat* (1963), pp. 135–36. According to Dale-Green (p. 41), Osiris was also associated with the cat; in view of the very tentative identification of Onuphrius with Osiris, it is tempting to regard the incident of his burial by two lions not as a late addition to his legend, inserted by analogy with Paul of Thebes, but as a detail proper to it, which has disappeared from our extant early versions. This conclusion, however, is tenuous at best.

walls.[66] The saint's quest, as we have seen, was both exterior and interior—real and symbolic.[67] Much the same is true of the quest of the medieval knight.[68] The climax of medieval epic, like that of the martyr's passions, occurs in public space—the battlefield, the praetor's court. In the romances a *tertium quid* becomes important. The drama is enacted in a space "betwixt and between," neither of this world nor wholly of the next. In Arthurian romance, this is usually either the forest, particularly Broceliande, or a magic (and uninhabited) island.[69]

Although the notion of the mysterious island as the locus of romance is as old as the *Odyssey*, the use of the theme in medieval literature is strongest in those works influenced, directly or indirectly, by hagiography. The *Navigatio Sancti Brendani* is an immediate parallel. This extremely popular religious fantasy tells of the adventures of a group of sixth-century Irish monks who spend seven years sailing in the North Atlantic in quest of the *terra repromissionis sanctorum*, the Promised Land of the Saints,[70] and visiting on the way many miraculous islands. Ultimately the saint and his crew do reach the promised land, a world rich in fruit where the sun never sets. In the *Queste del saint Graal*, also, Perceval encounters his friendly lion on an island which he reached by mysterious means.

The hero frequently sets forth in disguise (le Chevalier *au lion*, le Chevalier *de la charrette*, le *Bel Inconnu*;[71] compare the frequency

66. Compare Jerome's praise of Asella, cited above, p. 81. For romance, see Ménard, "Le Chevalier errant" (1976), p. 292.

67. See above, chapter 4, section 4, "Secret Flight."

68. See Ménard, "Le Chevalier errant," p. 298; also Saly, "L'Itinéraire intérieur" (1976).

69. For the latter, the influence of the Irish *Imrama* and accounts like the *Navigatio Sancti Brendani* are probably important.

70. Ed. Selmer (1959).

71. Other disguised heroes are found in *Cligès*, *Partenopeus de Blois*, and *Ipomedon*. The successful use of disguise seems to be one of the *differentiae* between epic and romance. Medieval epic heroes do not, or cannot, successfully disguise themselves for long (see Suard, "Le Motif de déguisement" [1980]). In ancient epic the use of disguise leads to tragedy (wearing another's armor leads to the death of Patroclus in the *Iliad*, and to the deaths of Euryalus and Turnus in the *Aeneid*). Only Odysseus, a proto-romance hero, can effectively conceal his identity.

of the motif of mistaken identity, d^1, or disguise, b, in the hagiographic romances). The prominence of disguise heightens the importance of recognition scenes. The disguise motif may be compared to rites of passage in which the liminars are stripped of distinguishing clothing and other attributes of culture. All are made equal. The romance heroes are not equal, but their anonymity guarantees that the renown they win is due to their own merits and not to respect for their inherited wealth or status.

Medieval heroes leave home for many reasons; some leave to seek a bride, a fief,[72] reputation, revenge, or even the Grail. These goals, however, are found in the forest or in a foreign court. The popular American fantasy of marrying the "boy (girl) next door" does not hold good here. Other heroes are forced to depart. A number of medieval works contain heroes who are exiles—the *Waltharius* and the *Ruodlieb*, to give only two examples written in Latin. Susan Wittig notes for Middle English romance the obligatory "motifeme" (or "motif," to use the terminology of Albert Lord) of exile.[73] For the material that she considers, Wittig remarks upon the validity of an anthropological interpretation of this phenomenon, which ensures an exogamous marriage for the hero.[74]

For hagiography, some other interpretation has to be found, but it is important that the motif remains the same, whatever its specific meaning for the work in question. Saints seek virginity, not marriage. We have seen the frequency of the motif of flight from marriage, a^1, and secret flight, a^2. In fleeing marriage, the saint rejects not only a spouse and an accompanying, well-defined social role chosen for him or her by parents but also an entire set of values concerning the importance of this world. But as many of the lives, particularly those of women, make plain, the saint will literally espouse another, celestial bridegroom and another, better set of values.[75] This spiritual marriage is truly exogamous. In tales of vir-

---

72. For a discussion of the search for these goals in real life, see Duby, "Les 'Jeunes' " (1964).

73. Wittig, *Stylistic and Narrative Structures* (1978), p. 120.

74. Ibid. 184.

75. For the popularity of such tales, particularly in Old French martyr narratives, see Hyan, "Dualistic Narrative" (1983).

gin martyrs, an almost obligatory motif is an assault, always successfully thwarted, on the saint's virginity.[76] Again, the detail serves
to underline the importance of virginity. Secret flight ensures that
the traveler goes alone, just as an exile is usually sent away by himself, bereft of companions. This fact encourages virginity, or at least
chastity, during the journey.

Yet another object of the quest is the search for something lost. In
the tales of the saints there is a pervasive nostalgia for Paradise and
for man's state before the Fall. The ability to live in amicable relations with the wild beasts is, I believe, the primary emblem of this
lost condition, although other activities of the hermits, such as the
practice of virginity and of ascetical fasting, are connected with it as
well. If the object of the quest is to recover Paradise and to return to
Adam's state before the Fall, then virginity is a necessary concomitant. In Eden Adam and Eve were virgins. They were sexually im-
mature. Many contemporary romances, whether written for children or adults, have children (or other virginal characters) for
heroes. Such fantasies reveal a nostalgia for the innocence and purity thought to be possessed only in childhood, before the advent of
sexuality. In a number of secular romances the adventure concerns
the explicit search for something lost[77]—for a lost or stolen girl in
the Greek romances, or a lost reputation (Chrétien de Troyes' *Erec
et Enide*), or a combination of the two, a loss of reputation that
brings about the loss of a wife's esteem (*Yvain*). During these
quests, the married heroes appear not to engage in sexual activity.

One of the characteristics of the romance mode, according to
Northop Frye, is the introduction of "a world in which the ordinary
laws of nature are slightly suspended."[78] Romances tell of unusual
experiences—miraculous knowledge of names, animal guides, the
ability to survive without food or water—and such events transpire
in unfamiliar places. Very few tales of the extraordinary, whether

76. Farrar, "Structure and Function" (1973), p. 84. In Hrothswitha's *Pelagius*,
the saintly hero has to withstand the homosexual attentions of the villanous Saracen
ruler.

77. A popular folklore motif; cf. Thompson, *Motif-Index* (1955), where items H
1385.1–3 concern the search for a lost woman.

78. *Anatomy of Criticism*, p. 33.

fairy tale or science fiction, occur in familiar surroundings. Like the initiand in a tribal rite of passage, the hero or heroine has to leave the safety of the known, of family and friends, and explore an unknown land. He or she has to become "a stranger in a strange land." So too does the follower of Christ or the *xenos monachos*, the monk-stranger. It is in this unknown world, in liminal space, that the ritual struggle takes place.

We have seen the tripartite nature of all *rites de passage*, as they move from separation to *limen* to aggregation. In a similar fashion, the romances posit a tripartite spatial division—this world, betwixt and between (the desert, the island, the forest), and the next (or a return to this world of the traveller in a changed, and improved, status). The plots also display a threefold movement, which may be variously described. The progression may be from

    1. STRUGGLE > RITUAL DEATH > RECOGNITION[79]
      agon   *pathos*   *anagnorisis*
                  or
    2. CIVILIZATION > SAVAGERY >   SALVATION
                 or
    3. PROHIBITION > VIOLATION >   RESTITUTION

The first of these patterns, which is the pattern of comedy as well, is adduced by Northrop Frye for romance, which he refers to as "The Mythos of Summer." He notes its applicability to the life cycle of the dying and rising god (whether Adonis or Christ). The martyr's *passio* might also be seen as conforming to this formulation. The hermit, too, struggles to leave the civilized world, undergoes a surrogate form of death, and in the end is recognized (usually by a traveler) as a saint. The fairy tale of Sleeping Beauty follows the same paradigm as she is "mysteriously threatened, suffers death or sleep similar to death. But she is awakened again and begins to flourish—and with her, the world about her."[80] The second pattern is particularly descriptive of the spatial movement of the hermit's *vita*. He leaves the *oikoumenē* for the desert and then attains

79. Ibid., p. 187.
80. Lüthi, *Once Upon a Time* (1976), pp. 23–24.

heaven. A schematic representation of the plot of *Yvain* conforms to this pattern as well. Yvain flees society after his rejection by Laudine, goes mad in the forest, and eventually, with the aid of Lunete and the lion, regains his wife's respect and love. The third pattern conforms to a Proppian analysis of folktale. The purely fictional life of Macarius fits this description as the saint sins with the diabolic bride, atones by being buried alive, and then is restored to his pristine condition and rewarded by a vision of Christ. The three formulations, however, are not restrictive, and may be applied, with varying degrees of accuracy, to more than one genre. What is important is the pervasiveness of the pattern.

THE PERSISTENT DREAM

The journey does not terminate with the few medieval works discussed here. Tales of quests continue to be written and to be read with eagerness; if we can judge by the number of science fiction books and films today, their popularity may be greater than ever. The objects of the quest may differ, but certain constants remain as men and women continue to search for knowledge, for identity, for sanctity, and for peace. The quest, moreover, can become obsessive. The Quaker painter Edward Hicks (1780–1849), for one, painted nearly one hundred canvases depicting that Peaceable Kingdom in which the lion and the lamb shall lie down together, and a little child shall lead them. In the background he often portrayed William Penn's treaty with the Indians as an image of fair behavior worthy of redeemed man.

Indeed, the quest for the New World was often seen in terms of a search for Paradise, and Columbus, at least, thought that he had found it. Believing that he had reached the shores of the far east, Columbus wrote to Ferdinand and Isabella from the Gulf of Paria near the mouth of the Orinoco:

There are great indications of this being the terrestrial Paradise, for its situation coincides with the opinions of the holy and wise theologians . . .; and, moreover, the other evidences agree with the supposition, for I have never either read or heard of fresh water coming in so large a quantity, in close conjunction with the water of the sea; the idea is also corroborated by the blandness of the temperature; and if the water of which I speak does not proceed from the earthly Paradise, it seems to be a still greater wonder. . . .[81]

Columbus was neither the first nor the last to think he had found Paradise. According to William Warren, the African adventurer Livingstone believed that when he succeeded in finding the sources of the Nile he would stand on "the site of the primeval Paradise."[82] In his book *Paradise Found*, Warren himself claims to have discovered the true location of the Garden of Eden at the North Pole.

In an article published in 1922, "The Location of the Garden of Eden," W. F. Albright apologized for his seeming "presumption" in adding "yet another study" to what he categorized as "this time-worn subject."[83] He writes optimistically:

The days are long since over when men looked back with a wistfulness born of oft-repeated disillusionment to the vanished beauties of the world in which mankind was cradled. We now realize that the only terrestrial paradise will be created by our own efforts, directed along the lines of healthy progress. Yet there is a rare charm in the romantic stories with which men beguiled their fancies and sought peace from the turmoil of a war-ridden land, or from the economic stress which has ever dogged our footsteps as we progress towards civilization.

If today one must speak with a less positivistic certainty about mankind's "healthy progress," one must also acknowledge with Albright the universal appeal of the search. As he goes on to point out, these are not the only psychological bases for the "motive of Paradise," and he notes the romantic nostalgia for childhood that accompanies many paradise reveries. But whatever the reasons, the quest is deeply rooted in the unconscious. And only in the rarest cases is the search successful. Regardless of the outcome, the quest does, and must, continue. The process is more important than the attainment of the goal. In terms of a tripartite structure, it is the middle term that is dramatically dominant.

81. *Select Letters of Christopher Columbus*, translated by R. H. Major (London, 1860), quoted by Warren, *Paradise Found* (1886), p. 5. See also Eliade, *The Quest* (1969), p. 90; also Williams, *Wilderness and Paradise*.
82. Warren, *Paradise Found*, pp. 21–22.
83. "The Location" (1922–23), p. 15.

According to Mircea Eliade, the quest for paradise is a quest for one's primordial beginnings.[84] Perhaps this is why images first of death, then of the womb and rebirth, and finally of children figure prominently in such tales. In the *Gospel of Pseudo-Matthew*, cited earlier, it was the *child* Jesus who enjoyed dominion over the lions and played with them. The familiar prophecy from Isaiah depicts a child leading the wild beasts (this prophecy was, to be sure, known to the author of *Pseudo-Matthew*).

Many children's stories and works of science fiction narrate quests that conform closely to the paradigms described above. C. S. Lewis's popular children's fantasy, *The Chronicles of Narnia*, for instance, relates the adventures of a group of children in an enchanted world, ruled over by the lion Aslan, a little-disguised, allegorical figure of Christ. In the first volume, *The Lion, the Witch, and the Wardrobe*, four children go through a large, dark wardrobe and find themselves in a magic land of talking animals[85] and evil witches. They set out on their journey, forgetting to take any provisions with them. Luckily they encounter some kindly beavers who feed them (motif b^1).[86] The animals lead the children to Aslan (animal guides, motif b^2). Aslan knows the children's names (miraculous knowledge, motif d^2). Like the lion of myth, Aslan is both "good and terrible."[87] He aids his friends, the innocent animals and the children, but destroys the evil witch and her cohorts. In the final volume of the *Chronicles of Narnia, The Last Battle*, there is great emphasis put upon the fact that Aslan "is not a Tame Lion."[88]

One final example of the persistence of the quest for the peaceable kingdom: *Le Lion*, a popular novel by the French writer

---

84. Eliade, *The Quest*.

85. According to St. Basil, in the terrestrial paradise animals are gentle and can talk; Graf, *Miti, leggende e superstizioni* (1892), ch. 3, "Gli abitatori del paradiso terrestre."

86. Lewis, *The Lion* (1950), pp. 69 ff. The evil witch also gives food, magical Turkish delight, to one of the children.

87. "People who have not been to Narnia sometimes think that a thing cannot be good and terrible at the same time," Ibid., p. 123.

88. *The Last Battle* (1956), pp. 16, 20. In an interview reported in *The New Yorker*, January 9, 1984, p. 28, Ringling Brothers Circus' animal trainer, Gunther Gebel-Williams, claimed that it is possible "to train lions and tigers but not to tame them."

Joseph Kessel. The book tells the tale of Patricia, the daughter of a game warden in Kenya, who has befriended an orphaned lion cub named King. King, who has grown into a magnificent animal, does not remain a pet but is returned to live in the wild with his own kind. He retains his love for the young girl, and they continue to play together. The people and the king of the beasts live in harmony together—until sex enters the picture. The native Masai are not at all sure that Patricia is not magic, and a young warrior wants to marry the girl. According to his tribal rules, to attain this honor he has to undergo a rite of passage, killing a lion with only his native weapons. The upshot of this confrontation is tragedy—the death of the lion (killed by Patricia's game-warden father to save the life of the native), and the destruction of Patricia's African paradise. The novel ends with the girl being sent out of the bush to a European school, to grow up.

The narrator is an anonymous traveler. His very lack of identifying characteristics makes him an ideal narrator; he speaks for everyone. He descends to the famed wilderness of an African game preserve—famed but dangerous all the same, for the animals retain their allegiance to the wild. When he arrives, he senses something special, almost magical, about the place. He is in the grip of an overwhelming, instinctive nostalgia: "It seemed to me that I had found again a paradise that I had dreamt or known in the times of which I had lost the memory. I touched its threshhold. And was unable to cross it."[89] He must *see* what is going on. He goes out walking:

I had reached the limit of the thorn bushes. I had only to leave their cover, confront the bright, humid sun, in order to know, on their consecrated territory, the friendship of the savage beasts.

    Nothing could prevent me any longer. The reflexes of caution, of self-preservation, were suspended in favor of an instinct as obscure as it was powerful that impelled me toward the *other* universe.[90]

89. Kessel, *Le Lion* (1958 [1978]), p. 15: "Il me semblait que j'avais retrouvé un paradis rêvé ou connu par moi en des âges dont j'avais perdu la mémoire. Et j'en touchais le seuil. Et ne pouvais le franchir."
90. Ibid., p. 16: "J'avais atteint la limite des épineux. Il n'y avait qu'à sortir de leur couvert, aborder le sol humide et brillant pour connaître, sur leur terrain con-

Like many of the works discussed in this study, *Le Lion* does not belong to the first rank of literature. Perhaps for that reason it is all the more revealing. "Popular" literature, whether hagiographic romance or a work like *Le Lion*, appeals to commonly held and indeed deep-rooted aspirations. It conveys these without excessive subtlety by means of a readily grasped mode of symbolic discourse. The narrator in *Le Lion* cannot take the step into that desired *other* world alone. It is forbidden (p. 17). For all the purity of his motives, he can only enter the magical world with Patricia. He protests: "I do not want to disturb the beasts. . . . But only live a little with them, like them."[91] For man—for adults in this modern fantasy world—such a life is not possible. But the wish remains, with all its potency.

---

sacré, l'amitié des bêtes sauvages. Rien ne pouvait plus m'en empêcher. Les réflexes de la prudence, de la conservation étaient suspendus au bénéfice d'un instinct aussi obscur que puissant et qui me poussait vers *l'autre* univers" (Kessel's italics).

91. Ibid., p. 20: "Je ne veux pas inquiéter les bêtes. . . . Mais seulement vivre un peu avec elles, comme elles."

Appendix

TABLE OF THEMES AND MOTIFS

THEME A: Circumstances preceding departure
flight from marriage, a^1
the "more" motif, a^2
secret flight, a^3
search for penance, a^4

THEME B: The journey
ability to survive without food or water, b^1
unusual guides, b^2
symbolic death, b^3
disguise, b^4

THEME C: Discovery of a place
an empty cave or cell, c^1
discovery of dead body, c^2

THEME D: Encounter (discovery of a person)
mistaken identity, d^1
miraculous knowledge of identity, d^2
unusual appearance, d^3
miraculously provided food, d^4
other miracles, d^5
uncorrupted body, d^6

THEME E: The tale

THEME F: The request
denied, f^1

THEME G: Burial
burial by lions, g^1

Bibliography

ABBREVIATIONS USED

AA.SS   Acta Sanctorum (References to AA.SS are by the volume number of the month in roman numerals and by the volume number in the continuous series in arabic figures, followed by the day of the saint.)

AB   Analecta Bollandiana

AJP   American Journal of Philology

AMS   Acta Martyrum Sincera

BHG   Bibliotheca Hagiographica Graeca

BHL   Bibliotheca Hagiographica Latina

BHO   Bibliotheca Hagiographica Orientalis

CB   Classical Bulletin

CCM   Cahiers de Civilisation Médiévale

CCSL   Corpus Christianorum, Series Latina

CSCO   Corpus Scriptorum Christianorum Orientalium

CSEL   Corpus Scriptorum Ecclesiasticorum Latinorum

DACL   Dictionnaire d'archéologie chrétienne et de liturgie

GRBS   Greek, Roman and Byzantine Studies

JRS   Journal of Roman Studies

JTS   Journal of Theological Studies

JWCI   Journal of the Warburg and Courtauld Institute

M&H   Medievalia et Humanistica

MGH   Monumenta Germaniae Historica

MLR   Modern Language Review

MP   Modern Philology

PG   Patrologia Graeca

PL   Patrologia Latina

PMLA   Publications of the Modern Language Association

PQ   Philological Quarterly

RAM   Revue d'ascétique et du mystique
RHR   Revue de l'histoire des religions
RLR   Revue des langues romanes
RPh   Romance Philology
VC   Vigiliae Christianae
ZfrSL   Zeitschrift für französiche Sprache und Literatur

PRIMARY SOURCES

Aelian. 1959. *On the Characteristics of Animals.* Ed. A. F. Scholfield. Cambridge, Mass.: Harvard University Press. Loeb Classical Library.

Amélineau, E. 1884. "Voyage d'un moine égyptien dans le désert." *Recueil de travaux relatifs à la philologie et à l'archéologie égyptiennes et assyriennes* 6: 166–94.

———. 1894. *Histoire des Monastères de la Basse-Egypte.* Paris: Leroux.

Bartelink, G. J. M., ed. 1974; rpt. 1981. *Vita di Antonio.* Rome: Fondazione Lorenzo Valla, Mondadori Editori.

Boneta y la Plana, Joseph. 1680. *Vidas de Santos y Venerables Varones de la Religión.* Saragossa: Domingo Gascón.

Budge, E. Wallis. 1915. *Miscellaneous Coptic Texts in the Dialect of Upper Egypt.* London: British Museum and Longmans and Co.

———. 1928. *The Book of the Saints of the Ethiopian Church.* 4 vols. Cambridge: Cambridge University Press.

Chariton. 1979. *Le Roman de Chairéas et Callirhoé.* Ed. Georges Molinié. Paris: Les Belles Lettres.

Charles, R. H., ed. 1913; rpt. 1964. *The Apocrypha and Pseudepigrapha of the Old Testament.* 2 vols. Oxford: Clarendon Press.

Chrétien de Troyes. 1914; rpt. 1970. *Arthurian Romances.* Trans. W. W. Comfort. New York: Dutton.

———. 1974. *Le Chevalier au Lion.* Ed. Mario Roques. Paris: H. Champion.

Colgrave, Bertram, ed. 1968. *The Earliest Life of Gregory the Great. By an Anonymous Monk of Whitby.* Lawrence, Kans.: University of Kansas Press.

———. 1956. *Felix's Life of Saint Guthlac: Introduction, Text, Translation and Notes.* Cambridge: Cambridge University Press.

Cunningham, Maurice P., ed. 1966. *Aurelii Prudentii Clementis Carmina.* CCSL, 126. Turnhout: Brepols.

Dagron, Gilbert, ed. 1978. *Vie et miracles de sainte Thècle: Texte grec, traduction, et commentaire.* Brussels: Société des Bollandistes.

Dawes, Elizabeth, and Norman H. Baynes, trans. 1948. *Three Byzantine Saints.* Oxford: Blackwell.

Eusebius. 1926; rpt. 1975. *Ecclesiastical History.* Trans. J. E. L. Oulton. Loeb Classical Library. Cambridge: Harvard University Press.

Elliott, Alison Goddard, ed. 1983. *The Vie de saint Alexis in the Twelfth and Thirteenth Centuries.* North Carolina Studies in Romance Languages and Literature, 221. Chapel Hill: University of North Carolina.

Festugière, A. J. 1970. *Vie de Théodore de Sykéon.* 2 vols. Subsidia hagiographica, 48. Brussels: Société des Bollandistes.

Flusin, R. 1983. *Miracle et histoire dans L'oeuvre de Cyrille de Scythopolis.* Paris: Etudes Augustiniennes.

Heidel, Alexander. 1963. *The Gilgamesh Epic and Old Testament Parallels.* Chicago: University of Chicago Press.

Homer. 1951. *The Iliad.* Trans. Richmond Lattimore. Chicago: University of Chicago Press.

James, Montague Rhodes. 1924. *Apocryphal New Testament.* Oxford: Clarendon Press.

Kessel, Joseph. 1958; rpt. 1978. *Le Lion,* Paris: Gallimard, Collection Folio.

Kim, H. C., ed. 1973. *The Gospel of Nicodemus.* Toronto: Pontifical Institute.

Lepage, Yvan G., ed. 1978. *Les Rédactions en vers du Couronnement de Louis.* Geneva: Droz.

Lewis, C. S. 1950; rpt. 1970. *The Lion, the Witch, and the Wardrobe.* New York: Collier Books.

———. 1956; rpt. 1970. *The Last Battle.* New York: Collier Books.

Luck, Dom Edmund J., O.S.B., ed. 1880. *The Life and Miracles of St. Benedict, by Gregory the Great, from an old English version by P. W.* London: R. Washbourne.

Merwin, W. S., trans. 1959. *The Poem of the Cid.* Ed. Ramón Menendez Pidal. New York: New American Library.

Michel, Charles, ed. 1924. *Protévangile de Jacques, Pseudo-Matthieu, Evangile de Thomas.* Paris: Picard.

Musurillo, Herbert. 1972. *The Acts of the Christian Martyrs.* Oxford: Clarendon.

Natalibus, Petrus de. 1519. *Catalogus Sanctorum et gestorum eorum ex diversis voluminibus collectus.* London: Jacob Saccon.

Pauphilet, Albert, ed. 1980. *La Queste del saint Graal.* 2nd ed. Paris: H. Champion.

Petitmengin, Pierre, et al., eds. 1981. *Pélagie la pénitente: Métamorphoses d'une légende.* Vol. I: "Les textes et leur histoire." Paris: Etudes Augustiniennes.

Pseudo-Callisthenes. 1955. *The Life of Alexander of Macedon.* Trans. Elizabeth Hazelton Haight. New York: Longmans.

————. 1969. *The Romance of Alexander the Great by Pseudo-Callisthenes*. Trans. Albert Mugrdich Wolohojian. New York: Columbia University Press.

Pseudo-Turpin. 1937. *The Pseudo-Turpin, edited from Bibliothèque Nationale, Fonds Latin, MS 17656*. Ed. H. M. Smyser. Cambridge, Mass.: The Mediaeval Academy of America.

————. 1960. *Història de Carles Magnes e de Rotllà: Traducció Catalana del segle XV*. Ed. Martí de Riquer. Barcelona.

Raoli, Horazio. 1705. *Vita di Sant' Honofrio Heremita*. Anagni: Angelo Mancini.

Rodríguez, Isidoro, and D. José Guillén. 1950. *Obras completas de Aurelio Prudencio*. Madrid: Editorial Católica.

Rutebeuf. 1977. *Oeuvres complètes*. 2 vols. Ed. Edmond Faral and Julia Bastin. Paris: Picard.

Selmer, Carl, ed. 1959. *Navigatio Sancti Brendani Abbatis*. Publications in Medieval Studies, 16. Notre Dame: University of Notre Dame Press.

Storey, Christopher, ed. 1968. *La Vie de saint Alexis: Texte du Manuscrit de Hildesheim (L)*. Geneva: Droz.

Surius, Laurent. 1875–80. *Historiae seu vitae sanctorum juxta optimam coloniensem editionem, nunc vero ex recentioribus et probatissimis monumentis numero auctae, mendis expurgatae et notis exornatae, quibus accedit Romanum martyrologium breviter illustratum, tauriensi presbytero e congreg. clerr. regg. S. Paulli curante*. Turin: Petri Marietti.

Swan, Charles, and Wynnard Hooper, trans. 1876; rpt. 1959. *Gesta Romanorum, or Entertaining Moral Stories*. New York: Dover Publications.

Synaxarium Alexandrinum. 1922. CSCO, vol. 78, Scriptores Arabici, Series tertia, vol. 18. Rome: Karolus de Luigi.

Talbot, C. H., ed. 1959. *The Life of Christina of Markyate: A Twelfth-Century Recluse*. Oxford: Clarendon Press.

Thomas, Antoine, ed. 1974. *La Chanson de Sainte Foi d' Agen*. Paris: Honoré Champion.

Veilleux, Armand, trans. 1980. *Pachomian Koinonia*. Vol. I. *The Life of Saint Pachomius and his Disciples*. Kalamazoo: Cistercian Publications.

Vielliard, Jeanne. 1938. *Le Guide du pèlerin de Saint-Jacques de Compostelle*. Macon: Protat Frères.

Walker, Alexander, trans. 1870. *Apocryphal Gospels, Acts, and Revelations*. Ante-Nicene Christian Library. Vol. 16, Translations of the Fathers to 325 A.D. Edinburgh: T.-T. Clark.

Whitehead, F. 1975. *La Chanson de Roland*. Oxford: Blackwell.

Xenophon of Ephesus. 1926. *Les Ephésiaques, ou le Roman d'Habrocomès et d'Anthia*. Ed. Georges Dalmeyda. Paris: Les Belles Lettres.

SECONDARY WORKS

Aigrain, René. 1953. *L'Hagiographie: Ses sources, ses méthodes, son histoire*. Paris: Bloud et Gay.

Albright, W. F. 1922–23. "The Location of the Garden of Eden." *American Journal of Semitic Languages* 39: 15–31.

Altman, Charles. 1975. "Two Types of Opposition and the Structure of Latin Saints' Lives." *M&H* 6: 1–11.

Amy de la Bretèque, F. 1980. "L'Épine enlevée de la patte du lion. Récit médiéval et conte populaire (Essai d'analyse morphologique)." *RLR* 84: 53–72.

Arbesmann, Rudolf. 1949–50. "Fasting and Prophecy in Pagan and Christian Antiquity." *Traditio* 7: 1–71.

Badawy, Alexander. 1978. *Coptic Art*. Cambridge, Mass.: MIT Press.

Baker, A. T. 1916–17. "La Vie de sainte Marie l'Egyptienne." *RLR* 59: 145–401.

Bandera Gómez, C. 1969. *El 'Poema de mio Cid': Poesía, historia, mito*. Madrid: Gredos.

Baroin, Jeanne. 1980. "A propos du cerf épique." *Mélanges de langue et littérature françaises du Moyen Age et de la Renaissance offerts à Charles Foulon II. Marche Romane* 30: 5–15.

Barnard, L. W. 1974. "The Date of S. Athanasius' *Vita Antonii*." *VC* 28: 169–75.

Barnes, Timothy D. 1968. "Pre-Decian *Acta Martyrum*." *JTS* 19: 509–31.

Barton, George Aaron. 1902. *A Sketch of Semitic Origins*. New York: Macmillan.

Bate, A. T. 1916–17. "La Vie de sainte Marie l'Egyptienne." *RLR* 59: 145–400.

Beatie, Bruce. 1971. "Patterns of Myth in Medieval Narrative." *Symposium* 25: 101–22.

Bettelheim, Bruno. 1977. *The Uses of Enchantment: The Meaning and Importance of Fairy Tales*. New York: Knopf.

Bibliotheca Hagiographica Graeca. 3d rev. ed. 1957. Ed. F. Halkin. Subsidia hagiographica, 8a. Brussels: Société des Bollandistes.

Bibliotheca Hagiographica Latina. 3 vols. 1898–1901; rpt. 1949. Subsidia hagiographica, 6. Brussels: Société des Bollandistes.

Bibliotheca Hagiographica Orientalis. 1910; rpt. 1959. Ed. Paul Peeters. Subsidia hagiographica, 10. Brussels: Société des Bollandistes.

Bibliotheca Sanctorum. 1961–70. Ed. Iosepho Vizzini. Rome: Istituto Giovanni XXIII.

Bichon, Jean. 1976. *L'Animal dans la littérature française au XIIème et au XIIIème siècles*. 2 vols. Université de Lille: Service de reproduction des thèses.

Boas, George. 1948. *Essays on Primitivism and Related Ideas in the Middle Ages*. Baltimore: Johns Hopkins University Press.

Bosquet, G. H. 1958. "Des animaux et de leur traitement selon le judaïsme, le christianisme et l'islam." *Studia Islamica*, 9: 31–48.

Bossy, Michel-André. 1980. "Heroes and the Power of Words in the *chansons de geste*" (abstract). In A. G. Elliott, "The Myth of the Hero: Classical and Medieval Epic (A Report on a Conference)." *Olifant* 7: 235–47.

Boureau, Alain. 1981. *Les Formes narratives de la Légende Dorée de Jacques de Voragine*. Thèse du Troisième Cycle, Ecole des Hautes Etudes en Sciences Sociales. Paris.

Bourgain, L. 1879. *La Chaire française au XIIe siècle*. Paris: Société général de librairie catholique, V. Palmé.

Bremond, Claude. 1964. "Le message narratif." *Communications* (Paris) 4: 4–32. Paris: Editions du Seuil.

Brennan, B. R. 1976. "Dating Athanasius' *Vita Antonii*," *VC* 30: 52–54.

Brodeur, Arthur Gilchrist. 1924. "The Grateful Lion." *PMLA* 39: 485–524.

Brown, Arthur C. L. 1905. "The Knight of the Lion." *PMLA* 20: 673–706.

Brown, Peter. 1971. "The Rise and Function of the Holy Man in Late Antiquity." *JRS* 61: 80–101.

———. 1981. *The Cult of the Saints: Its Rise and Function in Latin Christianity*. Chicago: University of Chicago Press.

———. 1983. "The Saint as Exemplar in Late Antiquity," *Representations* 1, no. 2: 1–25.

Browning, Robert. 1980. "The 'Low Level' Saint's Life in the Early Byzantine World." In Sergei Hackel, ed., *The Byzantine Saint*, p. 117–27. Oxford: University of Birmingham Fourteenth Spring Symposium of Byzantine Studies.

Burger, André. 1948–49. "La Légende de Roncevaux avant la *Chanson de Roland*." *Romania*, 70: 433–73.

Cabriol, J., and H. Leclerc. 1907–53. *Dictionnaire d'archéologie chrétienne et de liturgie*. Paris: Lotouzet et Ané.

Cahier, Charles. 1867. *Caractéristiques des saints dans l'art populaire*. 2 vols. Paris: Poussielgue.

Calame, Claude. 1976. "L'Univers Cyclopéen de l'Odyssée entre le carré et l'hexagone logiques." *Versus* 14: 105–12.

Campbell, Joseph. 1949; 2d ed., rpt. 1972. *The Hero with a Thousand Faces*. Bollingen Series, 17. Princeton: Princeton University Press.

Canart, Paul. 1966. "Le Nouveau-né qui dénonce son père: Les avatars d'un conte populaire dans la littérature hagiographique." *AB* 84: 309–33.

Carp, Teresa. 1980. *"Puer-senex* in Roman and Medieval Thought." *Latomus* 39: 736–39.

Cary, George. 1956. *The Medieval Alexander.* ed. D. J. A. Ross. Cambridge: Cambridge University Press.

Cassin, Elena. 1951. "Daniel dans la 'fosse' aux lions." *RHR* 139: 127–61.

———. 1975. "Le Semblable et le différant." In L. Poliakov, ed., *Hommes et bêtes.* Paris: Mouton.

Casson, Lionel. 1974. *Travel in the Ancient World.* London: Allen and Unwin.

Cauwenbergh, Paul van. 1914. *Etude sur les moines d'Egypte depuis le concile de Chalcédoine (451) jusqu' à l'invasion arabe (640).* Paris/Louvain: Geuther.

Chadwick, Henry. 1967; rpt. 1981. *The Early Church.* Pelican History of the Church, I. London: Penguin Books.

Childress, Diana J. 1978. "Between Romance and Legend: 'Secular Hagiography' in Middle English Literature." *PQ* 57: 311–22.

Chitty, Derwas J. 1962. *The Desert a City.* Oxford: Blackwell.

Chotzen, Th. M. 1932–33. "Le Lion d'Owein (Yvain) et ses prototypes celtiques." *Neophilologus* 18: 51–58, 131–36.

Church, F. Forest. 1975. "Sex and Salvation in Tertullian." *Harvard Theological Review* 68: 83–101.

Coleiro, E. 1957. "St. Jerome's Lives of the Hermits." *VC* 11: 161–78.

Colliot, Régine. 1979. "Aspects de l'ermite dans la littérature épicoromanesque des XIIe et XIIIe siècles." In *Mélanges de Langue et littérature françaises du moyen-âge offerts à Pierre Jonin: Senefiance* (Aix-en Provence) 7: 159–80.

Cosquin, Emmanuel. 1881. "Contes populaires lorrains." *Romania* 10: 117–93, 543–80.

Crist, Larry. 1975. "Deep Structures in the *chansons de geste.* Hypotheses for a Taxonomy." *Olifant* 3: 3–35.

Cross, J. E. 1978. "Mary Magdalen in the *Old English Martyrology*: The Earliest Extant 'Narrat Josephus' Variant of her Legend." *Speculum* 53: 16–25.

Crum, W. E. 1915–17. "Discours de Pisenthios sur saint Onuphrius." *Receuil de l'orient chrétien* 10: 38–67.

Curtius, Ernst Robert. 1963. *European Literature and the Latin Middle Ages.* Trans. Willard R. Trask. New York: Harper Torchbooks.

Dale-Green, Patricia. 1963. *The Cult of the Cat.* London: Heinemann.

De Caluwé, Jacques. 1976. "La 'Prière épique' dans les plus anciennes chansons de geste françaises." *Oliphant* 4: 4–20.

Delcourt, Marie. 1958. "La complexe de Diane dans l'hagiographie chrétienne." *RHR* 153: 1–33.

Delehaye, Hippolyte. 1906; 2d ed., rpt. 1927. *Les Légendes hagiographiques.* Brussels: Société des Bollandistes.

————. 1906; rpt. 1962. *The Legends of the Saints.* Trans. Donald Attwater. New York: Fordham University Press.

————. 1909; rpt. 1975. *Les Légendes grecques des saints militaires.* New York: Arno Press.

————. 1912. "Saints de Thrace et de Mésie." *AB* 31: 161–300.

————. 1921; rpt. 1966. *Les Passions des martyrs et les genres littéraires.* Subsidia hagiographica, 20. Brussels: Société des Bollandistes.

————. 1923. *Les Saints stylites.* Subsidia hagiographia, 14. Brussels: Société des Bollandistes.

————. 1926. "La personnalité historique de S. Paul de Thèbes." *AB* 44: 64–69.

————. 1934. *Cinq Leçons sur la méthode hagiographique.* Subsidia hagiographica, 21. Brussels: Société des Bollandistes.

————. 1934. "Un groupe de récits 'utiles à l'âme.'" *Mélanges Bidez: Annuaire de l'Institut de Philologie et d'Histoire Orientales* 2: 255–66.

Dembowski, Peter F. 1976. "Literary Problems of Hagiography in Old French." *M&H* 7: 117–30.

Deonna, W. 1950. "Salva me de ore leonis: A propos de quelques chapiteaux romans de la cathédrale Saint-Pierre à Genève." *Revue belge de philologie et d'histoire,* 28: 479–511.

Derouet, Jean-Louis. "Les Possibilités d'interprétation sémiologique des textes hagiographiques." *Revue d'histoire de l'église de France* 62: 153–62.

Detienne, Marcel. 1972; rpt. 1981. "Between Beasts and Gods." In R. L. Gordon, ed., *Myth, Religion and Society,* pp. 215–28. Cambridge and Paris: Cambridge University Press and Editions de la Maison des Sciences de l'Homme. Originally published as "Entre Bêtes et Dieux." *Nouvelle revue de psychanalyse,* 6 (1972), 231–46.

————. 1972. *Les Jardins d'Adonis. La mythologie des aromates en Grèce.* Paris: Gallimard.

D'Evelyn, Charlotte. 1967. Review of Theodor Wolpers, *Die englische Heiligenlegende des Mittelalters* (Tübingen, 1964). In *Speculum* 42: 213–17.

Devereux, George. 1970. "The Structure of Tragedy and the Structure of the Psyche in Aristotle's *Poetics.*" In Charles Hanly and Morris Lazerowitz, eds., *Psychoanalysis and Philosophy.* New York.

Dictionnaire de spiritualité ascétique et mystique, doctrine et histoire. 1932– . Ed Marcel Viller. Paris: G. Beauchesne.

Doble, G. H. 1943. "Hagiography and Folklore." *Folk-Lore* 54: 321–33.

Dodds, E. R. 1965. *Pagan and Christian in an Age of Anxiety*. Cambridge: Cambridge University Press.

Dolbeau, François. 1979. "Un Example peu connu de conte hagiographique: La Passion des saints Pérégrin, Mathorat, et Viventien." *AB* 97: 337–54.

Dronke, Peter. 1984. *Woman Writers of the Middle Ages*. Cambridge: Cambridge University Press.

Droogers, André. 1980. "Symbols of Marginality in the Biographies of Religious and Secular Innovators." *Numen* 27: 105–21.

Duby, Georges. 1964. "Les 'Jeunes' dans la société aristocratique dans la France du Nord-Ouest au XIIe siècle." *Annales. Economies, Société, Civilisations*, 19: 835–46.

Earl, James Whitney. 1971. "Literary Problems in Early Medieval Hagiography." Dissertation, Cornell University.

Eco, Umberto. 1966; rpt. 1981. "James Bond: une combinatoire narrative." *L'Analyse structural du récit. Communications* (Paris) 8: 83–99.

Eliade, Mircea. 1954. *Cosmos and History: The Myth of the Eternal Return*. Trans. Willard Trask. Bollingen Series 46. New York: Pantheon Books. Originally published as *Le Mythe de l'Eternel Retour: Archétypes et répétition*. Paris: Gallimard, 1949.

——. 1969. *The Quest: History and Meaning in Religion*. Chicago: University of Chicago Press.

Eliez, Annie. 1967. *Le Lion et l'homme, des origines à nos jours*. Paris: Picard.

Elliott, Alison G. 1977. "Saints and Heroes: Hagiographic Poetry in Latin and Old French." Dissertation, University of California, Berkeley.

——. 1978. "The Martyr as Epic Hero: Prudentius' *Peristephanon* and the Old French *Chanson de Geste*." *Proceedings of the Patristic, Medieval, and Renaissance Conference* 3, pp. 119–36. Villanova, Pa.

——. 1982. "The Power of Discourse: Martyr's Passion and Old French Epic." *M&H* n.s. 11: 39–60.

Esbroeck, Michel van. 1980. "Le saint comme symbole." In Sergei Hackel, ed., *The Byzantine Saint*. pp. 128–40. Oxford: University of Birmingham Fourteenth Spring Symposium of Byzantine Studies.

Farrar, Raymond S. 1973. "Structure and Function of Representative Old English Saints' Lives." *Neophilologus* 57: 83–93.

Festugière, A. J. 1942. *La Sainteté*. Paris: Presses Universitaires.

——. 1955. "Le Problème littéraire de l' *Historia Monachorum*," *Hermes* 73: 257–84.

——. 1959. *Antioche païenne et chrétienne: Libanius, Chrysostome, et les moines de Syrie*. Bibl. des Ecoles Françaises d'Athènes et de Rome, 194. Paris: E. de Boccard.

———. 1960. "Lieux communs littéraires et thèmes de folk-lore dans l'Hagiographie primitive." *Wiener Studien* 73: 123–52.

———. 1961. *Les Moines d'orient: Introduction au monachisme oriental.* Paris: Editions du cerf.

Firth, Raymond. 1973. *Symbols, Public and Private.* Ithaca: Cornell University Press.

Foerster, W. Ed. 1902. *Yvain (der Löwenritter).* Halle a. S.: M. Niemeyer.

Fontaine, Jacques. 1975. "Le Mélange des genres dans la poésie de Prudence." In *Etudes sur la poésie latine tardive,* pp. 1–23. Originally in *Forma futuri (Mélanges M. Pellegrino),* pp. 755–77. Torino: Bottega d'Erasmo.

———. 1975; rpt. 1980. *Etudes sur la poésie latine tardive d'Ausone à Prudence.* Paris: Les Belles Lettres.

Frappier, Jean. 1967. *Les chansons de geste du cycle de Guillaume d'Orange.* 2 vols. Paris: Société d'Edition d'Enseignement Supérieur.

———. 1969. *Etude sur Yvain ou le Chevalier au Lion de Chrétien de Troyes.* Paris: Société d'Edition d'Enseignement Supérieur.

Frazer, Sir James George. 1926. *Atys et Osiris: Etude de religions orientales comparées.* Trans. Henri Peyre. Paris: Paul Aeuther.

———. 1930. *Myths of the Origin of Fire.* London: Macmillan.

Frend, W. H. C. 1959. "The Failure of the Persecutions in the Roman Empire." *Past and Present* 16: 10–30.

———. 1965. *Martyrdom and Persecution in the Early Church.* Oxford: Blackwell.

Frye, Northrop. 1957; rpt. 1973. *Anatomy of Criticism: Four Essays.* Princeton: Princeton University Press.

———. 1976. *The Secular Scripture: A Study of the Structure of Romance.* Cambridge, Mass: Harvard University.

Gaiffier, Baudouin de. 1947. "Intactam Sponsam Relinquens: A propos de la vie de S. Alexis." *AB* 65: 157–95.

———. 1960. "Notes sur le culte de Sainte Marie-Magdaleine." *AB* 78: 161–68.

———. 1967. "*Sub Daciano Praeside*: A Study of Some Spanish *Passios*." *Classical Folia* 21: 3–21.

———. 1971. *Recherches d'Hagiographie Latine.* Subsidia hagiographia, 52. Brussels: Société des Bollandistes.

Gallais, Pierre. 1974. "Remarques sur la structure des 'Miracles de Notre Dame.'" *Epopées, légendes et miracles: Cahiers d'Etudes Médiévales,* vol. 1, pp. 117–34. Montréal/Paris: Bellarmin.

Gatto, Giuseppe. 1979. "Le Voyage au Paradis: La Christianisation des traditions folkloriques au moyen âge." *Annales. Economies, Société, Civilisations.* 34: 929–42.

Gennep, Arnold van. 1911. *Religions, moeurs et légendes.* 3 vols. Paris: Mercure de France.

————. 1960. *The Rites of Passage.* Trans. Monika B. Vizedom and Gabrielle L. Caffee. Chicago: University of Chicago Press.

Gerould, Gordon Hall. 1905. "The Hermit and the Saint." *PMLA* 20: 529–45.

Gieysztor, Alexander. 1974. "*Pauper sum et peregrinus:* La légende de saint Alexis en occident: Un idéal de pauvreté." In Michel Mollat, ed., *Etudes sur l'histoire de pauvreté (Moyen âge-XVI siècle),* pp. 125–39. Paris: Publications de la Sorbonne.

Goldziher, Ignace. 1880. "Le culte des saints chez les musulmans." *RHR* 2: 257–351. Reprinted in S. M. Stern, ed., *Muslim Studies,* 2, pp. 255–341. London: Allen and Unwin, 1971.

Grabar, André. 1966. *L'Age d'or de Justinien: L'univers des formes.* Paris: Gallimard.

Graf, Arturo. 1892. *Miti, leggende, e superstizioni del medio evo.* 2 vols. Turin: Loescher.

Grant, Mary A. 1967. *Folktale and Hero-Tale in the Odes of Pindar.* Lawrence, Kans.: University of Kansas Press.

Grégoire, H. 1904. "La vie anonyme de S. Gérasime." *Byzantinische Zeitschrift* 13: 114–35.

Greimas, A. J., and F. Rastier. 1966. "The Interaction of Semiotic Constraints." *Yale French Studies* 41: 86–105.

Günther, Heinrich. 1976. "Psicologia della leggenda: Aspetti e problemi." In Sofia Bresch Gajano, ed., *Agiografia altomedievale.* Bologna: Il Mulino.

Guillaumont, Antoine. 1968–69. "Le dépaysement comme forme d'ascèse dans le monachisme ancien." *Annuaire de l'Ecole Practique des Hautes Etudes,* pp. 31–58. Cinquième Section, Sciences religieuses.

————. 1972. "Monachisme et éthique judéo-chrétienne." *Recherches de Science Religieuse* 60: 199–218.

————. 1975. "La Conception du désert chez les moines d'Egypte." *Revue de l'Histoire des Religions* 188: 3–21.

————. 1978. "Esquisse d'une phénoménologie du monachisme." *Numen* 25: 40–51.

Hackel, Sergei, ed. 1980. *The Byzantine Saint.* Oxford: University of Birmingham Fourteenth Spring Symposium of Byzantine Studies.

Hägg, Tomas. 1983. *The Novel in Antiquity.* Berkeley and Los Angeles: University of California Press.

Haidu, Peter. 1972. *Lion-Queue-Coupée: L'Ecart symbolique chez Chrétien de Troyes.* Geneva: Droz.

Halkin, François. 1971. "Sainte Tatiana: Légende grecque d'une 'martyre romaine.'" *AB* 89: 265–309.

Harnack, Adolf. 1905. *Militia Christi; die christliche Religion und der Soldatenstand in den ersten drei Jahrhunderten.* Tübingen: J. C. B. Mohr.

Hartman, Louis F., and Alexander A. Di Lella. 1978. *The Book of Daniel.* The Anchor Bible, vol. 23. Garden City, N.Y.: Doubleday and Co.

Heffernan, Thomas J. 1975. "An Analysis of the Narrative Motifs in the Legend of St. Eustache." *M&H* 6: 63–89.

Heiserman, Arthur. 1977. *The Novel Before the Novel: Essays and Discussions about the Beginnings of Prose Fiction in the West.* Chicago: University of Chicago Press.

Henry, Albert. 1939. "Sur l'épisode du lion dans le *Poema de Myo Cid.*" *Romania* 65: 94–95.

Hook, David. 1976. "Some Observations upon the Episode of the Cid's Lion." *MLR* 71: 553–64.

Hopkins, E. W. 1924. *Origin and Evolution of Religion.* New Haven: Yale University Press.

Hummel, Edelhard L., C. M. M. 1946. *The Concept of Martyrdom According to St. Cyprian of Carthage.* Catholic University of America Studies in Christian Antiquity, 9. Washington, D.C.: Catholic University of America.

Hyan, Theresa M. 1983. "Dualistic Narrative in Old French Martyr Poems." *RPh* 37: 49–56.

Igarashi-Takeshita, Midori. 1980. "Les Lions dans la sculpture romane en Poitou." *CCM* 23: 37–54.

James, E. O. 1968. "The Tree of Life." *Folklore* 79: 241–49.

Janet, Pierre. 1926. *De l'angoisse à l'extase: Etude sur les croyances et sentiments.* 2 vols. Paris: Félix Alcan.

Jauss, H.R. 1970. "Littérature médiévale et théorie des genres." *Poétique* 1: 79–101.

———. 1970–71. "Literary History as a Challenge to Literary Theory." *New Literary History* 2: 7–37.

Johnston, Oliver M. 1907. "The Episode of Yvain, the Lion, and the Serpent in Chrétien de Troies." *Zeitschrift für französische Sprache und Literatur* 31: 157–66.

Kassel, R. 1960. "*Acta Pauli.*" *Revue d'Histoire et de Philosophie Religieuses* 40: 45–53.

Kay, Sarah. 1978. "Ethics and Heroics in the 'Song of Roland.'" *Neophilologus* 62: 480–91.

Keller, Thomas. 1980. "Iwein and the Lion." *Amsterdamer Beiträge zur älteren Germanistik* 15: 59–75.

Kohler, Erich. 1974. *L'Aventure chevalresque: Idéal et réalité dans le roman courtois.* Trans. Eliane Kaufholz. Paris: Gallimard.

Krappe, Alexander H. 1942. "Guiding Animals." *Journal of American Folklore* 55: 228–46.

————. 1947. "St. Patrick and the Snakes." *Traditio* 5: 323–30.

Kuehne, Oswald R. 1922. *A Study of the Thaïs Legend, with Special Reference to Hrothsvitha's "Paphnutius."* Philadelphia: University of Pennsylvania Press.

Künstle, Karl. 1926. *Ikonographie der Heiligen.* Freiburg im Breisgau: Herder.

Kurtz, Benjamin P. 1926. *From St. Anthony to St. Guthlac.* University of California Publications in Modern Philology 12. Berkeley: University of California Press.

Labande, E. R. 1955. "Le 'Credo' épique: A propos des prières dans les chansons de geste." In *Recueil de travaux offert à M. Clovis Brunel,* vol. 2, pp. 62–80. Paris: Société de l'Ecole des Chartes.

Labriolle, Pierre de. 3rd ed.; 1947. *Histoire de la littérature latine chrétienne.* Paris: Les Belles Lettres.

Ladner, Gerhart B. 1967. "*Homo Viator*: Mediaeval Ideas on Alienation and Order." *Speculum* 42: 233–59.

Laistner, M. L. 2d ed.; 1957. *Thought and Letters in Western Europe.* Ithaca, N.Y.: Cornell University Press.

Le Goff, Jacques. 1970. "L'Occident médiéval et l'océan indien: Un Horizon onirique." Reprinted in *Pour un autre Moyen Age,* pp. 280–98. Paris: Gallimard, 1977.

————. 1970. "Culture ecclésiastique et culture folklorique au moyen âge: Saint Marcel de Paris et le dragon." In *Pour un autre Moyen Age,* pp. 236–79.

————. 1977. *Pour un autre Moyen Age. Temps, travail et culture en Occident.* Paris: Gallimard.

————. 1981. *La Naissance du Purgatoire.* Paris: Gallimard.

————. 1964. *La Civilisation de l'Occident médiévale.* Paris: Arthaud.

Leach, Edmund. 1969. *Genesis as Myth and Other Essays.* London: Cape.

————. 1967. "Magical Hair." In John Middleton, ed., *Myth and Cosmos: Readings in Mythology and Symbolism,* pp. 77–108. Austin: University of Texas. Originally published in *The Journal of the Royal Anthropological Institute,* 88, 2 (1958): 147–64.

Leach, Edmund, and D. Alan Aycock. 1983. *Structuralist Interpretations of Biblical Myth.* Cambridge: Cambridge University Press and Royal Anthropological Institutes of Great Britain and Ireland.

Leclercq, Dom Jean. 1961. *Etudes sur le vocabulaire monastique du moyen âge: Studia Anselmiana* 48. Rome: "Orbis Catholicus," Herder.

Lévi-Strauss, Claude. 1958; rpt. 1967. "The Story of Asdiwal." Trans. Nicholas Mann. In Edmund Leach, ed., *The Structural Study of Myth and Totemism*. pp. 1–47. London: Tavistock.

Lodolo, Gabriella. 1977–78. "Il tema simbolico del paradiso nella tradizione monastica dell'occidente latino (secoli VI–XII): Lo Spazio del simbolo." *Aevum* 51: 252–88. "Lo svelamento del simbolo." *Aevum* 52: 177–94.

Lorrie, L. Th. A., S. J. 1955. *Spiritual Terminology in the Latin Translations of the Vita Antonii*. Nijmegen: Dekker and van de Vegt.

Lot, Ferdinand. 1931; rpt. 1961. *The End of the Ancient World and the Beginnings of the Middle Ages*. Trans. Philip and Mariette Leon. New York: Harper Torchbooks.

Lowe, J. 1931. "The First Christian Novel: A Review of the Pseudo-Clementines." *Canadian Journal of Religious Thought*, 7: 292–301.

Lüthi, Max. 1970; trans. 1976. *Once Upon a Time: On the Nature of Fairy Tales* (translation by Lee Chadeayne and Paul Gottwald of *Es war einmal . . . vom Wesen des Volksmärchens*). Introduction by Francis Lee Utley. Bloomington: Indiana University Press.

MacCormack, Sabine. 1981. *Art and Ceremony in Late Antiquity*. Berkeley/Los Angeles: University of California Press.

Mackean, W. H. 1920. *Christian Monasticism in Egypt to the Close of the Fourth Century*. London: Society for Promoting Christian Knowledge.

Maddox, Donald. 1973. "Pilgrimage Narrative and Meaning in Manuscripts L and A of the *Vie de saint Alexis*." *Romance Philology* 27 (1973): 147–57.

———. 1978. *Structure and Sacring: The Systematic Kingdom in Chrétien's Erec et Enide*. French Forum Monographs, 8. Lexington, Kentucky.

———, and Sara Sturm-Maddox. 1978. "Le Chevalier à l'oraison: Guillaume dans *Le Couronnement de Louis*." In *Charlemagne et l'épopée romane*, pp. 609–15. Actes du VIIe Congrès International de la Société Rencesvals. *Congrès et Colloques de l'Université de Liège*, 76. Liège.

Malone, Edward E., O.S.B. 1950. *The Monk and the Martyr: The Monk as Successor of the Martyr*. Catholic University of America Studies in Christian Antiquity, 12. Washington, D.C.: Catholic University of America.

Malone, Kemp. 1928. "Rose and Cypress." *PMLA* 43: 397–446.

Marrou, Henri Irénée. 1956. *A History of Education in Antiquity*. Trans. George Lamb. New York: Sheed and Ward, 1956. French edition: *Histoire de l'Education dans l'Antiquité*, third ed. Paris: Editions du Seuil.

———. 1977. *Décadence romaine ou antiquité tardive?* Paris: Editions du Seuil.

Maury, L.-F.-Alfred. 1863. *Croyances et légendes de l'antiquité*. Paris.

Ménard, Philippe. 1976. "Le Chevalier errant dans la littérature arthurienne: Recherches sur les raisons du départ et de l'errance." In *Voyage quête, pèlerinage dans la littérature et la civilisation médiévales. Sénéfiance* 2: 291–310.

Meredith, Anthony. 1976. "Asceticism—Christian and Greek." *JTS* 27: 313–32.

Meslin, Michel. 1972. "Le phénomène religieux populaire." In Benoît Lecroix and Pietro Boglioni, ed. *Les Religions populaires: Colloque International, 1970*. Quebec: Presses de l'Université de Laval.

Messenger, Ruth E. 1946. "Mozarabic Hymns in Relation to Contemporary Culture in Spain." *Traditio* 4: 149–77.

Monod, Victor. 1936. "Le Voyage, le déracinement de l'individu hors du milieu natal constituent-ils un des éléments déterminants de la conversion religieuse?" *Revue d'Histoire et de Philosophie Religieuses* 16: 385–99.

Morino, Claudio. 1952. *Ritorno al Paradiso di Adamo in S. Ambrogio: Itinerario spirituale*. Vatican City: Tipografia Poliglotta Vaticana.

Musurillo, Herbert. 1956. "The Problem of Ascetical Fasting in the Greek Patristic Writers." *Traditio* 12: 1–64.

———. 1962. *Symbolism and the Christian Imagination*. Dublin: Helicon.

Nagy, Gregory. 1974. *Comparative Studies in Greek and Indic Meter*. Harvard Studies in Comparative Literature, 33. Cambridge, Mass.: Harvard University Press.

———. 1979. *The Best of the Achaeans*. Baltimore: Johns Hopkins University Press.

Neytor, André. 1979. *Les Clefs païennes du christianisme*. Paris: Les Belles Lettres.

Neumann, Erich. 1963. *The Great Mother*. Bollingen Series, 47. New York: Bollingen Foundation.

Nichols, Stephen G. 1977. "A Poetics of Historicism? Recent Trends in Medieval Literary Study." *M&H* 8: 77–101.

———. 1980. "Sign as (Hi)story in the *Couronnement de Louis*." *Romanic Review* 71: 1–9.

Nock, Arthur Darby. 1933. *Conversion: The Old and the New in Religion from Alexander the Great to Augustine of Hippo*. Oxford: Blackwell.

Noonan, John T., Jr. 1965; rpt. 1967. *Contraception: A History of its Treatment by the Catholic Theologians and Canonists*. New York: Mentor.

Nuffel, Pierre van. 1973. "Problèmes de sémiotique interprétative: L'Épopée." *Lettres Romanes* 27: 150–62.

Ogle, M. B. 1916. "The Stag-Messenger Episode." *AJP* 37: 387–416.

O'Leary, DeLacy. 1937. *The Saints of Egypt*. London: Society for Promoting Christian Knowledge.

Oldfather, William Abbott, ed. 1943. *Studies in the Text Tradition of St. Jerome's Vitae Patrum*. Urbana: University of Illinois Press.

Olsen, Alexandra Hennessey. 1980. "'De Historiis Sanctorum': A Generic Study of Hagiography." *Genre* 13: 407–29.

Papachryssanthou, Denise. 1970. "L'Office ancien de Pierre l'Athonite." *AB* 88: 27–41.

———. 1974. "La Vie ancienne de saint Pierre l'Athonite." *AB* 92: 19–61.

Patch, Howard Rollin. 1950. *The Other World According to Descriptions in Medieval Literature*. Cambridge, Mass.: Harvard.

Patlagean, Evelyne. 1968. "Ancienne hagiographie byzantine et histoire sociale." *Annales. Economies, Société, Civilisations* 23: 106–26.

———. 1976. "L'Histoire de la femme déguisée en moine et l'évolution de la sainteté féminine à Byzance." *Studi Medievali* 17: 597–623.

Pavlovskis, Zoja. 1976. "The Life of Saint Pelagia the Harlot: Hagiographic Adaptation of Pagan Romance." *Classical Folia* 30: 138–49.

Payen, Jean-Charles. 1967. *Le Motif du repentir dans la littérature française médiévale*. Geneva: Droz.

Peebles, Bernard M. 1951. *The Poet Prudentius. Boston College Candlemas Lectures on Christian Literature*, 2. New York: McMullen Books.

Peeters, Paul. 1906. Review of Francesco Maria Esteves Pereira, *Vida de santo Abunafre (S. Onuphrio): Versão ethiopica*. Lisbon: 1905. *AB* 25: 203–4.

———. 1907. Review of B. Turaiev, "Légende copte-ethiopienne sur S. Cyr." *AB* 26: 125–26.

———. 1920. "La Légende de S. Jacques de Nisibe" *AB* 38: 285–373.

———. 1943. "S. Syméon Stylites et ses premiers biographes." *AB* 61: 29–71.

Peña, Ignace, Pascal Castellana, and Romuald Fernandez. 1975. *Les Stylites Saints*. Publications du "Studium Biblicum Franciscanum," Collectio minor, no. 16. Milan: Centro Propaganda e Stampa.

Penco, Gregorio. 1964. "Il Simbolismo animalesco nella letteratura monastica." *Studia Monastica* 6: 7–38.

Penido, M. T.-L. 1932. "Une Théorie pathologique de l'ascétisme." *La Vie Spirituelle* 31: 35–54.

Perry, Ben Edwin. 1967. *The Ancient Romances*. Berkeley and Los Angeles: University of California Press.

Philpot, Mrs. J. H. 1897. *The Sacred Tree, or the Tree in Religion and Myth*. London: Macmillan.

Pickford, T. E. 1975. "*Apollonius of Tyre* as Greek Myth and Christian Mystery." *Neophilologus* 59: 599–609.

Poliakov, Léon, ed. 1975. *Hommes et bêtes.* Paris: Mouton.

Poncelet, Albert. 1890. *La Science Catholique* 4: 269–71, 632–45.

Propp, Vladimir. 2nd rev. ed. 1968. *The Morphology of the Folktale.* Trans. Laurence Scott. Austin: University of Texas Press.

Quasten, Johannes. 1950. *Patrology.* Vol. 1, "The Beginnings of Patristic Literature." Utrecht/Brussels: Spectrum.

Raglan, Lord. 1956. *The Hero: A Study in Tradition, Myth, and Drama.* New York: Vintage Books.

Raynaud de Lage, Guy. 1972. "L'Inspiration de la prière 'du plus grand péril.'" *Romania* 93: 568–70.

Réau, Louis. 1956. "Iconographie du prophète Elie." In *Elie le prophète selon les écritures et les traditions chrétiennes,* vol. 1, pp. 233–67. *Etudes Carmélitaines.* Bruges: Desclée de Brouwer.

———. 1958. *Iconographie de l'art chrétien.* Vol. 3, "Iconographie des Saints." Paris: Presses Universitaires.

Reardon, B. P. 1982. "Theme, Structure and Narrative in Chariton." In John J. Winkler and Gordon Williams, eds., *Later Greek Literature,* pp. 1–27. Yale Classical Studies, 27. New York: Cambridge University Press.

Reitzenstein, Richard. 1916. *Historia Monachorum und Historia Lausiaca: Eine Studie zur Geschichte des Mönchtums und der frühchristlichen Begriffe Gnostiker und Pneumatiker.* Göttingen: Vandenhoek and Ruprecht.

Resch. P. 1931. *La Doctrine ascétique des premiers maîtres égyptiens du quatrième siècle.* Paris: Beauchesne.

Rice, Eugene F. 1985. *St. Jerome in the Renaissance.* Baltimore: Johns Hopkins University Press.

Ring, Grete. 1945. "St. Jerome Extracting the Thorn from the Lion's Foot." *Art Bulletin,* 27: 188–96.

Ringbom, Lars-Ivar. 1958. *Paradisus Terrestris: Myt, Bild och Verklighet.* Copenhagen: Munksgaards. (English summary, pp. 435–46.)

Roques, Mario. 1928. "Le lion vaniteux." *Romania* 55: 258–60, 552–54.

Rosenberg, Bruce A. 1979. "Folkloristes et médiévistes face au texte littéraire: Problèmes de méthode." *Annales. Economies, Société, Civilisations* 34: 943–55.

Rosenthal, Constance L. 1936. *The Vitae Patrum in Old and Middle English Literature.* Dissertation, University of Pennyvania.

Rousseau, Philip. 1978. *Ascetics, Authority, and the Church in the Age of Jerome and Cassian.* Oxford: Oxford University Press.

Rowland, Beryl. 1974. *Animals with Human Faces: A Guide to Animal Symbolism.* London: Allen and Unwin.

Rudder, Orlando de. 1982. "La Vie de sainte Marie l'Egyptienne." *Médiévales* 1: 39–47.

Rush, Alfred C. 1941. *Death and Burial in Christian Antiquity*. Washington, D.C.: Catholic University of America.

———. 1972. "Death as a Spiritual Marriage: Individual and Ecclesial Eschatology." *VC* 26: 81–101.

Saintyves, P. 1907. *Les Saints, successeurs des dieux: Essais de mythologie chrétienne*. Paris: Emile Nourry.

———. 1908. *Les Vierges mères et les naissances miraculeuses*. Paris: Librairie critique.

———. 1930. *En Marge de la légende dorée: Songes, Miracles et Survivances. Essai sur la formation de quelques thèmes hagiographiques*. Paris: Emile Nourry.

———. 1934. "Le Thème des animaux sauvages domestiqués par les saints et sa signification allégorique." *L'Ethnographie* 34: 51–61.

Salomonson, J. W. 1979. *Voluptatem Spectandi non Perdat sed Mutet*. Amsterdam: North Holland Publishing Company.

Saly, Antoinette. 1969. "Le Thème de la descente aux enfers dans le 'credo' épique." *Travaux de linguistique et de littérature de Strasbourg* 7, vol. 2, pp. 47–63.

———. 1976. "L'Itinéraire intérieur dans le Perceval de Chrétien de Troyes et la structure de la quête de Gauvain." In *Voyage, quête, pèlerinage dans la littérature et la civilisation médiévales. Sénéfiance* 2: 355–61.

Sauneron, Serge. 1964. "Les Animaux fantastiques du désert: Remarques de philologie et d'étymologie." *Bulletin de l'Institute Française d'archéologie orientale du Caire* 62: 15–18.

Saxer, Victor. 1959. *Le culte de Marie Magdalen en occident des origines à la fin du moyen âge*. Paris.

———. 1979. *Saints anciens d'Afrique du Nord*. Vatican.

Sbordone, Silvia. 1978. "Caratteristiche strutturali di alcune vite di santi dei secoli III–IV." *Koinōnia* 2: 57–67.

Schapiro, Meyer. 1944. "The Religious Meaning of the Ruthwell Cross." *Art Bulletin* 26: 232–45.

Schierling, Stephen P., and Marla J. 1978. "The Influence of the Ancient Romances on the *Acts of the Apostles*." *CB* 54: 81–99.

Schmitt, Jean-Claude. 1976. "'Réligion populaire' et culture folklorique." *Annales* 31: 941–53.

———. 1979. *Le Saint lévrier: Guinefort, guérisseur d'enfants depuis le XIIIe siècle*. Paris: Flammarion.

Schnapp-Gourbeillon, Annie. 1981. *Lions, héros, masques: Les Représentations de l'animal chez Homère*. Paris: Maspero.

Shook, Laurence K. 1960. "The Burial Mound in *Guthlac A*." *MP* 58: 1–10.

Smith, Macklin. 1976. *Prudentius' Psychomachia: A Reexamination.* Princeton: Princeton University Press.

Söder, R. 1932. *Die apokryphen Apostelgeschichten und die romanhafte Literatur der Antike.* Stuttgart: W. Kohlhammer.

Spitzer, Leo. 1938. "Le lion arbitre moral de l'homme." *Romania* 64: 525–30.

Ste. Croix, G. E. M. de. 1954. "Aspects of the 'Great' Persecution." *Harvard Theological Review* 47: 75–113.

———. 1963. "Why were the Early Christians Persecuted?" *Past and Present* 26: 6–38.

Stebbeins, E. C. 1973. "Les Origines de la légende de saint Alexis." *Revue Belge de Philologie et d'Histoire* 51: 497–507.

Stevens, John. 1973. *Medieval Romance: Themes and Approaches.* London: Hutchinson University Library.

Strycher, Emile de, S. J. 1961. *La Forme plus ancienne du Protévangile de Jacques.* Subsidia hagiographica, 33. Brussels: Société des Bollandistes.

Suard, François. 1980. "Le Motif du déguisement dans quelques chansons du cycle de Guillaume d'Orange." *Olifant* 7: 343–58.

Te Velde, H. 1980. "A Few Remarks upon the Religious Significance of Animals in Ancient Egypt." *Numen* 27: 76–82.

Thomas, A. 1905. "Le Roman de Goufier de Lastours." *Romania* 34: 55–65.

Thompson, Stith. 1955. *Motif-Index of Folk Literature.* 6 vols. Bloomington, Indiana: Indiana University Press.

Todorov, Tzvetan. 1968. "Introduction," *Le Vraisemblable. Communications* 11. Paris: Editions du Seuil.

———. 1978. *Poétique de la prose.* Paris: Editions du Seuil.

Tristram, Henry Baker. 1884. The Survey of Western Palestine. *The Fauna and Flora of Palestine.* London: Committee of the Palestine Exploration Fund.

Tubach, Frederic C. 1969. *Index Exemplorum: A Handbook of Medieval Religious Tales.* FF Communications, 204. Helsinki: Suomalainen Tiedekatemia.

Turcan, Robert. 1963. "Le Roman 'initiatique': A propos d'un livre récent." *RHR* 163: 149–99.

Turner, Victor. 1969. *The Ritual Process.* Harmondsworth: Penguin Books.

———. 1974. *Dramas, Fields, Metaphors: Symbolic Action in Human Society.* Ithaca: Cornell University Press.

Turner, Victor, and Edith Turner. 1978. *Image and Pilgrimage in Christian Culture.* Oxford: Blackwell.

Uitti, Karl D. 1973. *Story, Myth, and Celebration in Old French Narrative Poetry, 1050–1200.* Princeton: Princeton University Press.

Vaccari, Alberto. 1920. "Le antiche vite di S. Girolamo." In *Miscellanea Geronimiana: Scritti varii pubblicati nel XV centenario dalla morte di San Girolamo*, pp. 1–18. Rome: Vatican.

Vauchez, André. 1977. "'Beata stirps': Sainteté et lignage en occident aux XIIIe et XIVe siècles." In Georges Duby and Jacques LeGoff, eds., *Famille et Parenté dans l'occident médiéval*, Vol. 30, pp. 397–407. Rome: Collection de l'Ecole Française de Rome.

———. 1981. *La Sainteté en occident aux derniers siècles du moyen âge, d' après les procès de canonisation et les documents hagiographiques*. Bibliothèque des Ecoles Françaises d'Athènes et de Rome, 241. Rome.

Vidal-Naquet, Pierre. 1975. "Bêtes, hommes et dieux chez les Grecs," in Léon Poliakov, ed., *Entretiens sur le racisme*, pp. 129–42. Paris/The Hague: Mouton.

Viller, Marcel. 1925. "Martyre et perfection." *RAM* 6: 3–25.

———. 1925. "Le Martyr et l'ascèse." *RAM* 6: 105–42.

Vööbus, Arthur. 1958. *A History of Asceticism in the Syrian Orient*. Corpus Scriptorum Christianorum Orientalium 184, Subsidia 14. Louvain.

Waddell, Helen. 1934. *Beasts and Saints*. London: Constable.

Walpole, A. S. 1922. *Early Latin Hymns*. Cambridge: Cambridge University Press.

Warren, William. 1886. *Paradise Found: The Cradle of the Human Race at the North Pole*. Boston: Houghton Mifflin.

Williams, Charles Allyn. 1925, 1927. *The Oriental Affinities of the Legend of the Hairy Anchorite*. 2 vols. Urbana: University of Illinois Press.

Williams, George H. 1962. *Wilderness and Paradise in Christian Thought: The Biblical Experience of the Desert in the History of Christianity and the Paradise Theme in the Theological Idea of the University*. New York: Harper and Brothers.

Wilmart, André. 1938. "Les Rédactions latines de la vie d'Abraham ermite." *Revue Bénédictine* 50: 222–45.

Wilmotte, Maurice. 1923. *De l'origine du roman en France: La tradition antique et les éléments chrétiens du roman*. In *Mémoires, Académie Royale de Belgique* 18, no. 5. Brussels: M. Lamertin.

Wit, Constant de. 1951. *Le Rôle et le sens du lion dans l'Egypte ancienne*. Leiden: E. J. Brill.

Wittig, Susan. 1978. *Stylistic and Narrative Structures in the Middle English Romances*. Austin: University of Texas Press.

Wittkower, Rudolph. 1942. "Marvels of the East: A Study in the History of Monsters." *JWCI* 5: 159–97.

Wortley, John. 1976. "The Passion of St. Themistocles." *AB* 94: 22–33.

Zumthor, Paul. 1972. *Essai de poétique médiévale*. Paris: Editions du Seuil.

Index

Abbâ Nâfer, 51. *See also* St. Onuphrius
Abraames (monk), 139
Abraham (hermit), 127, 128; *Vita Abrahae* 127–130. *See also* Maria Meretrix
Abraham of Qidana, 86, 92–94, 96, 97, 98, 99, 104–5, 131, 132, 176–77
Abunâfer, 51. *See also* St. Onuphrius
Acepsimus (hermit), 177
Achilles (in Homer), 23, 80, 168, 169
Achilles Tatius, 104n
Acta. See Acts (of Martyrs)
Actaeon, 168
Acts (of Martyrs), 9, 11, 18, 25, 26, 28, 30, 31, 33, 38, 41, 146, 186
Acts of Paul and Thecla, 48–50, 176
Adam, 99, 133, 137, 140, 141, 143, 165, 207
Adonis, 208
Aelian, 150, 151, 158, 198, 200n
Agolant (in *Pseudo-Turpin*), 186
agon, 24, 208
Aigialos (in *Ephesiaca*), 47
Ajax, 80
Albright, W. F., 210
Alexander the Great, 122. *See also Romance of Alexander the Great*
Alexis, St., 80, 87, 92; *Life of*, 174
Altman, Charles F., 16, 17, 24, 45, 181, 182
Ambrose, St., 96, 141, 144, 147, 164, 165
Amélineau, E., 51
Ami et Amile, 182
Ammonius (hermit), 140
Anastasis (church of), 123
Anbā Hūb, 158
Andreas (in *Peregrinatio*), 57

Androcles (and the lion), 150, 151, 158, 198
angel, 54, 57, 61, 62, 63, 65, 67, 69, 117, 118, 133, 159, 161, 172, 173. *See also* guide
angelikos bios, 161, 169, 170
Anicetus, St., 149
anima, 82
animals, 144–67, 168–70, 169, 170, 193–213; guides, 65, 211; helpful, 152–60. *See also* centaurs; dragon; lions
Anthia (in *Ephesiaca*), 46–47, 85, 126.
Antigone, 79
Antony, St., 12, 44–45, 77, 79, 85, 99, 104, 106, 108, 131, 136, 153, 176; in *Life of Paul*, 67, 72, 83, 84, 116, 126, 144, 161, 180; disciple of St. Simeon, 12, 88–89, 157; *Life of* (*Vita Antonii*), 4, 44, 82, 88, 108, 116, 138, 152. *See also* Athanasius
Aphraat, (Syriac father), 153
Apocryphal Acts of Thomas, 50
Aristotle, 72, 90, 168, 169
Artemis, 46, 49, 201
Arthurian romance. *See* romance
ascent, 131–67
Asdiwal. See *Story of Asdiwal*
Asella, 81, 82
askēsis, 43, 45
Aslan, 211
Astion (martyr), 12, 16, 21, 22, 87
Atalanta, 168
Athanasius, 44, 45, 88, 99, 106, 107, 116, 138, 153. *See also* St. Antony, *Life of*
Augustine, St., 143; *Confessions*, 4

Babylon, 124
baptism, 122; by blood, 19, 31

Barlaam and Josaphat, 12, 74
Baroin, Jeanne, 201
Basil, St., 3, 12, 166
Bel Inconnu, 205
Benedict, St., *Life of*, 3, 88, 177
Bethlehem, 123
Bichon, Jean, 194
binary opposition, 19, 30–31, 36–38, 45, 85, 182
Blandina (martyr), 20, 147
Bollandists, 9, 10
Book of Enoch, 135
Book of Tobit, 117
Booth, William, 174
Bossy, Michel-André, 185
Bramimonde (Saracen queen), 38
Brendan, St., 205
bride, 64, 65, 66
Broceliande (forest), 205
Brown, Peter, 6
Browning, Robert, 91
Buddha, 12, 174
burial, 54, 60, 61, 62, 67, 72, 104–16, 105, 164, 176, 202–3. *See also* cave; death; tomb

Caesaraugusta, 28, 29
Callisthenes, Pseudo, 120
Callisto, 168
Calogrenant (in *Chevalier au lion*), 83
Camino de Santiago, 183. See also *Codex Calixtinus*
Campbell, Joseph, 10, 73
Canczon de sancta Fides, 184, 186, 189
Carpus, St., 20, 149
Cassian, John, 141, 177
Cassin, Elena, 166
Cavaliere d'Arpino, 78n
cave, 51, 52, 54, 55, 59, 60, 61, 62, 63, 65–66, 67, 97, 107, 108, 133, 135, 140, 172, 174. *See also* burial; tomb
centaurs, 169. *See also* animals; culture vs. nature
Cesari, Guiseppe, 78
Chançun de Willame, 183
chanson de geste, 18, 182
Chanson de Roland, Le, 23, 38, 182, 183
Chariton, 104n

Charlemagne (in *Pseudo-Turpin*), 186
Chevalier au lion, 182, 196–200, 202, 205. *See also* Chrétien de Troyes; *Yvain*
Chevalier de la charrette, 205
childhood, 77–81, 210–13
Chiron (centaur), 169. *See also* centaurs
Chitty, Derwas J., 136
Chrétien de Troyes, 182, 196–200, 207. *See also Chevalier au lion*; *Yvain*
Christ Jesus, 6, 21, 33, 44, 50, 78, 79, 113, 116, 135, 160n, 161, 163, 164, 167, 173, 174, 187, 188, 189, 199, 208, 211
Christina, St., 162
Chronicles of Narnia. See Lewis, C. S.; *Narnia Chronicles*
Cid. *See Poema de mio Cid*
Cinderella, 80, 159
Circe, 196
city, 82. *See also* desert; polis
Clement of Alexandria, 44, 144
Clement of Ancyra, 150
Clement I (Pope), 47–48
Clementine Recognitions, 48
Clothar, 87
clothing, 98–99; dress code, 98
Codex Calixtinus, 183
cogitatio, 83
Colosseum, 146
Columba, St., 194
Columbus, Christopher, 209–10
communitas, 173, 178. *See also* liminality; Turner, Victor
confessors, 43
Conon (martyr), 20, 22
Constantine: Edict of Milan, 44; peace of (313 A.D.), 18, 42, 143
Copres (monk), 162
Corsolt (in *Couronnement*), 186, 187, 189–90
Council of Nicaea, 48
Couronnement de Louis, Le, 182, 187, 189
Crist, Larry S., 36, 37
crusades, 13, 184
culture vs. nature, 95, 97, 132–37, 140, 165, 170, 173, 208–9
Cyprian, St., 18, 40, 136

Cyriacus, St., 156, 163
Cyril of Scythopolis, 156, 163

Dacian (governor of Tarragona), 27,
    28, 29, 30–31, 33–34, 36, 186
Damascene, John, 153
Damasus (Pope), 149
Daniel (Old Testament), 151–53, 161,
    204
Dante, 115, 159, 179
Daria, 148–49, 192
Dasius (martyr), 20
date palm. See palm tree; tree of life
death: symbolic, 75, 76, 104–16, 172,
    175–79, 176. See also velut mortuus
Decius (emperor), 104
Delehaye, Hippolyte, 2, 3, 10, 26, 71
Delphi, 85
Dembowski, Peter, 9
descent, 103–30, 189. See also sleep
desert, 82, 83, 85, 88, 90, 91, 106,
    125, 138, 169, 170, 172, 174, 204,
    208. See also polis
D'Evelyn, Charlotte, 3
devil, 78; and St. Macarius, 111–15
Diocletian (emperor), 9, 26, 27, 147,
    149
Dionysius (Bishop of Alexandria), 104
disguise, 119–20, 177–78, 205n
Divine Comedy, 159
Doble, G. H., 9
Domitilla, Catacomb of, 152
dragon, 50, 125, 128, 157, 162. See
    also animals
dress. See clothing
Droogers, André, 173–75

Earl, James, 2
Eco Umberto, 7
Eden, 115, 133, 142, 194, 207, 210
Edict of Milan. See Constantine
Egypt, 42. See also Flight into Egypt
Electra, 79
Eleutherios, St. 150, 161
Eliade, Mircea, 171, 181, 211. See also
    quest
Elijah (Old Testament), 54, 125, 160n,
    161
Enoch. See Book of Enoch
Ephesiaca, 46–47, 50, 85
Ephrem of Syria, St., 12, 86, 93, 98,
    128, 177

epic, 13, 23, 26, 29, 36, 37, 184, 186,
    205; homeric, 196
epic passions, 46
Epictetus (martyr), 12, 16, 21, 22
"Epistle to Diognetus," 19
Erec et Enide, 207. See also Chrétien
    de Troyes
Eros, 46
Eucherius of Lyons (Bishop), 137
Eugenia, St. (martyr), 12, 21, 79, 81
Eulalia, St. (martyr), 1, 24, 35, 39–40,
    85, 185
Eumorphio (soldier), 33
Euphraxia (mother of Euphrasia), 86n
Euphrosyne, St., 80, 86, 119, 120. See
    also Smaragdus
Eusebius, 104, 147
Eustache, St., 182
Eustochium, 139. See also St. Jerome
Euthymius, St., 157, 163
Evagrius, 12, 44
Eve, 95, 140, 141, 142, 143, 207
Ezekiel, 145

Fabian, Bishop of Antioch, 104
fairy tale, 77. See also Grimm's Fairy
    Tales
Fall, 99, 103, 137, 151, 165, 207
fasting, 131, 132–35, 141, 160, 167,
    207. See also food
Felicitas, 18, 147. See also Passion of
    Perpetua and Felicitas
Felix (monk), 4
Ferragut (in Pseudo-Turpin), 186, 190
Festugière, A. J., 84, 133
Fides, St. See Canczon de sancta Fides
Firth, Raymond, 98–99
Flavius (servant of St. Sabas), 156
Fleming, Ian, 7
flight. See marriage; secret flight
Flight into Egypt, 81, 163
folklore, 7
folktale, 80
Fontaine, Jacques, 27, 29
food, 100–101, 137–42; miraculous,
    160–62; raw, 138–40, 168. See also
    fasting; omophagy; xerophagy
France, Anatole, 182. See also Thaïs
Francis, St., 144
Frappier, Jean, 198–99
Frazer, James, 139

Frye, Northrop, 14, 103, 115, 181, 207, 208

Gaiffier, Baudouin de, 10
Galahad, 201
Ganelon (in Chanson de Roland), 38
Gatto, Giuseppe, 202
Gawain, 83
Genesis, Book of, 135
George, St., 8, 16, 27
Gerasimus, St., 155, 163, 165
Gesta Romanorum, 197
Girart de Vienne, 188
Golden Age, 194; in Hesiod, 165
Goldziher, Ignace, 166
Golfier de Lastours, 197
Golgotha, 123
Gómez, C. Bandera, 192
Gordius, St., 3
Gospel of Nicodemus, 188
Gospel of Pseudo-Matthew, 81, 163, 211
gradational structure, 17, 45–51, 75, 85, 126
Grail, 200, 206
Green Knight, 83
Gregory Nazianzen, 179
Gregory of Nyssa, 118
Gregory of Tours, 5
Gregory Thaumaturge, 118
Gregory the Great, 3, 16, 145, 163; Life of, 6. See also St. Benedict
Greimas, A. J., 37
Grimm's Fairy Tales, 159
guide, 54, 63, 66, 69, 85, 116–19, 159, 161, 201. See also angel; animals
Guillaume (in Couronnement de Louis), 184, 186, 187, 188, 189–90. See also Mariage Guillaume I
Guillaume d'Angleterre, 182. See also Chrétien de Troyes
Guillaumont, Antoine, 106
Guthlac, St., 4; Life of, 4

Habrocomes (in Ephesiaca), 46–47, 85
Hägg, Thomas, 49
hagiography, nature of, 1–15. See also Laistner, M. L.
hair, 61, 65, 67, 70, 98, 99, 170
Harrowing of Hell, 187–89
Hector, 168

Helenus (Abbot), 162
Heracles, 80. See also Hercules
Heraklambon (in Peregrinatio), 57
Hercules, 190. See also Heracles
hermit, 192–93
hero, 1, 7, 10, 13, 14, 15, 16, 27, 28, 29, 73, 77, 80, 83, 171, 181, 185, 189–204
Hicks, Edward (painter), 209
Hilarion, St., 12
Hippomenes (and Atalanta), 168
Historia Lausiaca, 13, 106, 139, 157. See also Palladius
Historia Monachorum, 85, 162. See also Rufinus
Historia Religiosa, 13, 88–89, 107, 139, 140, 159. See also Theodoret
history, and hagiography, 2–6
Homer, 168, 184, 194; homeric epic, 196
Honofrius. See St. Onuphrius
Hook, David, 192
Horace, 30
horizon of expectation, 8
Hroswitha, 107
Huesca, 28
Hyginus and Sergius (monks), 123
Hymn of the Soul, 50

Ignatius, St., 146, 147, 194
Iliad, 168, 194, 196
imitatio Christi, 29, 43, 79, 131
initiation rites. See rite of passage
interior mons, 42, 82, 104, 174
Isaac, 80

Jacob of Nisibis, 139, 140
James Bond, 7
Jason, 8on
Jauss, H. R., 184
Jerome, St., 4, 5, 7, 43, 66, 71, 72, 73, 74, 79, 81, 84, 86, 88, 116, 139, 141, 142, 144, 154, 164, 178, 198, 201. See also Eustochium; St. Malchus, Life of; Paul of Thebes, Life of
Jerusalem, 24, 79, 87, 90, 123, 124
Joannes (Abba), 69, 70
Joannes (in Peregrinatio), 57
Job, 107, 153
John Calybite, 87
John Chrysostom, 170

John the Baptist, 54, 80, 84, 107, 137–38
Jordan (the lion), 155
Joseph (Old Testament), 80
Joseph of Arimathea, 200
journey, 59, 60, 61, 62, 67, 81, 85–91, 120–26, 131, 170, 176. See also quest
Julian (monk), 140
Julian the Apostate, 124
Justin Martyr, 18, 19

Kessel, Joseph, 182, 212. See also Le Lion
Kimbongu (Zaire prophet), 174
kleos aphthiton, 23

Laistner, M. L., 1, 2, 4
Last Days of Pompeii, 146
Last Judgement, 183, 189
Laudine (Chevalier au lion), 209
Lawrence, St., 28, 39, 186
Leach, Edmund, 8, 76, 173. See also liminality
Legenda aurea, 21
Léger, St. See Vie de saint Léger
Lévi-Strauss, Claude, 10, 76
Lewis, C. S., 182, 202, 211. See also Narnia Chronicles
Licinius, St., 87
Life of. See under particular name
liminality, 168–80, 193, 204–9. See also Leach, Edmund; Turner, Victor
Lion, Le, 182. See also Kessel, Joseph
lioness. See lion
lions, 4, 49, 64, 65, 72, 97, 99, 100, 108, 109, 113, 133, 137, 145–167, 147, 148–49, 150, 152–53, 154, 163–67, 168, 170, 191, 194–213. See also Androcles; animals, guides; Daniel; Jordan
Livingstone, David (explorer), 210
locus amoenus, 133
Loomis, Laura, 8
Lord, Albert, 206
Lot, Ferdinand, 4
Lunete (Chevalier au lion), 209
Lyons, 20

Macarius of Alexandria, 139
Macarius the Egyptian, 157, 177
Macarius the Roman, St., 12, 64, 86, 92–93, 94, 96–101, 104–5, 109, 115–16, 124, 131, 132, 136, 137, 159, 161, 164, 165, 169, 170, 176, 200, 201, 202, 204, 209; Life of (Vita Macarii), 58, 65–66, 82, 122, 166; Story of, 63–66; temptation of, 110–15. See also devil; marriage
Macedonius (Syrian monk), 139
Maddox, Donald, 23, 24, 43, 188
Malchus, St., 12, 43, 86, 116; Life of (Vita Malchi), 43, 86, 154
Malone, Edward E., 43
Mamas, St., 160n
Marbod of Rennes, 87
Marcianus (monk), 106, 107
Maria Meretrix, 127–30, 174
Mariage Guillaume I, 190
Marina, St., 119, 120
Mark, St. (Evangelist), 145
Mark of Termaqa (Mark the Athenian), 68. See Also Mark the Athenian
Mark the Athenian, St., 68, 135, 136, 176; Life of, 58; story of, 68–70
marriage, 82, 86, 87, 96, 97, 104, 109, 175, 206; and St. Macarius, 109–15; flight from, 92–102, 206. See also secret flight; wedding
Marrou, Henri, 6
marturein, 22, 24, 36
martyr: and saint, 18–41, 43–45; and wild beasts, 145–51
martyrium dicere, 185
Marx, Karl, 174
Mary. See Virgin Mary
Mary Magdalen, 174
Mary the Egyptian, 12, 67–68, 71, 75, 99, 108, 119, 127, 142, 164, 165, 169, 174, 202; Life of, 58
Maximilian (martyr), 20
Maximus (magistrate), 25, 32. See also Veteran Julius
megatext, 13
Mercurius, St., 124
Messenger, Ruth, 36
metamorphosis, 120, 168
militia Christi, 20, 26
Milton, John, 142
Mohammed, 135, 174
Monk of Eynsham, 179
monomyth, 73
Montalembert, Charles F. R., 194

"more" motif, 59, 83–85
Moschus, John, 13, 91, 155. *See also*
  Pratum Spirituale
Moses, 160n, 173, 189
Mount of Olives, 123
Mount Sinai, 173
Mozarabic liturgy, 36
Musurillo, Herbert, 131–32
Mycenae, 167
myth, 7, 10, 12, 73, 169, 171, 189–
  204; Egyptian, 203

Narcissus, 115
Narnia Chronicles, 182, 211. *See also*
  Lewis, C. S.
nature. *See* culture vs. nature
Navigatio Sancti Brendani, 205
Nazareth, 21, 22
New World, 209. *See also* Paradise
Nichols, Stephen G., 184, 185
Nile, 210
Nilus (Abbot), 141
Nonnus (Bishop), 90
Novatian, 140
novel. *See* romance
Nuffel, Pierre van, 37

Odysseus, 80, 205n
Odyssey. 205. *See also* Homer
Oedipus, 80
Oliver (in *Chanson de Roland*), 183
Olivier (in *Girart de Vienne*), 188
Olympius (Abbot), 91, 175n
omophagy, 138–39. *See also*
  xerophagy; food; culture vs. nature
Onuphrius, St. 1, 11, 12, 51, 58, 60,
  60–62, 63, 71, 74, 75, 78, 90, 108,
  118, 125, 131, 135, 136, 161, 164,
  169, 170, 175, 176, 202; story of,
  53–64; *Vita Onuphrii*, 51, 57, 58,
  71
oral poetry, 8
oral tradition, 8
Origen, 84, 137
Osca, 28
Osiris, 13, 204n
Ounnofer, 13. *See also* St. Onuphrius
Oxyrhynchus, 57, 62

Pachomius, St., 12, 79, 162
paideia, 6
Palestine, 42

Palladius, 13, 106, 139, 157. *See also*
  Historia Lausiaca
palm tree, 52, 54, 55, 61, 63, 67, 135;
  date palm, 173. *See also* food; tree
Panteleemon, St., 149
Paphnutius (Abbot), 177
Paphnutius, St., 55, 60–62, 66, 71, 74,
  75, 83, 84, 90, 108, 118, 125, 126,
  133, 161, 170, 176, 180, 199; story
  of, 51–64, 52, 53, 55. *See also*
  Peregrinatio Paphnutii
Papylus, St. (martyr), 20, 149
Paradise, 57, 64, 70, 81, 110, 124,
  131–67, 133–35, 143, 151, 156,
  161, 166, 170, 207, 209–12. *See
  also* New World; Peaceable Kingdom; spring; tree
passio, 9, 11, 12, 16, 17, 19, 21, 23,
  24, 36, 42, 43, 103, 181, 182, 185–
  87, 191, 193
passion, 184
Passion of Perpetua and Felicitas
  [Felicity], 118, 147
Patrick, St. *See St. Patrick's Purgatory*
Patroclus (in Homer), 205n
Paul, St., and Thecla, 48–50
Paul of Thebes, 4, 8, 12, 71, 72, 74,
  79, 83, 86, 104, 105, 108, 135, 159,
  161, 164, 169, 176, 180, 202, 203,
  204; *Life of* (*Vita Pauli*), 58, 66,
  66–67, 71, 72, 84, 116, 144, 179
Paul the Deacon, 165
peace of Constantine. *See* Constantine,
  peace of
Peaceable kingdom, 144–67, 209–12.
  See also Golden Age; Hicks,
  Edward; Paradise
Peeters, Paul, 71, 72, 88
Pelagia, St., 90, 119, 127
Penn, William, 209
Perceval, 200, 201, 205
Peregrinatio Paphnutii, 51–58, 57, 58,
  74, 84, 176
Peristephanon, 5, 24, 27, 85, 185,
  186, 189. *See also* Prudentius
Perpetua, 18, 143, 147. *See also Pas-
  sion of Perpetua and Felicitas*
Perseus, 80
Peter, St., 21, 48
Philomorus (hermit), 140
Pliny, 151
Poema de mio Cid, 182, 188, 191–92

polis, 43, 167, 168, 172, 173, 204. See
    also city
Polycarp, St. (martyr), 20
ponos, 165
Poros, 122
Poseidonius (hermit), 140
Pratum Spirituale, 13, 91, 154, 155.
    See also Moschus, John
Probus, St., 150
Propp, Vladimir, 10, 83, 209
prostitutes, 127, 174
Protevangelicum of James, 80, 161
Prudentius, 28–31, 33, 34, 36, 39, 41,
    184, 185, 189. See also Peris-
    tephanon
"Pseudo-Map" cycle, 200
Pseudo-Matthew. See Gospel of
    Pseudo-Matthew
Pseudo-Turpin Chronicle, 183, 186,
    190
Psyche, 80, 159
psychopompos, 118, 172, 202, 204
puer-senex, 59, 78, 80, 81, 87, 157
Purgatorio, 115
Pythagoras, 169n

quest, 120–26, 205. See also Eliade,
    Mircea; journey
Queste del saint Graal, 182, 200,
    205

Raglan, Lord, 77
Raphael (Archangel), 116–19
raw food. See food, raw
rebirth, 76, 110
redundancy, 8, 75; repetition, 57
Regulus (in Horace), 30
Rencesvals (in Chanson de Roland),
    183, 190
repetition. See redundancy
Resurrection, 187
rhetoric, 3
rite of passage, 208–9, 212; rites de
    passage, 95, 110, 171, 175, 178–79,
    208; initiation rites, 175, 177. See
    also van Gennep, Arnold
Roland: in Chanson de Roland, 23,
    183; in Girart de Vienne, 188; in
    Pseudo-Turpin, 186, 190
Romance of Alexander the Great,
    120–22
romance, 8, 13, 14, 18, 42–76, 103,

120–26, 126, 130, 180, 189, 192–
    93, 204; Arthurian, 83, 205
Romanus (hermit), 140
Romanus, St. (church of), 183
Rome, 24
Rowland, Beryl, 157
Rufinus, 162. See also Historia
    Monachorum
Ruodlieb, 206
Rutebeuf, 202

Sabas, St., 156
St. Patrick's Purgatory, 179
Salomonson, J. W., 151
Saly, Antoinette, 188
Samuel (Old Testament), 80
Sanctus (martyr), 20
Saragossa, 28, 29
Saturus (martyr), 118, 147. See also
    Passion of Perpetua and Felicitas
Schnapp-Gourbeillon, Annie, 196
Schniewind, J., 75
secret flight, 85–91, 92, 175, 206–7.
    See also wedding; Paradise
Serapion (Abbot), 68, 69, 117, 135,
    136, 161, 176. See also Mark the
    Athenian
Sergius and Hyginus (monks), 123
sex, 137–42
Shaw, George Bernard, 158
Sheol (realm of the dead), 118
Simeon Metaphrastes, 13, 51, 86, 90,
    93, 98, 146, 150, 157
Simeon Priscus, 139, 140, 159
Simeon Stylites, St. (the elder), 12, 77,
    79, 88–89, 100, 105, 157, 164
Simon. See Simeon
sleep, 115. See also descent
Sleeping Beauty, 80, 208
Smaragdus, 119, 120. See also St.
    Euphrosyne
springs, 135; and Paradise motif, 133–36
stag, 201
Ste. Croix, G. E. M. de, 27
stomach, 104n
Story of Asdiwal, 76
Sturm-Maddox, Sara, 188
Subiaco, 88
Susa, 167
Symeon. See Simeon
Synaxarium Alexandrinum, 158
Syria, 42

Tacitus, 151
Tarragona, 29, 31
Telemachus, 80
Terence, 142
Tereus, 168
Tertullian, 141, 143, 146
Thaïs, 107, 127, 174; by Anatole France, 182
Thebaid, 52
Thecla, St., 48–50, 83, 119, 148, 149
Thelxina (in Ephesiaca), 47
Theoctista of Lesbos, St., 71
Theodore of Sykeon, St., 107
Theodoret, 13, 88–89, 106, 139, 140, 159, 160, 177. See also Historia Religiosa
Theophilus: in Peregrinatio, 57,; one of Three monks, 63, 83, 122, 123–24, 125. See also St. Macarius
Theseus, 80
Thomas. See Apocryphal Acts of Thomas
Three monks, (in Life of St. Macarius), 66, 74, 89–90, 98, 100, 101, 116, 122, 132, 159, 171, 176
Timotheus, 52, 53, 63, 74, 75, 84, 135, 176. See also St. Paphnutius
Tobias, 117. See also Book of Tobit
Tobit. See Book of Tobit
Todorov, Tzetvan, 184. See also vraisemblance
tomb, 67, 103, 105, 106–8, 136, 176. See also burial; cave; death
Trajan (emperor), 146
tree, 133; of life (date palm), 70, 135. See also palm; paradise
Trophimus, St., 150
Turner, Victor, 172, 173, 178. See also liminality
Turpin, Archbishop (in Chanson de Roland), 183

Valentia, 28, 29
Valerius (Bishop), 28, 30, 38, 39
van Gennep, Arnold, 171, 179
vegetarianism, 168. See also food
velut mortuus, 61, 69, 108, 118, 125, 199. See also death
Verba Seniorum, 57, 58, 68, 154, 177
Vergil, 85, 184
Vestal virgins, 113n
Veteran Julius, 18, 25, 27, 41

Vie de saint Léger, 184
Vincent of Saragossa, St., 11, 27–33, 36, 38, 39, 162, 186
Virgin Mary, 81, 135, 162
virginity, 92, 95, 137, 142–44, 149, 167, 172, 206–7
vita, 9, 11, 12, 14, 16, 17, 18, 21, 103, 181, 182, 191, 193
Vita Abrahae. See Abraham (hermit)
Vita Antonii. See St. Antony
Vita Macarii Romani. See St. Macarius the Roman
Vita Malchi. See St. Malchus
Vita Onuphrii. See St. Onuphrius
Vita Pauli. See Paul of Thebes
Vitae Patrum, 11, 12, 13, 79
Vivien (in Chançun de Willame), 183
voluptas, 100, 137–42
Vööbus, Arthur, 139
vraisemblance, 184–86. See also Todorov, Tzetvan

Waldes, 174
Waltharius, 206
Warren, William, 210
wedding, 65. See also marriage
Whitby, Monk of, 6, 7
William of Aniane, St., 190
William IX of Aquitaine, Duke, 84n
Williams, Charles, 74
Wilmotte, Maurice, 198
Wittig, Susan, 8, 206
"Wooing of Emer" (Celtic tale), 202
Works and Days, 165

Xenophon of Ephesus, 46. See also Ephesiaca
xerophagy, 138. See also food; culture vs. nature; omophagy
Xystus (Pope), 39

Yvain, 83, 196–200, 207. See also Chevalier au lion; Chrétien de Troyes

Zeno (monk), 106, 140
Zosimas, St., 75, 83, 84, 99, 108, 119, 120, 125–26, 142, 176, 202, 203; story of, 67–68

theories of the firm

London School of Economics handbooks in economic analysis

theories of the firm

Malcolm C. Sawyer

Reader in Economics, University of York

St. Martin's Press

New York

For information write: St. Martin's Press, Inc.,
175 Fifth Avenue
New York,
N.Y. 10010
Printed in Great Britain
First published in the United States of America in 1979

ISBN 0–312–79703–6

Library of Congress Cataloging in Publication Data
Sawyer, Malcolm C
  Theories of the firm.

  Bibliography: p.
  Includes index.
  1. Production (Economic   theory) 2.   Business
enterprises. 3. Microeconomics. I. Title.
HB241.S284 1979   338.5   79–14662
ISBN 0–312–79703–6

contents

page

preface

part one

chapter 1   **introduction**   3
1.1   the importance of theories of the firm   3
1.2   contents of this book   7
1.3   the definition of firm and industry   10

chapter 2   **perfect competition and monopoly**   13
2.1   cost conditions   13
2.2   the theory of perfect competition   18
2.3   problems of perfect competition   20
2.4   the theory of monopoly   22
2.5   discriminating monopoly   25
2.6   bilateral monopoly   26

chapter 3   **the theory of monopolistic competition**   29
3.1   the model of monopolistic competition   29
3.2   criticisms of monopolistic competition   38

chapter 4   **classical theories of oligopoly**   42
4.1   introduction   42
4.2   the oligopolistic nature of industry   44
4.3   classical theories of oligopoly   45
4.4   the Cournot model   46
4.5   the leader/follower model   50
4.6   comparisons of the leader/follower and
      the follower/follower models   50

4.7	the von Stackelberg model	52
4.8	the price leadership model	53
4.9	general models	54
4.10	market shares model	54
4.11	collusion	55
4.12	the kinked demand curve theory	56
4.13	the theory of games approach	58
	appendix to chapter 4	64
4.14	an extension to the Cournot model of oligopoly	64
4.15	the theory of games	64

chapter 5 — **the impact of barriers to entry** — 70

5.1	the nature of barriers to entry	70
5.2	the limit-pricing model	72
5.3	capacity as an entry barrier	76
5.4	dynamic limit pricing	78
	appendix to chapter 5	80
5.5	the Kuhn-Tucker theorem	80
5.6	Gaskins' model	81

part two

chapter 6 — **introduction to part two** — 85

chapter 7 — **managerial theories of the firm** — 89

7.1	background to the managerial theories	89
7.2	theory of Scitovsky	91
7.3	theory of Baumol	92
7.4	theory of Williamson	97
7.5	theory of Marris	101
7.6	comparison of theories based on growth and profit maximization	110
	appendix to chapter 7	116
7.7	an extension to Williamson model	116
7.8	extensions to Marris model	117

chapter 8   **behavioural theories of the firm**   121
                        8.1   satisficing   121
                        8.2   full-cost pricing   123
                        8.3   the behavioural theory of the firm   128
                        8.4   *X*-inefficiency   130

chapter 9   **radical critique and radical alternatives** 133
                        9.1   the theory of countervailing power   134
                        9.2   monopoly capital   135
                        9.3   Rothchilds' theory   137
                        9.4   the new industrial state   139

chapter 10   **the debate over the motivation of firms** 142
                        10.1 concepts of profits   142
                        10.2 ability of firms to maximize profits   144
                        10.3 the managerial revolution again   146
                        10.4 are firms forced to maximize profits?   148
                        10.5 differences between owner-controlled
                                and manager-controlled firms   152
                        10.6 implications for efficiency   154

notes   155

references   165

index   169

preface

This book grew out of courses of lectures on the theories of the firm given to second- and third-year economics students at University College London. Comments made by the several generations of students attending those lectures influenced their content and presentation and now the contents of this book.

There appears to be a movement towards authors of text books making explicit their own views on their subject, rather than pretending to have no preferences amongst the various approaches discussed. I gladly support this movement by stating that my preferences lean towards the importance of the theories explored in Chapters 5 and 9, even though they provide only partial views of the manner in which firms operate.

I would like to thank Brian Henry for comments on the first draft which have led to considerable improvements and Christine Robinson for typing the manuscript.

part one

chapter 1

introduction

1.1 The importance of theories of the firm

The productive efficiency and, to a lesser extent, the distributive equity in a private-enterprise economy crucially depends upon the behaviour and performance of firms. By firms we mean all non-government producers of output for sale. This book deals with many of the theories of the firm which have been proposed. These theories are first outlined, and then their predictions are analysed and their weaknesses examined.

This book is concerned with theories of firm behaviour under a private-enterprise system in developed economies. How firms operate under other situations is not considered, although the models used here may be applicable to other situations. Even the operation of firms under private enterprise may indicate a wider scope than is actually achieved, since the theories examined are Anglo-Saxon in origin and may not be relevant to, say, the Japanese context.

This book is also restricted to *theories* of the firm, and there is little mention of empirical work. The only reference to 'reality' comes with some theories whose development is intertwined with observations on how firms actually operate. The omission of any consideration of empirical results is for three reasons. Firstly, there are great difficulties in devising tests which adequately discriminate between the competing theories, and further complications in obtaining data with which to undertake the appropriate tests. Secondly, such work that has been done yields conflicting results. Thirdly, and arising from the first two points, an adequate and comprehensive examination of the evidence (with formulation of the appropriate tests) deserves a book to itself, and could not be undertaken properly within the length of this study. I have sought rather to provide a comprehensive coverage of the theories of the firm.

As the title of the book indicates, there is more than one theory of the firm. By the end of the book, it will be realized that there are a multitude of theories. Why so many? Many reasons can be suggested. A first one is that there are a wide variety of firms, ranging in size from 'one-man' businesses to those which employ hundreds of thousands. Firms also differ in terms of the type and range of products which they make, and in terms of the number of owners (ranging from one person through to many thousands of shareholders in large quoted companies). Whilst some writers feel that the size of the firm makes no basic difference to the manner in which the firm operates, others do not share that view and have advanced various theories to apply to firms of different size. The most notable example of this latter view being the development of theories intended to apply when the number of shareholders becomes very large and the shareholders are no longer in day-to-day (nor, some would argue, year-to-year) control of the firm, with the managers being able to pursue their own interests which may conflict with the interests of the shareholders.

A second and similar reason for the number of theories is that the industrial context in which firms operate varies. For example, the number of firms in the industry, the relative size of the firms, the nature of the product, etc., may be features which influence firm behaviour. We will see that the assumptions about the number of firms in the industry and the ease of entry of new firms into that industry also vary and that these variables generate different theories.

Reference has already been made to the difficulty of testing the theories. This has meant that, so far, no empirical consensus has emerged by which certain theories are seen as clearly in conflict with the available evidence.

A further major concern is the balance of power between the consumers and producers. The perfect-competition approach has often, rather misleadingly, been described as incorporating consumer sovereignty, whereby the wishes of the consumer are uppermost. That system, however, should be seen as one which indicates a balance between the interests of consumers and producers reached in conditions of equilibrium. But other theories would indicate that the producers have the upper hand and that producer, rather than consumer, sovereignty is the order of the day.

An alternative (but similar) way of viewing this is to say that under a private-enterprise system the price mechanism coordinates the demands of consumers and producers, and through which resource allocation and income distribution are determined. In particular, consumers and producers are seen as responding to the prices of goods and services and factors of production in making their decisions as to what to buy and what to produce. Economic efficiency will require, at least, that prices are appropriately set to encourage the producers and consumers to respond in a manner which leads to overall economic efficiency. Thus, there is considerable interest in how prices are determined. Are they determined by the interplay of demand and supply, or are they set without much restriction by large firms?

However, it is not sufficient to work out how prices are set (and even that
remains an open question), for in addition one must know who or what
determines the nature of the goods produced (e.g. high-quality or low-
quality goods), how consumers' perceptions of the goods produced are
determined (e.g. are they moulded by advertising?), and how the nature of
the goods produced changes over time through product innovation.

As already indicated, there are a multitude of theories of the firm, and this
naturally invites one to ask whether there is any way of distinguishing
between the various theories. A number of rather fundamental problems
present themselves at this juncture. Firstly, the various theories do not
always have the same purpose. For example, the neoclassical theories are
mainly concerned with making predictions on equilibrium prices and
changes in those prices, without much attempt or pretence of 'realism'. In
contrast, the behavioural theories (discussed in Chapter 8) can be seen as
attempting to provide a fairly realistic theory of pricing decision-making in
disequilibrium situations. For example, Machlup (1967) writes:

> 'The model of the firm in that theory (perfect competition) is not . . .
> designed to serve to explain and predict the behaviour of real firms;
> instead, it is designed to explain and predict changes observed in prices . . .
> as effects of particular changes in conditions (wage rates, interest rates,
> import duties, excise taxes, technology etc.). In this causal connection the
> firm is only a theoretical link, a mental construct helping to explain how
> one gets from the cause to the effect'.

A second problem is that the theories may be intended to relate to
particular situations. For example, the theory put forward by Galbraith in
The New Industrial State (discussed in Chapter 9) is not intended to apply to
the small dairy farmer (to use Galbraith's example) but only to the large
corporations, which Galbraith sees as dominating the American economy.
Thus it may be difficult or impossible to compare theories if the population
of firms to which they are intended to apply only overlap to a limited extent
or even not at all.

There is the related problem that when numerous theories are presented,
each relating to a somewhat different situation, rules are needed (or another
theory) to indicate which theory is to be applied to a given industry. For
example, Chapter 4 shows that there are many theories of oligopoly. But, so
far, there has been no indication as to when one of these theories, rather than
another, might best be applied.

One school of thought has argued that a major (if not the only) role of the
theory of the firm is to predict price and quantity supplied changes from

specified changes in the economic environment (e.g. the level of demand for a product, change in taxation, etc.). Machlup (1967) writes:

'Let us ... pose four typical questions and see which of them we might expect to answer with the aid of "price theory" (i.e. theories of the firm). (1) What will be the prices of cotton textiles. (2) What prices will the *X* corporation charge. (3) How will the prices of cotton textiles be affected by an increase in wage rates. (4) How will the *X* corporation change its prices when wage rates are increased.

'Conventional price theory is not equipped to answer any but the third question; it may perhaps also suggest a rebuttable answer to the fourth question. But questions 1 and 2 are out of reach'.

Such a view illustrates the dominant methodology of 'positive' economics in which a given theory is not judged in any sense by the realism of its assumptions, but solely by its ability to predict successfully the 'real world'.[1] Thus heavy reliance is placed on prediction and none on explanation.[2] The theories presented in Part Two of this book and some of them in Part One do not yield many unambiguous predictions, but they may be able to provide some explanations of how the world (or at least firms) works. However, 'positive' economic methodology emphasizes the ability of a theory to predict and, if possible, to predict with the minimum of assumptions. Moreover, it asserts that theories are able to generate predictions, and if possible create different predictions so that the theories can be confronted.

At this point a number of problems must be noted. Firstly, what is the subject of the predictions, or what ingredients of firm behaviour are we interested in predicting? The flavour of the quote from Machlup given above is that it is the prediction of prices and quantities. In the debate with Galbraith (see Chapter 9) over the New Industrial State, Solow (1967) says:

'The world can be divided into big thinkers and little thinkers. ... Economists are determined little thinkers. They want to know what will happen to the production of houses and automobiles in 1968 if Congress votes a 10 per cent surcharge on personal and corporate tax bills, and what will happen if Congress does not. ... Big think and little think are different styles'.

By limiting ourselves to the prediction of prices, quantities and the like, many important contributions of some theories will be overlooked. Further, making predictions the sole concern gives an edge to the perfect-competition view of the world; since that theory does provide prediction, albeit of a limited nature, with relatively little trouble. It also means that since that theory is limited to predictions on price and quantity any comparisons between theories tend to be limited to those variables.

A second problem is to derive the requisite predictions with which to make comparisons. As will be partially seen in later chapters, theories often tend to come up with similar predictions in a qualitative sense. Thus the theories will often predict the same direction of change for a variable, following a specified change in another variable. Quantitative predictions will differ. But since they depend upon a number of usually unknown numerical values of parameters, comparisons of quantitative predictions are not usually possible.

A third, but related, problem is the inability of some theories to make predictions. This has been a particular criticism of the theory of monopolistic competition (Chapter 3), but it applies more generally.

Fourthly, there are difficulties in constructing situations whereby the predictions can be tested. The predictions are usually of the form, 'if X changes, then Y changes in a predicted direction', with all other variables held constant. Further, a change in Y which is predicted relates to changes in its equilibrium value. In a world where many things are changing, such comparisons are difficult to undertake.

1.2   Contents of this book

The book is in two parts, and, as will be explained below, there are some basic differences between the approaches used in the two parts of the book.

Part One covers mainly traditional theories of the firm with the one central theme that firms seek to maximize profits (usually short-run profits). The context in which the firms operate is different in the various theories, and as a result their actions and the overall outcome differ. But firms are assumed to have the same motivation.

Chapter 2 provides a review of the theories of perfect competition and monopoly–the former a situation of free entry by new firms into the industry, and the latter a situation of a single firm with no threat of entry. This chapter also reviews cost curves. The theory of monopolistic competition, discussed in Chapter 3, attempts to combine one element of monopoly (the firm produces a unique product and hence faces a downward-sloping demand curve) with elements of perfect competition (free entry and firms producing close substitutes). In Chapter 4 theories of oligopoly (where the number of firms is small but more than one) are discussed. The small number of firms generally leads to a marked dependence of one firm's profits on the actions of its rivals, and the central theme of Chapter 4 is the impact of this interdependence. However, in Chapter 4 one underlying assumption is that the existing firms are protected by barriers to entry from new firms coming into the industry. In Chapter 5 that assumption is relaxed, and we investigate the impact of the threat of new entrants on the behaviour of the existing firms. This chapter removes the 'all or nothing' assumption about barriers to entry which have been made in the previous three chapters, where theories have either assumed that there were complete barriers, so that no new firms could come into the industry, or that there were (at least in the long run) no impediments to new firms entering.

The theories of the firm considered in Part Two have three central themes. Firstly, they are theories of oligopoly/monopoly in that they all assume that there are some barriers against new firms entering the industry, which allows existing firms to earn above normal profits if they so wish. Secondly, firms are treated as organizations and the goals of the firm are built up from a consideration of the interests of groups within that organization. A third point arises from these two, that firms of this kind pursue objectives other than maximization of profits. A factor reinforcing this is often taken to be the 'managerial revolution', whereby it is argued that firms are not controlled by their owners (who are seen as rather dispersed shareholders) but by managers who have an interest in pursuing objectives other than profit maximization.

In Part Two, Chapter 6 provides a general introduction in which the remarks in the previous paragraph are further elaborated. Chapter 7 deals with three theories which retain the maximization of stated objectives as the underlying assumption, but since the objective is not profits (nor directly profit-related), the firms pursue these other objectives subject to constraints on the amount of profits which they must generate. The retention of the maximization principle means that the firm strives to achieve cost minimization as an adjunct to its maximization procedure.[3]

Chapter 8 relaxes the maximization postulate, replacing it by the idea of satisficing, which means that firms strive to reach what they regard as satisfactory levels in certain key variables, such as profits, sales, growth, etc. Whereas the theories in Chapter 7 build up the objectives of the firm by a consideration of the objectives, aims and drives of the various groups within the firm but arrive at an objective which is then maximized, these theories in Chapter 8 argue that the last part of the argument cannot be performed to turn the problem into a maximization one.

Chapter 9 has less of a common thread than earlier chapters, and the only common feature is that the theories discussed here can be considered 'radical' theories of the firm, which within a much broader framework present views of the firm which are essentially critical of the existing order. These theories often accept that there has been a 'managerial revolution' with its consequent changes in firm behaviour, place some emphasis on the interdependence between firms, and investigate the wider impact of large firms on the overall economic and political environment.

In Chapter 10 the threads of the previous chapters are drawn together. In particular, the question of whether profit maximization is a meaningful concept is discussed and also to what extent it can be said that firms are forced to maximize profits. This involves a consideration of the pressures on the firm, and what room for manoeuvre they have. The pressures on the firm can come from the capital market, by lack of finance, or the threat of take-over if the firm does not achieve some rate of profit. The pressures may also come from the product market with existing firms being threatened by new entrants.

There are a number of basic distinctions between the two parts of the book which may not have emerged from the above discussion. There is, first, a difference in the underlying concept of the firm. In Part One, the concept of the firm is largely based on the single entrepreneur controlling the firm in his own interests. It may be recognized that firms are often large organizations, but the view is maintained that even large firms are, in a sense, merely 'inflated' entrepreneurs. This enables the retention of the assumption that the firm has a single objective, that the objective is profits, and that the entrepreneur is able to enforce his decisions on his workforce. In a sense, the firm is viewed as a 'black box', with inputs being fed in and outputs emerging, and with the outputs being as large as is technically feasible (given the inputs and the state of knowledge). In contrast, the underlying concept in Part Two is of an organization for which the objectives have to be deduced, and which may have difficulties in achieving technical efficiency. Thus, in Part Two, the theories make some attempts to prise open the 'black box', even though they find different contents in the box when it is opened.

There is a further difference of concept between the two parts. In Part One, the firm is closely linked with the product it produces. Although it is rarely spelt out, the firm and the product are practically synonymous. So far as the analysis is concerned, the firm produces a single product. The firms considered in Part Two are not identified with the products which they produce, but are treated as entities in their own right. A firm is, then, basically a block of capital which currently happens to produce a certain range of products, but is not in any way limited to that range. It may move into or out of industries and product ranges as seems appropriate to the firm.

Another distinction is that the theories in Part One are essentially theories of industry rather than theories of the firm. Deriving from the first consideration above (with the firm treated as the 'black box'), the major emphasis in Part One is on how firms interact within an industry. In contrast, the theories in Part Two are mainly concerned with individual firm behaviour, and one of the main weaknesses of these theories lies in a neglect of the interaction between firms.

These rather basic differences between the theories in the two parts of this book reinforce the difficulties mentioned above of making comparisons between the theories.

A final difference is more methodological in character. The theories in Part Two are often built on observation of actual firm behaviour, and make more attempt at 'realism' than the theories in Part One. In contrast, the theories of Part One would generally pride themselves not on their realism, but on their analytical convenience and their ability to make testable predictions. This distinction cannot be an absolute one. Any theory must make some assumptions which do not incorporate all aspects of reality and to some extent, therefore, are unrealistic.

1.3   The definition of firm and industry

The last part of this chapter now considers the rather mundane problems of how firms and industries are to be defined.

One definition of a firm could be any person or collection of people who turn inputs into outputs. But this view could be taken as including households, seen as converting the input of income and household labour, etc., into the output of consumption goods, etc. Within the context here, the definition is restricted to those organizations or individuals which produce marketable output. This also means the exclusion of many forms of government activity as well.

That defines the functions of a firm; it is still necessary to say where the boundary of a firm is. One view of where the boundary lies arises from the following consideration. A contrast can be made between coordination through the decentralized price mechanism and coordination by central decision-making. Coase (1937) writes:

'For instance, in economic theory we find that the allocation of factors of production between different uses is determined by the price mechanism. The price of factor A becomes higher in X than in Y. As a result, A moves from Y to X, until the difference between the prices in X and Y, except in so far as it compensates for other differential advantages, disappears. Yet in the real world we find that there are many areas where this does not apply. If a workman moves from department Y to department X, he does not go because of a change in relative prices, but because he is ordered to do so.'

Thus, within the firm, resources are allocated by the controllers of the firm, though they may take market prices into account when making their decisions. The firm makes contact with the market when inputs are purchased and when output is sold. The boundary of the firm is then seen as the interface between central decision-making within the firm and the price mechanism.

This approach places emphasis on the coordinating role of the entrepreneur. But in line with the theories considered in Part Two, we may want to replace that by coordination (or attempts at coordination) by managers, interest groups, and others within the firm.[4] In this case, it would be more appropriate to talk of coordination by consent than by command.

Whilst for many firms it is clear where the boundary lies, this is not always the case. For example, a holding company which owns several units could, under this approach, be regarded as many firms if the holding company did not coordinate the activities of its various units and, whilst providing supervision of them, essentially allowed them to operate in an independent manner. Elements of fuzziness would be introduced if the holding company allocated capital between the units but otherwise did not allocate resources between them, or if there was some trading between the units with the prices determined by the holding company.[5] An example from the other end of the spectrum would be where one firm is the major or sole customer of another, and the power of the one firm over the other is such that in many respects resources within the two firms were allocated centrally, even though' they were nominally under separate ownership.

Another definition of the firm has already been emerging and in many respects this is the one which underlies the theories of the firm presented in Part Two. There, the firm is presented in terms of a legal definition, based on the ownership of the assets of the firm. As such a firm can be regarded as a block of capital, which is invested in different activities, of which the boundaries of the block are laid down by legal requirements.

In most of the theories in Part One, firms are grouped together into industries. But how are industries defined? One view, which underlies the theories of perfect competition and monopoly, is that the boundaries of an industry are self-evident, and are drawn in terms of the product produced by the firms within it. In other words, firms which produce the same product are placed in one industry. In those cases where only one firm produces the goods, it is in a monopoly situation. It is put more formally as: firms in an industry are producing a homogeneous product. But this begs the question of what is meant by the same product. An oft quoted example of a perfectly competitive industry is the wheat industry: there are numerous producers, not one of which is of any significant size relative to the total industry, and each one is producing the same product – wheat. But there are different grades of wheat, which are purchased for delivery at different places and at different times, and these could all be regarded as distinct products. The general problem raised here has been more explicitly faced under the context of the theory of monopolistic competition (see Chapter 3).

The notion of defining an industry in terms of the products produced is retained by the theory of monopolistic competition but it is recognized that there is not usually product homogeneity. Looking at many manufactured products we find product heterogeneity, at least in terms of different brand names, and usually slight differences in quality, product characteristics, etc. An industry could then be defined in terms of a group of close substitutes in demand. More formally, an industry could be defined in terms of the firms producing goods, which have cross-elasticities in demand (between themselves) greater than some predetermined number X. Whilst this definition has been around for a long while, no one has ventured to state precisely the value of X !

A possibly more common sense, but less precise, view would be to regard an industry as a group of firms who feel that their own destinies are interwoven. This may have two aspects. Firstly, where there are a large number of firms the feeling may be one of 'sink-or-swim' together. Secondly, where the numbers are few, whilst a general change in demand would affect all firms in that industry, there is some feeling that one firm's success would be at the expense of other firms.

chapter 2

perfect competition and monopoly

In this chapter the theories of perfect competition and monopoly are reviewed. These topics are not given as full a treatment as other topics in the belief that they have been covered in previous courses of study.[1] Our review of these theories is intended to draw out certain salient features of their analysis for later use. But before looking at these theories, cost curves are briefly discussed. The last part of the chapter deals with some extensions of the theory of monopoly.

2.1 Cost conditions

Firms are viewed as purchasing inputs (such as labour and raw materials) and producing outputs which are then sold to consumers and other producers. The objectives of the firm in undertaking production are discussed later in the book, and for this part of the book the assumption is that firms seek to maximize some concept of profits. The cost curves are intended to show the costs of the inputs for different levels of output. Two types of cost curves are used here, namely, average and marginal costs. Average costs are total costs of some or all the inputs divided by the level of output, whilst marginal cost refers to the incremental cost of producing a little bit more output. In formal terms, average cost is C/q, and marginal cost dC/dq (that is, the first derivative of C with respect to q), where C is costs and q is level of output. The particular type of average costs in which interest is usually shown are the average of the costs of those inputs whose usage is variable during the decision period being considered. However, the average and marginal cost curves have to be related to specified circumstances. How marginal costs, and hence average costs, change as output changes depends upon how much flexibility the firm is assumed to have. Some inputs which the firm purchases can be bought off the shelf as required and do not involve any commitment to future use. In contrast, the current purchase of some inputs will involve commitments to purchase in the future, e.g. labour hired today will often involve commitments through custom, contract or labour law to hire again tomorrow. It is usually 'capital' (covering machinery, buildings, vehicles, land, etc.) which is placed most firmly in this category. The validity of that action will depend upon the type of capital asset involved (clearly cars can be more easily varied than electric power stations) and the second-hand market in that asset. If a piece of machinery could be bought today and sold tomorrow without the firm suffering any capital loss or having to pay any buying and selling costs, then the amount of machinery used could be varied from day to day. Another constraint on the flexibility of the firm's use of inputs arises from the time taken to purchase some inputs and put them into full use. Clearly much capital equipment is made to order, so that there are delays in obtaining the equipment. But there are also likely to be delays in hiring labour, and in the time that labour takes to become familiar with the operations of the firm which hires it. The short run period usually refers to a period during which the use of labour input can be varied, but for which the capital equipment is fixed. Although we shall follow this usage, it should be remembered that in practice some labour inputs will take longer to adjust than some capital inputs. However for the short run, inputs of materials and labour are assumed to be variable whilst the input of capital is taken as fixed. The average variable and marginal cost curves for the short run are drawn in figure 2.1 with the assumption that price of inputs is fixed to the firm. The costs included in the average variable cost curve are only those of variable inputs. The average variable cost curve turns upwards at point *B* to reflect the onset of diminishing returns to the variable factors being applied to a fixed amount of capital.

Reference is often made to the capacity of a factory; is it possible to give

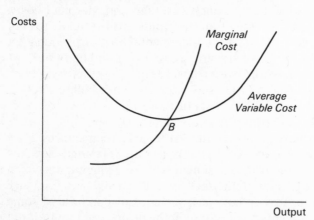

figure 2.1   Average variable and marginal cost curves

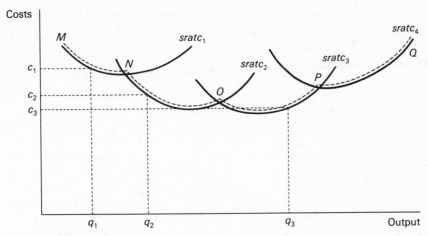

figure 2.2 Long-run average cost curve

that concept any meaning in this context? The curves have been drawn without any obvious physical limit being placed on the level of output produced with a particular piece of capital input. But from the diagrams it is apparent that the costs of additional output rise without limit. This points to an 'economic' definition of capacity, and the one usually used is that capacity is the quantity of output for which average costs are at a minimum, i.e. the point B in figure 2.1.

We now derive the long-run cost curve. Since capital is a variable input in the long run, the cost of capital is included in total costs. First suppose that the capital input can only be supplied in four sizes, and that the average total cost curves for these four sizes are portrayed in figure 2.2. A firm which wanted in the long run to produce an output q_1 would find that the lowest costs would be achieved by operating the capital equipment which corresponds to the cost curve $sratc_1$. Its average costs would then be c_1. Similarly, if the firm planned on producing q_2, it would find that lowest costs were reached by operating along $sratc_2$, with costs c_2. By considering each possible level of output, the long-run cost curve is generated as the dotted line in the diagram and labelled $MNOPQ$.

Now we remove the restriction that there are only four possible sizes of capital input, and instead assume that the size of the capital input can be continuously varied. As the number of possible capital input sizes is increased, the range of output for which any one capital input size is the one with lowest average costs becomes smaller. At the limit when there are an infinite number of possible capital input sizes (which corresponds to our assumption that the capital input is continuously variable), at most, one point of any short-run average cost curve will be part of the long-run average cost curve.[2] Further, a short-run cost curve cannot be below the long-run cost curve; for if it were, then for some output that short-run cost curve would have lower costs than the long-run cost curve, which is contrary to the basis on which the long-run cost curve is derived. Thus, any short-run cost curve has, at most, one point in common with the long-run cost curve. This is illustrated in figure 2.3, and the long-run cost curve is the 'envelope' of the short-run cost curves.

It can be seen that, except for one size of capital input (which corresponds to $srac_3$ in figure 2.3), the installed size of the capital input will not be operated at full capacity (that is where short-run average costs are at a minimum). For example, if the size of capital input which leads to $srac_1$ is built to produce q_1, it will be operated at below capacity. The full capacity for $srac_1$ is output level q_2, but for that level the cost curve $srac_2$ yields lower costs.

The shape of the long-run average cost curve indicates whether the production is subject to increasing, constant, or decreasing returns to scale. In figure 2.3, there are increasing returns (decreasing unit costs) up to W, constant returns at W and decreasing returns (increasing unit costs) thereafter. Whether the point W occurs at an output which is small in relation to total demand for the product or not is a matter of considerable importance in terms of the type of industrial structure one would expect to emerge and the forms of industrial policy advocated. The forces influencing the shape of the long-run average cost curve is discussed by Pratten (1971).

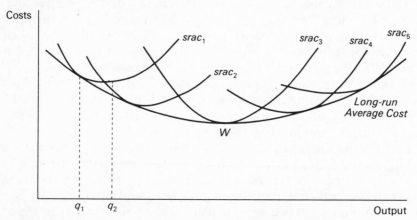

figure 2.3   Long-run and short-run average cost curves

The above discussion relates to a firm which operates only one factory (capital input). The multi-plant firm can now be brought into the picture. First take the case where the firm has two plants which have identical cost curves (which are $srac_1$ in figure 2.4), and there are no costs or benefits associated with operating two plants *per se*. The curve $srac_{1+2}$ describes the average costs which result when the output is produced equally in the two plants. It is the inflation of $srac_1$ (and of $srac_2$ which is identical) by a factor of two, so that for any given level of average costs, say c_1 in figure 2.4, the output which can be produced for that cost is doubled for $srac_{1+2}$ as compared with $srac_1$. There are four ranges of output level to be considered and these are illustrated in figure 2.4. Up to the output level q_0, the average costs decline with output when it is produced in a single plant, and it can be seen by a comparison of $srac_1$ with $srac_{1+2}$ that lower costs result from concentrating output in a single plant rather than splitting it between the two plants. Over the range q_0 to q_1, the average costs of output within one plant are rising, but costs in one plant are still below costs from producing in two plants. The third range of q_1 to $2q_0$ sees the firm splitting output between the two plants, and operating subject to declining average costs. The fourth range is from $2q_0$ onwards where both plants are operated but subject to rising costs. The analysis for *n* identical plants would be similar.[3]

The second point is a more important one. A firm which could continue to duplicate plants, each of which had the same cost curve and which did not incur any costs of coordination of the plants, could expand indefinitely at close to constant costs. In such a case, there would be little in the way of cost

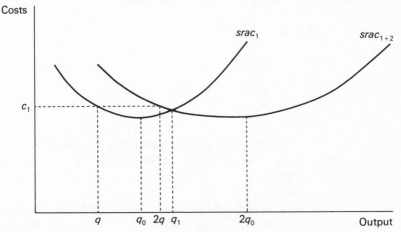

figure 2.4   Cost curves for single-plant and double-plant operation

rises limiting the expansion of the firm. Thus an important consideration in views on firm size would be not only whether there are economies of scale as plant size increases, but also whether there are significant costs of coordination and differences in costs across plants operated by the same firm.

2.2   The theory of perfect competition

The theory of perfect competition analyses a situation where there are a large number of small firms who produce an identical product for which there is a single market price which is not influenced by the actions of any individual firm. So the firms are price-takers, and they seek to maximize profits. There is no impediment against new firms entering the industry and each firm faces identical cost conditions which include average costs rising at a level of output which is small relative to the total market. This last assumption helps to maintain the first assumption, as will be made clearer below.

In the short run, the 'capital' of the firm is fixed and this means that the number of firms is fixed. Thus firms outside the industry with zero capital in the industry cannot change their capital equipment (i.e. cannot enter the industry) and firms in the industry cannot leave it. Then the firm faces the problem of maximizing $\pi = pq - C(q)$, where π is the profits of the firm over this short-run period for which it is making its decision, p is the market price, q the level of output, and C the relevant total costs.[4] The price is fixed to the firm, and costs depend upon the level of output q. The firm has only to decide on the level of output.

The maximization of this profit function requires

$$\frac{d\pi}{dq} = p - \frac{dC}{dq} = 0$$

$$\frac{d^2\pi}{dq^2} = -\frac{d^2C}{dq^2} < 0 \quad \text{i.e.} \frac{d^2C}{dq^2} > 0$$

so that output is adjusted to bring price and marginal cost into equality, and marginal costs are rising rather than falling. The diagrammatic representation of this is given in figure 2.5 with the second condition leading to output q_1 rather than q_2.

This describes short-run equilibrium for the individual firm. In the long run, firms can adjust their capital stock, thus enabling firms to enter or leave the industry. The free-entry assumption leads to a long-run equilibrium

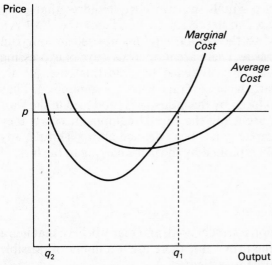

figure 2.5   Output levels for which price = marginal cost

condition that economic profits are zero; otherwise firms would be entering or leaving the industry. Zero profits (where profits refer to excess of revenue over all costs including the cost of capital) yields the long-run condition that price equals average cost. The simultaneous achievement of the profit-maximizing condition (that price equals marginal cost) and the no-

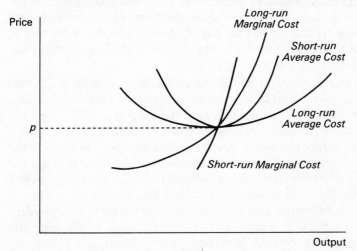

figure 2.6   Long-run equilibrium price under perfect competition

entry/exit condition (that price equals average cost) requires that price settles down at the level indicated in figure 2.6. In that figure the short-run cost curves, which correspond to the capital equipment used in long-run equilibrium, have also been drawn. There are numerous ways of expressing this long-run equilibrium result. Firstly, each firm (in this case, all are assumed to be identical) operates where average costs are minimized. Thus the level of output which is produced by the industry is produced in the least cost manner. Secondly, firms are using the capital equipment which they have to 'full capacity', as full capacity has been defined above. Thirdly, any decreasing costs have been fully exploited by the firms moving to the base of the average cost curve.

2.3   Problems of perfect competition

The model of perfect competition is widely used, and many believe that it is a particularly useful theory of the firm.[5] But there are a number of possible objections to it which need to be investigated.

The theory of perfect competition is essentially a theory of equilibrium, and in particular, with firms acting as price-takers. It does not incorporate any explanation of *how* prices change. This can be summed up: 'If all firms are price-takers, how do prices ever change?'[6] Within the model set up above, there is no way for prices to change, but the movement to long-run equilibrium would require prices to change. Recently, attempts have been made to relax the assumption of perfect information and then to build models which would have a price-change mechanism. The essence of such models is that firms have a limited monopoly position in the short run, in that they can raise their price without losing all their custom, and lower their price without demand increasing without limit.[7]

The theory of perfect competition has proceeded on the basis that all firms have the same cost curves and face the same demand conditions (the same price). The individual firm examined can then be thought of as the representative firm of the industry, with the experience of other firms paralleling that of the firm examined. An alternative interpretation is that the firm examined is the 'marginal' firm in the industry, in the sense that it is the firm on the margin of leaving the industry since it is only just earning normal profits. The other, non-marginal, firms would be earning supernormal profits.[8] However, their output decision rule would be the same if they wished to maximize profits (equate marginal cost to price), but in the long-run equilibrium their profits would be above the normal level. For, by assumption, firms not in the industry would have cost curves if they entered the industry which would never yield even normal profits. In other words, their average cost curves lie everywhere above the prevailing price.

The assumptions of perfect competition include that of increasing costs setting in at a level of output which is small relative to the industry total. The presence of economies of scale would undermine perfect competition in at least two ways. Firstly, whichever firms were larger would have lower costs and could expand either by reinvesting their profits (which from lower costs are larger than for the small firms), or by a departure from price-taking by setting a price lower than that which can be matched by the smaller firms. Secondly, the marginal cost curve lies below the average cost curve, as indicated in figure 2.7, when there are economies of scale. Thus the rule of equating price and marginal cost would generate losses for the firm, since average costs are greater than marginal cost (price) for any level of output.

Thus competitive conditions, in terms of a large number of small firms in an industry, and the existence of unexploited economies of scale and/or of decreasing short-run costs facing the firm, would appear to be incompatible. The belief that it was often observed that such situations did coexist in the same industry is often labelled the Sraffa paradox,[9] and the theory of monopolistic competition discussed in the next chapter can be thought of as an attempt to explain the Sraffa paradox.

The profit-maximizing condition of price equals marginal cost leads to a firm's supply curve since from that condition the amount a firm wishes to

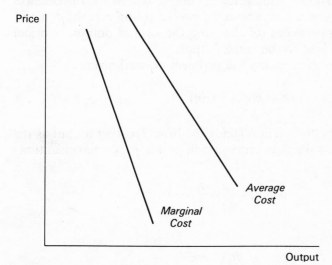

figure 2.7   Average and marginal cost curves under increasing returns

supply at any given price can be easily ascertained. The supply curve for the firm becomes coincident with the marginal cost curve (above the average variable cost curve); and the industry supply curve is obtained by the summation of the firm supply curves. The existence of a supply curve is a powerful tool in the perfect-competition armoury for it enables predictions on price and output movements to be made for specified changes which shift either the demand or the supply curves.

2.4   The theory of monopoly

The theory of monopoly (one seller) is in many respects at the other end of the spectrum to perfect competition. It deals with a situation where there is one firm in the industry who sets the price in order to maximize profits. There are barriers to entry into the industry, such that there is no threat to the existing firm.

The monopolist faces a downward-sloping demand curve, which relates the price charged and the quantity demanded. The firm can choose either price or quantity, but not both; once one of these variables has been fixed by the firm, the consumers via the demand curve determine the other. It is conventional to set up the problem in terms of the monopolist choosing the level of output which maximizes profits, rather than choosing the price. In this model whether output or price is deemed to be the one chosen by the firm does not affect the final result, and the level of output is used for convenience. But if the monopolist was unsure about the precise position of the demand curve, then the two approaches (of choosing the level of output or price) would not necessarily lead to the same output.

The monopolist is seen as facing the problem of maximizing

$$\pi = p(q).q - C(q)$$

where $p(q)$ inverse demand function facing the firm. Treating output as the decision variable, yields the first-order condition for profit maximization:

$$\frac{d\pi}{dq} = p(q) + \frac{dp}{dq} - \frac{dC}{dq} = 0$$

which can be written

$$p\left(1 + \frac{q}{p} \cdot \frac{dp}{dq}\right) = \frac{dC}{dq}$$

which is
$$p = \frac{dC/dq}{1 - 1/e}$$

where e is the elasticity of demand.[10]

This condition is usually expressed as the firm equates marginal revenue (the $p + dp/dq.q$ term) with marginal cost (dC/dq) by varying its output. The last expression indicates that the extent to which price exceeds marginal cost depends upon the elasticity of demand. It also follows that the monopolist operates where the elasticity of demand (e) exceeds unity. For if e were less than one, the indicated price would be negative; at e equals unity, price would be infinite. The basic reason for this is that when the elasticity of demand is less than unity, the marginal revenue (of increasing output) is negative, so that the firm would gain by reducing output since that would reduce costs and increase revenue. Thus the firm would never find its optimal (in profit terms) to operate where the elasticity of demand is less than unity.[11]

It can also be seen that as the elasticity of demand increases, price relative to marginal cost falls. At the limit where elasticity of demand tends to infinity, price equals marginal cost.

In the theory of perfect competition, it was possible to derive supply curves for the industry for various time periods. The device of a supply curve means that the impact of a change in demand on price and quantity is predictable. But it is only under the circumstances of perfect competition where a supply curve can be drawn, and where the impact of a change in demand is predictable without further information. This can be illustrated easily in the case of monopoly, but a similar analysis would appertain for the theories of monopolistic competition and oligopoly discussed below.[12]

In the context of monopoly, output is determined by marginal revenue equals marginal cost. Changes in demand, besides shifting the demand curve inwards or outwards, may also change the relationship between price and marginal revenue, i.e. the elasticity of demand may change.[13]

The supply curve of perfect competition indicates a one-to-one relationship between price and quantity supplied. It is easy to show that this one-to-one relationship does not hold under monopoly (nor under any of the theories which incorporate price-makers). The easiest way of demonstrating this is given in figure 2.8, where the price p_1 is associated with output q_1 when demand curve D_1 prevails, and with q_2 when demand curve D_2 holds. Thus a change in demand from D_1 to D_2 would lead to a rise in demand at the initial price, no change in price but a rise in quantity supplied.

If the manner in which the demand curves changed and the position of the cost curves were fully specified, then it would be possible to predict the outcome of the specified change in demand. But if one were only told that demand at the initial price had, for instance, risen, then the consequences cannot be definitely predicted, and in a theory such as the one discussed here, one is restricted to such limited qualitative information.

The theory of monopoly discussed here is an analysis of a situation where one firm controls an industry. It can, however, be more widely interpreted. The major assumptions made are that the firm takes no account of how its price and output might affect new entrants coming into the industry nor of how its price and output affect other firms and how they respond to that price

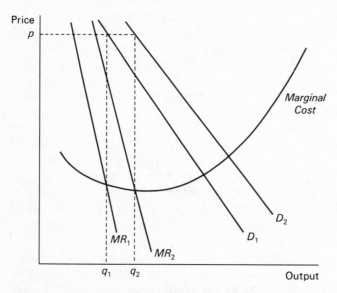

figure 2.8 Two alternative profit-maximizing outputs

and output. In the case of monopoly, this type of behaviour fitted in with the assumptions made of barriers to entry into the industry and control of the industry by the firm. This latter assumption really means that there are no close substitutes for the product of the firm in question. In other contexts, the analysis derived for monopoly may carry over, if the firm believes (rightly or wrongly) that similar conditions apply in its case.

Two extensions of this analysis of monopoly now follow: firstly, where the monopolist sells the same product in two distinct markets; secondly, where the monopolist sells to a single buyer (a monopsonist).

2.5   Discriminating monopoly

The first extension being made from the above analysis of monopoly is usually known as the case of the discriminating monopolist. The monopolist must have some means of keeping the two (or more) markets separate; otherwise it could be expected that middlemen would intervene to ship the monopolist's output from the low-price market to the high-price market. The markets may be in different countries, and movement between the two markets may be limited by transport costs, tariffs and the imposition of contracts on the distributors by the monopolist preventing shipping between markets. Another type of example would arise in the case of personal services which by their nature cannot be resold.

Consider the case where the monopolist sells in two markets, with costs dependent on total output. The demand conditions are given by $p_1(q_1)$ in market one and by $p_2(q_2)$ in market two. Thus the monopolist seeks to maximize $\pi = p_1(q_1)q_1 + p_2(q_2)q_2 - C(q_1 + q_2)$.

The first-order conditions yield

$$\frac{\partial \pi}{\partial q_1} = p_1(q_1) + \frac{\partial p_1}{\partial q_1} \cdot q_1 - \frac{\partial C}{\partial q_1} = 0$$

$$\frac{\partial \pi}{\partial q_2} = p_2(q_2) + \frac{\partial p_2}{\partial q_2} \cdot q_2 - \frac{\partial C}{\partial q_2} = 0$$

which are merely the marginal revenue equals marginal cost condition applied to both markets. Manipulation yields

$$p_1(1 - 1/e_1) = \frac{\partial C}{\partial q_1}$$

$$p_2(1 - 1/e_2) = \frac{\partial C}{\partial q_2}$$

where e_1, e_2 are the elasticities of demand in markets one and two. The marginal cost of q_1 and q_2 will be the same since from the production side they are identical products. Hence

$$\frac{p_1}{p_2} = \frac{1 - 1/e_2}{1 - 1/e_1}$$

so that the price will be higher in the market with the lower elasticity of demand.

2.6   Bilateral monopoly

In the building up to the bilateral monopoly (one buyer/one seller) case, first consider the case of a single buyer facing many sellers of the product in question. For the monopsonist (single buyer), as the scale of purchase increases, so does the price paid for it face an upward-sloping curve for the good. The demand curve of the buyer, whether determined from utility or profit considerations, can be interpreted as indicating the amount which the buyer would want to buy for each given marginal cost of purchase.[14] In figure 2.9 we have the supply curve of the many sellers (based on their marginal cost of production), the marginal cost of purchase curve facing the buyer (derived from the sellers' supply curve), and the demand curve. The outcome is the purchase of an amount q_1 at a marginal cost to the purchaser of m_1, but at a price of p_1. For the buyer wishes to purchase an amount q_1, and to induce that supply to be forthcoming requires a price p_1.

The case of one seller and one buyer is usually known as bilateral monopoly, and within the context of the type of economic theory considered here, it is often regarded as having an indeterminate outcome. Figure 2.10 has the curves necessary for the analysis. From the monopoly side, with one seller facing a demand curve, the outcome would be a price p_a and quantity q_a. From the monopsony side, with one buyer facing a supply curve, the

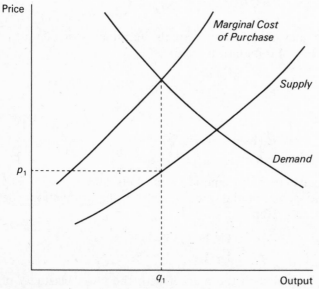

figure 2.9   Monopsony

outcome would be a price p_b and quantity p_b. The combination of one buyer with one seller is then said to leave the outcome on the price side indeterminate within the range p_a and p_b, with the precise outcome determined by the relative bargaining skills of the two participants. Further, even when the price has been decided the quantity which is traded has also to be determined.

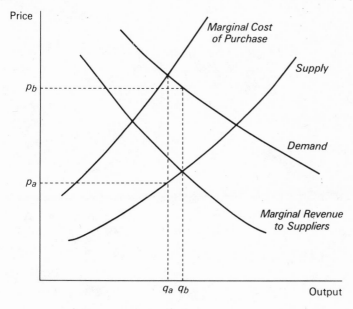

figure 2.10   Bilateral monopoly

The theories of perfect competition and monopoly share certain common features, despite their apparent antithesis. In each case, the firm operates in isolation in that its actions do not affect other firms. In the case of perfect competition, the firm adjusts its output to bring marginal cost in line with price. The only point of contact between one firm and another is through price, and by assumption no single firm can influence price. Thus in changing its output, the firm has no noticeable impact on the price, and consequently no noticeable impact on its competitors. For monopoly, and impact on other firms, is ruled out by the nature of the situation being considered.

A second common feature between perfect competition and monopoly is that the nature of the good being produced is taken as fixed. Thus these theories do not comprehend changes in the nature of a product, nor industries where there is no external given product but the firms have to design their own product, nor advertising which changes consumers' perceptions of products.

Some account, however, is taken of interdependence between firms and of product change in the theories discussed in the next two chapters.

chapter 3

the theory of monopolistic competition

3.1 The model of monopolistic competition

The theories of perfect competition and monopoly which were discussed in the previous chapter can be seen as representing the two polar extremes of a large number of firms with free entry on the one hand and with a single firm with no possibility of entry on the other. The theory of monopolistic competition has been presented as based on the view that most, if not all, real world industrial arrangements contain elements of both competition and monopoly. However, the important part of the argument is that the chemistry of a situation which contains elements of both competition and monopoly does not lead to an outcome somewhere between perfect competition amd monopoly, but contains features not present in either of the polar cases.

The theory of monopolistic competition is based on the book of the same name by Chamberlin (1933). The theory of monopolistic competition presented in most textbooks (including this one) forms only part of the analysis by Chamberlin. He looked at two types of situation: that with a small number of firms and that with a large number of firms. His analysis of the small number case helped revive the analysis of Cournot, Bertrand, Edgeworth, etc., of the situation of oligopoly. Some of these theories are examined in the next chapter.

Of central importance in the analysis of monopolistic competition is the idea that firms in an industry are producing products which are similar but not identical to each other. Thus in contrast to the assumption made in the theory of perfect competition that firms within an industry produce a homogeneous product (indeed the industry is defined in terms of that homogeneous product), in the theory of monopolistic competition the products produced are assumed to be heterogeneous. The assumption is not that the products are necessarily physically different (though they may often be so) but rather that, as far as the consumers are concerned, the products can be differentiated from one another. This differentiation may consist solely of differences in the brand name attached to physically identical products or of real differences in the characteristics of the product. The product differentiation and differences between consumers in their tastes, perceptions of products, etc., lead to a number of closely related conclusions. There is the possibility that similar products may be sold for different prices. Those consumers with a strong preference for brand X over brand Y will be prepared to pay more for X than for Y. Thus the producer of X can charge more for his product than the going price for Y and still retain some custom. So each firm faces a downward-sloping demand curve for its own product. Firms are price-makers in that they have to decide what price they will charge for their product. In the limited sense described in the last three sentences, the firm under monopolistic competition can be said to be in a monopoly position. Indeed the short-run analysis of monopolistic competition is analogous to that of monopoly.

This now leads back to the original point: monopolistic competition contains elements of both competition and monopoly. The monopoly element is that the firm has a monopoly in terms of the product which it produces. Thus it is assumed that it is not possible for another firm to enter the industry and exactly replicate the product of any existing firm. The competitive element is supplied by two features: first, in contrast to monopoly, each product has a number of close substitutes; secondly, there is free entry into the industry in the long term.

The recognition of product differentiation introduces the extra decision to be made by the firm on the nature of the product it produces. More accurately, the firm has extra decisions to make about the exact nature of the product, its packaging, advertising and marketing, etc. A possibly extreme case would be the decision of a car manufacturer on model specification, marketing etc. In the analysis below, all these decisions are compressed into one and labelled in general terms as the product 'characteristic' decision.[1]

The model of monopolistic competition will now be described, some of the conclusions reached by the theory will be investigated, and then some of the criticisms which have been made of the theory will be examined.

The model is designed for an industry in which there are a large number of firms who produce similar but distinct goods. There is free entry into the industry, so that when there are supernormal profits, firms offering new products are drawn into the industry. Conversely, when there are subnormal profits some firms leave the industry. Further, although differentiated goods are being produced within the industry, all firms still face the same cost and demand conditions. Essentially, it is assumed that some unit of measurement exists for each product such that when these units are used, the cost and demand curves of each product are the same.[2] This assumption is often referred to as the 'uniformity' assumption.

Finally, it is assumed that the effect of any firm's price or characteristic change is spread widely and thinly over all the other firms so that no other firm is substantially affected by one firm's action. This 'symmetry' assumption helps to rule out the possibility of interdependence between small groups of firms within the industry. If a small, interdependent group existed, then a situation more akin to oligopoly would prevail. This kind of oligopolistic situation will be considered in the subsequent chapters.

In terms of the assumptions made above, the model of monopolistic competition resembles perfect competition in many respects. The assumptions of large numbers of firms, free entry into the industry, and the 'uniformity' assumption are equivalent to the assumptions made in perfect competition. Since firms are price-takers under perfect competition, the impact of one firm's actions (level of output) does not affect any other firms as one firm's output is assumed to have no impact on the common price level. So a 'symmetry' assumption is implicit in perfect competition. However, the model of monopolistic competition diverges from perfect competition in that the firms are producing differentiated goods, and each one faces a downward-sloping demand curve.

The firms are assumed to be short-run profit-maximizers, so that the ith firm faces the problem of maximizing:

$$\pi_i = q_i(p_i, p, d_i, d) - C_i(q_i, d_i)$$

where π_i are the profits of firm i, p_i, q_i, d_i are the price, quantity and product characteristics of the firm i, respectively, and p, d the vectors of prices and product characteristics of the products of other firms.

The demand function $q_i(p_i, p, d_i, d)$ is a formalized way of saying that the quantity of its product which a firm can sell depends upon the price charged for its own product, the prices charged by its competitors, and the product characteristics of the firm's product and of its competitors' products. For the individual firm, there are four decision variables which influence the level of profits: its costs, its own price, product characteristics, and quantity. But (e.g. price and quantity via the demand curve), only two of the variables can be independently determined by the firm since these are interrelated. Since costs are determined by level of output and product characteristics it is usual to treat costs as one of the passive variables. The three remaining variables are linked through demand conditions. Here the quantity of output will be treated as the passive variable and price and product characteristics are taken as the decision variable of the firm.

The same basic results would follow from considering price and quality as the decision variables.[3] However, a further problem of interpreting the demand function still remains. In the function $q_i(p_i, p, d_i, d)$ for given values of the other variables, price is a negative function of quantity. In respect of price in the short run, the problem facing the monopolistic competitive firm is analogous to that facing the monopoly. But, and this is a central problem for the analysis of this chapter and the next one, is it reasonable to take the price and characteristics of other firms' products as fixed when picturing the firm's price/quantity-making decision? The same type of argument will also apply to the firm's decision-making process with regard to product characteristics.

There are, at least, three reasons for thinking that when one firm's price changes, then the prices of other firms will not remain fixed. Firstly, in focusing on the representative firm, then whatever forces have shifted its cost and demand curves (leading to it having to make its profit-maximizing decision afresh), could well have operated on many other firms in the industry. For example, a rise in the cost of a particular input is likely to have affected other firms as well as the firm being considered. Secondly, since the price of each firm enters the demand curve of all the other firms, as one price changes so change the demand conditions facing the other firms. Thirdly, a move by one firm may trigger off reactions by other firms. For example, a move by one firm may be regarded as aggressive by other firms who then respond to try to isolate the 'aggressor'. In the context of monopolistic competition, with many firms in the industry, the second and third reasons are ruled out by assumption. These factors, however, will play an important role in the theories of oligopoly considered in the next chapter. These reasons do indicate that how one firm thinks other firms will respond to, say, a price change may depend upon the circumstances of the industry. The first reason given above for some interdependence operates in the context of monopolistic competition.

In the short run, the firm seeks to maximize profits by changing price and the product characteristics of output (and so its quantity and costs vary), with the firm taking the price and product characteristics of its competitors as fixed. Thus the firm under review maximizes

$$\pi_i = p_i \cdot q_i(p_i, p, d_i, d) - C_i(q_i, d_i)$$

with respect to p_i and d_i, assuming that p and d are constant. The first-order conditions are:

$$\frac{\partial \pi_i}{\partial p_i} = \frac{\partial q_i}{\partial p_i} \cdot p_i + q_i - \frac{\partial C_i}{\partial q_i} \cdot \frac{\partial q_i}{\partial p_i} = 0$$

$$\frac{\partial \pi_i}{\partial d_i} = \frac{\partial q_i}{\partial d_i} \cdot p_i - \frac{\partial C_i}{\partial q_i} = 0$$

The first condition states that for a given set of products the firm equates the perceived marginal revenue gained from price change with the marginal cost of the output change induced by the price change. The marginal revenue is described as perceived since it depends upon the firm's perceptions of what other firms will do. In this case, the perceptions are that other firms will do nothing in response to the firm's actions. The second condition indicates that the firm equates the marginal revenue gained from varying product characteristics with the marginal cost of these variations.

If the firm under consideration is a representative firm, then as it is changing its price, other firms will be changing their price. In one sense it is reasonable for the firm to assume that its pricing policy has no impact on what other firms do. Nevertheless, the price and product characteristics of other firms do change and would have changed anyway. Thus the firm's belief that other prices and product characteristics remain unchanged is not borne out in practice and so it does not move along the demand curve along which it expected to move. In other words, its perceived demand curve, which generated the perceived marginal revenue function in the two first-order conditions, does not turn out to be the demand function along which the firm actually moves. As the firm changes its price, other firms are changing their price by the same sort of amount. Thus the demand curve along which the firm finds itself moving is the one with other prices changing at the same pace as the firm's own price. So that the demand curve along which the firm moves is not $q_i(p_i, p, d_i, d)$ with p constant, but it is subject to p always changing to the same extent as p_i does.

In figure 3.1 two demand curves are drawn. The dd curve corresponds to the perceived demand function used in the above maximizing procedure, that is with all other prices including the prices of competitors assumed constant. The DD curve is the demand curve for the prices of competitors changing with the price of the firm whose demand curve is drawn. The dd curve is more elastic than the DD curve, reflecting that a price rise along the dd curve will lose more custom than if the firm moves along the DD curve. In the former case, there is a loss of demand for the firm's product to both its competitors and to other industries. Whereas in the latter case, only the second loss operates. These demand curves focus on price and quantity, and implicitly the product characteristics of all firms' output is assumed constant.

In figure 3.1 the firm, under the behavioural assumptions given above, would price at p_0 anticipating to sell q_0 (having equated the marginal revenue

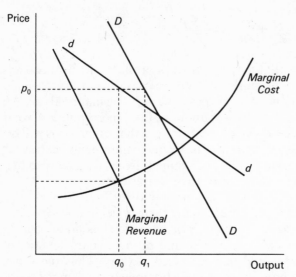

figure 3.1   First-round profit maximization under monopolistic competition

derived from the *dd* curve with the marginal cost). But when other firms change their price, the firm finds that at price p_0 it sells q_1. Thus its expectations are not fulfilled, and so the outcome is not a profit-maximizing one.

Short-run equilibrium requires both that the firm is maximizing profits (under its assumptions about other firms' prices) and that its expectations about other firms' prices are fulfilled in practice. This would occur when the intersection of the appropriate *dd* and *DD* curves was at the same output as the intersection of the corresponding marginal revenue curve and the marginal cost curve. This is drawn in figure 3.2 and provides the short-run equilibrium position for the monopolistic-competitive firm with respect to price.

A shift in other firms' prices means that the demand function for the representative firm, derived from the assumption that other prices are held constant, changes: in the diagram the *dd* curve shifts. Holding to the behavioural assumption made above the firm would go through the decision-making process again to determine its new profit-maximizing price, subject to other prices being assumed constant. But once again, the firm's expectations are likely to be falsified in the outturn.

So far, only the profit-maximizing price has been considered and nothing has been said as to whether the resulting profits are positive or negative. In

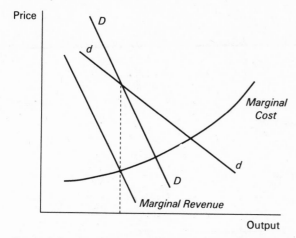

figure 3.2   Short-run equilibrium under monopolistic competition

the long run, there is assumed to be free entry into and free exit out of the industry, so that profits in the industry (and hence for the representative firm) move to the normal level. As firms move into or out of the industry so the demand function facing the individual firm is likely to shift, i.e. if other firms move in, a shift to the left is likely and if other firms leave, a shift to the right. Little can be said about the exact way in which the industry moves towards this long-run equilibrium. Instead the characteristics of this long-run equilibrium position are described.

For long-run equilibrium the short-run equilibrium conditions must hold, and there must also be the condition that there are only normal profits. This gives: average revenue equals average costs (including normal profits). In other words, the output at which marginal revenue equals marginal cost, and at which the *dd* and *DD* curves intersect, will be a long-run equilibrium output if the average cost equals average revenue (whether calculated from the *dd* or *DD* curve need not be specified here since the two calculations would yield the same result). The long-run equilibrium output is illustrated in figure 3.3 at q_e, with price p_e. The key feature of this equilibrium is that the *dd* curve is tangential to the average cost curve.[4]

Since the long-run equilibrium is being considered, it would be appropriate to deal in terms of long-run costs, with the firms adjusting the scale of operation as appropriate. The long-run average cost curve is the envelope of the short-run cost curves (as indicated in Chapter 2), so that the short-run cost curve in use for output q_e has the long-run cost curve, as well as

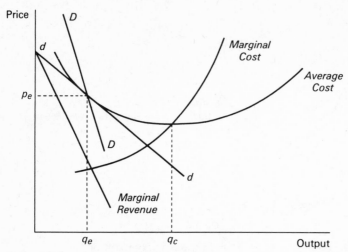

figure 3.3   Long-run equilibrium under monopolistic competition

the *dd* curve, tangential to it in the long-run equilibrium position as illustrated in figure 3.4.

The so-called 'tangency solution' can be expressed in a number of alternative ways. In terms of the short-run cost curve, for a particular set of capital equipment, it can be said that the firm operates with surplus capacity. It will be recalled that full capacity is defined as *the level of output at which*

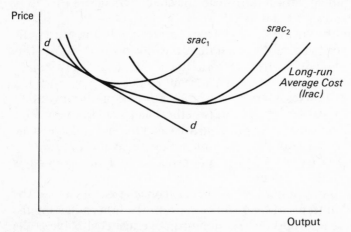

figure 3.4   Long-run equilibrium under monopolistic competition, with long-run costs

average costs are at a minimum (alternatively where average cost equals marginal costs). The long-run equilibrium output is less than the full capacity/output and the firm is operating with excess capacity (on this definition of full capacity). In terms of long-run costs, the firm by using the plant-size yielding cost curve $srac_1$ (in figure 3.4) rather than the plant-size yielding cost curve $srac_2$ is not fully exploiting the available economies of scale. For if the firm operated plant 2, it would be lower down its long-run cost curve and fully exploiting the available economies of scale.

Another way of looking at this result is to say that firms under monopolistic competition do not operate, in long-run equilibrium, where average costs are at a minimum. This can be contrasted with the long-run equilibrium condition of perfect competition. But it has also to be noted that the cost curves here are drawn for the production of output with particular product characteristics. It is, therefore, difficult to make comparisons between the cost conditions under perfect competition and those under monopolistic competition. Where an industry is producing an essentially homogeneous product, with these products differentiated by a label and through advertising, it can be expected that the cost curves will be higher than they would be under perfect competition. With essentially homogeneous products, perfect competition would be a feasible proposition. When the range of products in an industry are in some essential way heterogeneous then there is not a feasible situation of perfect competition with which to compare the existing monopolistic-competitive industry.

The analysis above has been mainly focused on price and quantity with product characteristics left on the sidelines. Throughout, however, the firm has also been adjusting its product characteristics in accordance with the first-order conditions on page 33. In terms of the final position reached, the product characteristics included in the demand and cost curves need to be interpreted as those which are maximizing profits for the firm. In the real world, one may expect that the speed of the response of other firms to a firm's price change would be faster than it would be for a product characteristic change. Furthermore, the speed of response would be different for different types of product characteristics.

The theory of monopolistic competition has, by grafting some elements of monopoly onto competition, provided a possible explanation for the 'Sraffa paradox' referred to in the previous chapter. Firms will, in the long-run equilibrium position, operate where their cost curves (whether short-run or long-run) are downward-sloping. Thus firms may be operating in a region of decreasing costs but are unable to expand further. Their expansion is cut off by the lack of demand for their product at the prevailing price, so that any expansion in output will lead to a drop in price which more than offsets any gain to the firm in terms of lower costs.

3.2   Criticisms of monopolistic competition

The theory of monopolistic competition has often been the centre of much controversy.[5] The first area of criticism has been the definition of the industry being used. The industry (or in Chamberlin's terminology, the group) is defined as firms producing goods which are similar but not identical. But how similar are they to be, and is there any stopping point before all goods in the economy are included? More technically, the goods included are those which have large cross-elasticity of demand with each other (i.e. they are close substitutes for one another). The problem then becomes one of choosing some number X, so that goods which have cross-elasticity of demand exceeding X are included in the same group, whereas those with cross-elasticity of demand below X are placed in different groups. But the value of X has never been specified (and even if it were, problems of estimating cross-elasticities would be enormous); nor do we know whether any value of X could be specified so that water-tight compartments of close substitutes would result.

This problem has sometimes been suggested as one specific to monopolistic competition.[6] But it is easy to see that defining industries in the real world of differentiated products is likely to be difficult. Even if the theory of perfect competition is thought applicable to an industry, that industry still has to be defined. In the real world, the appropriate definition of an industry is not self-evident in the manner implicitly assumed in perfect-competition or monopoly theory.[7]

The practical importance of the 'excess capacity' result depends to a large extent on the elasticity of the *dd* curve and the slope of the cost curve. It can be argued that since firms are producing close substitutes the own-price elasticity of demand for any particular firm will be very high. A small change in the price charged by the firm will generate large changes in demand. With high elasticity of the *dd* curve it becomes close to horizontal, and so the difference in price under monopolistic competition and under perfect competition becomes small.

For the individual firm, the loss of output under a regime of monopolistic competition as compared with a perfect-competition regime depends upon the slope of the cost curve. For a given elasticity of the *dd* curve, the loss of output will be greater the shallower the slope of the cost curve. But account would also have to be taken of the number of firms in the industry. The smaller output per firm will be partially offset by there being more firms in the industry, and the cost comparisons would involve comparing regimes with different number of firms at different levels of capacity utilization.

Another major thrust of criticism has been aimed at the lack of testable predictions yielded by the theory of monopolistic competition. For example, Stigler (1949) writes that from the theory of monopolistic competition 'we cannot make a single statement about economic events in the world we sought to analyse'. The types of predictions which monopolistic competition is unable to make are those concerned with the changes in price, quality and product characteristics which would follow a change in demand or a change in costs. In contrast, the theory of perfect competition is able to make predictions (which may, of course, be incorrect) on how prices and output would react. Before discussing the reason for the inability of monopolistic-competition theory to make such predictions two points arise. Firstly, this lack of predictive power may not be as major a weakness in a theory as many of the proponents of the 'positive' economics school would argue. Secondly, the theory is able to make one major prediction: that of excess capacity. This is potentially testable, even though there are major problems in estimating cost conditions.

There are three basic reasons why the impact of, say, a change in demand on prices and output cannot be predicted in the theory of monopolistic competition. Firstly, under monopolistic competition, as under a situation of monopoly, the firm (and hence the industry) does not have a supply curve. The impact of a change in demand depends upon the precise manner in which the demand curve changes, and how the marginal revenue curve is affected. This was explored in the previous chapter on page 23. Secondly, a firm can respond to a change in demand by changes in price and changes in product characteristics. In the demand function facing the firm, it has only been assumed that the demand is influenced by price and product characteristics, without making any assumptions about the relative importance of the two variables. Thus, for example, it has not been ruled out that a change in demand leads to the firm making adjustments only to the quality of the product and not changing price. This line of argument is explored more fully in Archibald (1961). Thirdly, the eventual impact on the long-run equilibrium position will depend not only on how firms react in terms of price and product characteristics, but also on which firms enter or leave the industry in response to changes in profits which are generated by the change in demand.

It has also been argued that the firms are strangely myopic in their behaviour. Each time they maximize profits, they do so believing that other firms' prices and product characteristics will be unchanged. Yet each time they find that other firms' prices and product characteristics do change. Although not a part of the original theory, an adaptation to that theory could be made whereby the firms would make their decisions essentially using a demand function which incorporated more realistic assumptions about the movement of the prices and product characteristics of other firms. Then in the above analysis, the demand curve *dd* based on all other prices constant would be replaced by another demand curve, say, *ee* based on another assumption about other firms' prices and product characteristics. Indeed, a whole family of theories could be generated, for each of which the assumptions incorporated in the *ee* curve would be different. One of these variants would be to use the *DD* curve itself as an *ee* curve. Then the firms would incorporate into their decision-making process an assumption about other firms' prices which turn out to be justified. Each of these variants would yield a similar equilibrium configuration, in the sense that the long-run equilibrium position would include a tangency between the *ee* demand and the relevant average cost curve. If the *DD* curve were thought appropriate (because it is less elastic than the *dd* curve) then the resulting degree of excess capacity would be greater with the use of the *DD* curve than with the *dd* curve.

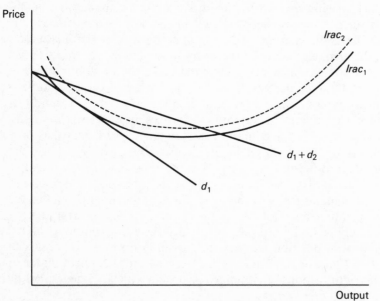

figure 3.5   Illustration of pre- and post-merger positions

There are some reasons for thinking that monopolistic competition may evolve into a situation of oligopoly. Firstly, if the symmetry assumption does not hold entirely, then sub-groups of firms may begin to realize their interdependence with one firm's price change having a noticeable impact on the profits of other firms in the sub-group. If this occurs, then in a sense, the monopolistic-competitive industry breaks up into a number of linked oligopolies.

Secondly, from the long-run equilibrium position the firms have a profit incentive to merge together. Suppose two firms make similar products which are sufficiently similar to be able to add together the demand curves facing them. If they begin in long-run equilibrium, as illustrated in figure 3.5 for firm 1, then after the merger the 'new' firm faces a demand curve which is the summation of the demand curve of the two original firms. The cost conditions faced by the 'new' firm will depend upon the extra costs of producing the two types of goods rather than just one. So the long-run average cost curve for the new firm producing both goods may be higher than the cost curves of the original firms. But unless these joint production costs are fairly high, the 'new' firm by closing down one plant and by expanding along the new cost curve $lrac_2$ will be able to reap supernormal profits, whereas the two original firms were only able to earn just normal profits.

Before we come to a consideration of oligopoly, one further area of controversy must be briefly mentioned. Monopolistic competition differs from perfect competition basically in terms of product differentiation versus product homogeneity. They appear to be costs attached to monopolistic competition in comparison with perfect competition as evidenced by the excess capacity theorem. A key, but unresolved question, is whether there are benefits to consumers arising from differentiation which offset those costs, and further whether there will be any tendency for the 'optimal' degree of heterogeneity and level of quality to emerge.[8]

chapter 4
classical theories of oligopoly

4.1 Introduction

All of the rest of the theories of the firm examined in this book can be thought of as theories which are intended to apply in situations which have some of the features of oligopoly. There are a multitude of alternative theories of oligopoly. Consequently, not all theories of oligopoly are covered in this book.

Oligopoly, strictly interpreted, is *a situation where there are few producers;* the Greek origin of the word means few producers. Previous theories discussed in this book have looked either at one producer (monopoly) or a large number (perfect and monopolistic competition), and oligopoly is often considered to cover the situations between these two extremes. In that case, the 'few' producers may become 'many' producers, provided that 'many' is less than 'a large number'. This illustrates one weakness: 'few' is not explicitly defined; although in terms of the theories considered in this chapter, the answer would be that the number of firms in an industry is 'few' if one firm's actions have a significant influence on the profits of other firms. This also indicates that many theories of oligopoly may be valid in that each theory applies to a different situation especially in terms of the number of firms in the industry: for example two oligopolistic industries, one with ten firms and the other with fifty firms may operate in significantly different ways, in part because of the difference in the number of firms in the two industries. Further differences may arise from variations in the relative size of the firms involved. For example, two industries each with fifty firms but one dominated by a few firms and the other with roughly equal sized firms may behave differently.

The situation of oligopoly rests on the fewness of the number of firms. But another important ingredient is generally the presence of barriers against potential entrants coming into the industry. The barriers to entry help explain why there are only a few firms in the industry, and also serve to give the existing firms some room for manoeuvre and allow supernormal profits (actual or potential) to be not entirely bid away by new firms entering the industry in pursuit of those supernormal profits.

The theories of oligopoly which are considered in the remaining chapters of this book fall into four groups which place different emphasis on these two features of oligopoly (fewness of numbers and barriers to entry). The four groups are:

(a) *Theories which retain the assumption of short-run profits maximization but which make varying assumptions about how firms cope with the interdependence of their profits and the impact which any one firm's actions have on other firms' profits.* In particular, these theories vary in terms of the assumption made about the beliefs of the firms on the reactions of its rivals to its own changes in price or output. These theories are considered in this chapter.

(b) *Theories which stress that while there are some impediments to entry into the industry, these are not complete.* Existing firms may then take into account that whether or not new firms enter the industry can depend upon the actions and profits of the existing firms. The pricing policy of the existing firms will take into account the height of the barriers to entry into the industry. In this case, the interdependence which is stressed is that between existing firms and potential entrants. Chapter 5 looks at these theories.

(c) *Theories which focus on the possibilities provided by barriers to entry through potential supernormal profits for the firms to pursue non-profit objectives or not to pursue any particular objectives at all.* In other words, the pressure to maximize profits is reduced, and these theories provide various alternatives to profit maximization (Chapters 7 and 8). These theories generally ignore the interdependence between firms. This partly arises because these theories are usually more specifically theories of the firm than theories of an industry. For although generally going under the heading of theories of the firm, the theories discussed in the first part of the book are really theories of an industry, and how the firms in that industry gel together. But non-profit-maximizing theories essentially treat the firm in isolation in comparison with its treatment in the other profit-maximizing theories.

(d) *Theories which provide some linkages between the two features of oligopoly.* These theories tend to focus on the firms' reaction to interdependence, sometimes in terms of tacit collusion and sometimes in terms of rivalry. They also stress that existing firms strive to build up barriers to new entrants. Finally, these theories do not limit their analysis to price/output decisions of the firms, but seek to introduce the overall economic and political importance of many oligopolistic firms. These theories are discussed in Chapter 9.

4.2   The oligopolistic nature of industry

It can be argued that the dominant structure of modern industry, particularly manufacturing industry, is that of oligopoly. However, to prove such a statement is rather difficult. One would need evidence on the number of firms in each industry, on the barriers to new entrants and on the effective elasticity of demand facing the firms. The number of firms is relatively easy to report, and this will be done shortly, but it must be remembered that even when there are only a small number of firms in an industry, their actions may be highly constrained by ease of entry into the industry and/or firms being faced by a very high elasticity of demand. For then the situation facing each firm would be rather like the perfectly competitive situation. There is little evidence available on the ease of entry and on the elasticity of demand facing firms.

When reporting on the number of firms in an industry, the major problem is that firms vary in size within an industry: rather in contrast to the assumption made in the theory that firms are of roughly equal size. Thus it could be reported that there are, say, a hundred firms in an industry but that the largest five firms produce, say, 80 per cent of the output. Thus rather than

table 4.1   **Frequency distribution of industries by ratio of sales of five largest firms in the industry to total sales: 1968**

range (%)	number of industries	percentage of sales of manufacturing industries in these industries
0–10	—	—
10–20	8	2.49
20–30	20	4.75
30–40	27	8.86
40–50	34	9.75
50–60	45	12.60
60–70	35	12.75
70–80	39	9.30
80–90	46	9.64
90–100	70	29.87

Source: Aaronovitch and Sawyer (1975).

report the number of firms in an industry, the share of the largest five firms is reported to give some indication of the dominance on an industry of a few firms.[1]

4.3   Classical theories of oligopoly

The 'classical' theories of oligopoly are based on the assumption that firms seek to maximize short-run profits in situations where there are few firms and where there are barriers against new entrants. The case of firms producing a homogeneous product is analysed; the case of heterogeneous products, whilst being more realistic, introduces further complexities into the analysis without being an inherent feature of the analysis. As a general case, consider an industry with n firms (although we will often take $n = 2$ for simplicity), and the profit function for firm i as:

$$\pi_i = p(q_i + Q_i)q_i - C_i(q_i)$$

where $p(.)$ gives the inverse demand function, q_i the output of the firm i, and Q_i the output of all its rivals. $C_i(.)$ is the cost function of firm i. The product is assumed homogeneous so that a common price p prevails in the market.

The interdependence between firms is reflected in two ways. First, the output of other firms, through affecting the price, has an impact on firm i's profits. Second, as one firm changes its output, this affects other firms, who in turn reassess their output decision. Thus, the level of Q_i may depend upon the level of q_i; further, the firms may take the impact of q_i on Q_i into account when making their output decision. This is explained in greater detail below.

The first-order profit-maximizing condition yields:

$$\frac{d\pi_i}{dq_i} = \left[\frac{\partial p}{\partial q_i} + \frac{\partial p}{\partial Q_i} \frac{\partial Q_i}{\partial q_i} \right] q_i + p - \frac{\partial C_i}{\partial q_i} = 0$$

The two aspects of interdependence discussed immediately above are reflected in this equation by the terms $\partial p / \partial Q_i$ and $\partial Q_i / \partial q_i$. The first term indicates the impact on the price prevailing in the industry of the output changes by firms other than firm i. The second term reflects the belief of firm i on the response of other firms to its own output changes.

This profit condition is, again, an application of the familiar rule: marginal revenue equals marginal cost. The marginal revenue term is more complicated than before and comes in two parts. The first, $\partial p / \partial q_i \, q_i + p$, is the direct impact of firm i's output change (and looks very much like the marginal revenue term of the monopolist). The second, $q_i \, \partial p / \partial Q_i \, \partial Q_i / \partial q_i$, incorporates the impact on firm i's revenue of the reaction of other firms to firm i's output change.

This can be compared with the perfect-competition case where although Q_i affects the price level in the industry, it is assumed that $\partial p/\partial q_i$ and $\partial Q_i/\partial q_i$ are zero; under monopoly, there is only one firm so that Q_i is always zero.

In the context of oligopoly, firms are only able to maximize their perception of the profit function, for their maximization depends upon their belief about the reactions of the other firms. If those beliefs turn out to be incorrect, then their attempt to maximize profits will be frustrated.

It also follows from this that firms will only reach an equilibrium position when besides producing a profit-maximizing output subject to their beliefs about other firms' response to their output, those beliefs turn out to be correct. Thus equilibrium requires that each firm has beliefs about the other firms' responses which are justified in the outturn.

4.4   The Cournot (follower/follower) model

Historically, the first solution proposed to the theoretical problem posed by oligopoly in this framework is that of Cournot (1897). Ironically, having stressed the importance of interdependence, this solution ignores it by assuming that each firm has the belief that $\partial Q_i/\partial q_i = 0$: that is, that other firms will not change their output in response to firm i's output change. Hence, the condition (first-order) for profit maximization becomes:

$$\frac{d\pi_i}{dq_i} = \frac{\partial p}{\partial q_i} \cdot q_i + p - \frac{\partial C_i}{\partial q_i} = 0$$

which can be written

$$p\left[1 + \frac{q_i}{p}\frac{\partial p}{\partial q_i}\right] = \frac{\partial C}{\partial q_i}$$

and this first-order condition looks very much like the profit-maximizing condition under monopoly of marginal revenue equal to marginal cost. The only difference is that the value of $q_i/p \; \partial p/\partial q_i$ will be smaller in absolute value (the term itself is negative since $\partial p/\partial q_i$ is negative) than $Q/p \; \partial p/\partial Q$ where Q is the total industry output which would appear in the first-order profit-maximizing condition for the monopolist. Here firm i is only part of the industry, so that a large proportional change in its output may represent only a small proportional change in the output of the industry.

However, unlike the monopolist case, this is not the end of the story. For the first-order condition for firm i depends upon the level of output of its rivals (Q_i), which firm i assumes to be constant when making its profit-maximizing decision on output. But firm i has changed its output in this period and other firms may be doing likewise.

From this first-order condition it can be seen that the level of output chosen by firm i depends upon the level of output of his rivals (Q_i) which firm i assumes will be held at its current level in the future no matter what firm i does.

The output, which firm i believes will maximize its profits, is a function of Q_i. This function can, in principle, be obtained from

$$q_i \frac{\partial p}{\partial q_i}(q_i + Q_i) + p(q_i + Q_i) - \frac{\partial C_i}{\partial q_i}(q_i) = 0$$

to give a function of the general form $q_i = g(Q_i)$. This function is often described as the reaction function of firm i.

The behavioural assumption imposed upon the firms under the Cournot model is essentially the same as that laid upon the firms in the theory of monopolistic competition, where the *dd* curve is based on the prices of all other firms remaining constant. However, the situation is different. In the oligopoly case, a change in one firm's output leaves the other firms in a new situation, and their re-evaluation of their position leads to a change in output. In the monopolistic competition, other firms' prices change not in response to the actions of the 'representative' firm, but because they were undergoing similar experiences. However, in both the monopolistic-competition case and the Cournot solution, firms will generally find that their predictions about their rivals' reactions will be proven to be incorrect, which again can be seen as a major weakness of this theory. However, to find the equilibrium outcome, the firm can be imagined going through round after round of decision-making. At each stage, each firm assumes that the other firms' output is fixed, and under that assumption finds the level of output which its believes will maximize profits. But at each stage, the other firms respond and in fact change their output. Nevertheless, the process may be stable and converge on an equilibrium configuration of outputs, where each firm is satisfied with its position in that it believes that it is maximizing profits so that it has no need of changing its output. In that case, the firm's belief that its rivals will not change their output is justified in the outturn.

For each firm, its output decision is given by the procedure outlined above, and summarized by the reaction function $q_i = g_i(Q_i)$, with $Q_i = q_1 + q_2 + \ldots + q_{i-1} + q_{i+1} + \ldots + q_n$. Similar equations apply to the other $n - 1$ firms, and so we have n equations $q_j = g_j(Q_j)$, for $j = 1, 2, \ldots, n$ summarizing the output response of each of the n firms. The industry will be in equilibrium when no firm has any incentive to change its output. This will occur when the value of each q_k given by these equations in response to the prevailing Q_k has the same value as that which enters the Q_js (for $j \neq k$) which determine the output of the other $n-1$ firms. Thus in principle, the equilibrium outputs are given by solving these n equations for the n unknowns of $q_1, q_2, ..., q_n$.

The original analysis by Cournot related to a situation of a duopoly (that is with two firms) selling water from a spring where the water was obtained at zero cost, and the firms faced a linear demand curve for their homogeneous product. In order to illustrate the Cournot solution, we take a slightly more general case than that considered by Cournot, where n firms are producing a homogeneous product subject to constant costs and face a linear demand curve. Then for firm i, $\pi_i = (a + bQ)q_i - dq_i$, where $p = a + bQ$ is the demand curve for the industry, d the level of unit costs, and $Q = q_i + Q_i$. Then $d\pi_i/dq_i = (a + bQ) + q_i b (\partial Q/\partial q_i) - d = 0$ (equation A) is the first-order condition in this case. Since $\partial Q/\partial q_i = 1 + \partial Q_i/\partial q_i$, the Cournot behavioural assumption of $\partial Q_i/\partial q_i = 0$ is equivalent to $\partial Q/\partial q_i = 1$. Then $d\pi_i/dq_i = (a + bQ) + bq_i - d = 0$. Summing over all n firms gives

$$na + nbQ + b \sum_{i=1}^{n} q_i - nd = 0$$

and since $\sum_{i=1}^{n} q_i = Q$, this gives $Q = (n/n+1)(d - a/b)$

Under perfect competition, price equals marginal cost for profit maximization, and price equals average cost for the zero-profits condition. In this case, average and marginal costs are equal at d, and so price would equal d. The competitive output Q_c would be $d - a/b$. With n firms, the level of output under the Cournot model in equilibrium is $n/(n+1)$ of the competitive equilibrium output. For monopoly $n = 1$, and the level of output is one half of the competitive level; for duopoly $n = 2$, so that output would be two thirds of the competitive level, etc. As the number of firms (n) increase, the value of the term $n/n+1$ tends to unity, and hence the equilibrium level of output tends towards the competitive level.

In this simple case, the reaction functions of the firms can be derived from equation A above as:

$$q_i = \frac{d-a}{2b} - \frac{1}{2}Q_i.$$

Thus an increase in the other firms' output by one unit leads firm i to decrease its output by $\frac{1}{2}$ a unit.

The relatively simple case of duopoly (two firms) can be illustrated diagrammatically. In figure 4.1 the reaction functions of the two firms (1 and 2) as R_1 and R_2 are drawn, and the analysis is put in a sequential form. Suppose that firm 2 has an initial output of q_{21}, with firm 1 about to make a decision on its level of output. The reaction function for firm 1 (R_1) indicates the level of output which will maximize its output, given the output of firm 2. In this case output q_{11}, chosen by firm 1, can be read off from R_1.

At the next stage, firm 2 makes a fresh decision on output given the level of output q_{11} now being produced by firm 1. From R_2 firm 2's new profit-maximizing output (under the assumption of constant output of firm 1) is read off as q_{22}. We can now repeat this procedure round after round, first with firm 1 making a fresh decision, then firm 2. In figure 4.1, the path followed is indicated by the arrows, and it eventually converges on point A, which will be the equilibrium position.[2]

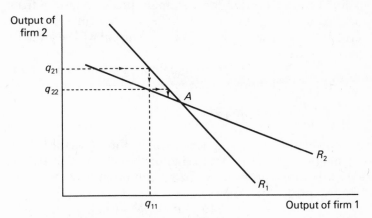

figure 4.1   Path to Cournot equilibrium

There is a further problem with the Cournot model in that the path to equilibrium was in the form of sequential decisions by the firms involved. Firm 1 held its output constant whilst firm 2 made its decisions; then firm 2 held its output constant whilst firm 1 made its decisions and so on. But as is shown in the Appendix to this chapter, neither equilibrium nor its stability is changed by allowing each firm to change its output each period (provided it assumes that the other firm holds to its previous period level of output).

The Cournot model has an equilibrium outcome, which in the simple case at least, was stable in that the system converged on that equilibrium configuration. But the model relied on firms holding to beliefs which were continually proved to be false. An obvious extension is to introduce firms learning from experience; but although obvious, this track has not yet led to a particularly satisfactory solution.

4.5   The leader/follower model

We next consider a model of duopoly which is often described as a leader/follower model. The Cournot model can be described as a follower/follower model, in that each firm takes a passive line in taking the output of the other firm as given. In the leader/follower model, one of the firms is assumed to keep to that passive role, whilst the other firm takes into account the fact that the other firm has adopted this passive role. It (the leader) takes a more active role and incorporates into its decision-making process its belief that the other firm will behave in the passive Cournot-like manner. Formally, for the leader firm (say firm 1), the term $\partial Q_1/\partial q_1$ here $= \partial q_2/\partial q_1$) in its first-order condition for maximum profit is derived from the reaction function of firm 2. For we and the leader firm know that whatever the level of output chosen by firm 1, firm 2's output will be given by the reaction function of firm 2.

The first-order condition for firm 2 to be maximizing profits is as before, since it is still operating as a follower. That is:

$$\frac{d\pi_2}{dq_2} = \frac{\partial p}{\partial q_2} \cdot q_2 + p - \frac{\partial C_2}{\partial q_2} = 0.$$

From this, its reaction function $q_2 = g_2(q_1)$ is derivable. Firm 1, as the leader, takes this reaction function into account to generate the value of the $\partial q_2/\partial q_1$ term, and hence its first-order profit-maximizing condition becomes:

$$\frac{d\pi_1}{dq_1} = \left[\frac{\partial p}{\partial q_1} + \frac{\partial p}{\partial q_2} \cdot \frac{\partial g_2}{\partial q_1} \right] q_1 + p - \frac{\partial C_1}{\partial q_1} = 0.$$

In this case, there is an equilibrium outcome, with two equations in two unknowns (q_1, q_2) to which the firms would move directly, and the expectations of the two firms are consistent. Although, expressed in terms of duopoly, it is fairly easy to see that it would generalize to the *n* firm case with one firm as leader and $n-1$ followers.

4.6   Comparison of the leader/follower and the follower/follower models

Taking the simple linear demand case again, with firm 1 as the leader, we have from above

$$q_2 = \frac{d-a}{2b} - \frac{bq_1}{2b}$$

as firm 2's reaction function. For firm 1

$$\pi_1 = (a + b(q_1 + q_2))q_1 - dq_1,$$

but it realizes that for changes in output by itself, firm 2 will respond according to its reaction function. Hence

$$\pi_1 = \left(a + bq_1 - \frac{d-a}{2} - \frac{bq_1}{2}\right)q_1 - dq_1$$

and then

$$\frac{d\pi_1}{dq_1} = a + \frac{d-a}{2} + bq_1 - d = 0$$

for the first-order condition for profits to be maximized. Then $q_1 = d - a/2b$, and also $q_2 = d - a/4b$. The total output will be $3(d-a)/4b$. Whereas it would be $2(d-a)/3b$ under the follower/follower regime. Prices will be lower in the leader/follower case to sell the higher output.

Under the follower/follower regime

$$q_1 = q_2 = \frac{d-a}{3b} \quad \text{and} \quad p = a + b\frac{(2/d-a)}{3\,3b} = \frac{2d+a}{3}.$$

$$\pi_1 = \pi_2 = \left(\frac{2d+a}{3} - d\right)\left(\frac{1}{3} \cdot \frac{d-a}{b}\right) = \frac{-1}{9b}(a-d)^2$$

(remember that $b < 0$). Joint profits of

$$\pi_1 + \pi_2 = \frac{-2(a-d)^2}{9b}.$$

Under the leader/follower regime,

$$q_1 + q_2 = \frac{3(d-a)}{4b}, \, p = a + b\frac{(3(d-a))}{4b} = \frac{3d}{4} + \frac{a}{4}$$

$$\pi_1 = \left(\frac{3d}{4} + \frac{a}{4} - d\right)\left(\frac{d-a}{2b}\right) = -\left(\frac{a-d}{8b}\right)^2$$

$$\pi_2 = \left(\frac{3d}{4} + \frac{a}{4} - d\right)\left(\frac{d-a}{4b}\right) = -\left(\frac{a-d}{16b}\right)^2$$

$$\pi_1 + \pi_2 = -\left(\frac{a-d}{b}\right)^2 \cdot \frac{3}{16}.$$

Overall profits are lower under the leader/follower regime than under the follower/follower regime, but the profits of the leader (firm 1) are higher than those of the follower (firm 2), and higher than firm 1 received in the follower/follower case. The follower (firm 2) loses out by firm 1 assuming the leadership role.

It is not possible to establish these results as completely general ones but it is likely that:

(i) the leader will be more profitable than the follower;
(ii) the leader will have higher profits than he would have obtained in a follower/follower regime.[3]

4.7   The von Stackelberg (leader/leader) model

In those cases when these results do apply, the firms involved will each have a profit incentive to act as leader and not as follower. But if each firm acts as leader assuming that the other will act as a follower, it is unlikely that there will be a mutually acceptable outcome. Each firm will plan a certain level of output which it thinks will yield it maximum profit, under the belief that the other firm will react as a follower. However, the other firm does not act the part of a follower as assumed, but also takes the role of leader.

This disequilibrium situation, which cannot be resolved if both firms persist in seeking to act as leader, is often named after its proponent, von Stackelberg (1952).

In terms of our simple case, each firm would choose an output of $d - a/2b$, for each acts as a leader assuming the other to be a follower. Then with total output of $d - a/b$ (coincidentally the perfect competitive level of output) price will be d, and with costs at d there will be zero profits. Thus in our particular example (and it is likely to happen more generally) the leader/leader situation generates lower profits than a situation involving some followership. This is not surprising in that a leader hopes to sell more than a follower. The more 'leaders' there are the higher will be the output in total, but the lower will be the price.

The leader/leader model can be viewed as firms striving for dominance in the industry, and engaging in warfare which reduces total profits. Similar remarks to those made above can be made here; with some learning by the firms involved the leader/leader situation (with firms cutting each others throats) is not likely to last indefinitely. Possible resolutions would be the emergence of a recognized leader in the industry (probably the winner of the struggle) and the realization of mutual interest and the development of some form of collusion (see below).

The leader/follower situation is often regarded as infeasible in the long term, in that the follower would not be content always to follow, given the lower profits which result. But leader/follower arrangements may seem plausible in industries which are characterized by a large disparity of size amongst firms. The firm which is the largest and considerably larger than others in the industry, is likely to be regarded (and regard itself) as the industry leader.

4.8 The price leadership model

The analysis above has been posed in terms of quantity adjustment, but when cast in terms of price adjustment the leader/follower model may have more appeal. This is the case of price leadership and can be analysed as follows.

The follower firms are assumed to operate as price-takers, so that whatever price is set by the leader firm it is accepted by these firms and they adjust their output in the light of that price to equate marginal cost with that price. For these follower firms, there is a supply curve which relates the amount they would supply for any price. The problem facing the leader is to maximize profits $\pi = p . q - C(q)$, where the quantity sold will be total demand minus supply by follower firms. Both total demand and follower firms' supply will depend upon the price chosen. Thus the leader supplies the residual demand. $q = D(p) - S(p)$, where $D(.)$ is the demand curve and $S(.)$ the supply curve of the follower firms.

Expanding the profits function above and writing it in terms of price gives

$$\pi = p . [D(p) - S(p)] - C[D(p) - S(p)],$$

which yields a first-order condition, with respect to price of

$$\frac{d\pi}{dp} = D(p) - S(p) + p\left(\frac{dD}{dp} - \frac{dS}{dp}\right) - \frac{dC}{dq}\left(\frac{dD}{dp} - \frac{dS}{dp}\right) = 0,$$

i.e.

$$\left(p - \frac{dC}{dq}\right) = \frac{D(p) - S(p)}{dS/dp - dD/dp} \quad \text{with} \quad D > S, \frac{dS}{dp} > 0, \frac{dD}{dp} < 0.$$

Then the extent to which the price leader can price above marginal cost depends upon the relative responsiveness of the supply of the follower firms and of total demand to price changes.[4]

4.9   General models

It would be reasonably easy to generate other theories of oligopoly within the general framework being considered here. This could be achieved in one of two ways. The follower/follower model could be extended to include cases when $\partial Q_i/\partial q_i$ was not taken as zero by the firms. Suppose, for example, that firms believe that $\partial Q_i/\partial q_i = a_i$ (a constant). Then in principle, we could solve the equation for firm i

$$\frac{d\pi_i}{dq_i} = p(q_i + Q_i) + q_i\left(\frac{\partial p^{\cdot}}{\partial q_i} + \frac{\partial p}{\partial Q_i}a_i\right) - \frac{dC}{dq_i} = 0,$$

to give a new reaction function T_i which indicates how firm i would react in terms of output to a given level of output produced by its rivals. If, as would happen in most cases, the assumption of the firms as to its rivals' output reactions were proven false in the outturn, then a similar problem would arise here as arose in the Cournot model. On each round firms would make predictions about their rivals' output changes which are not fulfilled. Nonetheless, it is still assumed that the firms do not change their method of making predictions. However, there will often be equilibrium configurations where output does not change. As long as firms predict no change in other firms' output in response to them not changing output, the firms' prediction will be fulfilled.

A second possibility is to design variants on the leader/follower theme, whereby the follower is assumed to have an objective other than short-run profit maximization which it follows oblivious of what other firms do, while at the same time the leader does take the follower firms' objectives thoroughly into account. One such model is the 'market shares' model, in which the follower wishes to maintain a particular market share, possibly in the belief that such a policy will aid long-run profits (non-profit objectives are discussed in Part Two). Then a follower firm i would operate so that its output was a constant share of the market, i.e. $q_i/(Q_i + q_i) = k$ (a constant), but treating Q_i as constant.

4.10   'Market shares' model

A leader firm (say firm 1) would know that its rivals are maintaining a constant market share. So far as it is concerned, $Q_1/(q_1 + Q_1) = K$ (a different constant) is how other firms adjust to its own output changes. So the leader firm faces a profit function $\pi_1 = p(q_1 + Q_1)q_1 - C(q_1)$ with $Q_1 = Kq_1/1 - K$ and the first-order condition for maximum profits is

$$\frac{d\pi_1}{dq_1} = \left(\frac{\partial p}{\partial q_1} + \frac{\partial p}{\partial Q_1}\frac{\partial Q_1}{\partial q_1}\right)q_1 + p\frac{\partial C}{\partial q_1} = 0$$

with $\dfrac{\partial Q_1}{\partial q_1} = \dfrac{K}{1-K}$. Put $\partial p/\partial q$ equal to the common value of $\partial p/\partial q_1$ and $\partial p/\partial Q_1$ and that gives

$$q_1\frac{\partial p}{\partial q}\left(\frac{1}{1-K}\right) + p - \frac{\partial C}{\partial q_1} = 0.$$

4.11 Collusion

The above discussion illustrates strongly that there is interdependence between the firms, in that the profits of any one firm depend upon the output and actions of other firms. Since by their actions firms are likely adversely to affect the profits of other firms, collusion of some form between firms may emerge. Collusion may take the form of formal agreements between firms over price, level of output, etc., or it might be arranged by unwritten agreements relying on a 'gentlemen's agreement' or solely on the mutual recognition of acting in concert. The extent of collusion is likely to be influenced by the legal environment (which may declare some types of agreement as illegal), the history of the industry concerned (the degree of past hostility etc.), and the gains thought to be made from colluding.

Full collusion would lead to the maximization of joint profits. Formally this would be:

maximize $\quad \pi = \displaystyle\sum_{i=1}^{n}\pi_i = \sum_{i=1}^{n}[p(Q)q_i - C_i(q_i)] = p(Q)Q - \sum_{i=1}^{n}C_i(q_i)$

where $Q = q_1 + q_2 + \ldots + q_n$ is total output, with respect to $q_1, q_2, \ldots, q_n$. This gives

$$\frac{\partial \pi}{\partial q_i} = \left(\frac{\partial p}{\partial Q}\cdot\frac{\partial Q}{\partial q_i} + p\frac{\partial Q}{\partial q_i}\right) - \frac{\partial C_i}{\partial q_i} = 0 \text{ for } i = 1, 2, \ldots, n$$

since

$$\frac{\partial Q}{\partial q_i} = 1, \text{ this gives } \frac{\partial p}{\partial Q}\cdot Q + p - \frac{\partial C}{\partial q_i} = 0 \text{ for } i = 1, 2, \ldots, n.$$

At this level, the problem is formally the same as that facing a multi-plant monopolist with n plants. The level of output is determined by equating marginal revenue and marginal cost. The allocation of output between the n firms (plants) is determined by the equalization of marginal cost across firms (plants).

The simple case leads here to the following outcome:

$$\pi = (a + bQ)Q - dQ$$

$$\frac{\partial \pi}{\partial q_i} = (a + 2bQ - d)\frac{\partial Q}{\partial q_i} = 0 \text{ for } i = 1, 2, ..., n$$

since

$$\frac{\partial Q}{\partial q_i} = 1, \text{ this gives } Q = \frac{d-a}{2b} \text{ and } p = \frac{a+d}{2}$$

which is not surprisingly the monopoly output and price. But in this simple case, since unit costs are constant and the same in all firms, there is no solution on how to allocate the output between firms.

With independent firms, even if the level and allocation of output which would maximize joint profits can be agreed upon, there remains the problem of how profits will be actually allocated between the firms. With any particular allocation of output to a firm, which it then sells at the market price, the firm will receive a certain profit. But in the interests of joint profit maximization, some firms may have their output severely restricted, and would expect to receive more profits than those which directly accrue to them. Thus some provision for side payments is likely to be necessary to them. In order to keep these low-profit firms in the cartel, there would need to be provision for payments from the high-profit firms to be made to them.

In practice, the extent of collusion between independent firms is likely to be limited by laws on restrictive practices and by the extent of the reallocation of output, etc., which may be implied by the collusive model. But if the profit gains from collusion are relatively large and/or if the costs of operating the collusive agreement are high, then firms have profit incentives to merge into a single firm.

4.12   The kinked demand curve theory

A theory which seeks to explain price stability rather than the level of price, but which can be considered within this general framework, is that of the kinked demand curve theory (Sweezy (1939)). The essence of this theory, which relates to oligopoly producing heterogeneous goods, is that firms consider that the reactions of other firms to a price change will be different for a price rise than for a price fall. In particular, it is argued that a firm believes that if it increases its prices, then its rivals will not follow that price rise, but will take the opportunity to increase their sales. But for a price

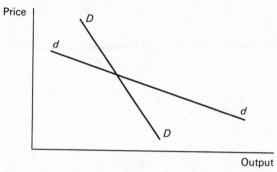

figure 4.2   The *dd* and *DD* curve in the kinked demand curve theory

reduction, the firm believes that other firms will follow suit, in the fear that if they did not their loss of sales would be heavy.

In figure 4.2, the two relevant perceived demand curves facing the firm, *dd* and *DD*, have been drawn. The *dd* curve relates the situation when the other firms' prices do not change in response to this firm's price change; the *DD* curve relates to the situation when those prices do change. Above the current price, the kinked demand curve theory argues that the *dd* curve is relevant. Below the current price it is argued that the *DD* curve operates. The kinked demand curve facing the firm which gives its name to the theory is drawn in

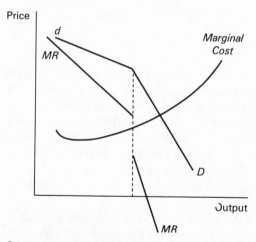

figure 4.3   The kinked demand curve and the consequent gap in the marginal
             revenue

figure 4.3 with the marginal revenue curve derived from it. The important point to notice is that the marginal revenue curve now has a gap in it. From profit-maximizing conditions, marginal revenue equals marginal cost, and hence the marginal cost curve passes through the hole in the marginal revenue curve at the current output.

It is then argued that there will be price stability under this regime. For it can easily be seen that shifts in the marginal cost curve which do not take the curve outside the gap in the marginal revenue curve will have no impact on price or output.

It can be argued that the extent of the price stability will, other things being equal, vary with the size of the gap. The size of the gap depends upon the difference in the relative slopes of the two perceived demand curves.[5] The gap will be larger

(i) the larger is the upward elasticity of perceived demand,
(ii) the smaller is the downward elasticity of perceived demand.

These models indicate some of the difficulties of constructing models of oligopoly, where interdependence is important. Further, since there are such a variety of models (and others could have been reported), one is left wondering how to choose between them. There has been no answer to that so far, and whilst it may be possible *ex post* to see that an industry seems to have behaved in accordance with one model rather than the others, there is no method of predicitng *ex ante* which industry will fit which model.

4.13   The theory of games approach

One further problem which we touched on lightly above is now brought to the fore. This problem is that of defining *ex ante* profits in the context of oligopoly where the outcome depends upon other firms' actions, so that any *ex ante* profits function must incorporate views on how other firms are going to react. This problem is highlighted in the theory of games, to which we now turn. The theory of games was developed by von Neumann and Morgenstern (1944). An introduction to their theory written within a few years of its appearance is contained in Hurwicz (1945) and a more recent and extensive discussion is in Bacharach (1976).

Besides highlighting the problems of placing any meaning on profit maximization, the theory of games (at least in some formulations) places an emphasis on the conflict of interests and on the interdependence of the oligopoly situation.

The theory of games starts from each player having a number of strategies open to him. The outcome of the game, as far as each player is concerned, depends not only upon the strategy it adopts but also on the strategy its rivals adopt. In the context of oligopoly theory, a strategy could be a change in price, the introduction of an advertising campaign, a change in the product characteristics, etc., or some combination of these types of activities. For each player, there is a well-defined 'pay-off' matrix which describes what the outcome will be for all combinations of strategies chosen by him and his rivals.

As an example, take the case where there are two players (hereafter referred to as firm A and firm B), and where firm A has m strategies, and firm B has n strategies. For firm A there is a pay-off matrix like this:

firm B's strategies

	b_1	b_2	b_3	b_4	...	b_n
a_1	x_{11}	x_{12}	x_{13}	x_{14}	...	x_{1n}
a_2	x_{21}	x_{22}	x_{23}	x_{24}	...	x_{2n}
a_3	x_{31}	x_{32}	x_{33}	x_{34}	...	x_{3n}
a_4	x_{41}	x_{42}	x_{43}	x_{44}	...	x_{4n}
...	...	...	...	...	...	...
...	...	...	...	...	...	...
a_m	x_{m1}	x_{m2}	x_{m3}	x_{m4}	...	x_{mn}

firm A's strategies

and also a pay-off matrix for B similarly with entries (y_{ij}) $(i = 1, 2, ..., m; j = 1, 2, ..., n)$.

The units of the xs in A's pay-off matrix and of the ys in B's pay-off matrix could be units of utility ('utils'), pounds of profits, etc. The entry x_{ij} in the pay-off matrix for A indicates the returns to A which result from A playing strategy i and B strategy j. Similarly, the entry y_{kl} in B's pay-off matrix indicates what would be the result to B of A playing strategy k and B playing strategy l. The particular type of game which is considered here is generally known as the 'two person zero sum game'. The two person part has already been introduced. The zero sum part refers to a game where the sum of the pay-offs to the two players, from any pair of strategies which they play, is always the same. In terms of the pay-off matrices above, this means that

$x_{ij} + y_{ij} = c$ (a constant) for all $i = 1, 2, ..., m;\ j = 1, 2, ..., n$. The zero sum element means that the conflict between the two players is total, since an increase in one player's returns can only occur with a corresponding decrease in the other player's returns. There are no gains to be made by cooperation or collusion between the players, since there are no other players in the model from whom these players can gain.

Now the theory of games will be treated as a theory of oliogopoly, and as such will refer to firms rather than players. The pay-off matrices refer to profits in monetary terms. With the zero sum game, it is only necessary to focus on one of the pay-off matrices, since the other one is linked in the manner indicated in the previous paragraph. There is a problem of interpreting profit maximization in this type of setting. Looking at firm A and its pay-off matrix for the moment, it can be seen that with appropriate choice of strategies by firm B any of the pay-offs could be obtained by firm A. But firm A has no way of foretelling with certainty which strategy firm B will choose. One solution would be for firm A to assign probabilities to firm B's choice, so that firm A thinks that there is probability p_1 of firm B using strategy b_1, p_2 of choosing strategy b_2, and so on through to probability of p_n using strategy b_n. For each of its own strategies, firm A could then calculate the expected outcome of that strategy. So that strategy 1 chosen by firm A would be expected to yield profits of $\sum_k p_k x_{1k}$ to firm A; strategy 2 would be expected to yield $\sum_k p_k x_{2k}$ and so on. Profit maximization could be interpreted as maximizing the expected outcome, and firm A would pick the strategy which leads to the highest expected profits.

This line of argument has a number of problems. First, how can firm A try to assign probabilities in the manner imagined above? Second, if firm B had an idea of what firm A was going to do, firm B's most profitable strategy would be to see which of its strategies would yield highest profits given the strategy chosen by firm A. Since one firm's gain is another firm's loss, this would leave firm A rather badly off. This argument may not have much force if the game is played once, but gains strength if many rounds of the game are considered.

An alternative approach to the objectives of the firm is to argue that firm A looks at the worst outcome which could result for each strategy (that is, if firm B did his worst as far as firm A is concerned), and uses the strategy which provides the best of the worse possible outcomes. In other words, firm A acts in a risk-averse manner, and seeks to limit the extent of the damage which it could suffer from the hands of firm B. To make this more concrete consider the following pay-off matrix:

firm B's strategies

		b_1	b_2	b_3
	a_1	2	8	1
firm A's strategies	a_2	4	3	9
	a_3	5	6	7

in a zero sum context where total profits always equal 10.

If firm A uses strategy a_1, the worst outcome, i.e. the one with the minimum profits, results from firm B using strategy b_3 and yielding 1 unit of profits. Strategy a_2 has minimum profits of 3 which arise from firm B using strategy b_2. Strategy a_3 has minimum profits of 5 arising from firm B using strategy b_1. Then if firm A seeks the maximum of these minimum profits, it chooses strategy a_3 which assures it of at least 5 units of profit. This choice of strategy is often referred to as the 'maximin' strategy, for fairly obvious reasons.

Now if firm B pursues the same policy, in general one would need to consider its pay-off matrix. But with the zero sum game, the corresponding entries in the two pay-off matrices sum to a constant. This means that, for example, if firm B looks at each strategy to see what is for itself the minimum profit outcome, this is equivalent to looking in firm A's pay-off matrix for the maximum profit (for A) outcome. For since firm A's and firm B's profits are in total always the same, when one is at a maximum, the other must be at a minimum. In terms of the pay-off matrix given above, the minimum profits for B (and so the maximum profits for firm A) would be: for strategy b_1 5 (i.e. the total profits of 10 minus firm A's profits of 5); for strategy b_2 2 (i.e. 10 minus 8); and for strategy b_3 1 (10 minus 9). On the basis of taking the maximum of these minimum profits, firm B would take strategy b_1. In terms of its own pay-off matrix (which we have not written down), the decision rule is again 'maximin', but in terms of A's pay-off matrix this becomes minimize the maximum profit (for firm A) or in shorthand, 'minimax'.

With the pay-off matrix used here, firm A decides on strategy a_3 and firm B on strategy b_1. Looking at this retrospectively, firm A sees that with firm B using b_1, the best it could do would have been to choose a_3, so in that sense it is satisfied with what it did. Firm B is likewise satisfied, for with firm A using strategy a_3, it could do no better than to choose strategy b_1.

As the reader may suspect, the numbers used in the pay-off matrix have been arranged to ensure such an outcome. Before considering extensions, it can be noted that one round of this game has produced a kind of equilibrium. However, let us change the pay-off matrix slightly to be:

firm B's strategies

	b_1	b_2	b_3
a_1	2	8	1
a_2	4	3	9
a_3	6	5	7

firm A's strategies

It can be calculated that using the same principles as above, firm A would adopt strategy a_3 and firm B strategy b_1. Now, if firm A knew what firm B was going to do, it would still have chosen strategy a_3; but if firm B knew that firm A was going to use strategy a_3, it would have gone for strategy b_2 which would have yielded a profit of 5 rather than the profit of 4 which results from the (a_3, b_1) pair of strategies.

Taking the process one round further, if firm B next time picks strategy b_2, firm A would be disappointed with the outcome if he chose a_3 again. For with b_2 used by firm B, firm A would be better off choosing strategy a_1 to yield a profit of 8 for itself. Thus, with this pay-off matrix there is no 'equilibrium' outcome as there was with the first example.

Within the theory of games, a solution to a game such as this has been proposed in terms of 'mixed strategies'. The basic idea here is that rather than a firm picking one strategy, it uses a mixture of strategies in the sense that whilst in any one round it can only use one strategy, it changes the strategies between rounds of the game. The choice of a particular strategy for a specific round is determined at random, so there is no element of 'he chose strategy i last time and I used strategy j, so he will think I'll choose k so I'll choose l...'. However, the mixed strategy consists of probabilities of choosing each strategy.

Returning to the general pay-off matrices used above, a mixed strategy for firm A would be probabilities $(p_1, p_2, p_3 ..., p_m)$ of choosing strategies $1, 2, ..., m$ for any particular round. These probabilities will in total, of course, sum to 1, and some of them may be zero with the corresponding strategies never chosen. The games considered above were a special case of mixed strategies where all but one of the ps were zero, and the odd one out equalled unity. Similarly, firm B would have a mixed strategy with probabilities $(q_1, q_2, q_3 .... q_n)$ of using strategies $(1, 2, 3, ..., n)$. It can then be shown (and an outline of the proof is given in the Appendix to this chapter) that there are mixed strategies for firms A and B which would yield a stable outcome, in the sense that a stable outcome was obtained from the first pay-off matrix above. Each firm observes that in the light of what the other firm is doing, its own actions are leading to the best outcome for itself.

The theory of games can be extended from the type discussed here to allow for more than two players and to include non-zero sum games. From either of these extensions an additional complication is introduced, namely, that of the formation of coalitions between the firms. When there are more than two firms, it may be possible for some of the firms to make agreements amongst themselves which lead to outcomes which favour the firms in the coalition at the expense of those outside. Similarly, when the game is a non-zero one, there are some mutual interests amongst the firms which may point towards agreement amongst the firms to take actions and choose strategies which increase total profits.

In this chapter, we began to explore some of the difficulties of constructing a theory for a situation of oligopoly, where there are considerable interactions between the firms, and where the firms have some discretion in what they do. A variety of theories have been put forward, and we may expect that their application to a specific situation may depend upon the history of the industry, the particular individuals and firms involved, as well as the number and size disparity of the firms.

appendix to chapter 4

4.14   An extension to the Cournot model of oligopoly

In the text it was indicated that the analysis of the Cournot model of oligopoly was based upon the firms taking turns at decision-making. Here we present the extension for the case where each firm responds to the other firm's output in the previous period, but in each period both firms are making fresh output decisions. Take the case of duopoly with linear reaction functions. Here, reaction function for firm 1 is: $R1 q_{1t} = a + b q_{2t-1}$, $b < 0$, and reaction function for firm 2 is: $R2 q_{2t} = c + d q_{1t-1}$, $d < 0$. Substitution yields difference equations for the two quantities as follows:

$$q_{1t} = (a + bc) + bd q_{1t-2}$$

$$q_{2t} = (c + ad) + bd q_{2t-2}$$

Both these equations have the general solution $q_{it} = A f^t + B(-f)^t + C_i$ ($i = 1, 2$) where $f = (bd)^{\frac{1}{2}}$, and the values of A and B depend upon the initial quantities: $C_1 = a + bc/1 - bd$ and $C_2 = c + ad/1 - bd$. The quantities q_{it} ($i = 1, 2$) will converge on C_i provided that $f < 1$, i.e. provided that $bd < 1$. This condition is also required for the equilibrium quantities to be positive.

In the case analysed in the text, where firms take turns with their output decisions, stability required that the slope of $R1$ was greater in absolute value than the slope of $R2$. Thus it was required that $1/|b| > |d|$, and since both b and d are negative this implies $1/b < d$ and hence $bd < 1$.

So the stability conditions are the same in both cases, though the path to the equilibrium outcome will be different.

4.15   Theory of games

We now outline the proof of the proposition that there is an unique outcome when both players used mixed strategies. First a numerical example is given then an outline of a general proof is provided.

For the numerical example, take the following pay-off matrix for firm (players) A and B in a zero sum game with total pay-off of 10:

firm B's strategies

	B_1	B_2	B_3	B_4
firm A's strategies A_1	2	5	7	4
A_2	4	1	6	9

With 'pure' strategies only, it can be easily shown that, under the minimax principle, A chooses strategy $A1$ and B chooses strategy $B1$. If A had known of B's plans, it would have been better for A to have used strategy $A2$.

In this example, with A having only two strategies available, a diagrammatic approach can be used. In figure A4.1, there is a representation of the pay-offs to A (and by subtraction for the constant total pay-off of 10 one can easily calculate B's pay-off) of the 8 possible outcomes. If A plays strategy $A1$, then reading off from the x axis from the points labelled $B1$, $B2$, $B3$, $B4$ indicates the pay-offs (to A) from strategy $A1$ combined with $B1$, $B2$, $B3$ and $B4$ respectively. Similarly for strategy $A2$ along the y axis.

Now let B mix his strategies. If, for example, firm B by the toss of a coin, uses either strategy $B1$ or $B4$, then on average for half the plays he uses $B1$ and for the other half $B4$. When firm A plays $A1$, the expected outcome will be $\frac{1}{2}$. 2

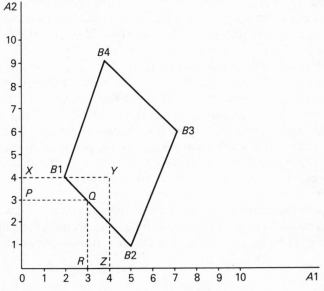

figure A4.1

$+\frac{1}{2}.4\,(\,=3)$ since the outcome of $(A1, B1)$ is 2 and of $(A1, B4)$ is 4. When firm A uses $A2$, the expected outcome is $\frac{1}{2}.4+\frac{1}{2}.9$ (i.e. 6.5). The point $(3, 6.5)$ will be halfway between the points labelled $B1$ and $B4$. More generally, any point on the line $(B1, B4)$ can be achieved (as an expected outcome) by a suitable choice of the probabilities of using $B1$ and $B4$.

This argument can be extended, and the lines between $B1, B2, B3$ and $B4$ and all the points within the lines represent expected outcomes which can be achieved with suitable probabilities assigned to each of the four possible strategies.

The objective for firm B is assumed to be that of looking at each strategy in terms of the best outcome that could result for firm A (which in this context is the worst outcome for firm B) and to choose the strategy which minimizes the 'best outcome'. Thus for any strategy, firm B has to examine the consequences of firm A playing $A1$ or $A2$ (or any combination of them). By playing strategies contained with the square $OXYZ$ in figure A4.1, firm B could contain firm A to receiving 4 units of profit at most. By 'shrinking' this square, we arrive at the square $OPQR$ and see that by playing the strategy corresponding to Q, firm A is contained to profits of 3, whether it plays $A1$ or $A2$ (and hence if it plays any combination thereof). This is reached by firm B using $B1$ with frequency 2/3 and $B2$ with frequency 1/3. For firm A it combines $A1$ and $A2$ with frequency f and $1-f$. Against $B1$, this would lead to an expected outcome of $2f+4(1-f)$; and against $B2$ to an expected outcome of $5f+2(1-f)$. The outcome for firm A is at a maximum when the expected outcome against $B1$ and against $B2$ are equal, i.e. when $2f+4(1-f)=5f+2(1-f)$, which gives $f=\frac{1}{2}$, and an expected outcome of 3. This pay-off to firm A is the same as the pay-off to firm A resulting from firm B's policy. Thus this provides a possible equilibrium outcome. It can be shown that it is an equilibrium outcome in that, given their opponent's mixed strategy, the one adopted by each side is the best available. For firm A, given that firm B plays the strategy corresponding to point Q in figure A4.1, it cannot obtain better than 3 units of profit, whatever combination of strategies it plays, given that both $A1$ and $A2$ separately give 3 units of profit. For firm B, the mixed strategy has been derived to ensure that it is the best strategy against whatever firm A does.

The more general proof requires an appeal to linear programming and we first quote the general result from linear programming. The primal problem is to maximize $a = p.q'$ where q is a vector of decision variables subject to

$$A.q' \le r'$$

$$q \ge 0$$

where p, q are $1 \times n$ vectors, A is an $m \times n$ matrix, and r is a $1 \times m$ vector. This can be written in terms of a $1 \times m$ vector of 'slack' variables u, as $A.q' + u' = r'$, $q \geq 0$ and $u \geq 0$.

A dual problem exists, namely

$$\text{minimize } b = r.s'$$

subject to

$$A'.s' \geq p'$$

$$s \geq 0$$

or in terms of a vector of slack variables

$$\text{minimize } b = r.s'$$

subject to

$$A'.s - l = p$$

$$s \geq 0 \quad p \geq 0$$

where the vectors r and p and the matrix A are common to the two problems.

The fundamental result in linear programming is that
(1) maximum a in the primal problem = minimum b in the dual
(2) $q.l = 0$ and $u.s = 0$.

Returning to the theory of games, the general problem facing firm A is to choose the frequency of use of the m possible strategies when faced with pay-off matrix P. Firm B has n strategies to use. For firm A, it has to choose the value of the vector $(q_1, q_2, \ldots, q_m)$ where the q_is are the frequency of use of each of the strategies, and so $q_1 + q_2 + q_3^+ \ldots q_m = 1$ and $q_i \geq 0$ for each i $= 1, 2, 3, \ldots, m$. The expected outcome if firm B plays $B1$ is $q_1 p_1 + q_2 p_2 + \ldots q_m p_{m1}$, where p_{ij} are the entries of the pay-off matrix. Looking at the worst outcome, on any particular round, firm A wishes to maximize L subject to

$$q_1 p_{11} + q_2 p_{21} + \ldots + q_m p_{m1} \geq L$$

$$q_1 p_{12} + q_2 p_{22} + \ldots + q_m p_{m2} \geq L$$

$$\cdots \cdots \cdots \cdots \cdots \cdots \cdots \cdots$$

$$q_1 p_{1n} + q_2 p_{2n} + \ldots + q_m p_{mn} \geq L$$

so that the expected outcome of at least L is obtained. In matrix notation this is $q.P - L \geq 0$.

Firm B chooses the value of $(v_1, v_2, \ldots, v_n)$, the frequency of the use of strategies $B1, B2, \ldots, Bn$, with $v_1 + v_2 + \ldots v_n = 1$, and $v_i \geq 0$ for $i = 1, 2, \ldots, n$. It wants to minimize the pay-off to firm A, and to maximize the pay-off to itself, and in an analogous manner firm B strives to minimize S subject to

$$v_1 p_{11} + v_2 p_{12} + \ldots + v_n p_{1n} \leq S$$
$$v_1 p_{21} + v_2 p_{22} + \ldots + v_n p_{2n} \leq S$$
$$\cdot \cdot \cdot \cdot \cdot \cdot \cdot \cdot \cdot \cdot \cdot \cdot \cdot \cdot \cdot$$
$$v_1 p_{m1} + v_2 p_{m2} + \ldots + v_n p_{mn} \leq S$$

and in matrix notation this is $v.P' - S \leq 0$.

Writing this problem out in full, in terms of slack variables, these become

$$\text{maximize } (1, 0, 0, \ldots, 0).(L, q_n q_2, \ldots q_m)$$

subject to

$$\begin{pmatrix} 1 & & & \\ \cdot & & & \\ \cdot & & -P & \\ \cdot & & & \\ 1 & & & \\ 0, & 1, & \ldots, & 1 \end{pmatrix} \begin{pmatrix} L \\ q_1 \\ q_2 \\ \vdots \\ q_m \end{pmatrix} + m = \begin{pmatrix} 0 \\ 0 \\ \vdots \\ 0 \\ 1 \end{pmatrix}$$

$$q_i \geq 0 \quad i = 1, 2, \ldots, m$$
$$m_i \geq 0 \quad i = 1, 2, \ldots, m$$

and minimize $(0, 0, \ldots, 1).(v_1, \ldots, v_n, S)$
subject to

$$\begin{pmatrix} 1, & \ldots, & 1 & 0 \\ & & & 1 \\ & -P' & & \vdots \\ & & & \vdots \\ & & & 1 \end{pmatrix} \begin{pmatrix} v_1 \\ v_2 \\ \vdots \\ \vdots \\ v_n \\ S \end{pmatrix} + p = \begin{pmatrix} 1 \\ 0 \\ \vdots \\ \vdots \\ 0 \end{pmatrix}$$

subject to $v_j \geq 0 \quad j = 1, 2, \ldots, n$
$\quad\quad\quad\quad\quad l_j \geq 0 \quad j = 1, 2, \ldots, n.$

A comparison of these two problems with the linear programming problem and its dual given above indicates that firm A's problem can be treated as a linear programming problem with firm B's problem as its dual. Thus, we can use the general linear programming results, so that

(1) max. L = min. S

(2) $q.l = 0$ and $u.v = 0$

The first result means that there is a stable outcome to this game in terms of mixed strategies. The second condition means that when a firm includes a particular strategy amongst those it uses, then the corresponding constraint on the other firm is binding. For example, if $q_i \neq 0$, so that strategy A_i is amongst those used, then the second condition requires that $l_i = 0$ and that in turn implies that $p_{i1}v_1 + p_{i2}v_2 + \ldots + p_{in}v_n - S = 0$.

Thus for firm B firm A's use of strategy A_i yields one of the worst outcomes, but for firm A it gives one of the best outcomes. It is assumed that firm A would use a strategy which yields a good outcome for itself.

chapter 5

the impact of barriers to entry

5.1 The nature of barriers to entry

In the theories so far considered, the assumptions made about entry into the industry under consideration have been of the 'all or nothing' variety. Under monopoly and oligopoly, the barriers against new entry into the industry were assumed to be so high that the possibility of new entry could be ignored. In contrast, under perfect competition and monopolistic competition there were no barriers against new entrants in the long run, and this ensured that profits were eventually bid down to their normal level. A related and unsatisfactory feature of the oligopoly theory is that there is no explanation provided of the number of firms in the industry; there are an unexplained n firms in the industry whose number does not change. In this chapter, first the nature of barriers to entry into the industry are briefly discussed, and second the 'all or nothing' assumption on barriers to entry of the earlier chapters is relaxed. The main thrust of the second part of the chapter is that existing firms may be able to influence the rate of entry into their industry by their activities.

Barriers to entry into an industry mean anything which prevents potential firms from competing on equal terms with existing firms. These barriers may be a result of the technical condition of production in the industry (like economies of scale) or in other ways to be treated as a datum of the industry; the barriers may be, in part at least, the result of the activities of the existing firms (for example, exclusive contracts made by producers with distributors).

The nature of the barriers to entry can be that existing firms are able to produce more cheaply than potential firms would,[1] and/or that after the entry of new firms life would be much harder for both the existing firms and the new firms than it is currently for the existing firms.

Barriers of entry can be conveniently divided into three types: those which are general to all industries, those which provide lower costs to existing firms, and those which operate by threatening post-entry problems to entrants.

Under the first head, the major entry barrier may arise from the capital market. If the typical new entrant is an untried new enterprise, finance capital may be difficult to obtain. The existing firm has a flow of profits which are reinvestable, if the firm wishes, which are not matched by any such flow in the new firm. The capital market may find it difficult to judge new firms to decide whether they are creditworthy (or, which comes also under our second heading, may charge the new firms a 'risk premium'). In lending finance capital, the banks are likely to ask for surety against the loans. When the finance capital is used to purchase land, buildings, machinery, etc., there is some physical item which may provide the necessary collateral, and which could ultimately be sold to partially offset the loan. But when the investment is in non-physical assets, problems are likely to arise. For example, investment in advertising to build up sales is not the type of asset which can be easily used as collateral. Another difficulty could arise if the investment is particularly risky, as would often be the case for investment in research and development.

This barrier to entry arising from the capital supply side is mainly operative on newly formed firms. However, it is less likely to afflict firms already operating in one industry which want to enter another industry.

The lower costs of existing firms vis-a-vis new entrants can arise from a variety of sources. A first possible source is where the existing firm has accumulated knowledge of the industry (e.g. its techniques of production and demand conditions) so that it is more adept in that industry than a newcomer would be. This could be summed up by saying that the existing firms have learned the job ('learning by doing') and are now more efficient, i.e. have lower costs than a new firm would have.

Secondly, the existing firms may, through ownership or long-term contracts, have control over the supply of vital factors of production. In those industries where there are a few key inputs (for example, coffee beans in the manufacture of instant coffee), control over the inputs will give the existing firms a head start over new rivals. This head start may reflect itself in the new firm having to pay more for the input or having to revert to using inferior quality inputs.

Thirdly, in a similar manner, the existing firms may have control over the distribution outlets for its goods. For example, in the United Kingdom petrol market, a large proportion of petrol stations are either owned by or under long-term 'solus' agreements with the petrol manufacturers.

The fourth way arises from product differentiation. If, by fair means or foul, existing products have an established clientele who have a 'taste' for existing products over potential products, this may enable existing products to be sold for a higher price than new products could be sold. Of course, making meaningful price comparisons between different goods is difficult, and in formal terms what is meant is that the cost/revenue ratio is lower for the existing firms than it would be for new firms because of the demand conditions facing the two groups of firms.

The final point interacts with the first group of barriers discussed. If existing firms have made past investments in advertising, research and development and productive capacity which in some way are more than strictly necessary, this has the effect of raising the capital requirements of new firms entering the industry. The 'extra' advertising may have created stronger preferences amongst consumers for the products of existing firms with the result that any new firm has got to 'shout more loudly' to overcome the advertising of existing firms. These factors raise the costs of new entrants (as well as raising the costs of existing firms) and increase both the capital requirements and the problems of raising the funds.

The long-run competitive price level in an industry would be set where there are no supernormal profits. In the case where existing firms have a cost advantage over potential entrants, the price which can be charged by existing firms without inducing entry into the industry is not where price equals unit cost, but a price up to the level of unit costs of potential firms. Thus existing firms are able to earn a unit profit equal to the difference between their costs and the costs of the potential entrants.

The third grouping revolves around price changes which would be consequent upon new firms entering the industry. If a new firm enters the industry on a significant scale, it will affect the price of goods produced by that industry, and also may affect the costs of the industry. On the latter point, a rise in costs following entry could occur if the industry was an important customer in some markets (its inputs) and the entry of a new firm by increasing the demand for inputs would help to bid up the price of the inputs. Similarly, on the price side, if the new firm adds significantly to industry output, the price in the industry will have to drop to allow demand to absorb the increase in supply. In this case (post-entry) the existing firms are worse off, and the position for the new firm is also less favourable than it was for the existing firms.

5.2   The limit-pricing model

How much of a barrier to entry these post-entry price and cost changes pose depends upon the size at which the new firms enter, the responses of the existing firms, and the elasticity of demand. The last feature enters in determining how much of a price fall would follow from a given increase in supply. We now look at this more formally using a model presented by

Modigliani (1958) (based on ideas in Bain (1956) and Sylos Labini (1962)).

The model focuses on the interplay between existing firms and potential firms. For simplicity, the number of existing firms is taken as one; this monopoly situation means that there are no oligopolistic interdependence problems between existing firms to be considered. This assumption could be interpreted as treating the existing firms as one group who have sorted out their internal relations. We now focus on their external relations. The output of existing and potential firms is treated as homogeneous, and all firms have access to the same cost conditions.

Often reference is made to the limit price. But it would be better to talk of a limit price being one of many possible limit prices. Assumptions have to be made by the architect of any particular theory of limit pricing on the behavioural assumptions made by the original firms and by the potential entrants.

The situation is rather like that analysed in the previous chapter under the classical theories of oligopoly, but with the difference that the margin of interdependence is between an existing firm and potential entrants. As there, the theory has to make assumptions about how firms believe that other firms will react to their behaviour. In the Modigliani model considered below, the model is akin to the leader/follower model of the classical oligopoly theory.

The limit price is the price level which rules when potential entrants are on the borderline between entering and not entering the industry. In other words, these potential entrants believe that, after entry, they can earn just normal profits. They are then on the margin since by the definition of normal profits, they could earn the same return without the bother of entering the industry.

How much profit a potential entrant can earn after entry depends not on the current price being charged but on the post-entry price. The post-entry price will depend upon (via the demand curve) the post-entry output of the new entrants and the existing firms. The existing firms can vary their output as they wish in response to new entrants. From the point of view of the potential entrant, the most optimistic situation would be one where the existing firms held their output constant following entry, and that the entrant was the only one entering the industry.[2] Thus, in order to exclude entry, the existing firms set their price so that with sufficient output to satisfy the demand at the price set, the potential entrants believe that they could only obtain normal profits after entry, even if output of existing firms remains the same after entry.

This analysis is based on a scenario in which the original firm acts on the assumption that potential entrants make their calculations on whether to

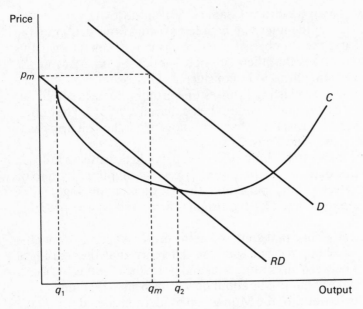

figure 5.1   Derivation of residual demand curve

enter the industry under the belief that post-entry output by the original firm would not be changed. Further, the original firm believes that if the post-entry price would yield only normal profits for the new firm then that firm will not actually enter the industry.

In figure 5.1, the industry demand curve (D) and the cost curve facing any firm (C) are drawn. If the original firm prices at p_m and produces to satisfy the consequent demand of q_m, then any firm contemplating entry into the industry, and holding the belief that the original firm will hold output constant at q_m, faces a residual demand curve drawn as RD. As in many cases above, the demand curve (in this case the residual demand curve) facing the firm is only drawn subject to assumptions about other firms' behaviour. The residual demand curve is merely the industry demand curve (D) minus the current level of output of the original firm (q_m).

As drawn in figure 5.1, over a range of output (q_1 to q_2), it would be profitable for the potential entrant to actually enter the industry (subject to the belief of the original firm maintaining output at the initial level).

The limit price, by definition, will leave the potential entrant on the margin of entering the industry; that would occur in terms of our diagram when the residual demand curve facing the potential entrant is tangential to the cost curve. Such a situation is portrayed in figure 5.2, where the limit price is p_L and the dominant firm produces q_L if it wishes to prevent any entry into the industry.

The nature of the barrier to entry in this case is that of economies of scale, and the cost curves have been drawn exhibiting declining costs over the region near the demand curve. In order to enter the industry, when there are economies of scale, the entrant has to come in in a big way to be able to obtain some, if not all, of the lower costs associated with having a large output. But the extra output, being significant relative to the existing output, will have a noticeable impact on price.

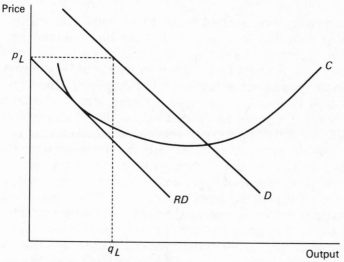

figure 5.2   Determination of limit price

We can get some feel for the order of magnitude involved by taking a simpler case. Suppose that the optimal scale of production is q_0, with unit costs at that output of k, and that because of the shape of the cost curve any firm entering has to do so with production level of at least q_0.[3] Then the competitive price $p_c = k$ (following from zero supernormal profits), and the competitive output would be $q_c = D(p_c) = D(k)$ where $D(.)$ is the demand curve in the industry. An indication of the barrier to entry posed by this optimal scale is given by $s = q_c/q_0$. The existing firms could raise price and reduce output without inducing entry into the industry provided that they did not leave room for an entrant to come in to produce q_0 (or more). For we have assumed that it is prohibitively expensive to produce below q_0, and following the behavioural assumptions made above, after entry a potential firm believes that the existing firms will hold their output constant. Then the existing firms to avoid entry must produce at least an amount $q_l = q_c - q_0$ $= q_c(1 - q_0/q_c) = q_c(1 - 1/s)$. The limit price p_l is then the price which would bring forth demand of q_l. With an elasticity of demand of e, this will be approximately $p_c(1 + 1/eS)$.[4] Thus the limit price is above the competitive price to an extent which depends upon S and e; measures of the economies of scale and the elasticity of demand.

5.3   Capacity as an entry barrier

The model of limit pricing incorporated beliefs by potential entrants that existing firms would hold their pre-entry output constant following new entry into the industry. However, if existing firms could encourage the belief that their post-entry output would be greater than their pre-entry output, they may be able to charge a higher price without inducing entry. One way of encouraging that type of belief would be for existing firms to install a capacity greater than that required for current output, but which could be brought into production following entry to provide increased output. This capacity also provides the potential entrants with an estimate of what the existing firms could do in the event of their entry. In the short run, the capacity of the existing firms places an upper limit on their response to entry. From the point of view of the existing firms, capacity has a benefit and a cost. The benefit is the deterrent effect on potential entrants, whilst the cost is the cost of the excess capacity in terms of interest payments, rent etc.

Spence (1977) provides an analysis of this type of situation, and here we take the simplest case of those which he looks at. The costs of production are the direct costs of production $C(x)$, where x is the level of output, plus the costs of the capacity installed which are $r \cdot k$, where r is the unit capacity costs (in terms of interest, rent etc.) and k the capacity level (measured in units of output). The amount of capacity installed does not affect the level of direct production costs, and the amount of capacity installed forms an upper limit on production. Total costs are $C(x) + r \cdot k$.

After entry, the output of the industry is estimated by potential entrants to be $k + y$, where y is the output of the new entrants, and k the output (existing capacity) of the existing firms. The post-entry price will then be $P(k + y)$, where $P(.)$ is the inverse demand function for the industry. The costs of the entrants will be $C(y) + ry$ if they install capacity to produce y, with the entrants operating at full capacity to minimize costs. Entry is profitable if post-entry price is greater than average costs, i.e. if

$$P(k+y) > \frac{C(y)+ry}{y}.$$

The value of k, the capacity which bars entry, is given by the minimum value of k which ensures that for all values of y,

$$P(k+y) \le \frac{C(y)+ry}{y}.$$

The existing firms seek to maximize profits, which are given by $\pi(x, k) = R(x) - C(x) - rk$, with respect to its two decision variables x and k. The two constraints on the existing firms are that $x \le k$ (i.e. production cannot be greater than capacity) and $k \ge \bar{k}$ where $\bar{k}$ is the capacity of existing firms (and hence estimated post-entry output by them) at which new firms would believe it profitable to enter the industry. The Kuhn-Tucker theorem[5] yields the following first-order conditions for this optimization with inequality constraints problem:

$$\frac{dR}{dx} - \frac{dC}{dx} = \lambda$$

$$r = \lambda + \mu$$

$$\lambda(k - x) = 0$$

$$\mu(k - \bar{k}) = 0$$

$$\lambda, \mu \ge 0$$

where λ and μ are the Lagrangian multipliers. Three separate cases arise. In case 1, $\mu = 0$, $\lambda = $ r, so that $dR/dx - dC/dx = r$. Capacity is fully utilized, and this is the same outcome as would occur without threat of entry, with marginal revenue and marginal cost ($dR/dx = dC/dx + r$) being equated. In case 2, $\lambda = 0$, $\mu = r$ so that $k = \bar{k}$ and $x < k$. The entry considerations determine capacity, but output is below capacity.

Since there is excess capacity, costs are greater than the minimum which for output of x would be $C(x) + rx$. Thus costs of $r(k - x)$ above the minimum are incurred in order to bar entry into the industry. Case 3 has $\lambda \ne 0$, $\mu \ne 0$ and then $x = k = \bar{k}$. Here entry considerations determine capacity, but firms operate at full capacity. In this case if the threat of entry were removed, capacity and output would both fall.[6]

The next step is to investigate the established firms' response to a limit price and the possibility of entry. There are three options available. First, the existing firm may charge a limit price now and in the future, thus blockading entry but reducing short-term profits. Second, it may opt to go for maximum profits in the short term and neglect entry possibilities. The third option is to charge a price above the limit price but seek to control the rate of entry into the industry.

The model which is briefly examined below portrays the firm deciding between the three options on the basis of which will lead to the maximum discounted value of future profit to the firm, in the context where the firm is, and remains the price-leader in the industry, even after substantial entry into the industry. It is fairly clear that an additional reason for seeking to block entry into one's industry is a fear of the disruptive consequence (as far as existing firms are concerned) of new entrants. In the narrower context of the model considered below, this would mean a fear by the initial firm that it would not be able to dictate price after the entry of new firms into the industry.

5.4 Dynamic limit pricing

The model based on limit pricing which is now described is based on Gaskins (1971), and is more fully discussed in the Appendix to this chapter. The initial firm seeks to maximize

$$V = \int_0^\infty e^{-rt}(p(t)-c)(f(p)-x)dt$$

where p is the price, c the firm's average cost, $f(p)$ the demand function for the industry, x the output of new firms, and r the rate of discount. The demand for the original firm is the total demand for the industry ($f(p)$) minus any supplied by entrants into the industry.

In this model, the costs of production are constant, and the existing firm has a cost advantage over new entrants. The price $p(t)$ determined by the initial firm directly influences current profits and the discounted profits, but affects future profits through influencing entry into the industry. This model takes the case where entry into the industry, measured in terms of output produced by other firms, changes in response to the difference between $p(t)$ and the limit price p_L; in particular,

$$\dot{x}(t) = k(p(t)-p_L)$$

where $\dot{x}(t)$ is the rate of change of $x(t)$.

The incorporation of the rate of change of the output of 'new' firms into the maximization process requires the use of the optimal control theory.[7] But the essence of the first part of the solution is straightforward. The original firm making a price change would have to balance the change in profits directly resulting from the price change with the change in profits arising indirectly from the price change through changes in the other firms in the industry (i.e. through changing $\dot{x}(t)$, and thereby x). The value-maximizing conditions, for each time t, is that the marginal profit direct gain from a price change is equal to the marginal value loss (now and in the future in present value terms) arising in the indirect manner indicated.

Over time, the output of 'new' firms is changing in line with the equation for $\dot{x}(t)$ above, and from the first-order conditions an equation for rate of change of price can be obtained. Of more interest is the long-run market share of the initially dominant firm. This is given by

$$m = \frac{(f(p) - x)}{f(p)} = \frac{k(p_L - c)}{f(p_L) \cdot r} - \frac{f'(p_L)}{f(p_L)} \cdot p_L \left(1 - \frac{c}{p_L}\right)$$

As an extreme case, it can be seen that if $p_L = c$ so that no effective barrier to entry existed, then $m = 0$. This arises from the following consideration. If the initial firm blockades entry, it would charge a price $p(t) = p_L = c$, and thus never gain any profits. The only way to earn profits is to charge a price higher than $p_L = c$, but that will induce entry into the industry.

In the other cases, how much (if any) of its market share the firm will relinquish depends upon the discount rate (r), the responsiveness of entry to price (k), the cost advantage of the initial firm ($p_L - c$), and the elasticity of demand at the limit price.

Models which analyse entry into the industry and existing firms' policy towards entry and entry prevention are still in their infancy. In particular, they have not begun to tackle the interdependence problems between existing and potential firms, and those between firms initially in the industry and those which enter the industry.

appendix to chapter 5

5.5 The Kuhn-Tucker theorem

The problem is to maximize $F(x_1, x_2, ..., x_n)$ subject to the m inequality constraints

$$g_1(x_1, x_2, ..., x_n) \leq 0$$
$$g_2(x_1, x_2, ..., x_n) \leq 0$$
$$\cdot$$
$$\cdot$$
$$\cdot$$
$$g_m(x_1, x_2, ..., x_n) \leq 0$$

and that $x_i \geq 0$ for $i = 1, 2, ..., n$.

The form of the constraints is quite general, since by suitable manipulation (including subtraction from zero, etc.) any constraint can be written in this way:

Form $G(x_1, x_2, ..., x_n, \lambda_1, ..., \lambda_m) = F(x_1, x_2, ..., x_n) + \sum_{j=1}^{m} \lambda_j g_j(x_1, x_2, ..., x_n)$.

The first-order conditions are then:

$$\frac{\partial G}{\partial x_i} \leq 0 \text{ for } i = 1, 2, ..., n \left(\text{i.e. } \frac{\partial F}{\partial x_i} + \sum_{j=1}^{m} \lambda_j \frac{\partial g_j}{\partial x_i} \leq 0 \right)$$

$$\frac{\partial G}{\partial \lambda_j} \leq 0 \text{ for } j = 1, 2, ..., m \text{ (i.e. } g_j \leq 0)$$

$$x_i \cdot \frac{\partial G}{\partial x_i} = 0 \; i = 1, 2, ..., n \text{ and } \lambda_j \frac{\partial G}{\partial \lambda_j} = 0 \; j = 1, 2, ..., m.$$

These last two conditions mean that only when the first derivative condition (e.g. $\partial G / \partial x_i \leq 0$) is operative (so that $\partial G / \partial x_i = 0$) can the corresponding variable (x_i) be non-zero. Finally $x_i \geq 0$, $i = 1, 2, ..., n$ and $\lambda_j \geq 0$, $j = 1, 2, ..., m$.

5.6 Gaskins' model

The objective of the firm is to maximize

$$V = \int_0^\infty e^{-\rho t}(p-c)(f(p)-x)dt$$

where p is price, c unit cost (assumed constant), x the output of other firms, $f(p)$ the industry demand curve, and ρ the rate of discount. This maximization is subject to $dx/dt = k(p-p_L)$ where p_L is the limit price, and k a constant, and is with respect to $p(t)$. Below f' and f'' are used to indicate first and second derivatives of f respectively.

We form the Hamiltonian $H = e^{-\rho t}[p(t)-c][f(p(t))-x(t)] + \lambda_1(t)k[p(t)-p_L]$. The first-order conditions for a maximum are:

$$\frac{\partial H}{\partial \lambda_1} = \frac{dx}{dt} \text{ which gives } k(p(t)-p_L) = \frac{dx}{dt} \tag{1}$$

$$-\frac{\partial H}{\partial x} = \frac{d\lambda_1}{dt}(t) \text{ which gives } \frac{d\lambda_1}{dt}(t) = e^{-\rho t}(p(t)-c) \tag{2}$$

$$\frac{\partial H}{\partial p(t)} = 0 \text{ which gives } e^{-\rho t}[(f(p)-x)+(p-c)f'(p)]+\lambda_1(t)k = 0. \tag{3}$$

The condition $\partial H/\partial p = 0$ indicates that, at every instant, price is chosen to maximize H. Equation 3 indicates that the firm balances the (discounted) direct gain from a marginal price change at time t with the indirect loss which comes from the entry induced by that price change. The $\lambda_1(t)$ term can be regarded as the shadow price of these indirect changes.

From equation 3, we have

$$\lambda_1(t) = -\frac{e^{-\rho t}}{k}[(f(p)-x)+(p-c)f']. \tag{4}$$

Differentiation with respect to t gives:

$$\frac{d\lambda_1}{dt}(t) = \rho\frac{e^{-\rho t}}{k}[(f(p)-x)+(p-c)f'(p)]+\frac{e^{-\rho t}}{k}\left[\frac{dx}{dt}-2f'(p)\frac{dp}{dt}-(p-c)f''(p)\frac{dp}{dt}\right]. \tag{5}$$

Combining equations 2 and 3 yields

$$(p(t)-c) = \frac{\rho}{k}[(f(p)-x)+(p-c)f'(p)]+\frac{1}{k}\left[\frac{dx}{dt}-2f'(p)\frac{dp}{dt}-(p-c)f''(p)\frac{dp}{dt}\right]$$

and solving for dp/dt, and substituting for dx/dt from equation 1 gives

$$\frac{dp}{dt} = \frac{k(p_L - c) + \rho[x - f(p) - (p - c)f'(p)]}{[-(p - c)f''(p) - 2f'(p)]}.$$

Assuming that there is an equilibrium outcome, then dp/dt and dx/dt will be zero. The market share of the original firm, $m = f(p) - x/f(p)$, since $f(p)$ is the total industry demand, and x the output supplied by the entrants. From $dx/dt = 0$, we get the equilibrium price $p_e = p_L$. From $dp/dt = 0$, we have

$$k(p_L - c) + \rho[x - f(p_L) - (p_L - c)f'(p_L)] = 0,$$

and hence

$$\frac{k(p_L - c)}{f(p_L)} = \rho\left[\frac{f(p_L) - x}{f(p_L)} + \frac{(p_L - c)f'(p_L)}{f(p_L)}\right].$$

This gives $$m_e = \frac{f(p_L) - x}{f(p_L)} = \frac{k/\rho\,(p_L - c) - f'(p_L)(p_L - c)}{f(p_L)}.$$

Thus if $p_L = c$, the market share of the original firm tends towards zero. In this case, the only way to make any profit is to charge a price above c and hence above p_L. But that induces entry into the industry.

chapter 6
introduction to part two

In Part One, firms were assumed to seek to maximize profits; the theories varied by the type of environment within which the firms operated. Part Two focuses on alternatives to profit maximization, and finishes in Chapter 10 with a review of the debates on the objectives of firms.

The theories of the firm which are based on profit maximization have an underlying view of the firm as controlled by one person or a small group of like-minded people who have complete control over the firm and its workforce and to whom any financial surplus will accrue. These controllers may supply some factors of production and/or they may hire some in the market place. But whichever they do, the outcome will not be affected, with any factors of production supplied by the controllers priced at opportunity cost, and the controllers interested in the excess of revenue over opportunity cost. The firm could be run by an entrepreneur who supplied no other factors, by the suppliers of capital, or by the suppliers of labour, provided that the objective remains the maximization of the economic profit.[1]

The theories considered in the following three chapters, in different ways, offer alternative views as well as alternative theories of the firm.

There are two other common features of the theories considered in this part of the book. The first one is that they are theories of firms rather than of industry. Although the theories considered in Part One were described as theories of the firm, it would have been more accurate to describe them as theories of industry, using the representative firm as part of the technique of analysis. The theories in this part of the book often relate to large firms operating in many industries, and do not take much account of the interplay between firms within an industry. Secondly, the often implicit assumption is that firms operate in an oligopolistic environment at least insofar as there are barriers against new competition which leaves the existing firms with potential, but generally unattained, supernormal profits. These potential supernormal profits lift the pressure on the firms to maximize profits in order to survive and allows them to pursue other objectives if they so wish. Firms considered in this part generally do wish to do so.

The managerial theories, considered in Chapter 7, are derived to apply to the modern large-scale corporation. One key characteristic of such firms is that a large number of shareholders legally own the company and have the legal title to any surplus, but the decisions on the allocation of the profits is not made directly by the shareholders.

'The policy of the company is the responsibility of the directors, and the shareholders do not have the power to change this policy but may only remove the directors from office. The directors may appoint and dismiss employees but not each other. That right is reserved to the shareholders. However, the managing director is held to be an employee, and thus responsible to his colleagues' (King (1977), p. 28). The managerial theories are designed to describe corporations where there are a large number of shareholders, each with a small proportion of the shares, and having little effective say in the appointment of directors or their subsequent actions.

This characteristic is specific to corporations, that is, a firm with a large number of shareholders. But in many situations, some of the owners of a firm may have problems in ensuring that the activities of the firm conform to their wishes. This is not a new problem just relating to the large corporation. For example, Pollard (1968) writes:

> There is here a further factor to be considered, which loomed much larger in eighteenth and early nineteenth century minds than in our own, but which ought on that account not to be entirely neglected. That was the view, based on bitter experience as well as on fashionable economic reasoning, that a system of large scale management was to be avoided at all costs because managers who had to be given any measure of power or responsibility were not to be trusted.
>
> Adam Smith, denying in a famous passage the ability of salaried managers to administer honestly and well any but the most routine and easily checked business, argued, as usual, not merely from philosophical principles, but from a wealth of practical experience relating, in particular, to joint stock companies:
>
> 'The directors of such companies (he accuses), being the managers rather of other people's money than of their own, it cannot well be expected that they should watch over it with the same anxious vigilance with which the partners in a private copartnery frequently watch over their own. ... Negligence and profusion ... must always prevail, more or less, in the management of the affairs of such a company'.[2]

The managerial theories of the firm are based on an examination of the interests of the managers/directors of the firm, from which are derived the objectives of the managers which are translated into the objectives of the firm. The pursuit of these objectives is not unconstrained, for the managers/directors are answerable to their firm's shareholders, directly or indirectly. The direct threat posed by shareholders would be to vote to replace the directors. An indirect threat, but probably of more significance, is that current shareholders can sell their shares. By doing so, as will be seen, they may open the way for a take-over bid and/or make the raising of finance capital more difficult for the firm.

The term 'managerial revolution' usually refers to the situation discussed above, whereby ownership has become divorced from control. But the control is now assumed to lie with the directors rather than the shareholders. The growth of scale of companies, which accompanied the managerial revolution, gives rise to growth in importance of managers in general, often termed lower and middle management.

The increased role of management generates problems of effective control of the organization by the directors and/or owners. The behavioural theories (considered in Chapter 8) view the firm as a large organization. Within the organization, there can be groups with conflicting interests. For example, the production managers may be mainly interested in promoting their own interests by increasing the quantity of output, whilst the sales department may be more interested in sales revenue. The former may then favour a low price to promote demand and hence output, whilst the latter may favour a higher price if that maximizes sales revenue. The behavioural theories place emphasis on this aspect of a firm as an organization, and the consequences of that for the way in which firms make decisions on price, output etc., and the impact on the nature of those decisions.

In the behavioural approach (and to a lesser extent in the managerial theories), emphasis is placed on the internal relations of the firm, with little heed paid to the external relations between firms. In contrast, the theories considered in Part One assumed that within the firm there was no problem of implementing the decisions of the firm's controllers. In particular, it was postulated that the firm's controllers wanted to maximize profits, determined what was necessary to do that, and then those decisions were effectively implemented. The emphasis for theories in Part One was entirely on the external relations of the firms, particularly how firms interact with one another within an industry.

The theories considered in Chapter 9 have some common strands but also contain some major points of difference. These theories can be loosely described as radical alternatives, and have three common themes. First, the theories relate to large firms operating in oligopolistic circumstances. Secondly, the firms being considered are capitalist firms with residual profits accruing to the shareholders of the company. Thirdly, the firms are sufficiently large to have a noticeable impact on the economic and political environment within which they operate, and that these firms will seek to mould that environment in directions which are advantageous to themselves. In particular, firms do not constrain themselves to operate only in the market place, but will strive to influence political decision-making.

In Chapter 10, we hope to compare and contrast, on a theoretical plane, the basic approaches to the firm which have been discussed in the first nine chapters. The first aim is to highlight the crucial differences between the theories. In this way, it may be possible to point to ways in which empirical evidence could be used to resolve some of the disputes. But some of the differences are likely to be such that they cannot be resolved in this way (or at least not in the foreseeable future). A second aim is to further illustrate that the theories differ in their view of the world (particularly their view of the firm) and in their objectives. In this case, theories cannot easily be discriminated between on the grounds of which fit the facts best (or least badly), but a view has to be taken on which approach appears to be the most fruitful.

chapter 7

managerial theories of the firm

7.1 Background to the managerial theories

The theories of the firm examined in this chapter share the common theme that the controllers of the firm pursue non-profit objectives, generally subject to achieving a certain level of performance in a profit-linked variable. These theories are theories of oligopoly, in that potential supernormal profits are assumed; but the interdependence characteristic of oligopoly is largely ignored. The stimulus for many of these theories was not the emergence of oligopoly so much as the belief that a 'managerial revolution' has occurred through which the managers who control the firm do not own it, and the owners do not control the firm. This is often alternatively stated as the divorce of ownership and control.

One of the earliest, and the most influential, works on the 'managerial revolution' was that of Berle and Means (1932). Their book, published in the early thirties, argued that they were observing the transition between a time when firms were essentially owner controlled and a time when large firms would be manager controlled. Amongst the largest two hundred non-financial firms in 1929, they argued that eighty-eight were manager controlled, sixty-eight were owner controlled (either minority, majority, or private ownership), forty-one were owner controlled via a legal device, one was in management/minority owner control, and two were in receivership.

Owner control was defined as a situation where a well defined group owned more than 20 per cent of the shares of the company and manager control defined as a situation where no well defined group held more than 10 per cent of the shares of the company. Implicitly, it was argued that where a small coherent group held more than one fifth of the shares, then that group would exert close control over the management of the firm to ensure that the objectives of the owners would be pursued. Conversely, when share ownership is widely dispersed, there is little incentive for any single shareholder to try to monitor the management, and shareholders then tend to play a passive role within the company.

Larner (1966) updates (and partially corrects) the earlier work of Berle and Means and, on a similar basis to theirs, indicates that the trends foreseen by

Berle and Means had largely materialized, with nearly 85 per cent of the largest two hundred American non-financial corporations under manager control.[1,2,3]

At one level, the 'managerial revolution' can be seen as an application of the principle of the division of labour, whereby the same group of individuals no longer have to supply both managerial skills and capital. When expressed like this, it would seem likely that some element of divorce of ownership and control has always been present, even if it is more pronounced in the twentieth century than in the nineteenth. But in terms of the theory of the firm (and also of views of how the firm affects the economy), any managerial revolution would only be of significance if it affected either the main aims of the firm or the achievement of those aims. In other words, if managers have different objectives to those of the owners and are able to pursue those objectives unhindered by the owners, then changes in the firm's behaviour could result. Further, the objectives of the owners and the managers must conflict over some range if any change results from the emergence of the managerial revolution. For example, it could be argued that managers look to high income and owners to high profits; but if the managers believed that their income was closely linked to profits by, say, performance-linked salaries or by some payments in the form of shares in the company, then pursuit of higher personal incomes by the managers may well lead to the pursuit of profits for the firm.

There have been, in some sense, two managerial revolutions and it is essential to separate them. The first one, which underlies much of the work discussed in the next chapter, refers to the increased importance of non-manual and particularly supervisory labour relative to manual labour within most sectors of the economy, i.e. the increased role of managers as that term is generally understood. The second one, which is the focus of this chapter, refers to the divorce of ownership from control whereby the crucial decisions for a corporation are taken by people who have little ownership interest in the company. Thus it is the composition of the board of directors and where the power within such boards lies that is under consideration.

The theories considered rely on the existence of barriers to entry into the industries in which their firms operate, so that potential supernormal profits are available to the firm. For if the firm could at most only earn normal profits, then it would have to maximize profits in order to survive. All the theories here assume that the controllers of the firm are maximizers, but differ in terms of which variables the controllers are thought to seek to maximize. In general, the controllers cannot maximize their utility regardless of what happens to profits, and so some constraint on profits or a profit-linked variable is introduced.

7.2   Theory of Scitovsky

Before coming to those theories which are explicitly linked to the managerial revolution, the model of Scitovsky (1943) is considered. In this model, the entrepreneur is treated as an individual and, in common with the standard treatment of the individual in micro-economics, he is assumed to maximize a utility function. In a manner analogous to the treatment of the individual and the derivation of the labour supply curve, the entrepreneur's utility function has two arguments: income and leisure.[4] The sales revenue of the entrepreneur depends upon how much labour he puts in; the costs will also vary since more labour by him requires more of other inputs. The postulated revenue and cost curves are drawn in figure 7.1 as curves R and C. The profit curve is obtained by subtraction of costs from revenue. Some of the indifference curves derived from the utility function $U(Y, L)$ (where Y is income and L leisure) are plotted as I_1, I_2 and I_3. Utility is maximized at point M since the entrepreneur is faced with the income/leisure trade-off defined by the profit curve. We can note that profit maximization would lead to operation at point N, and in a utility maximization framework could only be reached by indifference curves of the shape J_1. This latter utility function would contain only profits as an argument, and the entrepreneur would be assumed to gain no satisfaction from leisure.

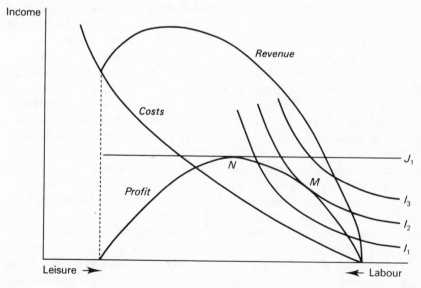

figure 7.1   The Scitovsky model.

7.3   Theory of Baumol

The theory of Baumol (1959) has at its centre the view that managers seek to maximize sales revenue of the firm subject to earning an acceptable level of profits for the firm. Before presenting the formal model, we look at some of the reasons suggested for this objective and constraint. Baumol's theory is one of oligopoly but where, it is argued, interdependence is largely ignored, particularly in day-to-day decision-making. It can be ignored by firms, and consequently in the theory, for a number of reasons. Firstly, the large firm produces hundreds of products, and would be in potential conflict with numerous firms to different extents via these products and would find it virtually impossible to take all the dimensions of interdependence into account.

Secondly, the complexity of large organizations means that proposals are often started at points in the organization far removed from the makers of the final decisions. The decision-making process is then too clumsy and slow moving for interdependence between firms to have much impact on the decisions made. Partly as a result of the first two reasons, firms tend to adopt a rule of thumb approach to pricing and other policies which will generally not incorporate rules about other firms' reactions. The rule of thumb may be to increase sales as much as possible.

It is also argued that there are advantages to the firm in being large. In particular, the larger the firm, the easier the raising of capital and it is able to borrow funds at a lower rate of interest. Thus to some extent the drive to expand the size of the firm is also in the interests of future profits.

There are rather more direct reasons for the firm and its controllers receiving benefit from increased sales. From the point of view of the firm as an organization, there are a number of reasons why it should be concerned about its sales volume. Declining sales bring problems of consumers shunning a product when it falls in popularity; banks and the money market will be less receptive and there are dangers of the firm with declining sales losing distributors. Further, personnel relations are likely to be more difficult when firing rather than hiring workers is the norm.

These reasons would point the firm towards at least a concern about sales, although it has been argued that they might equally apply to the firm seeking to maximize profits subject to a sales constraint.[5]

Baumol argues that since the managers' salaries appear to be more closely linked to sales than to profits, personal self-interest would lead them to promote sales. Also, if the firm benefits from increased sales as argued in the previous paragraph, the contribution of a manager to a firm, his promotion prospects, and his standing in the firm may be judged in terms of sales.

These are derivative reasons for striving to increase sales. Finally, we come to sales as an objective in their own right. Baumol's argument for this is essentially that in his role as an economic consultant he has observed that sales, rather than profit, seem to be the objective of the managers. Further that when conflicts between sales and profits arose sales were generally placed above profits as an objective.

Thus a wide range of reasons have been put forward for believing that the firm will maximize sales. Some of them can be interpreted (and have been) as indicating that sales maximization in the short run is a route to long-run profit maximization. It can be argued that sales maximization acts as a rule of thumb for day-to-day decision-making, which leads to profit maximization.[6] Or that in the interests of long-term profits there are gains from lower capital costs which derive from increased size.

The sales revenue maximization is not without limits, for that would lead to negative profits. Instead, a minimum acceptable profit level is laid down. Baumol sees this as being determined by the need to be able to raise finance in order to pay for future expansion of sales. This finance may come directly from retentions of profits by the firm or through some external sources. In the former case, the profit requirement is direct. Whereas in the latter case, it is indirect in that current profitability will be necessary to impress the capital market. Profits here are seen as a means to the end of further sales, and not as an end in themselves. If the capital market is severe in its judgement on firms' profitability before providing new finance, then the profit constraint may be rather tight on the firms, and its ability to diverge substantially from profit maximization may be limited; this question is more fully explored in Chapter 10.

The formal model can be expressed in the following terms: the large corporation seeks, in the short term, to maximize sales revenue $p \cdot q$, where p is price and q quantity, subject to profits being at least of size $\bar{\pi}$. The demand for the firm's output is summarized by price $p = p(q, v)$, with the price depending upon the quantity to be sold and the amount of advertising, v, undertaken by the firm. Its costs depend upon output and advertising, i.e. $C = C(q, v)$. Thus the firm seeks to maximize $p(q, v) \cdot q$ subject to profits of $p \cdot q - C(q, v) \geq \bar{\pi}$, with q and v as its decision variables.

Before undertaking the formal analysis of this, we note that the profit constraint could be set so 'tight' that either it is unattainable whatever the firm does so that the firm cannot operate or that the profit limit can only be obtained by the firm maximizing profits. In the following analysis we shall assume that neither of these circumstances arises.

The Lagrangian $L = p(q, v)q + \lambda(p(q, v) \cdot q - C(q, v) - \bar{\pi})$ can be formed, and the Kuhn-Tucker theorem[7] yields the first-order conditions:

$$\frac{\partial L}{\partial q} \leq 0 \quad q \cdot \frac{\partial L}{\partial q} = 0 \tag{1}$$

$$\frac{\partial L}{\partial v} \leq 0 \quad v \cdot \frac{\partial L}{\partial v} = 0 \tag{2}$$

$$\frac{\partial L}{\partial \lambda} \geq 0 \quad \lambda \cdot \frac{\partial L}{\partial \lambda} = 0 \tag{3}$$

$$q, v, \lambda \geq 0.$$

For the firm to be in operation requires that $q \neq 0$, and we will assume that it undertakes some advertising so that $v \neq 0$. The conditions (1) and (2) then become $\partial L/\partial q = 0$ and $\partial L/\partial v = 0$. Writing these conditions out in full (with $R(q,v) = p(q,v) \cdot q$):

$$0 = \frac{\partial L}{\partial q} = \frac{\partial R}{\partial q} + \lambda \left(\frac{\partial R}{\partial q} - \frac{\partial C}{\partial q} \right) \tag{4}$$

$$0 = \frac{\partial L}{\partial v} = \frac{\partial R}{\partial v} + \lambda \left(\frac{\partial R}{\partial v} - \frac{\partial C}{\partial v} \right). \tag{5}$$

From equation 3, we can see that either $\lambda = 0$ or $\partial L/\partial \lambda = 0$ (or both). If $\lambda = 0$ then from equation 5 we would have $\partial R/\partial v = 0$. This would mean that the marginal revenue from advertising falls to zero, and that possibility is ruled out by Baumol. Thus it is assumed that advertising will always increase revenue (though the marginal costs of that advertising may be far in excess of the extra revenue). This line of argument leads to $\lambda = 0$ being ruled out, so that $\partial L/\partial \lambda = 0$, which is that the profit constraint, $R(q,v) - C(q,v) - \bar{\pi} = 0$ (6), is binding on the firm.

The first-order conditions for the sales-revenue maximizer are then equations 4, 5 and 6, and the output and advertising which results will be referred to as Q_c and v_c respectively.

The profit-maximizing firm would produce an output Q_m, and advertise at a level v_m which is given by the conditions:

$$\frac{\partial R}{\partial q} = \frac{\partial C}{\partial q}$$

$$\frac{\partial R}{\partial v} = \frac{\partial C}{\partial v}.$$

Rewriting equation 4 as $(1+1/\lambda)\,\partial R/\partial q = \partial C/\partial q$, with λ positive, indicates that the sales revenue-maximizer operates where marginal revenue is less than marginal cost. We cannot make a definite comparison between the sales-revenue maximizer's output and that of a profit-maximizer, since the level of advertising influences marginal revenue (and perhaps marginal cost). But, for a given level of advertising, the sales-revenue maximizer will produce a larger output than the profit-maximizer. For the profit-maximizer produces an output such that marginal revenue equals marginal cost; a larger output leads to a fall in marginal revenue and a rise in marginal cost (under the conventional assumptions) thus leading to output where marginal revenue is less than marginal cost, which is the range where the sales-revenue maximizer operates.

For a given level of advertising, full unconstrained maximization of sales revenue would lead to an output Q_s where $\partial R/\partial q = 0$. The sales-revenue maximizer with the profit constraint produces Q_c with $\partial R/\partial q = (\lambda/\lambda +1)\partial C/\partial q$ and so marginal revenue is positive. With declining marginal revenue, this implies $Q_c < Q_s$.

These arguments are summarized in figure 7.2, where the curve labelled MR_λ is the curve of $(1+1/_\lambda)MR$.

The conclusions are summarized in figure 7.3, which relates to the output

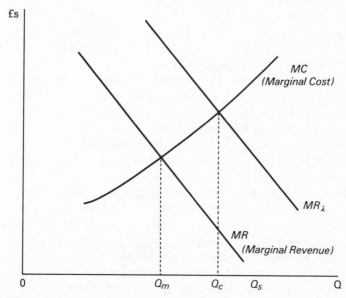

figure 7.2   The relationship between Q_m, Q_c and Q_s

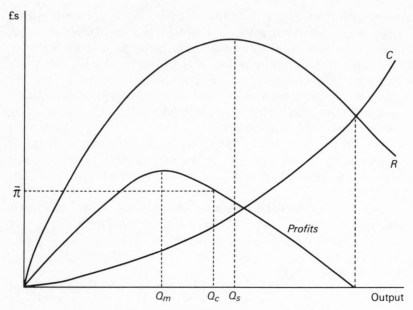

figure 7.3   Outcome from model of Baumol

decision, using the same notation as above. In this figure, a given level of advertising has been incorporated in the revenue, cost, and profit curves. As before, we have that Q_c is less than Q_s, and both of these are larger than Q_m.

The interesting predictions of the theory follow from this result that the profit constraint is binding on the firm. For then, any changes which depress profits will cause the firm to respond to restore profits to the minimum acceptable level. In particular, a rise in fixed costs (such as rent or interest rates) will push down profits and the firm will have to respond by raising price, reducing output, and reducing advertising to restore profit levels. This stands in contrast to the prediction of the profit maximization model, where a change in fixed costs unrelated to output has no impact on price.

One interpretation of the results is that the managers are able to trade in any profits above the minimum acceptable level for an increase in sales revenue, through using any 'excess' profits to finance advertising and sales promotion.[8] It is, then, clear that as far as the managers are concerned, profits *per se* yield them no utility or benefit, whereas sales revenue does (for all the reasons listed above). But, literally interpreted, the managers are prepared to trade in any amount of profits above the acceptable level for any increase in sales revenue however small. This line of argument points towards envisaging the managers maximizing a utility function, whose arguments included sales revenue and profits. And in some respects the model of Williamson examined below does that.

Although intended to apply to a multi-product firm, the form of analysis so far has been in terms of one product only. If the number of products produced by the firm was greater than one, a similar analysis would apply to a multi-product firm provided that the number of products is constant (noting, however, that the outcome would be complicated if some of the products produced by the firm were substitutes for each other). However, if the assumption of a fixed number of products is relaxed, then the sales-revenue maximizer may look rather like a profit-maximizer.[9,10] Suppose that the firm is currently producing just one product. In the analysis described above and summarized in figure 7.3 the firm produces at level Q_c. But if the firm could produce a second product, it could reduce its output of the first product back to Q_m, leaving it with some profits above the acceptable level, and start producing a second product. Production at the profit-maximizing level would add to sales, without detracting from profits. Thus the introduction of this second product pushes back the time when the profit constraint begins to bite on the firm's sales expansion. It would be faced with a similar choice after introducing the second line. It would continue to maximize profits on each line and introduce new products until the profits on the last product introduced is zero. But, it could be added that the sales-maximizer would continue to introduce further products which added to sales but detracted from profits; this is, of course, similar to its course of action on the level of production where it adds further production which adds to sales but subtracts from profits.

Finally, one can make the point that if firms were really interested in sales, they would move into areas such as retail distribution where sales are high relative to profits; sales have to be interpreted as a proxy for size.

7.4   Theory of Williamson

The model of O. E. Williamson (1964), to which we now turn, can be seen as a generalization of the Baumol model, though there are notable differences in the reasoning behind the formal model. The general model (of which Williamson examines a number of variants) is based on the notion that managers seek to maximize a utility function subject to reported profit exceeding some minimum acceptable level. The utility function is a function of staff employed, emoluments of the managers and 'discretionary' profits.

Williamson's theory is based on the notion that managers have considerable room for manoeuvre. He argues that there is a consensus amongst organization theorists that the important immediate determinants of management behaviour are salary, status power and prestige, and security. In order to bring these motives into a formal model, Williamson introduces the notion of 'expense preference', whereby managers have a positive preference for some types of expenses. Three forms of expenses are included under the 'expense preference' heading: staff, emoluments, and discretionary profits. On the first item, the managers have preference for increased staff as a means of increasing their power and often salary, in addition to making promotion prospects within the company more favourable. The emoluments here refers to the portion of management salaries which is discretionary, that is, economic rent of the managers paid over and above the minimum needed to keep them in their present employment. Finally, discretionary profits are profits above the minimum performance constraint. This is included in the belief that future expansion will be tied to such profits, and that managers gain satisfaction from self and organizational achievement, and that profits are a measure of success.

The most general model presented by Williamson hypothesizes that managers seek to maximize a utility function:

$$U(S, M, \pi - \pi_0 - T)$$

subject to $\pi - \pi_0 - T \geq 0$, where S is staff costs, M managers emoluments, π actual profit, π_0 minimum post-tax profit and T taxes.

Williamson first asserts that the constraint (that discretionary profits are not negative) will not be binding. This assumption has the following interpretation. If the firm were operating close to the profit constraint, then a reduction of £x in staff costs and managers' emoluments and a corresponding increase of £x in discretionary profits would yield a net gain in utility to the managers. For then, in striving to increase their utility, managers would increase discretionary profits above zero. The reasonableness, or otherwise, of this assumption is very difficult to evaluate. The precise analysis of Williamson depends on that assumption. But in the Appendix to this chapter, the consequences of dropping this assumption are explored. In terms of the conclusions drawn below from the first-order conditions, there are no basic changes.

At this stage we can note two essential differences between the models of Baumol and Williamson. First, the level of discretionary profits $\pi - \pi_0 - T$ enters the utility function of the firm in the model of Williamson. This circumvents the criticism made of Baumol's model, which implied that managers would go for a very small increase in sales even at the cost of a large drop in profits, provided profits were above the minimum level. Secondly, the profit constraint is taken as binding on the firm in the Baumol model, but not binding in the case of Williamson. In both cases, specific assumptions are made to lead to the conclusion about whether the constraint is binding or not.

If the constraint on discretionary profits is not binding, then it can be effectively forgotten, and we can proceed with the maximization procedure. The discretionary profits, labelled D, is $(1-t) . (P(X,S,E) X - C(X) - S - M - T) - \pi_0$ where P is price of output, X level of output, C production costs, E a parameter describing the state of the environment in which the firm operates, t the marginal tax rate, and T lump sum taxes.

The decision variables for the managers are S, M and X. The first-order conditions for maximum utility are:

$$\frac{\partial U}{\partial S} = U_1 + U_3 \frac{\partial D}{\partial S} = 0$$

$$\frac{\partial U}{\partial M} = U_2 + U_3 \frac{\partial D}{\partial M} = 0$$

$$\frac{\partial U}{\partial X} = U_3 \frac{\partial D}{\partial X} = 0$$

where $U_i (i = 1, 2, 3)$ are the first partial derivatives of U with respect to the three arguments of U. Manipulation and substitution yields:

$$\frac{X \partial P}{\partial S} = \frac{-U_1 + (1-t)U_3}{(1-t)U_3} = \frac{-U_1}{(1-t)U_3} + 1$$

$$U_2 = (1-t)U_3$$

$$\frac{X \partial P}{\partial X} + P = \frac{\partial C}{\partial X}$$

(assuming that U_3 and $1-t$ are non-zero).

The first condition indicates that the marginal revenue product of staff (the left-hand-side term) is less than the marginal cost of staff, which is unity in this model. For the term $-U_1/(1-t)U_3$ is negative, with U_1 and U_3 being assumed positive. Thus in respect of staff, the 'Williamson firm' is hiring more than the profit-maximizing firm would. For the profit-maximizer would hire staff until their marginal revenue product equalled marginal cost. The marginal cost of staff (at unity) is the same for the two firms, and so the marginal revenue product of staff is smaller for the

Williamson firm than for the profit-maximizer. With the assumption of declining marginal product this yields the result quoted.

The second condition is that the firm will take some of the actual profits in the form of emoluments, and that the amount will depend upon the tax rate as well as the firm's preferences.

The third condition looks like a profit maximization condition of marginal revenue equals marginal cost. Indeed it is; except that here, the costs involved are restricted to production costs.

It is possible to examine the impact of changes in the firm's circumstances on its decision variables. In the model as set up above, the firm's circumstances can change through a change in the environment in which it operates (for example, a change in the general level of demand), a change in the tax rate, or a change in the lump sum taxes. The impact of changes in these three variables on the three decision variables is given in Table 7.1, which is reproduced from Williamson (1964).

table 7.1 Comparative static responses for the Williamson model

		parameter		
		E	t	T
decision	X	+	+ ?	−
variable	S	+	+ ?	−
	M	+	+ ?	−

A favourable change in the environment (shifting the demand curve outwards) leads to a rise in output, staff, and emoluments. A rise in profits tax is likely to lead to a rise in output, staff, and emoluments, partly because the cost (in terms of forgone profits) of an increase in staff and emoluments is thereby reduced.

These changes relate to small changes in the parameters describing the firm's position and for the firm moving from one equilibrium to another. However much of the evidence produced by Williamson in support of his theory relates to a 'crisis' situation when there is a sharp fall in profits (through, say, an adverse change in the firm's environment), the firm, if it is to survive, then has to reduce costs. The firm finds that it is able to cut costs by reducing staff and emoluments which are above the level necessary for the operation of the firm. The firm in the Williamson model hires staff and pays emoluments above what is necessary for the current level of production. Consequently costs are higher and profits lower than they could be. When a crisis arises, and profits fall below the minimum level, there are costs which can be reduced to help restore profits. It can be said that the firm operates with some 'organizational slack', which is reflected in higher costs. In the next chapter other models will be discussed which also indicate that firms operate subject to a degree of slack, although the reasons given are different.

7.5   Theory of Marris

The theories of Baumol and Williamson shared a number of common features. They are theories which rely on short-period analysis, and which draw out the objective function of the firm from the interests of the organization and its members rather than from the interests of the directors of the firm. The theory of Marris (expounded particularly in Marris (1964)), whilst having certain similarities with the theories of Baumol and Williamson, does diverge from them in respect of the two common features of those theories just mentioned. Thus it is concerned with a long-run situation, and particularly the choice by the firm of a sustainable growth path. Another central feature is the decisions taken on the level of investment and the dividend payments of the firm. These are clearly 'top level' decisions which are likely to be taken by the board of directors rather than resulting from a build up of decisions taken by many different groups within a firm. In this respect, the theory of Marris is the most explicitly 'managerial revolution' orientated theory of those so far presented, and relies heavily on managers having interests which are at variance with the interests of the shareholders.

The theory has three parts: the assumptions on the motivation of the managers and how these motives are made operational within the theory; a view, essentially a neoclassical one, of how the stock market values the firm; and a theory of take-overs with the threat of a take-over being the main constraint on managers' behaviour.

The view on the stock market embedded in the theory is that the stock market valuation is determined by discounted future expected dividends. The firm is viewed as an ongoing business, so that the shareholders' interest in the firm is derived from its dividend payments, and not the 'worth' of the firm in terms of its capital equipment etc. Moneys retained by the firm for future investment become of direct benefit to the shareholders when that investment yields dividends to them. But there is an indirect benefit to the shareholders, for the anticipation of higher future dividends from the investment enhances the present market value of the firm and of their shares.

Initially we take the simplest case, where a firm's investment is financed by retained profits, and assume that the firm does not increase its debt or issue new shares to raise finance. Below, these assumptions will be relaxed.

Future dividends are discounted at the prevailing rate of discount to calculate their present value. Thus the market value of the firm becomes $V = \sum_{t=0}^{\infty} \frac{(1-r_t)P_t}{(1+i)^t}$, where P_t is the expected profits in period t, r_t the expected retention ratio (that is, the proportion of profits retained by the firm, in the main to finance future investment), and i the rate of discount (here assumed constant through time). Dividend payments expected in time t are then $(1-r_t)P_t$. It is assumed for the present that i, the rate of discount applied to the firm, is independent of the firm's behaviour, although this is also relaxed below.

The valuation ratio, v, is defined as the ratio of the market value of the firm to its book value. The latter is intended to correspond with the value of the capital equipment owned by the firm. The threat of a firm being taken over by another rests on the valuation ratio of the firm. A lower valuation ratio places a firm at a greater risk of being taken over. For with a lower valuation ratio, the amount a potential acquirer needs to pay per pound of capital equipment acquired is lower; thus making the firm a more attractive acquisition target.

In a capital market where any opportunity for profit is quickly known and acted on, and where the costs of acting are small, any fall in the valuation ratio below unity would trigger off a take-over bid. For with such a valuation ratio, a firm could be acquired for just less than the value of its capital equipment. In practice, it is expected that a take-over bid which involves the buying of at least 51 per cent of the company in one swoop will lead to a bidding up of the price of the firm.[11] Whilst some individuals buy and sell at the current price, the majority of shareholders are presumed to be content with the firm at its current price and are only prepared to sell for a higher price (since they are observed not to sell at the current price). The majority of the shareholders have to be enticed to part with their shares by the offer of a higher price. There are also likely to be considerable costs in making a take-over bid. For these two reasons, the valuation ratio may fall substantially below unity without triggering off a take-over bid.

In practice, the valuation ratio may be considerably above one because the book value of the firm does not adequately reflect the assets of the firm. This could arise through failure to revalue assets during periods of inflation, over-depreciation of assets, etc.

In this approach, firms can manipulate their market value and valuation ratio through their profitability and the retention ratio. Take-overs are considered unwelcome and the firm can avoid them by appropriate action on profitability and retentions.

On the motivation side, the interests of the managers leads the firm to maximize a utility function whose two arguments are growth and security. The line of argument for these two is similar to those used by Baumol and Williamson above. The desire for higher salaries, seeking power and prestige, lead to emphasis on the growth of sales. The main threat to the managers' security, particularly security of their employment, is argued to be the take-over of the firm. Following a take-over, the 'top' managers will be redundant for the simple reason that the acquiring firm will bring with it its own 'top' managers, and only one set of 'top' managers will be required. The risk of take-over rises as the valuation ratio and market value of the firm falls, so the managers have an interest in the valuation ratio. This, it is argued, will be reinforced by feelings of obligation toward shareholders whose interests are closely linked to the valuation ratio. So, in terms of observable variables, the utility function of the managers depends upon growth of sales and the valuation ratio.

The firm is looking to the long term and is interested in persistence of growth, rather than a sudden spurt which increases sales now but does not continue into the future. Thus the firm is concerned with *sustainable* growth. This would mean that the firm would not be interested in increasing sales in one time period if it adversely affected sales in subsequent periods. However, in looking at the future, the firm may see before it a number of new possibilities, all of which involve fluctuating growth rates. For example, a product is likely to have phases when demand is increasing rapidly followed by periods when growth slackens off (analysis of such demand is given in Marris (1964), Chapter 4). However, to simplify the analysis, the firm is portrayed as choosing between different growth rates, which if chosen would be constant throughout the foreseeable future. Besides making any mathematics easier, it also avoids tricky problems of comparing growth paths which 'cross over'.[12] A further simplification is that the production possibilities do not change over time, so that technical progress and substitution between inputs are ignored. In particular, the capital-output ratio is assumed constant.

Any variables relating to the firm's position which grow (such as sales, profits, capital stock etc.) do so at this constant rate. Thus with growth rate g, the profits in any period t become $P_0(1 + g)^t$, where P_0 is the initial value of profits. The retention ratio, being the ratio of two variables, retentions and profits, which grow at the same rate g, is expected to persist at the same level into the indefinite future. The valuation ratio of the firm in time period 0 then reduces to:

$$v = \frac{\text{Market Value}}{\text{Book Value}} = \sum_{t=0}^{\infty} \frac{(1-r)P_0(1+g)^t/(1+i)^t}{K_0} = \pi_0(1-r) \sum_{t=0}^{\infty} \left(\frac{1+g}{1+i}\right)^t$$

$= \pi_0(1-r)(1+i/i-g)$, with the last equation resulting from the summation of the geometric series $\sum_{t=0}^{\infty} (1+g/1+i)^t$.[13] K_0 is the initial book value of the firm and π_0 the initial rate of profit (P_0/K_0). This formula rests on the neoclassical assumptions on the determination of the firm's stock market valuation in terms of discounted future dividends.

There is a two-way relationship between the rate of profits and the rate of growth. On the one side, profits are the source of finance for growth, and with only internal finance being used, net investment equals 'savings' of the firm, which is retained profit. Thus $I = r.P$, and dividing through by the capital stock K, gives $I/K = r.P/K$, which is $g = r.\pi$.

The other side of the relationship is that profitability is a function of the rate of growth. In particular, it is asserted that there are 'costs of growth' which are charged against profits. Thus an attempt to raise the growth rate increases the costs of growth, and consequently depresses the rate of profits. These costs of growth would include, on the demand side, the costs of expanding demand for the firm (say, through advertising) and of developing new markets for the firm. There could also be costs of assimilation as new staff and equipment are taken on by the firm as it expands.[14] These costs of growth are here regarded as current, rather than capital, costs.

This discussion has emphasized the depressing impact of faster growth on profitability, so that $d\pi/dg < 0$, but there may be an initial range of g where this derivative is positive.

From the formula above for the valuation ratio, and with $g = r\pi$, we arrive at

$$v = \frac{(\pi(g)-g)(1+i)}{i-g}.$$

The shape of this curve is sketched in figure 7.4.

We note first that it is necessary to impose some conditions on i, g and π, for a meaningful value of v to be generated. The internal financing of investment ensures that $\pi \geq g$, with $v = 0$ if $\pi = g$ for then there would never be any dividends with all profits being reinvested. However, the condition $i > g$ has to be imposed. This could be imposed by fiat to ensure a reasonable value for v. An alternative would be to argue that the discount rate applied to a firm depends upon that firm's growth rate, under the argument that higher growth rates are subject to more uncertainty. Then i could be a function of g such that $di/dg > 0$, and such that i is always above g. Another alternative would be to argue that the costs of growth are such that the rate of profits falls as the rate of growth rises so that π would fall to equal g before g reached the level of i.[15]

The shape of the valuation ratio curve rests on the shape of the profitability growth curve. For

$$\frac{dv}{dg} = \frac{(1+i)}{(i-g)^2} \cdot \left[\frac{d\pi}{dg}(i-g) + \pi - i \right].$$

When $d\pi/dg$ is positive, dv/dg is also positive; when $d\pi/dg$ becomes negative (as g increases), at first dv/dg stays positive, but eventually becomes negative.

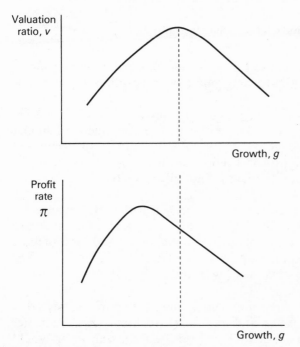

figure 7.4   Valuation ratio growth and profit rate growth curves

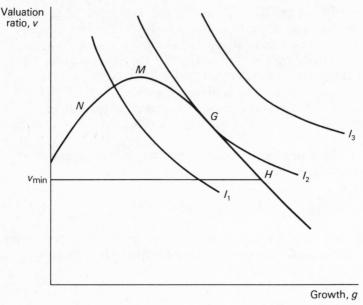

figure 7.5   The valuation ratio curve and managerial indifference curves

Thus the valuation ratio curve has the inverted U-shape that is drawn, and its turning point occurs after the turning point of the profitability curve as indicated in figure 7.4.[16]

A firm seeking a more rapid expansion of sales would find its market valuation ratio affected in two ways. Firstly, the requirement of higher retentions to finance the faster growth reduces dividends in the short run. But this is partially offset by the prospect of higher dividends some time in the future. Secondly, the more rapid expansion initially raises but later depresses the rate of profit.

On the motives side, the managers regard both growth and the valuation ratio as desirable. Their entry into the utility function generates indifference curves between these two variables of the traditional shape, and some of these are superimposed on the technical trade-off curve diagram in figure 7.5. The maximization of utility dependent on growth and the valuation ratio leads to an outcome at G.

In this context the notion of profit maximization has to be reinterpreted. If the initial size of the firm in terms of its capital stock is fixed (for further discussion on this, see below), then one period profit maximization would lead to maximization of the rate of profit. Since the turning point of the profitability growth curve occurs at a lower rate of growth than the turning point of the valuation ratio growth curve, this would entail operating at a point to the left of M in figure 7.5, at point N, say. But if profit maximization is taken as a shorthand for the interests of the shareholders, then in terms of their monetary interests that would lead to operating at M, where the valuation ratio, and hence with a given initial capital stock, the market value of the firm is maximized.

The above analysis focused on internal finance (that is, retained profits) as the sole form of finance for investment. Much of the discussion on the growth of firms has made this assumption under the belief that internal finance constituted the major form of finance and that making the analysis more complicated by the introduction of other forms of finance did not alter the basic conclusions. We now sketch the implications of, first, borrowing at a fixed rate of interest, and second, the use of new share issues as a form of finance. A more detailed analysis is given in the Appendix to this chapter.

The essential conclusion in the first case of borrowing at a fixed rate of interest is that there is no basic change to the analysis. The inverted U-shape of the valuation curve is retained, and under some assumptions, the decision on the amount of fixed interest borrowing can be separated from the decision on the growth rate.

In balanced-growth models, the debt of the firm grows at the same rate as the capital stock of the firm and as the shareholders' interest in the firm. So the extent of debt finance does not change over time. The valuation ratio for the firm becomes

$$v = \frac{(\pi - g) + d(g - j)}{1 - d} \cdot \frac{1 + i}{i - g}$$

where d is the 'gearing' of the firm (that is, the ratio of fixed interest debt to the capital employed by the firm), and j the rate of interest at which the firm can borrow. This rate, j, may be an increasing function of d, reflecting an increasing risk for the lenders as a firm increases its lending. The fixed interest payments have to be met out of the profits of the firm, and the greater the borrowing the greater the probability that in a bad year there will not be sufficient profits to meet the interest payments. The rate of discount applied by the market to this firm may also be an increasing function of the gearing ratio of the firm, again reflecting increasing risk as d increases. If, at least, one of these were not the case, then the firm could increase its valuation ratio indefinitely by shifting into debt finance, since as d moves towards unity, v becomes infinitely large.

For a particular value of the firm's gearing, say d^*, a valuation curve is determined. This valuation curve will have the same basic inverted U-shape as the no-debt valuation curve did. The analysis which was provided above for the no-debt case will carry through here provided two conditions are satisfied. First, the gearing of the firm, d, does not enter the utility function of the managers. It could be argued, for example, that a high gearing was more risky than a low gearing, and for that reason the managers preferred a low gearing, other things being equal. Second, the optimal gearing for the firm (in terms of that which yields the highest valuation ratio) must be independent of the growth rate chosen. This would occur if the valuation ratio curves of any two gearing ratios, say, d_1 and d_2, do not intersect. In figure 7.6, two valuation curves have been drawn which do not intersect. It can then be seen that whatever growth rate is chosen by the firm, the same gearing ratio (in this case d_2) would be chosen.

If, however, these two conditions are not satisfied, then the analysis becomes more complicated but the basic conclusions are not changed.

The possibility of new share issue as a source of finance can be shown to not be an effective one, at least in the context of balanced growth models of the firm. There are two strands to this argument. First, for a given growth rate, the relative use of internal finance and new share issue as a source of finance for investment can be shown to have no impact on the valuation ratio. Second, the firm is able to raise all the finance which it needs for any feasible growth rate from internal finance.

These conclusions are derived in a very limited context, namely of a firm

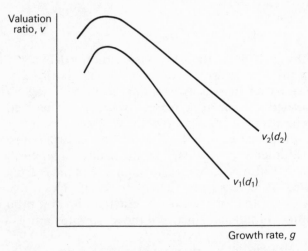

figure 7.6   Two valuation ratio curves for different gearing ratios

experiencing (and expected to experience) balanced growth, and in a world where there are no differential taxes as between dividends, retained profits, and capital gains and no uncertainty.

The 'irrelevance' of the source of finance here is an application of the theorem of Modigliani and Miller (1958), and the proof is outlined in the Appendix to this chapter. But the argument can be thought of in the following terms. Suppose that a firm was seeking to expand its capital base (its book value) by 10 per cent. What profit would it need to earn to maintain its current valuation ratio? Whether it raises the finance from its current shareholders by retaining profits, or by issuing new shares, the answer is the same. It has to increase profits by 10 per cent. Further, internal finance cannot finance a growth rate of more than the rate of profit, and with the 'irrelevance' of the source of finance it follows that new share issue cannot either. Thus the rate of profit sets an upper limit to the rate of growth of the firm.

These lines of argument indicate that the analysis can be restricted to the internal finance only case without any loss of generality and with some gain in analytical convenience.[17]

In this theory the shareholders' interests are identified with the valuation ratio, and by extension it is often argued that an owner-controlled firm would seek to operate at M in figure 7.5. But an owner whose interests were related to the eventual size of the firm would not operate in this manner. For example, an owner whose main preoccupation was the value of the firm on his retirement to provide him with a prosperous retirement or whose concern was with the size of his bequest to his children would be interested in size at some future date, and this would lead to some emphasis on growth. Indeed, an owner-controlled firm would be able to place more emphasis on growth than a manager-controlled firm since the owner-controlled firm is not threatened by take-over bids in that it can decide whether such a bid would be accepted. It would not be, as a manager-controlled firm would, in the hands of others (i.e. its shareholders).

The take-over in this model is a hostile act which is threatened on a reluctant victim. Where (as often seems the case) acquisitions and take-overs are by mutual consent of the parties involved, the threat to the managers' security posed by the take-over bid is absent.

The take-over process can also be viewed from the acquiring firm's side. As far as their motives are concerned, little can be said. The acquiring firm could be a profit or market value-maximiser who sees the opportunity presented by a low valuation ratio to enhance his profits. But that firm could be a growth-maximiser who sees the opportunity for fast growth at low cost. As far as the growth-maximizer is concerned, he would wish to generate as much growth as possible from a given pool of finance, and a low valuation ratio would offer the possibility of acquiring capital assets at $1/v$ of their book value.[18]

7.6   Comparison of theories based on growth and profit maximization

One way of discriminating between the theories based on profit maximization and those based on managerial motivation would be to try to make predictions about how the different types of firm would react in certain circumstances, and then to seek to test these predictions in practice. One major difficulty with such a procedure is that whilst it is possible to test the hypothesis that all firms maximize profits against the hypothesis that all firms follow some particular managerial theory, it is more difficult if the proposition is that some firms follow one path and other firms follow another path, for then the firms have to be presorted into their appropriate category. However, the immediate problem is to find ways of effectively distinguishing between the theories. Here, we try to do this in terms of the profit maximization theory and a variant of the theory of Marris, following the approach of Solow (1971). An alternative, but basically similar approach is contained in J H Williamson (1966). The variant of the theory of Marris which is used is that which treats the firm as seeking to maximize its growth rate subject to the constraint that its valuation ratio is maintained at a level which avoids any threat of a take-over.

There is a further reason for pursuing the comparison of different approaches. It is that in doing so a more formal presentation of the models themselves is necessary.

A fundamental point must be made at the outset. In considering long-run behaviour, particularly when the pursuit of growth is involved, the analytically easiest method to adopt is that of working with steady-state growth outcomes. That is to say (in this context) firms make decisions on prices, output, advertising or whatever in the initial period. Once those decisions are made, they become frozen through time. The variables (such as profits, capital stock) which grow (or decline) over time as a result, directly or indirectly, of the decisions made by the firm do so at a constant rate. So that a firm which strives to maximize growth of sales is interpreted as making decisions which generate the maximum growth of sales, say g_s, (subject to the constraints imposed on the firm) in the initial time period, and thereafter sales grow in every time span at this rate g_s.

A supplementary problem arises in the context of the theory of the firm, which is concerned with the relationship between the growth rate of the firm (say, g_f) and the growth rate of the economy (say, g_e). The logical extension of the steady-state growth approach is that any growth rate persists to eternity. Then if $g_f > g_e$, by the power of geometric growth rates, the firm will exceed, at some stage, any preassigned proportion of the size of the economy; conversely, if $g_f < g_e$ the firm will eventually decline to insignificance within the economy. Under the former case, the economy will find its growth rate pulled up towards g_f, and the firm cannot be treated as 'small' and its impact on the whole economy would have to be taken into account. So in this type of analysis, the assumption is that such an occurrence is a long way off, and that it can be ignored for the present purposes.

In devising a model, assumptions need to be made about the demand and cost conditions facing the firm. In the work of Solow, the demand conditions are expressed by $p = Q^{-1/n}$ (with p as price, Q as quantity) in the initial period, with n being the constant price elasticity of demand. Over the future, demand grows at a rate which is determined by the sales effort of the firm, subject to minimum growth rate (g_{min}) from no sales effort, which is linked to the growth rate of the economy and the income elasticity of demand for the firm's product. In other words, demand grows at rate $g(s)$, where s is the firm's sales expenditure, with $g(0) = g_{min}$.[19]

On the cost side, it is assumed that inputs are required in fixed proportions, which simplifies the analysis by not requiring consideration of the choice of techniques of production. Further, it is assumed that there are constant returns to scale. If, in contrast, the assumption were made that there were decreasing returns to scale, then the initial size of the firm and its subsequent growth would be dominated by cost considerations and motivation would have little role to play. In particular, Solow assumes that one unit of capital can be bought for m pounds, is subject to evaporative depreciation at the rate f per unit of time, and provides capacity to produce b units of output. Since labour and other current inputs are required in fixed amounts (per unit of output) and are purchased at constant prices, we can summarize current costs by setting them equal to a/b pounds per unit of output. With fixed input proportions, the growth rate of all inputs (including capital), output and sales become the same, so that we can talk of the growth rate of the firm without needing to specify which variable is measuring growth.

The value of the firm is taken as determined in the current instance by discounting future expected dividends. In any time t in the future, output is expected to be $Q_0 e^{gt}$, where Q_0 is the initial output level, and g the growth rate. Sales revenue will be $p \cdot Q_0 e^{gt}$, and from the demand conditions this can be written $Q_0^{1-1/n} e^{gt}$, which is abbreviated with obvious notation to

$Q_0^\theta e^{gt}$. The firm's production costs are $(a+mf)K_0 e^{gt}$, where the first part of the expression is the cost of non-capital inputs, and the second part is the depreciation of the capital stock, which had an initial size K_0. Before arriving at the dividends, the.firm finances future expansion out of profits (that is, sales revenue minus production costs). Future expansion has two types of costs. There are the costs of expanding demand through sales promotion, and this takes a fraction $s(g)$ of sales revenue. There is an underlying growth of demand (linked, say, to the growth of the economy) g_{min}, so that $s(g_{min}) = 0$. But it is expected that $ds(g)/dg > 0$ and $d^2 s(g)/dg^2 > 0$ so that these costs of growth increase at an increasing rate with higher growth rates. The other cost of expansion is new capital investment, which with fixed input proportions amounts to gK units of investment at total cost of mgK.[20] Thus, here production costs and expansion costs are separated out. In the analysis of Marris discussed above, expansion costs other than fixed investment and production costs were combined. The assumption in that analysis that $d\pi/dg < 0$ is equivalent to the assumption here that $ds/dg > 0$.

Now dividends equal profits minus finance for expansion, which gives dividends $= (b^\theta K_0 - (a+mf)K_0)e^{gt} - s(g)b^\theta K_0^\theta - mgK_0 e^{gt}$, i.e. $[(1-s(g)]b^\theta K_0^\theta - [a+m(f+g))K_0]e^{gt}$, which is written as $Z_0 e^{gt}$ for convenience in any time period t. The value of the firm is the discounted value of this dividend stream i.e. $\int_0^\infty Z_0 e^{gt} e^{-it} dt$ with i as the discount rate, which gives $V = Z_0/i - g$. For a positive and finite value of V to result, we can either assert that $i > g$ or that Z_0 becomes zero for some value of g which is less than i.[21]

The value of the firm is clearly a function of its initial scale K_0 and its growth rate g. These two variables are taken as the decision variable of the firm and it can be checked out that when the value of these two variables has been determined the value of all the other variables also become determinate.

When the alternative decision criteria and the impact on the behaviour of the firm are considered, we are faced with a severe problem in the case of the growth-orientated firm. If it has discretion over its original size, then in order to maximize growth, it would choose an infinitesimally small initial size and then grow dramatically. This does not correspond with the flavour of the managerial theories, which are intended to apply to firms who are already large with the consequent divorce between ownership and control. All that can be done is to assume that the initial size (and in particular K_0) is a datum. Once that is done, the following paradoxical situation arises. With K determined at K_0, the initial level of output (and hence price) becomes determined. Price is assumed set forever, so that it remains constant whilst output and capital grow in the future at whatever rate the firm decides. But with these initial values determined, the profits of the firm also become determined at $b^\theta K_0^{\cdot} - (a + mf)K_0$, no matter what the motives of the firm are. Reported profits may differ depending on the accounting practice used in reporting expenditure to promote future sales.[22] However, this result can be interpreted as follows. The firm having a pool of resources at its disposal (its profits) has to decide how these resources are divided out between the interests of the shareholders (proxied here by current dividends) and the interests of the managers (proxied here by retained earnings to finance future growth).

The growth-maximizer will pursue a growth rate at least as high as that of the value-maximizer, so that dividends and market value will be lower in the former case. But the higher growth rate of the growth-maximizer applies to dividends as well as capital, output, etc., so that at some time in the future the dividends of the growth-maximizer will overtake those of the value-maximizer, as will the value of the firm evaluated at some future date.

In order to be able to compare the value-maximizer and the growth-maximizer, the initial scale of operation is taken as given and g becomes the decision variable for the firm. For the value-maximizer, the condition $dv/dg = 0$ is required. From

$$V = \frac{Z_0}{i-g} \text{ we have } \frac{dv}{dg} = \frac{1}{(i-g)^2}\left[\frac{\partial Z_0}{\partial g}(i-g) + Z_0\right] = 0$$

with

$$Z_0 = [1 - s(g)]b^\theta K_0^\theta - [a + m(f+g)]K_0 \text{ and } \frac{\partial Z_0}{\partial g} = -\frac{ds(g)}{dg}b^\theta K_0^\theta - mK_0.$$

Manipulation yields

$$\frac{a - s(g) + (i-g)(-ds/dg)}{a + m(f+i)} = b^{-\theta}K_0^{1/n} = A$$

where A is a constant, and $n = 1/1 - \theta$ as before. The growth rate derived from this equation labelled g_v is the rate which maximizes the value of the firm.

For the growth-maximizer, with the take-over constraint binding so that the valuation ratio $v = \bar{v}$ (the level of the ratio at which a take-over is just avoided), we have $V = \bar{v}mK_0$. Combining this with $V = Z_0/i - g$, after manipulation we arrive at

$$\frac{1 - s(g)}{a + m[f + \bar{v}i + (1 - \bar{v})g]} = b^{-\theta}K_0^{1/n} = A.$$

The solution to this is labelled g_g and is the constrained maximum of the growth rate.

From these not very illuminating equations for g_v and g_g the responses of firms to changes in the parameters of this equation can be worked out. Solow provides an analysis of changes in the growth rate in the two cases consequent upon changes in price of capital goods, rate of discount, excise tax, and tax on profits. In all cases the qualitative change is the same for the two types of firm, although the quantitative change will differ. But to distinguish between the two types of firm on the basis of the quantitative changes will be very difficult since the size of change depends upon a number of parameters and functions whose values are very unlikely to be known.

As an illustration of this proposition, the case of a change in an excise tax on sales is taken. The above model must first be slightly amended to allow for an excise tax on sales at a rate z. Sales revenue (but not current or capital costs) are scaled down by a factor $(1-z)$. So that for the value-maximizer, the condition from immediately above now becomes

$$(1-z)\frac{[1-s(g)]+(i-g)(-ds/dg)}{a+m(f+i)} = A$$

and for the constrained growth-maximizer, the condition becomes

$$(1-z)\frac{1-s(g)}{a+m[f+\bar{v}i+(1-\bar{v})g]} = A.$$

The only decision variable is the growth rate, and to see how that would change for a change in the rate of excise tax, we calculate dg/dz for the two cases. For the value-maximizer, denoting the growth rate by g_v, we have

$$\frac{dg_v}{dz} = \frac{[1-s(g_v)]+(i-g_v)[-ds(g_v)/dg]}{(1-z)[-d^2s(g_v)/d^2g](i-g_v)}$$

and by substitution from above

$$\frac{dg_v}{dz} = \frac{A[a+m(f+i)]}{(1-z)^2(i-g_v)[-d^2s/dg^2(g_v)]}.$$

For the growth-maximizer, denoting the chosen growth path by g_g, we have

$$\frac{dg_g}{dz} = \frac{1-s(g_g)}{(1-z)(-ds(g_g)/dg)-Am(I-\bar{v})}$$

and again by substitution from above this equals

$$\frac{A(a+m(f+\bar{v}i+(1+\bar{v})g)}{(1-z)((1-z)(-s(g_g)-Am(1-v)))}.$$

Forming the ratio

$$\frac{dg_v}{dz}\bigg/\frac{dg_g}{dz}=\frac{a+m(f+i)}{a+m(f+\bar{v}i)+(1-\bar{v})g}\ \frac{(i-g_v)(d^2s/dg^2)(g_v)}{ds(g_g)/dg+Am(1-\bar{v})}$$

indicates that the two kinds of firm respond in qualitatively similar ways to changes in the excise tax, since this ratio is positive.

It can be tentatively concluded from this approach that if our interest is in making qualitative predictions about responses from firms to changes in taxes, interest rates, etc., then these different models are likely to give similar answers. Our conclusions must be tentative because of the highly simplified model which has been used. However, our interest might be in the size of the growth rates which result from different types of firms. An inspection of figure 7.7 indicates that the difference in the growth rate of a value-maximizer (operating at point M) and a growth-maximizer (operating at point H) depends upon the slope of the valuation curve and the extent to which the minimum valuation ratio (V_{min}) needed to avoid a take-over fall below the maximum.

This chapter has outlined three theories of the firm based on the idea that there is a separation of ownership from control in a large firm. The next chapter deals with theories which additionally drop the notion that firms are maximizers.

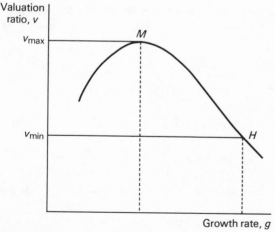

figure 7.7

appendix to chapter 7

7.7 An extension to Williamson model

The model of O. E. Williamson discussed in the text was based on the assumption that the profit constraint was not binding. Here that assumption is relaxed.

The firm is assumed to maximize $U(S,M,D)$ subject $D \geq 0$ where $D = (1-t)$ $(P(X,S)X - C(X) - S - M) - \pi_0$ is the discretionary profits; the symbols are those used in the main text. Setting up the Lagrangian $V(S,M,D,\lambda)$ $= U(S,M,D) + \lambda D$ from the Kuhn-Tucker theorem[1], the first-order conditions are

$$\frac{\partial V}{\partial S} \leq 0 \quad \frac{\partial V}{\partial M} \leq 0 \quad \frac{\partial V}{\partial X} \leq 0 \quad \frac{\partial V}{\partial \lambda} \geq 0$$

$$S\frac{\partial V}{\partial S} = 0 \quad M\frac{\partial V}{\partial M} = 0 \quad X\frac{\partial V}{\partial X} = 0 \quad \lambda\frac{\partial V}{\partial \lambda} = 0.$$

We shall assume that some output, staff and emoluments are necessary for any operation so that X, S and M are not zero. Then we have $\partial V/\partial S = 0$, $\partial V/\partial M = 0$ and $\partial V/\partial X = 0$.

Writing these in full, we have

$$U_1 + U_3(1-t)\left(\frac{\partial R}{\partial S} - 1\right) + \lambda(1-t)\left(\frac{\partial R}{\partial S} - 1\right) = 0 \qquad (1)$$

$$U_2 + U_3(1-t)(-1) + \lambda(1-t)(-1) = 0 \qquad (2)$$

$$U_3(1-t)\left(\frac{\partial R}{\partial X} - \frac{\partial C}{\partial X}\right) + (1-t)\left(\frac{\partial R}{\partial X} - \frac{\partial C}{\partial X}\right) = 0. \qquad (3)$$

From $\lambda(\partial V/\partial \lambda) = 0$, we have $\lambda.D = 0$, and then either $\lambda = 0$ or $D = 0$ (or both).

The analysis of Williamson essentially assumes that $D \neq 0$, so that $\lambda = 0$. The substitution of $\lambda = 0$ in the above conditions will yield the equations in the text. If $\lambda \neq 0$ so that $D = 0$, from equations 2 and 3 we have

$$U_2 = (U_3 + \lambda)(1 - t)$$

$$0 = (1 - t)(U_3 + \lambda)\left(\frac{\partial R}{\partial X} - \frac{\partial C}{\partial X}\right) = U_2\left(\frac{\partial R}{\partial X} - \frac{\partial C}{\partial X}\right).$$

Since $U_2 \neq 0$, $\partial R / \partial X = \partial C / \partial X$. This condition that the marginal revenue of production equals its marginal cost is the same as that derived for the unconstrained case.

From equation 1, we get that

$$\frac{\partial R}{\partial S} = \frac{-U_1}{(U_3 + \lambda)(1 - t)} + 1$$

and since $\lambda > 0$, $\partial R / \partial S < 1$.

Although the equation for $\partial R / \partial S$ differs from the one for the unconstrained case, the conclusion that $\partial R / \partial S < 1$ applies in both cases. Since unity is the price of S in this model, this condition is that marginal revenue of staff is less than its marginal cost.

7.8   Extensions to Marris model

Further analysis of the model of Marris is now outlined first for the case where fixed interest debt is used and then for the case when new shares are issued to finance new investment.

The fixed-interest debt case
The book value of the firm is K, which is financed by shareholders to the extent of S and by debt to the extent of D, so that $D + S = K$, with gearing $d = D/K$. Profits before interest payments are P, and the firm's earnings are $E = P - j.D$ where j is the rate of interest on debt. The rate of profit π is P/K. New investment, DK, is financed by an increase in the shareholders' interest DS, and by an increase in debt DD. Thus $DK = DS + DD$.

With balanced growth at a rate g, we have $DK = gK$, $DS = rE$ (retention ratio times earnings) and $DD = gD$ and hence $gK = rE + gD$. Dividends $= (1 - r)E = (1 - r)(P - jD)$. The market value of the firm is

$$(1 - r) \sum_{t=0}^{\infty} \frac{P_t - jD_t}{(1 + i)^t} = (1 - r)(P_0 - jD_0) \sum_{t=0}^{\infty} \frac{(1 + g)^t}{(1 + i)^t} = (1 - r)(P_0 - jD_0)\frac{1 + i}{i - g}$$

where the suffix 0 indicates the variable in the initial period.

The valuation ratio

$$v = \frac{\text{Market Value}}{S_0} = (1-r)\frac{P_0 - jD_0}{S_0} \cdot \frac{(1+i)}{i-g}.$$

Since

$$\frac{P_0}{S_0} = \frac{P_0}{K_0}\frac{K_0}{S_0} = \frac{\pi}{1-d}, \quad \frac{D_0}{S_0} = \frac{d}{1-d},$$

we have

$$v = (1-r)\frac{\pi - jd}{1-d}\cdot\frac{1+i}{i-g}.$$

From the financing equation, we have $g(K-D) = rE$ and then

$$r = \frac{g(1-D/K)}{E/K} = \frac{g(1-d)}{\pi - jd}.$$

By substitution for r, we arrive at

$$v = \frac{(\pi - g) + d(g-j)}{1-d} \cdot \frac{(1+i)}{(i-g)}.$$

As indicated in the main text, i and j may be functions of d, with di/dd and dj/dd non-negative.

Thus $v = v(g,d)$. If managers seek to maximize $U(v,g)$ subject to $v = v(g,d)$ with respect to g and d, the first-order conditions are:

$$\frac{\partial U}{\partial g} = \frac{\partial U}{\partial v}\frac{\partial v}{\partial g} + \frac{\partial U}{\partial g} = 0, \quad \text{i.e.} \quad \frac{\partial v}{\partial g} = \frac{-\partial U/\partial g}{\partial U/\partial v}$$

$$\frac{\partial U}{\partial d} = \frac{\partial U}{\partial v}\frac{\partial v}{\partial d} = 0$$

and since $\partial U/\partial v > 0$ (that is, utility increases with the valuation ratio), this implies $\partial v/\partial d = 0$. The first-order condition, for a given value of d, generates a condition analogous to that generated in the no-debt issue case. The second condition yields, for a given growth rate, the gearing which leads to the highest valuation ratio for the given growth rate. If the optimum gearing is independent of the growth rate, then that given value of the gearing, say d^*, can be inserted in the formula for the valuation ratio, and an analysis very similar to the no-debt case carries through.

The new share issue case
If M is the market value of the firm, and m the rate of increase of the number of shares in the firm, then the finance raised by share issue in one period is

mM. The financing of investment leads to the equation $DK = DS + mM$, so that $gK = rP + mM$, using the same notation as in the first part above. Dividing through by K gives $g = r\pi + mv$, since $v = M/K$, and from this $r = g - mv/\pi$. The new shares are assumed to be issued at the beginning of each period to finance the investment during that period. Thus at the beginning of the period 0, the initial shareholders' shares have been augmented by the first new share issue. In any period t in the future, total dividends are expected to be $(1-r)P_0(1+g)^t$. But the number of shares will have grown by a factor $(1+m)^{t+1}$, and so in period t, the dividends accruing to the initial shareholders will be

$$\frac{(1-r)P_0(1+g)^t}{(1+m)^{t+1}}.$$

The discounted value of these dividends provides the present value, i.e.

$$\frac{(1-r)P}{(1+m)} \sum_{t=0}^{\infty} \left[\frac{1+g}{(1+m)(1+i)}\right]^t \text{ which gives } \frac{(1-r)P(1+i)}{i+m+im-g}.$$

The valuation ratio is then

$$v = \frac{\pi(1-r)(1+i)}{i+m+im-g}.$$

Substituting for r from above gives $v = (\pi - g)(1+i)/i - g$, so that the division of finance between retentions and new issues does not affect v.

If the firm wishes to increase its growth rate, can it finance it? From $g = r\pi + mv$, after substitution for v, we have

$$g = \frac{\pi[r(i-g)+m(1+i)]}{i+m+im-g}.$$

Then

$$\frac{\partial g}{\partial r} = \frac{\pi(i-g)}{i+m+im-g} > 0$$

and

$$\frac{\partial g}{\partial m} = \frac{\pi}{(i+m+im-g)^2}$$

$$[(i+m+im+g)(1+i)-(r(i-g)+m(1+i))(1+i)]$$

$$= \frac{\pi(1+i)}{(i+m+im-g)^2} \cdot (i-g)(1-r) > 0$$

provided that $r < 1$.

So that an increase in either the retentions or new share issue would enable the growth rate to be raised, provided that $r < 1$. When $r = 1$, $g = \pi$, and $\partial g / \partial m = 0$. Thus the maximum growth rate of the firm is equal to the rate of profit, and it is not possible to grow faster than that. Up to that rate of growth, any finance can be obtained by retained earnings.

chapter 8
behavioural theories of the firm

8.1 Satisficing

The theories of the firm examined in the first part of the book viewed the firm as an entrepreneur who wanted to maximize profits and was able to do so. That view of the firm can be disputed, and it can be argued that firms are large organizations, and as such are not merely an entrepreneur magnified several fold. For a firm run by a single entrepreneur who receives any residual profit himself is likely to be a rather different animal from a firm which employs a large number of people and is controlled by individuals who do not have the title to any residual profits. The theories examined in the last chapter were developed as a response to the idea that the typical firm (at least in terms of the type of firm which produced the bulk of the economy's output) was now of the latter form. The theories which are examined in this chapter can also be seen in that light, but additionally place more emphasis on the large organization facet of the large corporation than the managerial theories did.

One of the first ideas which emerges from looking at the firm as a large organization is that it is difficult to talk of the objectives of a firm. Individuals can have objectives, and individuals in control of a firm may impose their objectives on the firm; this would be the underlying assumption of the preceding theories. If, however, the firm is seen as a coalition of groups with conflicting interests the picture changes. The impact of that view emerges in two ways. Firstly, whilst a small group of 'top' managers may still be taking the crucial decisions, the information on which those decisions are made and the implementation of the decisions may depend upon the actions of various other groups. In particular, groups may seek to supply information which points to a decision favourable to themselves; they may, within a certain range, more or less cooperate in the implementation of decisions.[1] Secondly, the conflicting groups may have their own representatives on, say, the board of directors and the decisions made by the board may then reflect the outcome of the battle between the various groups and their representatives.

One can think of the personnel, sales, and production divisions having conflicting interests in terms of the internal allocation of resources and also over the setting of prices, investment, etc. Then if the board of directors has the personnel manager, sales manager, and production manager as members, the conflict between the groups may be resolved at that level.

In these circumstances, it becomes difficult to talk of the objectives of the firm, or even of the board of directors. Its apparent objectives will change with changes in the objectives of the different groups and their relative power within the firm. This view of the firm points towards replacing the idea of maximization by the notion of 'satisficing' (that is, the organization aiming for a satisfactory, rather than an optimal, outcome). If we cannot talk of the firm's objectives, then we cannot talk of the maximization of objectives. But groups within the firm are assumed to have their own objectives, and hence it is possible to talk of those groups seeking to maximize their own objectives. However, it is likely that maximization attempts by each group would heighten the conflict between the groups, and full maximization by one group is unlikely to be attainable. It is rather more likely that the interests of the competing groups could be mutually reconciled if each was prepared to live with an acceptable outcome. This view is usually expressed under the heading of 'satisficing'.

The general notion of satisficing is that 'the motive to act stems from drives, and action terminates when the drive is satisfied. Moreover, the conditions for satisfying a drive are not necessarily fixed, but may be specified by an aspiration level that itself adjusts upward or downward on the basis of experience' (Simon (1959) p. 10).

Thus, if an economic agent is a satisficer, then provided the situation is regarded as satisfactory, the agent will not seek to make any changes to the situation. But the agent's idea of what is satisfactory may gradually change, particularly in the light of what appears to be possible. When a situation is not satisfactory, then effort is made to find changes which would lead to a satisfactory outcome. On the other hand, a maximizing agent would continue to make changes until the situation is reached which maximizes its interests. The extent of the difference between the two types of economic agent will depend upon how far what is satisfactory departs from the maximizing outcome.

Even when the firm is viewed as having objectives itself, the notion of satisficing may still be applicable. It can also be noted that the idea of satisficing runs at variance with the general view in economic theory that there is no satiation level which could place an upper limit on a maximization process. This is particularly so for consumer theory based on utility maximization, where one of the key assumptions is that of non-satiety, i.e. more of a good always yields an increase in utility.

In the context of the theory of the firm, there are two central questions, and we will return to these in Chapter 10. They are, firstly, how fast do the aspirations adjust to the attainable, and in particular do they adjust quickly to the maximum level so that individuals may believe themselves to be satisficing but are actually maximizing; secondly, what impact on the attainable is imposed by factors external to the firm, particularly the market environment within which the firm operates.

Another angle on the general view of satisficing is that a decision which would maximize the interests of the firm (whatever they were) would involve the collection of costly information by the firm, some of which (such as the response of rivals) may be unobtainable. The reaction to such a situation may be the adoption of rules of thumb such as 'fix advertising budget as x per cent of forecast sales', in contrast to making a maximizing calculation. These rules of thumb reinforce the satisficing view in two respects. Firstly, they may be cast in satisficing terms, such as price to obtain a satisfactory profit margin (and this particular view will be explored in more detail shortly). Secondly, the firm may be prepared to operate with its rules of thumb so long as they generate satisfactory outcomes, with the proviso that drastic action is likely to be taken if they no longer generate satisfactory outcomes, e.g. because there is a change in the market conditions leading to a sharp fall in sales/profits.

8.2   Full-cost pricing

We take as a simple example of satisficing the theory of full-cost pricing, which is generally associated with Hall and Hitch (1939).

This theory can be viewed as an elementary application of the notion of satisficing, although the development of that theory predates the use of the term 'satisficing'. Full-cost pricing can also be viewed as part of a family of theories which include target rate-of-return pricing and cost-plus pricing, and which see the level of prices as closely linked to costs.

The idea of full-cost pricing was developed by Hall and Hitch as a generalization of answers to a questionnaire answered by thirty-eight businessmen. The paper outlining the idea was later published as part of a collection of papers on the price mechanism, which shared a common theme that economic agents did not behave in the optimizing manner portrayed by economic theory.

The notion of full-cost pricing was expressed by Hall and Hitch (1939) as:

'price (is) based on full average cost (including a conventional allowance for profit)', and full average cost is determined as follows:

> 'prime (or 'direct') cost per unit is taken as the base, a percentage addition is made to cover overheads (or 'oncost' or 'indirect' cost), and a further conventional addition (frequently 10 per cent) is made for profit. Selling costs commonly and interest on capital rarely are included in overheads; when not so included they are allowed for in the addition for profits'.

Six basic reasons are given why firms follow this practice, and these are of some interest in relation to our earlier and later discussions. The six reasons are:

(i)   Producers cannot know their demand or marginal revenue curve because they do not know consumers' preferences and/or they are oligopolists who do not know the reactions of their rivals.

(ii) The firms do not know, but fear, that a price cut would be matched by their rivals.

(iii) The firms do not know, but fear, that a price rise would not be followed by their rivals.

(iv) Firms believe that the elasticity of demand for the products of the group of firms is inelastic, so that price lowering would be unprofitable for the group as a whole.

(v)   Prices are not raised much above the full-cost level because it is thought that this would lead to new entry into the industry in the long run.

(vi) Changes in price are frequently costly, a nuisance to salesmen, and disliked by consumers.

The first reason is a general one for firms being unable to maximize profits even if they wished to do so; it is a view expressed by, *inter alia*, Simon (1959) in his exposition of satisficing. The second and third reasons were used by Sweezy (1939) to develop the kinked demand curve theory (discussed in Chapter 4), and indeed the publication by Hall and Hitch predates Sweezy by three months.[2] The fifth reason can be linked up with the notion of limit pricing discussed in Chapter 5, and indeed the profit margin developed under that theory could serve as the conventional profit margin used in full-cost pricing.

It can be noted that some of the reasons put forward ((ii), (iii), and (vi)) point toward price stability. The full-cost principle by itself does not lead to price stability. Under profit maximization when the costs of making price changes are not considered, the condition of marginal revenue equal to marginal cost would require price and output changes whenever demand or cost conditions changed. But, at a general level, the same would be true for full-cost pricing. A change in demand would mean that at the prevailing price, there would be a change in the quantity demanded and supplied. As quantity changes, the 'prime' costs of the firm would change. Similarly a change in costs of inputs would lead to a change in price. Thus, by itself, full-cost pricing does not lead to price stability. But some of the reasons given by Hall and Hitch for full-cost pricing (and listed above) would indicate delays in adjusting price to the full cost. However, profit maximization (or any other approach) when price changes are costly would also lead to infrequent price changes.

The rule of thumb aspect of full-cost pricing would develop out of reasons (v) and (vi). If there are a large number of products produced by a firm, then the calculation of the profit-maximizing sector of prices could be extremely expensive, especially when the cross-elasticity of demand between the products, the reactions of rivals, etc., is taken into account.

There are three topics concerned with full-cost pricing which need to be examined. First, the level of output for which the costs are calculated has not been specified. In figure 8.1, we have drawn a conventional U-shaped cost curve, and above it the 'full cost' curve which indicates the price charged for any given output. One can see that unless the firm makes its calculations for output q_1 to arrive at price p_1, then the amount demanded (and presumably supplied) will be different from that used in the cost calculations. For example, if output q_2 is used, price p_2 is calculated, which leads to a demand

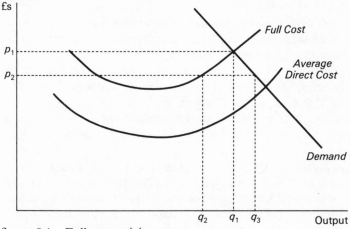

figure 8.1   Full-cost pricing

of q_3. Viewed in this manner, there would again be a gradual movement toward an equilibrium at (p_1, q_1).

Although not part of the original formulation, two alternatives to this problem have been suggested. The first one draws upon much empirical work done on the nature of short-run cost conditions facing a firm which has concluded that cost curves are often horizontal over the range of output where firms typically operate.[3] Then cost curves look more like the one portrayed in figure 8.2 than that given in figure 8.1. In such a case, the level of output for which the calculation of full cost is made may be immaterial.

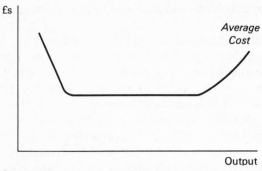

figure 8.2

A second alternative, which links in more closely with the ideas on price stability, is that the costs are calculated for a 'normal' level of output, which can be thought of as the level of output which the firm thought would be produced on average when the plant was built.[4] Thus, reverting back to figure 8.1, if the firm thought that q_1 would be the normal level, then it would price at p_1 and not change that price when the demand curve shifted, but allow output to bear the adjustment process.

A second area of concern with full-cost pricing, as well as with some of the other satisficing theories, lies with the question of what happens if the target is unobtainable (in this case, if the conventional margin for profit is not possible). For example, in figure 8.3, with the demand curve below the full-cost line, the firm could not obtain the full-cost price, but as drawn there, could cover direct costs.

Thirdly, comparisons with other models can be made. Profit maximization yields a price which is equal to (marginal cost)/$(1 - 1/e)$, where e is the elasticity of demand and where the elasticity of demand used here may incorporate the firm's beliefs about the reactions of its rivals to a price change. It can be seen that if the firm perceives the elasticity of demand as not changing over time (which may be quite a reasonable assumption), then price will follow marginal cost. Further, if the firm perceives its cost curves as having the shape portrayed in figure 8.2, then over a wide range average and marginal costs will be equal, and then price would follow average cost. Thus, under not implausible assumptions from profit-maximizing conditions, a pricing rule is generated which looks deceptively like the full-cost-pricing rule. The major difference is that under full-cost pricing overhead costs enter into the pricing rule directly, whereas under profit maximization they do not.

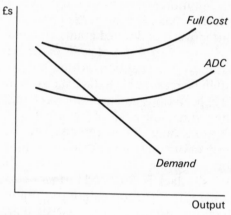

figure 8.3

Apart from theories based on profit maximization, many theories (including those examined in Chapters 5 and 7) would lead to outcomes superficially like the full-cost-pricing result, though reached by a different route. For example, under the limit pricing approach the conditions of entry into the industry and the elasticity of demand indicated a mark-up on costs for profit which would not induce entry into the industry. Provided that those conditions of entry and the elasticity of demand remain constant (or are perceived to remain constant), then the mark-up applied by the firms would remain constant. Likewise, the minimum acceptable profit in the Baumol theory of sales revenue maximization would provide an indication to the firm of the profit mark-up for which it aims. Of course, the role of the mark-up is rather different. In the full-cost pricing case it is the firm's target, with limit pricing the upper limit, which is guaranteed to avoid entry. In the sales revenue maximization case, it is the lowest profit margin which is acceptable to the shareholders.

8.3 The behavioural theory of the firm

The term 'behavioural theory of the firm' is often associated with a work by Cyert and March (1963), in which they, with a number of other contributors, outline such a theory. This approach is designed to analyse the process of decision-making within the large modern firm; this is done in terms of the variables that affect organizational goals, the variables that affect organizational expectations, and those that affect organizational choice.

Cyert and March argue 'that the goals of a business firm are a series of more or less independent constraints imposed on the organization through a process of bargaining among potential coalition members . . . Goals arise in such a form because the firm is, in fact, a coalition of participants with disparate demands, changing foci of attention, and limited ability to attend to all organizational problems simultaneously'. (p. 43). The goals of the firm change gradually over time as the nature of the coalitions within the firm changes. But in the short run, it will often be reasonable to take many of the goals of the firm as given, at least until expectations and aspirations change. The exception to the stability in the short run of the goals of the firm is when a crisis situation arises. In such cases, goals may change rapidly. This last point arises from the notion that the firm operates with some organizational slack, and that only if a crisis arises does the firm need to reduce the slack by drastic changes. The idea of organizational slack is discussed further below.

The goals which Cyert and March identify for a contemporary firm for price and output decisions are production, inventory, sales, market share, and profit. These goals are postulated in the models presented by them and one of these models is summarized below. The conflict over goals within the organization are never fully resolved for they reflect conflicts between different parts of the firm.

The choices made by the organization are argued to come about in the following manner. The criterion of choice is that the selected alternative should meet all of the demands of the coalition of conflicting interest groups within the firm. But of the alternatives which satisfy that criterion, the one chosen will tend to be the first satisfactory alternative considered, and not the one which in any sense maximizes the interests of the firm. If an existing policy satisfies the goal, there is little search made for alternatives; but when some of the goals are not satisfied there is intensive search made for an alternative which does satisfy the goals.

In the short run, the decisions made by the firm are mainly determined by the application of 'rules of thumb' and standard operating procedures.

The general approach is applied by Cyert and March to a specific case of one department in a large retail department store. This study is now outlined to indicate rather more concretely the implications of their approach. The organization makes decisions on price and output, but does so in a relatively independent manner. The two goals of the department are the sales objective and that of establishing a specified average target mark-up on the goods sold.

On the sales goal, the organization forms sales estimates that are consistent with its sales goal and develops a routine ordering plan for advance orders. As sales proceed, a feedback check on the sales objective is provided; if the sales objective is achieved, then reordering follows the standard rules. But if the goal is not reached, then a series of counter measures are taken. These measures include attempts to secure lower prices from suppliers and increased promotional budget, price reductions on goods, and search for new items to be sold at relatively low prices but with standard mark-up.

Similarly, this approach is taken with respect to the mark-up goal. If it is achieved, then no change is made. But if it is not achieved, then the department searches for ways to raise the mark-up through increased promotion, stocking of more high mark-up goods, etc.

Cyert and March provide further details on the mechanics of routine ordering and determination of the mark-up. There is not sufficient space to provide details here, but the following gives some flavour of them. The firm recognizes three pricing situations; normal, sales, and mark-down pricing. The normal pricing on standard items is set by the rule: *divide each cost by 0.6 and move the result to the nearest $0.95*. But if the good is not available to the competing local stores then the rule becomes: *calculate the standard price from the cost, then use the next highest price on the standard schedule.*

Cyert and March conclude that for the standard mark-up, this rule of thumb was able to predict correctly to the exact cent in 188 cases out of a sample of 197 prices. For sales pricing, the record was 56 correct to the exact cent out of 58 cases. For mark-down pricing, it was 140 correct out of 159.

In a follow-up study, Baumol and Stewart (1971) conclude that:

'our case study strongly suggests that the specifics of the rules of thumb do change with economic circumstances . . . More specifically, the predictive power of the original Cyert and March rules turns out to be rather less perfect than it was in the original study. Even after *ad hoc* modification in its parameters it does not achieve the degree of success which was attained by the original study. Yet the ability of the model, thus modified, to account to the penny for some 70 per cent of the price remains impressive. . . . The upshot, it seems to us, is to confirm the notion that much of routine economic decision-making does follow fairly simple rules of thumb, as the behavioral approach predicts'.

Two points arise on these pricing and output rules. First, these are not necessarily the rules actually operated by the firm, at least consciously, but are generalizations from observed behaviour. Second, there is some impingement of the external environment on the firm, through the impact of competitors (note the difference between standard pricing and exclusive goods pricing) and through mark-up revisions when sales are not up to expectations.

The example of the retail department store is likely to yield a relatively simple model as compared with one which would result from, say, a multi-product manufacturing firm. For example, the goals are reduced to two (price and sales) in this case, but may be as large as five in other cases.

8.4 X-inefficiency

A basic assumption for theories considered in earlier chapters was that, whatever the objectives of the firm, they operated with full technical efficiency. It was assumed when the cost curves of Chapter 1 were drawn that the firm bought inputs in proportions which minimized costs (for any given level of output) and converted the inputs into output in a manner which obtained the maximum output with those inputs. The realism of this was challenged by Leibenstein (1966) when he summarized evidence suggesting that typically firms did not achieve technical efficiency, and that losses from technical inefficiency (or as labelled by Leibenstein X-inefficiency) were much larger than losses from allocative inefficiencies.

In his 1966 paper, Leibenstein suggested four major reasons for the lack of X-efficiency. First, the contract for labour does not (and cannot) completely specify what is to be done by the labour hired. The hiring of labour is the hiring of time on the job, and the intensity of effort by labour is variable. Secondly, not all factors of production are marketable, so that some factors necessary for technical efficiency may not be available to the firm. In particular, there may be considerable market imperfections in the market for managers, with the qualities of a manager difficult to assess in advance. Thirdly, the production function is not completely specified nor completely known by the firm. Its previous experience and its willingness to experiment will be factors contributing to a firm's knowledge of its production function. But, if the firm does not know its production function, it may have difficulty reaching the production frontier. Fourthly, there is interdependence between firms and uncertainty about competitors' reactions. This leads to tacit cooperation and imitation between firms which, again, may prevent firms reaching the production frontier.

These are reasons for the existence of some inefficiency, but it does not indicate how much. Some limitations on the extent of inefficiency come from the pressure of competition and adversity. Competition of other firms can, by placing pressure on profit margins, restrain the degree of inefficiency. Adversity (arising from, say, a slump in demand) may trigger off efforts to reduce the extent of inefficiency. These reasons for technical inefficiency amount to little more than a list of reasons why firms are not cost-minimizers, and hence questions the notion of firms being maximizers at all.

In more recent work, Leibenstein (1975, 1976) has sought to spell out more fully the underlying theory of X-efficiency. One essential feature is that organizations (and households) are collections of individuals, each of whom has his own interests to pursue and whose contributions to the organization is variable. This line of thought was part of the underpinning of O.E. Williamson's (1964) theory and the behavioural approach. Leibenstein departs from those theories in stressing the variability of effort by the individual, rather than the mutuality (or otherwise) of individuals' interests within the organizations. Although Leibenstein seeks to go 'beyond economic man' (the title of Leibenstein (1976)), one could portray this approach as saying that each individual pursues his own interests, some of which contribute to the interests of the organization as a whole; but the individual is subject to constraints on his activities during his working hours, imposed by the organization. The 'tightness' of these constraints depends upon the nature of the job being done, the system of payment (e.g. payment by results, payment by time, etc.), and the type of organization. Two important factors in determining the tightness of the constraint are likely to be the strength of the competition in the markets where the firm operates, and its degree of success.

A number of the theories which have been considered incorporate some notion of 'organizational slack'. Firms do not operate on their production frontiers for various reasons, but could move much closer to it if forced by external events to do so. In the theory of O. E. Williamson (1964), the managers of the firm were interested in (i.e. they were arguments in their utility function) staff costs, managerial emoluments, and discretionary profits. Whilst production costs were assumed to be minimized for any given level of output, staff costs and managerial emoluments were not. Thus the organizational slack in that case, can be identified with the excess of staff costs and managerial emoluments above the necessary minimum.

Cyert and March (1965) regard organizational slack as 'payments to members of the coalition in excess of what is required to maintain the organization'. They add that

> 'many forms of slack typically exist; stockholders are paid dividends in excess of those required to keep stockholders (or banks) within the organization; prices are set lower than necessary to maintain adequate income from buyers; wages in excess of those required to maintain labor are paid, executives are provided with services and personal luxuries in excess of those required to keep them; subunits are permitted to grow without real concern for the relation between additional payments and additional revenue; public services are provided in excess of those required'.

The slack arises from the bargaining and decision process, and is not part of the objectives of the firm.

Leibenstein's degree of X-inefficiency is also closely linked to concepts of organizational slack. It arises in his theory through the pursuit of self-interest by labour, variation in effort, and incomplete monitoring of individuals.

The above indicates that whilst organizational slack has a role in each of these three approaches, and in all cases it indicates that firms respond to crisis by reducing the slack, nevertheless it occurs from rather different reasons in the three cases. For Williamson, it arises from pursuit of self-interest by managers; for Cyert and March, it arises from the nature of the bargaining process; for Leibenstein it arises essentially from effort variations. But they all point to non-minimization of costs, and so non-maximization of profits, although the theory of Williamson still leads to the minimization of production cost. The analysis of Leibenstein tends to imply that the losses through X-inefficiency to the firm are losses to society. But what are costs to the firm can often be benefits to the individual, and this comes out most clearly in the model of Williamson.[5]

The theories considered in this chapter dwell on alternative approaches to the conventional view of the firm as a maximizer. At one level, these theories can be considered as critiques of the other theories in this book which rely on firms being maximizers. But as theories in their own right, they map out a different perspective on the firm.

chapter 9

radical critique and radical alternatives

The theories of the firm considered in this chapter are rather a mixed bag of theories which share some common themes. However, they do have substantial differences and do not have the same degree of commonality as theories grouped together in previous chapters.

The theories discussed here share the view that many large firms have considerable market power, generally operating in the context of oligopoly, although they take different views on the constraints under which the firms operate. They take a rather broader approach to the firm, and tend to emphasize the impact of large firms on the economic, political, and social environment rather than focussing on price/output decisions of the firm. This means that they are not compact analytics of decision-making, but more in the nature of broad themes and ideas on the role of the firm. The objectives of the firm in these theories are various but do depart from profit maximization of the form assumed by the theories of Part One of this book. The precise role of profits does vary between the theories, sometimes acting as a constraint, sometimes playing a more central role. A final common point is that they generally take a less optimistic view of the efficiency of capitalism, and of the constraints on the power of large firms imposed by consumers and governments.

Four theories are considered. The first, usually labelled the theory of countervailing power, was put forward by J.K.Galbraith in his *American Capitalism* (Galbraith (1963)). Secondly, we look at the theory of Baran and Sweezy on *Monopoly Capital* (Baran and Sweezy (1967)). The third is taken from 'Price Theory and Oligopoly' by K.Rothchilds published in *Economic Journal* 1947. For the fourth theory we return to the writings of Galbraith on *The New Industrial State* (Galbraith 1968), which draws on a number of ideas explored in Chapter 7. In all cases we are summarizing in a short space, theories and ideas which were originally expressed at length, and inevitably some of the flavour of the original will be lost. Also, we have plucked out of these writings, ideas of interest to the theory of the firm, without paying much attention to the broader framework within which these ideas were originally presented. We hope to offset some of these losses by being able to relate these theories of the firm to each other and to the previous discussion. But our short summary cannot be a close substitute for reading the original works.

9.1   The theory of countervailing power

The central idea of the theory of countervailing power is that the emergence of oligopoly and monopoly amongst sellers has tended to induce the emergence of few buyers on the other side of the market, whose economic power counteracts the power of the few sellers. Thus a situation of bilateral monopoly or bilateral oligopoly arises. The traditional analysis of bilateral monopoly, which was outlined in Chapter 2, rested on the chance occurrence of such a situation. In contrast, Galbraith sees it as a response by one side of the market to power on the other side of the market. One reason for this would be that market power on one side of the market leads to monopoly profits for that side of the market, and that therefore the other side have an inducement to form a countervailing block to share some of those monopoly profits or to prevent themselves being exploited.

In the competitive environment, each firm is powerless. If one firm sought to charge a higher-than-competitive price it would find sales disappearing as other firms continued to charge a lower price. Thus, in this context, the power of one firm is held in check by other firms' willingness and eagerness to sell at the competitive price. With the emergence of oligopoly, cartels and monopoly, Galbraith argued that these competitive checks on a firm's power go, but tend to be replaced by countervailing power. Thus the provision of a check on the power of a single firm is transferred from its competitors to its firms or organizations on the other side of the market.

One of the features of the 'real world' which is ignored in most of the theories of the firm is that firms often sell to other firms, and not always to consumers. One way in which countervailing power emerges could be that amongst firms to whom a monopolist sells, there is a tendency towards the formation of a smaller number of firms to offset the monopoly position. And one of the main examples given by Galbraith of countervailing power is in the retail business. Large retail chains compete on prices charged to consumers, have considerable buying power, and face only a few suppliers. The presence of few suppliers, who initially were able to reap some monopoly/oligopoly profits, provides an incentive for the retailers to grow to try to combat the power of the suppliers. The producers of consumers' goods are likely to react to such a move by the retailers, and reactions could include further moves towards monopoly and extension of their activities into retailing.

The other major example given by Galbraith is in the labour market with the formation of trade unions in industries which are dominated by large firms. The strength of unions in the car, steel, rubber, and farm machinery industries where large firms predominate, is contrasted with their weakness in agriculture where small firms predominate.

9.2 Monopoly capital

The ideas of Baran and Sweezy on the theory of the firm come from their *Monopoly Capital*. Because they do not treat the firm in isolation from the rest of the economy and society (which is often done in theories of the firm), our discussion of only the motivation of firms and how they determine prices, investment etc., leads to the omission of many aspects of Baran and Sweezy's work.

Baran and Sweezy in Chapter 2 of *Monopoly Capital* focus on the role of the giant corporation, identified with the 150 or so largest firms in the economy which they are considering (the American one), who accounted for nearly half of total productive assets. The emphasis is on the giant corporation which it is believed has considerable economic power and which is accepted as the portent of the future. Baran and Sweezy accept that a managerial revolution has taken place, so that control of the giant corporation rests in the hands of management (by which they mean the board of directors and the chief executive officers). But the significance of this 'revolution' for them is rather different from that provided by the theories discussed in Chapter 7.

Primarily, Baran and Sweezy focus attention on three characteristic features of the modern corporation. Firstly, they point out that control rests with management with outside interests often represented on the board of directors to facilitate the harmonization of the interests and policies of the corporation with those of large customers, suppliers, bankers, etc. Even so, the real power is held by the 'inside' management, rather than the representative of the outside interests. Secondly, they hold that management is a self-perpetuating group and their responsibility to the majority of shareholders who do not participate in management is generally negligible. Thirdly, they maintain each corporation aims for and normally achieves financial independence through the internal generation of funds from retained profits. The corporation may still borrow from financial institutions, but it is not normally forced to do so.

They argue that corporations cannot be analysed as though they were an individual entrepreneur (such an approach was implicit in theories considered in Part One of this book). However, success for the individual manager generally comes from his promotion of the success of the corporation, and there are no conflicts of interests between managers and the corporation.

The underlying objective of the corporations (and hence the criteria by which managers are judged) is the achievement of profit. However, corporations have only limited information and are not able to achieve an absolute maximum profit as portrayed by traditional theory. Rather, the aim is the greatest increase in profits which appears possible in the given historic situation (subject to the proviso that today's increased profit does not ruin tomorrow's).

In contrast to the managerial theories, Baran and Sweezy do not see the emergence of a managerial class as changing the basic objective of the firm, which remains the reaping of profits. But the modern corporation is able to extract profits more effectively than the individual entrepreneur was able to. Technical developments, specialization within the corporation, etc., leads to the corporation being better equipped for the generation of profits than the small business.

The corporations aim for highest profits because the system within which they operate rewards profits and punishes losses. Profits may be valued in their own right or they may be the means to an end such as growth, prestige, etc. But at the motivation stage, profits take the centre of the stage.

It should be noted here (and this point will be reiterated in the next chapter), Baran and Sweezy are talking of the flow of profits in any given period. Those profits can then be divided between dividends and finance for further investment within the firm. In the context of the managerial revolution, profit maximization has been interpreted as the maximization of the present value of the firm, often equated with the present value of current and future dividends. Baran and Sweezy view the process in two stages: first, maximize (or at least obtain the largest increase in) the flow of profits; secondly, determine how these profits are distributed between retained earnings and dividends. In the latter context, Baran and Sweezy see the managers and the richer shareholders as having an interest in low dividends/high retentions, and the smaller shareholders in high dividends/low retentions. This could be interpreted as a coincidence of interest of richer shareholders and managers in promoting growth at the expense of the market value of the corporation.

The managers are interested in high retentions for many of the reasons outlined in Chapter 7, but also because they have an interest in postponing the receipt of the gains to themselves from their ownership of shares. Their ownership of shares arises partly through payment in share options, etc. and partly because they are often rich people in their own right. For tax reasons and to ensure a comfortable retirement, the postponement of some of the yield of shares until their retirement is preferred to receipt now in the form of dividends. Rich shareholders may also prefer retentions, generating capital gains, to dividends because of the lower rate of tax on capital gains as compared with the rate of tax of income.

In summary, the modern corporation is seen as a particularly efficient engine for the production of profits. The managerial revolution which helps promote the efficiency of this production may have changed the balance between dividends and retained earnings (though in which direction is not entirely clear).

9.3   Rothchilds' theory

The thrust of the approach of Rothchilds is on the determination of price under conditions of oligopoly. He recognizes that in some markets, prices are determined by the interplay of demand and supply and for those markets he accepts the analysis based on perfect competition. Rothchilds confines his attention to those industries where only a few firms dominate, and where demand/supply analysis is not appropriate. The first part of his paper provides a critique of many of the theories considered in Part One, and some of his arguments on this front will be considered in the following chapter.

There are two central features of oligopoly in Rothchilds' approach, which intertwine to produce a number of consequences. The first of these features is that oligopoly is a situation of potential warfare between the firms, although for most of the time an uneasy peace will reign. Thus, he believes, analogies from the literature on warfare may be useful. Secondly, oligopolists have some market power and are able to some extent to change the circumstances within which they operate. Thus, oligopolists do not feel that cost and demand conditions which they currently face are immutable but that they can be shifted to the advantage of the firms themselves.

A first result of these two features is that the objectives of the firm become a desire for *secure* profits. This arises under oligopoly, but not under conditions of perfect competition and monopoly. In the case of monopoly, by assumption, the firm is completely secure in its industry; in perfect competition, 'the security question is a very urgent one, the market conditions are such an overwhelming force that he cannot do anything to safeguard his position. All he can do is to try to make full use of every opportunity as it comes up'.[1] In many cases, the desire for security will lead to results which could have resulted from seeking to maximize profits. But in other cases, and Rothchilds instances the frequence of price adjustment, the two motives would lead to different conclusions. In the oligopoly case, he expects that 'price rigidity is an essential aspect of "normal" oligopolistic price strategy'. For reducing the number of price changes limits the chances of triggering off retaliatory action by rivals or stimulating new entry into the industry. Price is seen as the key parameter, rather like a crucial stronghold in battle which firms seek to hold for as long as possible, using advertising, quality changes, etc., to defend the price. But, when prices are fixed, what forces govern the level chosen? Oligopolists have some discretion and market power in setting prices, but this power can only be exercised within a range. The lower end of the range is set by the desire to avoid retaliation from competitors, and the upper end by the wish to avoid new entrants coming into the industry. Thus the upper end of the price range is similar to the notion of limit price discussed in Chapter 5. A further restriction on the price is given by the need to 'maintain the goodwill of the customer: i.e. ... maintain a protection against aggressive policies of rivals'. Then 'within these limits and the minimum which (the oligopolists) regards as essential for his continued stay in the industry, the oligopolist will try to quote that price which will promise him maximum profits.'

The desire for security and the existence of market power clearly influence the price set. But, the oligopolist looks further afield than price for security, and this provides a second consequence of the two features of oligopoly. Security may be aided by size and financial strength, so that one would expect the typical oligopolist to be 'over large', if judged by value maximization criteria. Other ways of increasing security come from extensions of the firm in both the forward and backward direction (that is forward into the output market of the firm, and backward into the input market of the firm). The forward extension particularly mentioned by Rothchilds is the use of advertising to 'immunize' consumers against rival invasion. Backward extension could involve control over supplies by vertical integration of the suppliers into the firm.

The third and final consequence is the extension of the activities of oligopolists into the political sphere. Rothchilds sums this up as 'oligopolistic struggle for position and security includes political action of all sorts right up to imperialism. The inclusion of these "non-economic" elements is essential for a full explanation of oligopoly behaviour and price'. These political activities include lobbying of government and legislature on tariffs, taxes, award of contracts etc.

9.4   The new industrial state

In many respects, the approach taken by Galbraith in *The New Industrial State* can be seen as a combination and extension of many of the ideas put forward by Marris (see Chapter 7) and Rothchilds (above).[2] One element of Marris's theory is the acceptance of the managerial revolution, and the change in objectives of the firm which that entails in the direction of maximization of growth of sales. One element of Rothchilds' theory is the great stress placed by Galbraith on the importance to, in his terminology, the 'technostructure' of independence from outside intervention and of security. In the theory of Marris, the desire for security was expressed in terms of avoidance of take-overs, whilst in the approach of Rothchilds it led to the firm seeking to control its environment. It is the last aspect which is subject to considerable extension by Galbraith, and the bulk of his book can be seen in terms of the firms seeking to control their environment, economic and political.

The theory provided by Galbraith, as was the case with Baran and Sweezy and with Rothchilds, is not intended to apply to all firms. Small firms operating in circumstances which can be reasonably described as atomistically competitive are excluded from consideration, and attention is paid to 'the world of the few hundred technically dynamic massively capitalized and highly organized corporations'.

An important concept in Galbraith's *The New Industrial State* is the technostructure. It consists of

'(those) from the most senior officials of the corporation to where it meets, at the outer perimeter, the white- and blue-collar workers whose function is to conform more or less mechanically to instruction or routine. It embraces all those who bring specialized knowledge, talent or experience to group decision-making. This, not the (top level) management is the guiding intelligence, the brain, of the enterprise' (Galbraith (1969) p. 80; words in parenthesis added).

The motivation of the technostructure is arrived at by similar arguments to those given in earlier chapters. The technostructure 'bans personal profit making', since if permitted, this would be very disruptive for the corporation. Further, profit maximization for the firm is also ruled out since the 'members of the technostructure do not get the profits that they maximize' (p. 125). Since 'the stockholders are without power, the board of directors is normally the passive instrument of the management; decisions, since complexity is usually associated with importance, are effectively the work of groups' (p. 155). Consideration is given to the various interest groups within the organization, in a manner similar to that provided by the behavioural theories of the firm. But Galbraith draws out two major interests of the technostructure. The first is for survival in order that it can preserve its autonomy, and this means that it must have a secure minimum level of profits. This minimum level provides for the traditional rate of dividends for the shareholders and a supply of finance for reinvestment. Otherwise, shareholders will seek to interfere and appeal to the outside suppliers of capital. Because it must ensure that this minimum level is achieved, the technostructure will try to avoid risk and go for safe investments.

The second interest is growth of sales, since growth 'as a goal is wholly consistent with the personal and pecuniary interests of those who participate in decisions and direct the enterprise'.

Thus, at the centre of the *New Industrial State*, there are the large corporations, run by the technostructure, and their objectives can be expressed as those which maximize growth of sales subject to earning a minimum level of profit. So far, we have an amalgam of many of the thoughts expressed in Chapters 7 and 8. But Galbraith departs from those theories when he extends the ways in which the technostructure seeks to make itself secure. The technostructure could be threatened by sudden shifts in demand, in supply, and in the prices which it charges or faces. Galbraith explores ways in which the technostructure seeks to control each of these.

Prices are managed to serve the interests of the technostructure of survival and growth. This leads to the absence of price competition between firms because of its dangers to the survival of the technostructure, which would result from an outbreak of competitive price cutting. Prices are set low enough to retain and expand demand for the firm's products, but high enough to provide profits to finance the growth of the firm. Once set, prices tend to remain fixed for considerable periods of time, so as to reduce the possibility of an outbreak of price competition, and to aid industrial planning with predictable prices.

The attempts to manage demand can be looked at in two parts: management of specific demand and management of aggregate demand. Control of specific demand is sought through advertising and its general moulding of demand, so that consumers buy what the technostructure wants to sell and at the prices which it finds beneficial. Whilst the technostructure is not able to completely determine demand, the system is closer to producer sovereignty than it is to consumer sovereignty. The growth of the role of the State contributes to the management of demand for the technostructure in two ways. In some high technology areas, which ordinarily would be high-risk areas, governments are the major or only purchaser, and often buys on long-term contract. This helps producers in those areas. More generally, the activities of the State striving to stabilize the aggregate level of demand would aid planning by the technostructure.

On the factor side, the technostructure has effective control over the supply of finance capital, since it generates internally from retained profits the finance which it needs for future expansion. This effectively insulates the technostructure from intervention from bankers and other possible sources of finance. In contrast with the theory of Marris, the technostructure does not face any take-over threat and only is required to finance its expansion.[3]

The other factor upon which the technostructure depends is qualified manpower, and this is provided mainly by the State. Once again, the interests of the technostructure are intertwined with the activities of the State.

This provides only a quick view of Galbraith's *The New Industrial State*, but its links with some of the previous discussion should be apparent. The theories discussed in this chapter have emphasized the power of large firms, vis-à-vis small firms, consumers, and the state. They have assumed this power, and discussed how the large firm uses its power. It is also a basic assumption that whilst these firms operate in an oligopolistic environment, they are aware of the dangers to themselves from vigorous rivalry, and tacit collusion arises.

The managerial theories considered in Chapter 7 (and also the behavioural theories of Chapter 8) treated the firm in isolation. This isolation was in respect of other firms and largely in respect of the general economic environment. The notion that firms accept the environment within which they operate is largely abandoned by the theories considered in this chapter. The emphasis on how the firms seek to manipulate the environment vary but the basic theme runs through all these theories. The theories differ in their attitude to the managerial revolution. One basic omission from these theories is any consideration of what happens if firms are not able to manipulate the environment as they wish or if the interests of competing firms clash.

chapter 10

the debate over the motivation of firms

This chapter has two major objectives: firstly, to compare the various theories of the firm (particularly in terms of their assumptions) and secondly, to evaluate the arguments that firms have no freedom of manoeuvre and finish up effectively maximizing profits.

There is little dispute that profits will play a central or near central role in influencing firm behaviour. Within the legal framework operating in Western economies, for a firm to be able to continue it must be able to finance its expenditure (costs) either by revenue or by injection of further finance into the company by its owners or creditors. It is unlikely that a firm will be able to continue for long to find injections of finance if its costs exceed its revenues. Thus, an excess of revenue over costs is generally required for continued operation. Further, profits provide a pool of funds which can be used for reinvestment in the company; access to external finance is likely to be enhanced by high profitability. Thus firms must pay some regard to profits. The key question is: how much regard has to be given to profits, and in particular, is it only profits that they consider?

In the discussion, it is necessary to distinguish between the size of the flow of profits and the uses made of those profits. But we start by looking at the concepts of profits which underlie various theories.

10.1 Concepts of profits

The concept of profits which lay behind much of the theories of Part One is that of 'economic profit'. Firms are portrayed as seeking to maximize the difference between revenue and the opportunity cost of the inputs used, including, of course, any inputs supplied by the owners of the firm. The owners of the firm are then assumed to be entitled to the economic profit. Note, however, that the owners of the firm may supply some capital, labour and management, but may supply only some, or none of them at all.

This concept of economic profits has to be distinguished from accounting profits, with the latter typically including any inputed return to the factors of production supplied by the owners of the firm. The distinction between these two concepts of profit will be important when the arguments about firms being forced to maximize profits in order to survive are considered below. In the context of the corporation, the concept of profit being used is that of accounting profits.

Profits are a flow and as such need to be measured per unit of time. The period over which accounting profits are measured will usually be a year, but the period for economic profits is left ambiguous (this is discussed further below). Whilst it is reasonably clear what is meant by short-run profits, when long-run profits are discussed the meaning is less clear. There are at least three different interpretations which can be placed on the phrase 'long-run profits'. Firstly, it can mean the profits per unit of time which can be earned from period to period in long-run equilibrium. Thus these profits are measured in the same time units as short-run profits, but refer to that level of profits which could be maintained indefinitely. Secondly, long-run profits can mean profits measured over a long period of time (perhaps to eternity), usually with some discounting of future profits. Thus long-run profits would be

$$\sum_{t=s}^{S+T} \frac{\pi_t}{(1+r)^t}$$

where π_t are the profits earned in time period t, discounted at a rate r over a time horizon extending over T periods. This time horizon over which the profits are discounted could be the future (and hence based on guesses about future profits) and used for decision-making purposes (see below), or to the past to measure the outcome of the firm's activities.

The third interpretation is designed to meet the requirements of the corporation, and in particular to place an interpretation on maximizing the interests of the shareholders. It can be said from one point of view that the interests of the shareholders lies in the market value of their shares being as high as possible. From another point of view it could be said that shareholders are interested not in profits *per se* but dividend payments, current and future.[1] These two points of view can be brought together by the idea that the market value of the corporation is determined by its discounted dividend payments. That is, market value equals

$$\sum_{t=0}^{\infty} \frac{d_t \pi_t}{(1+r)^t}$$

where d_t is proportion of profits paid out as dividends in period t. Then market value of the corporation shares is one interpretation of the long-run profits of the firm, with emphasis placed on the shareholders' interests.

10.2   Ability of firms to maximize profits

The above discussion relates to the concept of profits being used. In principle, these concepts of profits can be measured *ex post* to indicate the performance of the firm concerned. But in terms of the theories of the firm, it is the *ex ante* concept which is important. Firms are often assumed to maximize profits (however defined), and when that assumption is made it must refer to *ex ante* profits. The firm is pictured as facing a profit function which describes what the profit outcome would be from any course of action which the firm could take, and then that the firm chooses the action which leads to the largest profits. In the simpler cases of perfect competition and monopoly, the firm has only one decision variable: the level of output. In the less simple cases, there are more decision variables (for example, price, quality, and advertising).

In perfect competition the profit function $\pi(q)$ is given by $p.q - C(q)$, with price p, output q, costs C, and since the firm takes p as given, it need only know the cost function in order to know the profit function. It then varies the level of output to maximize profits, and of course operates where price equals marginal cost. This profit function describes the amount of profit which is anticipated from each course of action. After the action is taken, and the period to which it relates is over, then the firm can calculate the profits which have resulted from their action. But the major question is whether it is meaningful to talk of profit maximization. There are two basic aspects to this. Firstly, can firms obtain sufficient information about their profit function for them to be able to make the relevant calculations? Secondly, how do firms react to the uncertainty attached to any forecast of profits?

In the context of monopoly or perfect competition, if the firm is able to maximize profits, it must be able to obtain sufficient information on the demand and cost condition which it faces to make the relevant decision. If the necessary information is freely available, and if there are no costs of changing the level of output, then in order to maximize profits, the firm would move to the level of output for which marginal revenue equalled marginal cost. A firm which has been in the same market for a long while is likely to have a fairly shrewd idea of the nature of the demand curve which it faces, and of the cost conditions under which it operates. But the precision of the profit maximization condition will be lost if there are costs attached to moving to that position or if there is some lack of information about the cost and demand conditions.

The oligopoly situation is much more complicated. There, it is not only a matter of knowing the demand and cost condition, but also of being able to accurately predict the responses of one's rivals. There are two elements to this (as there is also to the forecasting of demand and cost conditions). Firstly, there is the problem of whether firms are able, on average, to forecast these things correctly. In a rapidly changing economic environment, it may be difficult for the firms to do so, as they may have little opportunity to learn about one situation before it has changed. Secondly, even if on average they are correct, how do they react to the probability (if not near certainty) that they will be wrong on any given occasion? In the presence of uncertainty about the outcome of the actions, the firm may decide to maximize expected profits. The firm then seeks to evaluate the probability of each outcome resulting from any particular action and weights the value of each outcome by the probability of it occurring. In other words, if the situation reoccurred a large number of times, the expected profit would be the average of the outcomes. But the firm may lay great stress on not going bankrupt, so that the outcome of making a loss is not merely entered into the calculations at the amount lost but at rather more.[2]

Another side of this is that the firm (its owners or its controllers) may not be 'risk neutral', as the maximization of expected profits would imply. For example, suppose a firm had the choice of two actions (say two levels of output) in the next period, one of which was expected to lead to 10 units of profit and the other to 12 units of profit, but that the latter outcome involved the possibility of a much wider spread of outcomes. Suppose, for concreteness, that the first action had a probability of 0.25 of yielding 9 units, 0.5 of yielding 10 units, and 0.25 of yielding 11 units, whilst that second action had probabilities of 0.4 of yielding 0 units, 0.2 of yielding 12 units, and 0.4 of yielding 24. Then one can see that it is, at least conceivable, that a firm might choose the first action rather than the second.

Thus, unless it can be reasonably assumed that firms are 'risk neutral' (that is, in this context look only at the expected returns of the action), the maximization of profits has no direct meaning in a world of risk.[3] We have seen above that in some theories the maximization of profits is replaced; in the theory of games it is replaced by the 'minimax' principle and in the theory of Rothchilds (1947) (Chapter 9) by the maximization of secure profits.

However, most of these criticisms could be applied to any theory which relies on maximization (whether of sales, growth of sales, or whatever). In certain instances, some of the difficulties of achieving a maximum are ruled out by assumption, as in the case of the theory of Baumol (1959) where the difficulties of oligopolistic interdependence are ruled out in that way.

The general line of counter argument to the proposition that firms are unable to maximize profits is that, in general, firms are not continually being plunged into totally new situations, but rather are in an ongoing situation to which they are able to gradually move to a profit-maximizing position. In other words, firms do not move straight to the maximizing position, as might be imagined from the theories, but rather move there gradually. The firms are then seen as making changes, examining the outcome for a change in profits, making further changes in response to the outcome, and so on. For example, under sales maximization, the firm would be seen changing the price and advertising, examining its impact on sales and on profits relative to the profit constraint. If sales revenue had been expanded by the course of action, and the profit constraint not yet hit, then the firm would make further changes in the same direction, re-examine, etc.

This process requires a number of preconditions if it is to work. Firstly, the environment in which the firm is operating must be sufficiently stable for this gradual seeking of the optimising position to be able to work itself out. Secondly, the variability of the outcomes following any particular action must be small. For example, if a monopolist faced a demand curve which shifted about (because of changes in the level of income, the weather, activities of other firms, etc.) so much that in making an increase in output from its current output there is a fifty-fifty chance whether profits rise or fall, then if the firm judges whether to further increase output, based on what happens to profits, there is a fifty-fifty chance that the firm will move in the wrong direction.

The notion that firms, for these reasons and others, cannot maximize anything underlies the theory of satisficing. The simple example of satisficing given in Chapter 8 (that of full-cost pricing) can be viewed as saying that whilst the firm knows its cost conditions, it does not know its demand conditions (partly because of oligopolistic interdependence), so that it retreats into relating price to what it knows: its costs.

10.3   The managerial revolution again

We now turn from consideration of whether firms are able to maximize (and indeed whether that is a meaningful concept) to whether firms *want* to maximize profits or whether firms are in some ways *forced* to do so.

One of the major arguments against the idea that firms wish to maximize profits has been associated with the idea of the managerial revolution. We saw in Chapter 7 that the theories of Baumol, Marris and Williamson based on objectives other than profit maximization had grown from the idea that there had been a separation of ownership and management in the corporation, with the managers in effective control and wishing to pursue non-profit objectives. So as part of this debate we need to consider again those 'managerial' theories.

Our first consideration is of the evidence of the extent of manager control in contrast to owner control. The influential data of Berle and Means (1932) and the follow up study by Larner (1966) have been quoted in Chapter 7. These statistics indicated the large influence of manager-controlled firms. Whilst the managerial theories have accepted this evidence, it has become increasingly questioned in two respects. Firstly, doubt has been expressed about the accuracy of the data reported by Berle and Means.[4] Secondly, the manner in which manager control was defined has been questioned.

We do not have enough space to examine fully the evidence here, but rather refer the reader to the recent useful summary by Nyman and Silberston (1978), who estimate that in 1975 amongst the largest firms in the United Kingdom (approximately the largest 250 firms) over 56 per cent were identified as owner controlled with the probability that some of the remaining 44 per cent were also owner controlled. They report Burch (1972) as finding that for the top 300 American firms, 45 per cent were probably under family control, 40 per cent probably manager controlled, and a further 15 per cent possibly under family control. These figures clearly indicate a different picture to those quoted earlier, and arise in part from different notions of control.

There are a number of aspects to the managerial revolution which must be borne in mind in trying to assess its influence. Firstly, it is widely agreed that the majority of shareholders only play a passive role in the company of which they are part owners. But that does not establish managerial control. Individuals (or families) with relatively small holdings (say, in the order of 8 to 10 per cent of the stock of a firm) may nevertheless feel it worthwhile to intervene actively in the running of the firm. A substantial presence on the board of directors by such minority shareholders would be sufficient to lead to policies on dividend payments, investment, etc., which were in the interests of those shareholders, if not of the others. Secondly, the managers may only own a very small fraction of the corporation for which they work, but that small fraction may still make them relatively wealthy individuals. Further it may mean that a substantial portion of their income is derived from shares of the corporation for which they work.[5] The importance of this remark depends upon the theory being examined. In the context of the theory of O. E. Williamson, where managers are assumed to have some discretion over their salaries, an individual manager would benefit directly from a rise in managerial salaries, but indirectly lose through the consequent reduction in profits and dividends. But since he would receive a much larger proportion of the salary increase than the proportion of the dividend reduction, the profit incentive arising from the share ownership may not be very great. But the picture is changed for the Baumol theory. There, the managers are seen to be keen to maximize sales revenue (subject to the minimum profit constraint) in order to enhance their salary indirectly. But when increased sales lowers profits, the managers would lose out from the reduction in profits and dividends from an increase in sales. So here, looked at from the income of the managers, whether they are biased towards sales or profits would depend upon the strength of the links between sales, profits and salary on the one hand, and the proportion of profits received by the managers through their share ownership.

Thirdly, similar patterns of share ownership by managers may give rise to different behaviour. One possibility would be that a manager had risen within the firm, and during that rise part of his salary had been paid in shares or share options. The other possibility would be an owner of shares who had used the influence of that ownership to arrange appointment as a manager. A person in the first situation may think much more 'managerially' than a person in the second situation would even though their share interests in their corporation were similar.

Another factor which may be of increasing importance is the nature of the shareholders. The discussion so far has tended to assume (implicitly, if not explicitly) that the shareholders are individuals and not other organizations. Yet institutions like investment trusts, unit trusts, banks either on their own behalf or as nominee holders, and pension funds are substantial shareholders. It has been estimated that for the United Kingdom direct shareholdings by individuals fell from 66 per cent of the total shareholdings in quoted companies in 1957 to 44 per cent in 1975. The holdings by financial institutions grew from 18 per cent to 38 per cent over that period (with the remaining holdings accounted for by charities, the public sector and overseas residents).[6] Particularly if a few of the institutions are prepared to act together, by their ownership stake in a corporation, they can (if they so wish) bring about large changes within that corporation.[7] The arguments and evidence about the significance of the managerial revolution do not yield any clear cut answers about the motivation of the corporation.

10.4   Are firms forced to maximize profits?

The argument that the objectives of the firm are largely irrelevant since survival and/or prosperity depend upon being able to maximize profits is now considered. This line of argument has to be examined in relation to the product market and the capital market. In the case of the product market, in the theories of perfect competition and monopolistic competition where no barriers to entry were assumed, in the long run firms were only able to earn normal profits. If firms did not maximize profits, their profits would fall below the normal level, and it was believed that subnormal profits would mean that a firm had to leave the industry. Thus survival in that context requires profit maximization and the absence of barriers to entry would dictate profit maximization.

This may be a case where the difference between economic profit and accounting profit is important. In the long-run situation, the firm is forced to maximize profits if it wishes to avoid negative economic profits. But survival in the real world would rely upon avoiding negative accounting profits. If the owners of the firm supply some or all of the factors of production, then there will be a difference between economic and accounting profits, such that the former is less than the latter. It would then be possible for a firm to continue in existence for a long time earning positive accounting profits but negative economic profits without being forced out of the market.[8]

Secondly, entry into the industry depends upon potential profits for the entrant. If the potential entrant judges his profit prospects by the profits of the industry at present, then the existing firms can reduce entry by reducing profits to the 'normal' level. Thus, for example, a firm which priced according to the full cost principle would earn the standard profit margin embodied in that principle. It would be able to continue to do so, if potential entrants observed that standard profit margin, and believed that was indicative of what they would earn if they were to enter the industry. Indeed, as indicated in Chapter 8, such an argument was put forward as a rationale for the full cost pricing principle. Under this line of argument, it might be expected that entry would be slowed down, but possibly not totally stopped, by existing firms earnings only a 'normal' level of profits.[9]

The pressure of these arguments is difficult to assess in the abstract, and empirical evidence is difficult to collect and to assess.

The pressures from the capital market on a firm to maximize profits can take two forms. Firstly, there is the threat of a take-over which plays a large role in the theory of Marris (1964), discussed in Chapter 7. Secondly, there may be pressures from the suppliers of finance capital (whether banks, institutions or individuals) on the firm to earn the highest possible profits.

The take-over threat arises when the share price of the firm falls relative to the potential value of the firm if it were operated to maximize its value. The value of the firm has been taken to be its present value of discounted future dividends, viz.:

$$\sum_{t=0}^{\infty} \frac{d_t \pi_t}{(1+r)^t}$$

where $d_t \pi_t$ are dividends in period t, and r the rate of discount.[10] The value of
the firm can fall below its potential maximum either by the dividend rate
being different from its 'optimal' level[11] or by the flow of profits being below
the maximum achievable. In the managerial theories of the firm, especially
the theory of Marris, stress was placed on the choice of the dividend rate[12] to
maximize growth, and this was at the expense of the market value of the firm.
Under many of the behavioural theories, the focus shifted towards the under-
achievement on the profits side.

For the present it does not matter how the divergence between the current
value of the firm and its maximum value arose. For the take-over mechanism
to work a number of conditions need to apply. Let us label the stock market
valuation of the firm as V_s, the discounted future dividends as V_d, and the
maximum value as V_m. Then for the take-over mechanism to work in the
context of a publicly quoted company, it is required that the relationship
between V_s and V_d is a close one. Further the market is required to operate so
that the extent to which V_d and V_m can move apart without a take-over being
triggered off is 'small'.

A scenario which would fit this would be one where the share price of a firm
was determined by (and equal to) the discounted future dividends, about
which there was general agreement in the market; that many others had
information about the potential of the firm under scrutiny; and that the costs
of making and effecting a take-over bid were minor relative to the share
prices involved.

This line of argument is only intended to apply to the large firm whose
shares are widely traded on the stock market, and to operate as a way of
ensuring that managers act in the interests of the owners. These interests are
taken to be synonymous with maximizing the value of the firm. This argument
clearly postulates a divorce of ownership and control, but with the stock
market operating to keep the firm as a profit-maximizer. When the managers
and the owners of the firm share an identity of interests this would not
operate in the same way. For then, the owners could pursue whatever policy
they wished, secure in the knowledge that the firm cannot be taken over
without their express consent. They may find that the value of the firm to
someone else is greater than the value to them, and this provides an
opportunity for them to profit by the sale of the firm.[13] But that would then
be a decision for the owners to make.

The other pressure from the capital market arises from the price at which finance capital is supplied to the firm. This price may be that charged by a bank or it may be the price which must be offered by the firm if it is to raise funds successfully from the market. If there is competition for funds, then it is expected that the price (of finance capital) will rise. If many firms are maximizing profits in similar situations to the firm we are considering, then the others will be earning a higher rate of profit than the firm in question. In the competition for funds, it is argued that those firms will be able to offer (if necessary) a higher price for the funds than the firm X. If there are sufficient of these profit-maximizing firms, relative to the finance available, then firm X will not be able to obtain any funds at a price which it has a prospect of paying. Although firm X is not then forced to maximize profits in order to survive, it would need to do so in order to expand. Then as the economy grows the non-profit maximizers would get left behind.

From this last argument it can be seen that the pressures on firm X to maximize profits would only arise if there are a large number of profit-maximizers around. If most firms were not profit-maximizers, then the pressures on any single firm would be reduced. This point also applies to many of the other arguments put forward to suggest that firms are forced to maximize profits. If most firms are maximizing profits, the pressures on the remaining firms is likely to be intense for them to fall into line or perish. But if most firms do not maximize profits, the pressures on any individual firm are light.

We have seen before that whilst some theories of the firm make an attempt at 'realism', others do not. This comes to the fore when it is argued that profit maximization is not to be taken as a literal account of the process by which firms make economic decisions, but rather that firms act *as if* they were profit-maximizers. For example, Friedman (1953) wrote:

'Unless the behaviour of businessmen in some way or another approximated behaviour consistent with the maximization of returns (i.e. profits), it seems unlikely that they would remain in business for long. Let the apparent immediate determinant of business behaviour be anything at all, habitual reaction, random chance, or what not. Whenever this determinant happens to lead to behaviour consistent with rational and informed maximization of returns, the business will prosper and acquire resources with which to expand; whenever it does not, the business will tend to lose resources and can be kept in existence only by the addition of resources from outside. The process of 'natural selection' thus helps to validate the hypothesis, or, rather, given 'natural selection', acceptance of the hypothesis can be based largely on the judgement that it summarizes appropriately the conditions for survival'. (Text in parenthesis added).

Two comments can be made here. Firstly, expansion requires finance, which is often directly or indirectly linked to profits. But these profits could arise from the maximization of profits and/or the earning of above average/normal profits in an oligopolistic environment where supernormal profits were available. Secondly, if the actions of the firm which are consistent with profit maximization are random, why should they be expected to persist? If the actions are habitual, will they be expected to be profit-maximizing in new as well as old situations?[14]

10.5   Differences between owner-controlled and manager-controlled firms

Although the impact of the managerial revolution on the view of how firms operate has influenced the above discussion, it has been rather peripheral. Now it comes back to the centre of the stage. The idea that the owners of the corporations are largely rentiers who have lent money to the firm but do not partake in any decision-making has led to a sharp distinction being drawn between owner-controlled firms and manager-controlled firms. And it is via this route that attempts have been made to subject some theories of the firm to empirical examination. Here the central proposition is examined in two stages. Firstly, do managers place more emphasis on sales and growth and owners more emphasis on market value and profit, as asserted by some of the 'managerial' theories? Secondly, is it correct to emphasize the conflict of interests between owners and managers? We examine then whether there is such a conflict of interests, and whether within the firm there could be other groups whose interests conflict in a more fundamental way.

The discussion at the end of Chapter 7 made it clear that the distinction between the owner-controlled firm and the manager-controlled firm came down to differences over the growth rate (of sales) and the accompanying retention ratio, but that the flow of profits in the initial time period would be the same in the two cases if all the costs of growth (including sales promotion costs) are regarded as investment and not as current costs. The manager-controlled firm placed emphasis on growth of sales, and were constrained to achieve a market value to avoid take-over, whilst owner-controlled firms were assumed to focus only on the market value. It is unfortunate that the ways of comparing these theories, which are at present available, do not enable any basic distinction to be made between growth of sales and growth of profits. It will be recalled from the end of Chapter 7 that the comparison of the alternative theories used a steady state growth model, in which sales and profits grew at the same rate. The growth-maximizer grows faster in terms of both sales and profits than the profit (more accurately, market value) maximizer, and that after some time, the profit flow, dividend flow, and market value of the growth-maximizer will exceed that of the profit-maximizer.

Whether the manager-controlled firm and the owner-controlled firm will act in the manner assumed can be questioned further. For the manager-controlled firm, the motivation under scrutiny is that of the board of directors and whether their objectives will be growth and sales rather than profits, was considered above. The owner-controlled firm may have many objectives other than maximization of market value. But the owners of a firm can always decline to accept a take-over bid, and so they can pursue policies which are not subject to the constraints which operate on the manager-controlled firm. Of course, it may still be postulated that for a large corporation where the shareholders appoint (in principle) directors as trustees to act on their behalf, that whether they do so can be judged by reference to the impact which the directors' actions and decisions have on the market value. But when the firm is owner controlled the owners may decide that their interests are not solely those of maximization of the value of the firm. For example, in the case of a business controlled and owned by one man, his objectives may be to maximize the capital value of the firm in n years time when he plans to retire, and this leads to a policy close to growth maximization. Although it is not a corporation, this firm can be thought of as pursuing a policy of high retentions (i.e. high savings and reinvestment out of profits) for growth. In this case, the owner-controlled firm would be more 'managerial' than any managerial firm subject to the take-over threat.[15]

Turning to the second question above, it can be argued that the owner/manager dichotomy may be exaggerated, and that the conflict of interests involved may be more like a three-way affair. In one corner are the shareholders who have no effective say in the running of the firm which they own, except that which can be expressed through buying and selling the shares. These 'outsider' shareholders will have no direct contact with the operation of the firm, and no early access to information concerning changes in the firm's fortunes (through, for example, a take-over bid). This can be contrasted with the second group, who can be labelled 'insider' shareholders.[16] This group includes individual shareholders with a seat on the board of directors, those with considerable influence over appointments to the board of directors arising from their large shareholdings or from a history of family involvement in the firm, etc.; individuals who are first managers but whose income has been partly in the form of shares in the firm; and institutions who have a large stake in the firm. In the third corner, there are the employees of the firm. The interests of many employees will be in wages and job security and consideration of those features has traditionally fallen outside the theory of the firm. The interests of the 'middle management' are again likely to be wages and jobs, but may also extend into 'empire building' considerations, improvements in the material conditions of work, etc. Many of these considerations were discussed in the theory of Williamson (1964) in Chapter 7.

10.6   Implications for efficiency

The debate over the role of profits and the objectives of the firm is important for its implications for the efficiency of the economy. We can examine this in terms of allocative and technical efficiency. The achievement of allocative efficiency (at least when judged according to the Pareto criteria) is brought about, under certain conditions such as the absence of economies of scale, by a system of perfect competition.[17] A system which approximates to perfect competition is likely to require profit maximization, free entry into the industry, and demand curves facing firms which are of very high elasticity. The absence of any of these is likely to threaten the overall efficiency of the system.[18] In situations of oligopoly with barriers to entry, the pursuit of profits is likely to lead to high profits for the oligopolists but not lead to allocative efficiency. But, if there is free entry into the industry, these high profits are bid away as new firms enter, and with high elasticity of demand leads to an approximation to perfect competition.

Technical efficiency of firms will generally follow from successful attempts by firms to maximize an objective, since that will involve minimizing costs. The exception to this is, as in the case of the theory of Williamson (1964), when some of the costs are elements in the objectives of the firm. But if a firm is a satisficer rather than a maximizer, then cost minimization will not generally result.

It is likely that profits are going to play a central role in any theory of the firm under a private-enterprise system. For the absence of profits would threaten the survival of the firm; the presence of profits enables expansion. So in a profit-based economy, profits will play a role. The key question, which remains unanswered here, is whether it plays the dominant role ascribed to it by profit maximization theories or a constraining role as in the managerial and some other theories of the firm. There is no consensus, and the debate over the role of profits is one which makes theories of the firm interesting to study.

notes

Chapter 1

1 The most well-known article advocating such an approach is Friedman (1953); but see also Lipsey (1962).

2 This line is put forward by, *inter alia*, Coddington (1972) and Leibenstein (1976) Chapter 1.

3 For if it did not minimize costs, then its profits would be lower than otherwise. By reducing costs, the firm would initially increase profits which would then be in surplus as compared with the minimum required. The firm would then have some profits to play with in pursuing its objective.

In one of the theories, an increase in certain costs (of some staff) is part of the objective of the firm; but the remaining costs would still be minimized.

4 This is intended to be a positive statement of how things are, rather than a normative statement of how things should be.

5 This enters a controversial area particularly if the units are operating in different countries. In those circumstances, goods passing between one unit and another do so with a price attached, the so-called 'transfer price'. This is necessary in order to determine in which country the profits have arisen. One possibility is that the central firm sets the price so as to minimize its overall tax bill on its profits. In this case, although one unit's output is sold at a price, that price is not the allocating mechanism.

Chapter 2

1 For example, these are covered by Lipsey (1962) and Samuelson (1977).

2 Those forms of capital input which never yield least cost output will not generate short-run cost curves which touch the long-run cost curve.

3 See Patinkin (1947).

4 In the short-run case, short-run variable costs.

5 'This ... defence is that the concept of perfect competition has defeated its newer rivals in the decisive area: the day-to-day work of the economic theories. Since the 1930s, when the rival doctrines of imperfect and monopolistic competition were in their heyday, economists have increasingly reverted to the use of the concept of perfect competition as their standard model of analysis. Today the concept of perfect

competition is being used more widely by the profession in its theoretical work than at any time in the past.' Stigler (1957).

6 See, for example, Arrow (1959).

7 See, for example, Phelps and Winter (1970).

8 The cost curves include the opportunity cost of the capital employed by the firm (i.e. 'normal profits'). Hence the cost curves will shift with changes in the capital employed by the firm. Consider firm X which initially is earning, say 20 per cent return on the capital employed in the firm of £1 million. The profits of the firm are then £200,000. If the opportunity cost of capital is, say 10 per cent, then prospective purchasers of the firm would be prepared to pay up to £2 million for the firm. For the profits of £200,000 would yield a 10 per cent return. If there are many potential buyers of firm X, then the market value of the firm will tend toward £2 million, rather than the original £1 million. If the firm were to change hands at £2 million (or the current owners revalued it at that figure), the subsequent cost curves would now include 'normal profits' of £200,000 rather than £100,000. In other words, the cost curves of firm X would have moved upwards to the extent which appears to eliminate supernormal profits.

9 Sraffa (1926).

10 The second-order condition is that

$$\frac{d^2\pi}{dq^2} = 2\frac{dp}{dq} + \frac{d^2p}{dq^2} \cdot q - \frac{d^2C}{dq^2} < 0.$$

The first part of this expression is the rate of change of marginal revenue. The second part is the rate of change of the marginal cost. The condition will certainly be satisfied if marginal revenue declines with output and if marginal cost increases with output, for then both parts of the expression will be negative.

11 If elasticity of demand were unity, marginal revenue would be zero, and a firm would find it optimal (in profit terms) to operate at that level of output only if marginal cost were also zero.

12 In the monopolistic competition and oligopoly cases, the prediction of the impact of a change in demand would require much more information than is the case for monopoly. Hence in those theories, the point being made here is reinforced.

13 As indicated above, marginal revenue $= p(1 - 1/e)$.

14 The utility-maximizing condition for a consumer facing prices which vary with the amount purchased, would be that the marginal rate of substitution between any pair of goods equals the ratio of the marginal cost of the goods. In consumer theory the marginal cost to the consumer of a good is usually taken as the price, since the consumer is assumed to be a price-taker. In the context being examined here, that assumption has been dropped. But from the above condition we can derive a demand curve which relates the amount of a good demanded in terms of the marginal cost of that good.

For a profit-maximizing firm, the demand for an input is dependent on the marginal revenue product of that input to the firm. Under profit-maximizing conditions, the firm would equate the marginal revenue product of an input to its marginal cost. This condition again forms the basis for the demand curve relating the amount demanded of the input with its marginal cost to the purchaser.

Chapter 3

1 It is more usual to talk of the quality rather than product characteristics decision. I prefer the proposed terminology for two reasons. Firstly, it does not seem accurate to talk of decisions over advertising, marketing, etc. (which are included under this head) as quality decisions. Secondly, products may be regarded as of similar quality but different product characteristics (e.g. cars with similar engine size).

2 Again using an example from the motor industry, this assumption would involve the existence of some number n such that if 1100 cc cars were measured not in number of cars but in number of blocks of n cars, then the demand and cost curves for a particular 1100 cc brand of car would look the same as the demand and cost curves for, say, a Rolls Royce.

3 Firms in practice are more likely to view price and quality rather than quantity and quality as the decision variables. In our analysis the two approaches yield the same basic results, but this is not necessarily the case when the demand function is not known with certainty.

4 This can be shown as follows. It is required that the firm is maximizing profits so that $dR/dq = dC/dq$ where R is the revenue function derived from the dd demand function (i.e. with other prices held constant). Further zero profits yields $R/q = C/q$. Combining the two conditions gives

$$\frac{dR}{dq} - \frac{R}{q} = \frac{dC}{dq} - \frac{C}{q}$$

which can be re-written as

$$\frac{q \cdot dR/dq - R}{q^2} = \frac{q \cdot dC/dq - C}{q^2}$$

which is

$$\frac{d}{dq}\left(\frac{R}{q}\right) = \frac{d}{dq}\left(\frac{C}{q}\right)$$

which is that the slope of the average revenue curve is equal to the slope of the average cost curve.

5 See, for example, the symposium in the *American Economic Review*, May 1964; the interchange between Archibald (1963), Friedman (1963) and Stigler (1963); and Demsetz (1959) and Barzel (1970).

6 For example, Stigler (1949).

7 Even with the examples often given of industries which are to be regarded as

perfectly competitive this remark applies. The wheat industry is an oft quoted example; but even here it could be argued that account should be taken of the different types of wheat, etc., grown in different parts of the world.

8 See, for example, Chamberlin (1957), Meade (1974).

Chapter 4

1 The measurement of the extent of oligopoly in an industry (often called the degree of concentration) presents more difficulties than indicated in the text. For a fuller discussion see Aaronovitch and Sawyer (1975) Chapter 4, and Hannah and Kay (1977).

2 In the simple case, with linear demand curves, we have for the two firms: R_1 is given by $q_1 = d - a/2b - q_2/2$ R_2 is given by $q_2 = d - a/2b - q_1/2$ which can be re-written as $q_1 = 2(d - a/2b) - 2q_2$. Thus the relative slopes of R_1 and R_2 are, in this case, those drawn in figure 4.1.

3 The leader firm operates so that:

$$\left[\frac{\partial p}{\partial q_1} + \frac{\partial p}{\partial q_2} \frac{\partial q_2}{\partial q_1} \right] q_1 + p = \frac{\partial C_1}{\partial q_1}$$

The follower firm operates so that:

$$\frac{\partial p}{\partial q_1} \cdot q_1 + p = \frac{\partial C}{\partial q_1}$$

Since $\partial p / \partial q_2$, $\partial g_2 / dg_1 < 0$, at a given price the left-hand side of these conditions will be greater for the leader than for the follower, and we can write this as $mr^l > mr^f$ where mr refers to marginal revenue (which is the meaning of the left-hand sides) and suffix l refers to leader, f to follower. With the same cost conditions for the two firms, the leader firm would produce a larger output to bring about the equality of marginal revenue and marginal cost than the follower firm would. Thus $q^l > q^f$; since the price is the same for both firms, this leads to $\pi^l > \pi^f$ where π refers to profits.

4 Put residual demand $R = D - S$, then we have

$$p - \frac{dC}{dq} = -\frac{R}{p} \frac{1}{\partial R/\partial p},$$

i.e. the mark-up of price over marginal cost is related to the elasticity of residual demand.

5 The size of the gap is the difference between the marginal revenue just below q_0 ($q_0 -$) and the marginal revenue just above q_0 ($q_0 +$). This equals

$$\frac{d}{dq}(pq)\bigg|_{q_0} - \frac{d}{dq}(pq)\bigg|_{q_0} = q_0 \left[\frac{dp}{dq}(q_0^+) - \frac{dp}{dq}(q_0^-) \right] + p(q_0^+) - p(q_0^-)$$

$$= q_0 \left[\frac{dp}{dq}(q_0^+) - \frac{dp}{dq}(q_0^-) \right].$$

Chapter 5

1 Broadly interpreted, this would include the case where a potential entrant could not obtain vital factors of production, which could be interpreted as only being available at an infinite price.

2 Obviously the implicit assumption is that potential entrants do not regard output reduction as within the range of possibilities. If more than one firm enters the industry, then output will be larger and price lower after entry than is envisaged in this theory.

3 This would assume that for production below q_0, production costs were very high, so that the cost curve has a very steep slope prior to q_0.

4 The difference between q_l and q_c is $-q_c/S$ and the relative difference moving from q_c is $-1/S$. With elasticity of $-e$, the relative difference in price (p_l, p_c) will be

$$\frac{1}{eS}$$

so that

$$\frac{p_l - p_c}{p_c} = \frac{1}{eS}$$

so that

$$p_l = p_c\left(1 + \frac{1}{eS}\right).$$

5 The Kuhn-Tucker theorem is given in the Appendix to this chapter.

6 In the entry-preventing case, with output x_c we have $dR(x_c)/dx - dC(x_c)/dx = \lambda = r - \mu < r$. Without threat of entry, profit maximization with output x_m would generate $dR(x_m)/dx - dC(x_m)/dx = r > dR(x_c)/dx - dC(x_c)/dx$. With usual assumptions on dR/dx and dC/dx this implies $x_m < x_c$.

7 For an introduction to the optimal control theory and its applications to economics, see Dorfman (1969).

Chapter 6

1 It is often assumed in the literature on labour-managed firms that such firms would seek to maximize output per head. See, for example, Meade (1972).

2 The quotation from Adam Smith is from Smith (1904), Vol. 2, pp. 233 and 245.

Chapter 7

1 Larner defined a manager-controlled firm as one in which no group controls more than 10 per cent of the shares.

2 For a rather different perspective on the extent of manager control, see Goldsmith and Parmelee (1940).

3 For further discussion, see Nyman and Silberston (1978).

4 For derivation of the supply of labour curve, see any textbook on labour economics, e.g. Rees (1973).

5 As argued by Fisher (1960).

6 For example, Peston (1959).

7 This theorem is outlined in the Appendix to Chapter 5.

8 This argument applies to the range over which increasing sales revenue leads to falling profits. Over the range where sales and profits rise together there is no need to trade in profits for sales.

9 Baumol (implicitly) assumes the number of products is fixed. See, for example, Appendix to Chapter 1 of Baumol (1959).

10 The line of argument which follows is based on Hawkins (1970).

11 There may be legal or quasi-legal requirements that if the bid attracts the support of more than a certain proportion of the shareholders, then the others must sell.

12 For example, how would we compare two growth paths, one of which had initially slow growth, then fast growth and finally, slow growth, with one which had fast, slow and then fast growth?

13 Recall that $\sum_{t=0}^{\infty} x^t = \dfrac{1}{1-x}$, if $|x| < 1$.

14 For a detailed discussion of these and other points, see Penrose (1959).

15 In real life, the market value of very high-growth firms (such as the so-called 'go-go' firms of the late sixties) with a growth rate above the level of interest rates, generally is liable to be unstable. The share price of such firms are also liable to large fluctuations.

16 When

$$i = i(g), \frac{dv}{dg} = \frac{1+i}{(i-g)^2}\left[\frac{d\pi}{dg}(i-g)+(\pi-i)-(\pi-g)\frac{di}{dg}\right].$$

With $di/dg > 0$, the turning point of the valuation curve occurs at a lower growth rate than that in the constant rate of discount case discussed in the text. Further, the turning points of the profitability curve and the valuation ratio curve may no longer be in the order indicated above.

17 This course of action has been followed by, *inter alia*, Marris (1971), Solow (1971), and J. H. Williamson (1966).

18 If the book value of the acquired firm is B, and valuation ratio v, then the acquiring firm pays vB to obtain B in capital assets; each pound spent on this acquisition yields $1/v$ in asset value.

19 J.H.Williamson (1966) assumes that price is fixed to the firm, and that this exacerbates the relative growth problem mentioned in the preceding paragraph, for the firm grows relative to the economy and the assumption of a given price becomes increasingly untenable.

20 Output is being increased at a rate g, and with fixed input proportions, all the inputs have to increase at the same rate so yielding net investment of gK.

21 Compare this with the discussion on p. 105 above. As g increases, the $-s(g)b^\theta K_0^\theta - mgK_0$ part of Z_0 becomes larger in absolute size, thus causing Z_0 to decline with increasing g.

22 Economists have generally argued that costs associated with expansion, whether in sales promotion or fixed capital, are not a current cost to be deducted from profits. But these investments then add to the capital stock of the firm, whether in the form of 'goodwill' or of fixed capital. There would then be items of current cost related to the depreciation of these assets. Thus if we are to regard sales promotion as a capital, and not a current cost, then depreciation of goodwill items should be deducted from the profits of the firm. In the discussion in the above paragraph, there would be no difference to the conclusions. For the owner-oriented firm and the growth-oriented firm would inherit from the past not only the same physical capital K_0 but also the same 'goodwill'.

In reality, it is likely that sales promotion in the form of advertising, marketing etc., will be regarded as a current cost. But sales promotion which takes the form of changing the product or introducing new products may be regarded as a capital cost (possibly under the heading of research and development).

Appendix to Chapter 7

1 For the Kuhn-Tucker theorem, see Appendix to Chapter 5.

Chapter 8

1 For a model of oligopoly which postulates that a firm's perceptions on the demand conditions and rivals' reactions depend on its internal structure, see Cyert and March (1955).

2 May and August 1939 respectively.

3 See, for example, Wiles (1961) Chapter 12.

4 For example, Godley and Nordhaus (1972).

5 For further discussion, see Parish and Ng (1972).

Chapter 9

1 Rothchilds (1947).

2 Whilst the reliance of Galbraith on the work of Marris is acknowledged by Galbraith, the links of Galbraith with Rothchilds is the interpretation of the present author.

3 A problem remains, which recurs in Chapter 10. If a minimum level of dividends has to be paid to the shareholders, and growth is internally financed, then the growth rate is determined by retained profits. In order to maximize the growth rate, the technostructure would maximize retained profits, and with fixed dividends, to maximize total profits.

Chapter 10

1 If the corporation continues in existence, then the shareholders' cash flow only benefits from profits when they are paid out to them as dividends.

2 If p_i is the perceived probability of outcome i, which would yield profit P_i, then the expected profit would be $\sum_{i=1}^{n} p_i P_i$ summed over all possible outcomes numbering n. But the firm may place utility $U(P_i)$ on the various outcomes, such that whilst the utility rises with profits, it does not do so in a uniform manner, and a very low utility is attached to a loss. Then the firm may be seen as minimizing $\sum_{i=1}^{n} p_i U(P_i)$ and this in general will not give the same outcome as the maximization of expected profits.

3 The terminology usually adopted in economics is that the presence of risk refers to situations when the outcome is unknown, but the probability of any outcome is known, so that the expected value of the outcomes can be calculated. Uncertainty refers to cases when the probabilities are not known so that the expected value cannot be readily calculated. We have been dealing with the former here; clearly the presence of uncertainty (in this definition) would make the difficulties discussed more intense.

4 'Berle and Means classified 88 out of the largest 200 corporations as under manager control in 1929. However, Zeitlin has pointed out that they actually provided no information on 44 of these, which they called 'presumably manager controlled' (Zeitlin p. 1081). Of the 43 (from a total of 106) *industrial* corporations classed as under manager control, Berle and Means classified 39 as 'presumably under manager control'. Of these 43 industrial corporations, no less than 33 were identified as having a definite centre of owner control by later studies (see Goldsmith and Parmelee (1940), NRC (1939), and Perlo (1957)). Thus only a very small number of industrial corporations can be identified as definitely under manager control in the 1930s in the USA.' (Nymans and Silberston (1978) p. 78; italic in original.)

5 See, for example the evidence of Llewelyn (1969) which suggests 50 per cent of income of directors as being linked to profit performance.

6 The source for these figures is King (1977) based on Moyle (1971) and the Royal Commission on the Distribution of Income and Wealth (1975). King (1977) gives a more detailed breakdown and also includes figures for 1963 and 1969. For the United States, personal holdings went from 85.7 per cent of the total in 1952 to 81.0 per cent in 1968 (source King (1977) based on Goldsmith (1973)).

7 For some examples, see Nyman and Silberston (1978).

8 If the owners of the firm were to withdraw their labour and capital, when they were earning negative economic profits, they would by definition receive a larger income from selling their labour and capital in the market place than they were in operating their firm. But there would not be forces compelling them to do so.

9 This differs from the limit pricing idea, which argues that the existing firms seek to propagate the idea that post-entry profits will be only at the normal level.

10 There could be a difference between the current value of the firm and the value

placed on it by a potential acquirer arising from the two using a difference rate of discount.

11 That is the level of dividends which would maximize the value of the firm.

12 Although it was discussed in terms of the retention ratio, the dividend ratio plus the retention ratio sum to unity.

13 As indicated in note 10 above, different groups may place a different value on the firm because of different views about future profitability, and on the appropriate discount rate; another consideration is that different taxes may apply to the different groups, leaving the post-tax profitability different.

14 For further discussion, see Winter (1964).

15 The take-over threat does assume that the shareholders are only interested in current market value. If, however, the firm were owned by individuals and institutions who were more interested in capital gains than in income (dividends), then even that assumption may not be always valid.

16 For further discussion on 'insider' and 'outsider' shareholders, see Aaronovitch and Sawyer (1975) Chapter 8.

17 For a discussion of Pareto criteria and allocative efficiency, see a text on welfare economics, such as Winch (1971).

18 The consequence of removing the high elasticity assumption can be seen in terms of the theory of monopolistic competition (Chapter 3 above).

references

AARONOVITCH S and SAWYER M (1974) 'The Concentration of British Manufacturing' *Lloyds Bank Review* 114.

AARONOVITCH S and SAWYER M (1975) *Big Business* Macmillan.

ARCHIBALD G C (1961) 'Chamberlin versus Chicago' *Review of Economic Studies* 24 (part of which is reprinted in Archibald (1971)).

ARCHIBALD G C (1963) 'Reply to Chicago' *Review of Economic Studies* 30.

ARCHIBALD G C (1971) *The Theory of the Firm* Penguin Books.

ARROW K (1959) 'Towards a Theory of Price Adjustment' in M Abramovitz (ed) *The Allocation of Economic Resources* Stanford University Press.

BACHARACH M (1976) *Economics and the Theory of Games* Macmillan.

BAIN J S (1956) *Barriers to New Competition* Harvard University Press.

BARAN P and SWEEZY M (1967) *Monopoly Capital* Penguin Books.

BARZEL Y (1970) 'Excess Capacity in Monopolistic Competition' *Journal of Political Economy* 78.

BAUMOL W J (1959) *Business Behaviour, Value and Growth* Macmillan.

BAUMOL W J and STEWART M (1971) 'On the Behavioural Theory of the Firm' in Marris and Wood (1971).

BERLE A A and MEANS G C (1932) *The Modern Corporation and Private Property* Macmillan.

BOULDING K E and STIGLER G J (eds) (1953) *Readings in Price Theory* Allen and Unwin.

BREIT W and HOCHMAN H (eds) (1968) *Readings in Micro-economics* Holt Rinehart and Winston.

BURCH P H (1972) *The Managerial Revolution Reassessed* Lexington Books.

CHAMBERLIN E H (1933) *The Theory of Monopolistic Competition* Harvard University Press.

CHAMBERLIN E H (1957) *Toward a More General Theory of Value* Oxford University Press.

COASE R H (1937) 'The Nature of the Firm' *Economica* 4 (reprinted in Boulding and Stigler (1953)).

CODDINGTON A (1972) 'Positive Economics' *Canadian Journal of Economics* 5.

COURNOT A (1897) *Récherches sur les Principles Mathematique de la Théorie des Richesses* published in English as *Researches into the Mathematical Principles of the Theory of Wealth* Macmillan.

CYERT R M and MARCH J G (1955) 'Organization, Structure and Pricing Behaviour in an Oligopolistic Market' *American Economic Review* 45.

CYERT R M and MARCH J G (1963) *A Behavioural Theory of the Firm* Prentice Hall.

DEMSETZ H (1959) 'The Nature of Equilibrium in Monopolistic Competition' *Journal of Political Economy* 67.

DORFMAN R (1969) 'An Economic Interpretation of Optimal Control Theory' *American Economic Review* 59.

FISHER F M (1960) 'Review of Baumol' (1959) *Journal of Political Economy* 68.

FRIEDMAN M (1953) *Essays in Positive Economics* University of Chicago Press (reprinted in Breit and Hochman (1968)).

FRIEDMAN M (1963) 'More on Archibald versus Chicago' *Review of Economic Studies* 30.

GALBRAITH J K (1963) *American Capitalism: The Concept of Countervailing Power* Penguin Books.

GALBRAITH J K (1969) *The New Industrial State* Penguin Books.

GASKINS D W (1971) 'Dynamic Limit Pricing: Optimal Pricing Under Threat of Entry' *Journal of Economic Theory* 3.

GODLEY W A H and NORDHAUS W D (1972) 'Pricing in the Trade Cycle' *Economic Journal* 82.

GOLDSMITH R W and PARMELEE R C (1940) 'The Distribution of Ownership in the 200 Largest Non-Financial Corporations. Investigations of Concentration of Economic Power' *Monographs of the Temporary National Economic Committee* 29 Government Printing Office Washington DC.

GOLDSMITH R W (ed) (1973) *Institutional Investors and Corporate Stock* National Bureau of Economic Research, New York.

HALL R L and HITCH C J (1939) 'Price Theory and Business Behaviour' *Oxford Economic Papers*.

HANNAH L and KAY J A (1977) *Concentration in Modern Industry: Theory, Measurement and the U.K. Experience* Macmillan.

HAWKINS C J (1970) 'On the Sales Revenue Maximization Hypothesis' *Journal of Industrial Economics* 18.

HURWICZ L (1945) 'The Theory of Economic Behaviour' *American Economic Review* 35 (reprinted in Boulding and Stigler (1953)).

KING M A (1977) *Public Policy and the Corporation* Chapman and Hall.

LARNER R J (1966) 'Ownership and Control in the 200 Largest Non-Financial Corporations, 1929 and 1963' *American Economic Review* 56.

LEIBENSTEIN H (1966) 'Allocative Efficiency vs. X-Efficiency' *American Economic Review* 56.

LEIBENSTEIN H (1975) 'Aspects of the X-Efficiency Theory of the Firm' *Bell Journal of Economics* 6.

LEIBENSTEIN H (1976) *Beyond Economic Man* Harvard University Press.

LLEWELLEN W G (1969) 'Management and Ownership in the Large Firm' *Journal of Finance* 24.

LIPSEY R G (1962) *Introduction to Positive Economics* Weidenfeld and Nicolson.

MACHLUP F (1967) 'Theories of the Firm: Marginalist, Behavioural, Managerial' *American Economic Review* 57.

MARRIS R (1964) *The Economic Theory of 'Managerial' Capitalism* Macmillan.

MARRIS R (1971) 'An Introduction to Theories of Corporate Growth' and 'The Modern Corporation and Economic Theory' both in Marris and Wood (1971).

MARRIS R and WOOD A (eds) (1971) *The Corporate Economy* Macmillan.

MEADE J E (1972) 'The Theory of Labour Managed Firms and of Profit Sharing' *Economic Journal* 82 (supplement).

MEADE J E (1974) 'The Optimal Balance between Economics of Scale and Variety of Products: An Illustrative Model' *Economica* 41.

MERMELSTEIN D (1970) *Economics: Mainstream Readings and Radical Critiques* Random House.

MODIGLIANI F (1958) 'New Developments on the Oligopoly Front' *Journal of Political Economy* 66.

MODIGLIANI F and MILLER M H (1958) 'The Cost of Capital, Corporation Finance and the Theory of Investment' *American Economic Review* 48.

MOYLE J (1971) 'The Pattern of Ordinary Share Ownership 1957–1970' *University of Cambridge, Department of Applied Economics Occasional Papers* 31.

NATIONAL RESOURCES COMMITTEE (1939) *The Structure of the American Economy* Government Printing Office Washington DC.

von NEUMANN J and MORGENSTERN O (1944) *Theory of Games and Economic Behaviour* Princeton University Press.

NYMAN S and SILBERSTON A (1978) 'The Ownership and Control of Industry' *Oxford Economic Papers* 30.

PARISH R and NG Y-K (1972) 'Monopoly, X-Efficiency and the Measurement of Welfare Loss' *Economica* 39.

PATINKIN D (1947) 'Multiplant Firms, Cartels and Imperfect-Competition' *Quarterly Journal of Economics* 60 (reprinted in Breit and Hochman (1968)).

PENROSE E (1959) *The Theory of the Growth of the Firm* Basil Blackwell.

PERO V (1957) *The Empire of High Finance* International.

PESTON M H (1959) 'On the Sales Maximization Hypothesis' *Economica* 26.

PHELPS E S and WINTER S G (1970) 'Optimal Price Policy under Atomistic Competition' in Phelps E S *et al Micro-economic Foundations of Employment and Inflation Theory* W W Norton.

POLLARD S (1968) *The Genesis of Modern Management* Penguin Books.

PRATTEN C F (1971) 'Economics of Scale in Manufacturing Industry' *University of Cambridge, Department of Applied Economics Occasional Paper* 28 Cambridge University Press.

REES A (1973) *The Economics of Work and Pay* Harper and Row.

ROTHCHILDS K W (1947) 'Price Theory and Oligopoly' *Economic Journal* 57 (reprinted in Boulding and Stigler (1953)).

ROYAL COMMISSION ON THE DISTRIBUTION OF INCOME AND WEALTH (1975) *Report 2 Income from Companies and its Distribution* HMSO.

SAMUELSON P A (1976) *Economics* 10th edition McGraw-Hill.

SCITOVSKY T (1943) 'A Note on Profit Maximization' *Review of Economic Studies* 11 (reprinted in Boulding and Stigler (1953)).

SIMON H A (1959) 'Theories of Decision-Making in Economics and Behavioural Science' *American Economic Review* 49 (reprinted in American Economic Association *Surveys of Economic Theory: Vol. 3* (1967) Macmillan).

SMITH A (1904) *Wealth of Nations* (ed E Cannan) Methuen.

SOLOW R M (1967) 'The New Industrial State or Son of Affluence' *The Public Interest* 9 Fall 1967 (reprinted in Mermelstein (1970)).

SOLOW R M (1971) 'Some Implications of Alternative Criteria for the Firm' in Marris and Wood (1971).

SPENCE A M (1977) 'Entry, Capacity, Investment and Oligopolistic Pricing' *Bell Journal of Economics* 8.

SRAFFA P (1926) 'The Laws of Returns Under Competitive Conditions' *Economic Journal* 36 (reprinted in Boulding and Stigler (1953)).

von STACKELBERG H (1952) translated by A Peacock *The Theory of the Market Economy* Wilham Hodge and Co.

STIGLER G J (1949) 'Monopolistic-Competition in Retrospect' *Five Lectures on Economic Problems* Macmillan.

STIGLER G J (1957) 'Perfect-Competition, Historically Contemplated' *Journal of Political Economy* 65.

STIGLER G J (1963) 'Archibald versus Chicago' *Review of Economic Studies* 30.

SWEEZY P M (1939) 'Demand Under Conditions of Oligopoly' *Journal of Political Economy* 47.

SYLOS LABINI P (1962) *Oligopoly and Technical Progress* Harvard University Press.

WILES P (1961) *Price, Cost and Output* Blackwell.

WILLIAMSON J H (1966) 'Profit, Growth and Sales Maximization' *Economica* 33.

WILLIAMSON O E (1964) *Economics of Discretionary Behaviour: Managerial Objectives in a Theory of the Firm* Kershaw.

WINCH D M (1971) *Analytical Welfare Economics* Penguin.

WINTER S G (1964) 'Economic Natural Selection and the Theory of the Firm' *Yale Economic Essays* Spring 1964.

ZEITLIN M (1974) 'Corporate Ownership and Control: The Large Corporation and the Capitalist Class' *American Journal of Sociology* 73.

index

Barriers to entry, 8, 42–3, 70–2, 90
Behavioural theories, 87, 128–30, 140

Capacity, 14–15, 16, 20, 76
Capacity, excess, 36, 38
Collusion, 55–6
Corporations, 86
Cost curves, 7, 13–18
Countervailing power, 133
Cournot model of oligopoly, 46–52, 64

Dividends 101–2, 106, 112

Economies of scale, 16, 21, 37, 75
Efficiency
    economic, 1, 2, 130, 154
    technical, 130

Firm, concept of, 8–9, 10–11
Follower-follower model of oligopoly, see Cournot model
Full-cost pricing, 123–7, 146

Games, theory of, 58–63, 64–9, 145
Gaskins' model, 78–9, 80–2
Gearing, 107–8, 117–18
Growth of the firm, 101–15, 117–20 (and passim)

Industry
    definition of, 10–12

Kinked demand curve theory, 56–8
Kuhn-Tucker theorem, 80, 94, 117

Leader-follower model of oligopoly, 50–2
Leader-leader model of oligopoly, see Von Stackelberg model
Limit-pricing model, 72–6, 78–9, 81–2, 127

Market shares model of oligopoly, 54–5
Managerial revolution, 8, 9, 87, 89–90, 101, 135, 139, 146–8, 152–4
Managerial theories, 8, 86–7, 89–120, 141
Maximization
    of growth, 101–15
    of profits, 7, 9, 18, 20, 22, 25, 31, 45, 46, 47, 50, 53, 54, 55, 77, 95, 110–15
    of sales, 92–7, 127
    of utility, 91, 97–101
Monopolistic competition 7, 12, 29–41, 47
Monopoly, 7, 22–4, 27–8, 29–30, 144
Monopoly capital, 133, 135–7
Monopoly
    bilateral, 26–7, 134
    discriminating, 25

New Industrial State, 5, 33, 134–5

Oligopoly, 5, 7, 42, 89, 92, 133, 137–8, 144
    classical theories of, 42–58, 64
Organizational slack, 101, 128, 131–2

Perfect competition, 4, 7, 18–22, 27–8, 29–30, 144, 155
Price determination
    in bilateral monopoly, 27
    in discriminating monopoly, 25
    in full-cost pricing theory, 124
    in limit-pricing model, 74–5
    in monopolistic competition, 32–3
    in monopoly 23
    in perfect competition, 20
    in price leadership model, 53
    in theory of Rothchilds, 138
Price leadership model of oligopoly, 53
Price rigidity, 56–8, 124–5
Product differentiation, 29–31, 41, 71–2
Profits, 58, 144–6, 148–52
    concepts of, 142–3
    secure profits, 137
    see also maximization of profits

Reaction function, 47–9
Retention ratio, 103

Sales revenue
maximization, *see*
maximization of sales;
theory of Baumol
Satisficing, 8, 121–3, 146
Shareholders, 4, 8, 86, 87,
88, 89–90, 102, 135–6,
139, 147–8, 153
Sraffa paradox, 21, 37

Take-overs, 9, 101–3, 109,
110, 149–50

Tangency solution, 36
Technostructure, 139–40
Theory of
Baumol, 92–7, 127, 145,
146, 148
Marris, 101–10, 117–20,
139, 149
Rothchilds, 133, 137–8,
139, 145
Scitovsky, 91
O. E. Williamson,
97–101, 116, 131–2,

146, 147

Valuation of firm, 101–2,
104, 112–13, 117–20,
143, 150
Valuation ratio, 102,
104–8, 110–15, 117–20,
160
Von Stackelberg model of
oligopoly, 52–3

X-inefficiency, 130–1